Developing .NET Enterprise Applications

JOHN KANALAKIS

W0235019

APress Media, LLC

Developing .NET Enterprise Applications
Copyright ©2003 by John Kanalakis

Originally published by Apress in 2003

ISBN 978-1-59059-046-1   ISBN 978-1-4302-0822-8 (eBook)
DOI 10.1007/978-1-4302-0822-8

Technical Reviewer: Phil Pledger

Editorial Board: Dan Appleman, Craig Berry, Gary Cornell, Tony Davis, Steven Rycroft, Julian Skinner, Martin Streicher, Jim Sumser, Karen Watterson, Gavin Wray, John Zukowski

Assistant Publisher: Grace Wong

Project Manager: Tracy Brown Collins

Copy Editor: Kim Wimpsett

Production Manager: Kari Brooks

Proofreader: Lori Bring

Compositor: ContentWorks

Indexer: Ron Strauss

Artist: April Milne

Cover Designer: Kurt Krames

Manufacturing Manager: Tom Debolski

Distributed to the book trade in the United States by Springer-Verlag New York, Inc., 175 Fifth Avenue, New York, NY, 10010 and outside the United States by Springer-Verlag GmbH & Co. KG, Tiergartenstr. 17, 69112 Heidelberg, Germany.

In the United States: phone 1-800-SPRINGER, email orders@springer-ny.com, or visit http://www.springer-ny.com. Outside the United States: fax +49 6221 345229, email orders@springer.de, or visit http://www.springer.de.

To family, friends, and new technology...

Contents at a Glance

Contents

About the Author

JOHN KANALAKIS is the senior director of software development at LoanCity
and is currently using .NET to power the mortgage industry. John has designed
and built a number of large-scale enterprise applications as well as application
frameworks.

Throughout his professional career, John has worked with a wide range of
programming platforms but has focused mainly on C++ and Java. Such applications include product requirements management, electronic component
supply-chain management, enterprise application integration, and catastrophe
simulation solutions.

John has largely been responsible for designing and implementing multi-
tiered and distributed computing applications with presentation layers available
as desktop applications, Web applications, and mobile device applications. John
has also written about, presented, and developed various Web service solutions
implemented in both Java and C#.

John keeps active within the developer community by writing white papers
and magazine articles, by participating in online developer forums, and by presenting at software-related conferences.

About the Technical Reviewer

PHIL PLEDGER has worked in the information technology field for more than 20 years, developing software for a diverse range of applications spanning from business systems to real-time process control systems. Phil has a bachelor's degree and master's degree in Computer Science from the University of Alabama. In 2002 he founded Idoneous Technologies (`http://www.idoneous.com`), a company aimed not just at custom software development but also at transferring software development knowledge to clients. Phil can be reached at `ppledger@idoneous.com`.

Acknowledgments

I AM ALWAYS AMAZED by the amount of work that goes into a publication such as this. It almost seems that organizing and writing the text is the easiest part. The real work is in the technical reviewing, project management, layout, and composition. The Apress team really needs to be acknowledged for the outstanding work done in order to turn this project into a reality. Special appreciation goes to Phil Pledger, Tracy Brown Collins, Kim Wimpsett, Gary Cornell, Kari Brooks, and Jessica Dolcourt.

Phil has done an excellent technical review of this book. I especially thank him for his patience as changes were made in a constant effort to improve the quality of this book. Phil always kept the reader's perspective in mind to ensure that this book provided the highest level of quality in its technical detail.

Tracy's contributions were immeasurable. As project manager, her responsibility was to keep everyone organized and on schedule. Her relentless insistence on deadlines balanced with forgiveness of delays made everything possible. Thanks to Tracy's terrific organization, this book was completed in a timely manner with the highest level of quality.

Kim is probably the best copy editor in the industry. Keeping my grammar in check cannot be an easy task, but she managed it well. She also helped to enforce a consistent chapter structure and significantly added to the overall readability.

Kari and Jessica have been especially helpful in guiding me through the production end of the book, moving from the original Word documents to the final book layout. They also were essential in managing all of the final production materials that add to the polished look to the book.

I would also like to credit Gary and Apress—I think they are one in the same. Apress is a remarkable publishing company with a high emphasis on quality. Gary's push for quality titles that are written clearly and accurately is terrific. As a buyer and reader of Apress books, I have never been disappointed.

I would also like to thank my family for their support, patience, and inspiration. Anke, Anneke, and Alyssa have always been a constant source of encouragement during the long nights and weekends dedicated to writing. And, finally, a special thanks to my parents, Mike and Mary; to my close family, Scott and Alex; and to the entire Kanalakis and Bruchs families.

Introduction

APPLICATION DEVELOPMENT IS USUALLY faced with several critical factors: time to market, ever-increasing quality, and cost of development. Time to market is critical in that any project that an individual or company may have in mind is probably already in the works elsewhere. When that is the case, everything comes down to being the first to deliver…even if it falls short. A Gartner Research study showed that competing products offering similar features will take the most market share if released sooner. The study further added that the product released first, even with fewer features, typically builds market share faster. The lesson of that study is that it is important to release a 1.0 version of a new product concept as quickly as possible and then follow up with feature add-ons over time.

Product consistency and quality are also critical to the success of products making their debut. Applications with modules that look differently can undermine the application user's confidence in the product. The lower their confidence in the application, the less they use the product and come to depend upon it. The same can be said at the code level. The more modules that are implemented consistently, the easier different developers can step in to investigate and resolve problems.

Cost of development is often measured by productivity, or how much code is created to accomplish specific application tasks. The best development platform for you to use will offer the most services related to your application. This has often been measured by the size of a platform's class library and its flexibility. Because the .NET Framework is rich with data access, presentation, communication, and networking services, it can save the enterprise developer a significant amount of time that would otherwise be required to build that foundation. In addition to providing a large resource library of functionality within the .NET Framework, Visual Studio .NET provides many time-saving tools. The integrated form and component designers save a lot of time when building Windows or Web forms. The IntelliSense feature saves time searching help files to obtain quick property and method information. Furthermore, the build manager makes configuring and building projects faster. Together, the .NET Framework and Visual Studio .NET significantly accelerates the time required to build complex business and enterprise applications.

Supporting Software Tools

The application development frameworks presented within this book place a lot of emphasis on business object classes. Chapter 2, "Accessing Data in ADO.NET," introduces business objects and explains their roles within the application framework. Although this is a scalable and flexible solution, there is one setback. It requires several C# code classes for each business object. In an effort to minimize that coding work, I have implemented an add-in for Visual Studio .NET 2003, called Business Object JumpStart.

After you download and install the Business Object JumpStart, you can seamlessly integrate it into Visual Studio. Just select Tools ➤ Business Object JumpStart from the Visual Studio menu and enter the attributes of your business object, as shown in Figure 1.

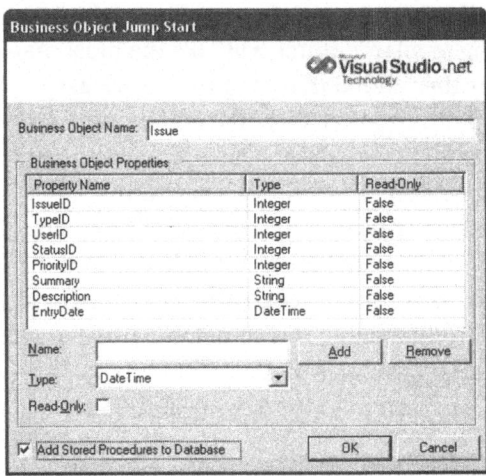

Figure 1. Adding business objects to your existing solution

After defining the new business object, click the OK button and take a break as the Business Object JumpStart adds a new class library project to your solution, creates all of the business object code in C#, and creates the database stored procedures that bind the business objects to the database. This handy tool trims a lot of mind-numbing coding from your development project and is based upon the examples within this book.

You can download the latest version of the Business Object JumpStart from the Downloads section of the Apress Web site (http://www.apress.com), or you can search the CNET Download.com Web site (http://www.download.com).

Planning Application Development

Building an enterprise application involves several steps. Chapter 1, "Introducing .NET and Enterprise Architecture," presents many of the specifics, especially with the types of documents you need to produce in preparation. Regardless of the specific documents you choose to implement, bear in mind two fundamental concepts: clear planning and consistent implementation.

Clear application planning is required so that everyone on the development team is working toward the same goal. The entire team must understand the application functionality. This is typically reflected within a business requirements document, user interface definition, and database schema definition. In addition to these fundamental documents, a high-level application design, a component-level design, and even individual class definitions are helpful, especially when parts of the application development will be outsourced to a different team.

Consistent implementation at the application level and the code level is just as important to the finished product. From the application level, it is important to take a close look the application's basic functionality. Try to identify areas of reuse that might be packaged into components. Also, applying style templates at the forms level will help ensure that each form is implemented consistently across the application. At the code level, specify coding guidelines for developers to follow. This should include consistent naming conventions for classes, enumerations, methods, properties, class variables, database tables, and database stored procedures. At the user interface level, this should include design templates describing how form controls must placed, which fonts must be used, and how controls should be sized.

With careful planning and a solid investment in application design, team members can work individually and make intelligent decisions that result in a great product.

Adopting an Application Framework

Every project of a reasonable scale should have an application framework. An application framework can be as simple as a set of templates or as complicated as a fully integrated code generator. An application framework is essentially a clearly defined pattern for building pieces of the application. Usually, the intention is that an application framework saves development time. The framework itself provides 80 percent of the application functionality, such as data access, presentation, and so on. The remaining 20 percent is your domain-specific application code. An important factor to be aware of is to not select a framework that completely locks you into it. A framework should be powerful enough to get you started but also flexible enough for you to outgrow it.

The frameworks presented within this book meet that expectation. They provide a great starting point for your application development, but they do not necessarily lock you into them. One way to identify a flexible framework is to look for abstractions. Functional abstractions, usually enforced through interfaces, provide a mechanism for you to replace the underlying implementation with your own custom code.

The Audience for This Book

This book is targeted at the intermediate-level software developer interested in building scalable and reliable business applications. General knowledge of the .NET Framework is required, and all source code examples are implemented in the C# language. For building a .NET knowledge foundation, I recommend the following books: *C# and the .NET Platform* by Andrew Troelsen (Apress, 2001) and *A Programmer's Introduction to C#*, Second Edition, by Eric Gunnerson (Apress, 2001).

The Structure of This Book

The purpose of this book is to outline the best practices for building a scalable enterprise application. Each chapter builds a small piece of an entire application. Rather than reference the same old sample applications that are bundled with the .NET Framework, such as Duwamish, Fitch & Mather Stocks, or Northwind, this book works toward building an enterprise application from the ground up. Each chapter focuses on a specific area of application development. You can read this book from one chapter to the next or selectively reference chapters for specific examples that match problems you might be facing.

Chapter 1, "Introducing .NET and Enterprise Architecture," sets the foundation for the book by defining an enterprise application and business processes. The chapter also briefly outlines the important stages of application development from requirements gathering to application deployment.

Chapter 2, "Accessing Data in ADO.NET," dives into the most important element of an application, the database. This chapter leads off with a review of ADO.NET and follows up with the implementation of a structured data access layer. This chapter also highlights the importance of business objects and how they can effectively insulate an application from changes to a data model.

Chapter 3, "Using Networking and Directory Services," introduces directory services, explains how they work, and shows how corporate enterprises use them to manage user accounts. This chapter introduces Active Directory, Microsoft's directory service solution, to build out a directory services business service that fits cleanly into the application framework and interacts with application business objects.

Chapter 4, "Applying Reliable Messaging," adds real-time messaging services to the application and explains how they can be leveraged to build out a scalable business tier based on asynchronous communication. This includes creating messages and queues that implement a framework for building out a sample distributed analysis engine.

Chapter 5, "Integrating Mail Services," presents e-mail services within the .NET Framework, including how they work, how enterprises applications use them, and how they can facilitate online collaboration between the users and the application. This chapter implements a messaging service that fits cleanly into the application framework and interacts with application business objects.

Chapter 6, "Automating Business Processes," takes a close look at business process automation and how it can be quickly added to an enterprise application with the help of Microsoft BizTalk Server. BizTalk provides tools that simplify process definitions that can span across multiple applications and execute for weeks. You can implement these processes using either the built-in BizTalk tools or the .NET managed code that is plugged in as an integration component.

Chapter 7, "Building Web Applications," implements the application's presentation layer with the use of Web forms, reflection, and data binding. The presentation layer finally adds the user interface to all of the services covered so far and relies upon templates and user controls to reduce errors and encourage reusability.

Chapter 8, "Developing Desktop Applications," implements an enterprise presentation layer as a desktop application. Desktop applications have different strengths and weaknesses when compared to Web applications. One thing both have in common, however, is the need for a structured development framework that minimizes errors and encourages reuse. The next chapter presents a framework for rapid application development that incorporates forms inheritance, user controls, application configuration files, and dynamic access to assemblies.

Chapter 9, "Using XML and Web Services," exposes to more details related to Extensible Markup Language (XML) and Web services. First, this chapter reviews what XML is and presents how it works. Second, the chapter shows how these concepts are broadened and used to create Web services that expose enterprise application functionality.

Chapter 10, "Integrating Reporting Services," describes the reporting services integrated with the Visual Studio .NET environment. The chapter begins with an overview of reporting and then breaks down the report-building steps. It covers everything necessary to build a typical enterprise report.

Chapter 11, "Deploying .NET Applications on Wireless Devices," takes the .NET Framework on the road and explores mobile application development. It covers developing mobile applications for two types of mobile applications: Compact Framework applications for Personal Digital Assistant (PDA) devices and Mobile Internet Toolkit applications for Web-enabled cellular phones. Both frameworks add mobile capabilities to the enterprise application.

Chapter 12, "Integrating .NET Applications," introduces application integration, .NET style. An introduction to application integration describes the value in interfacing existing applications with new .NET applications. Then, it shows how to assemble a new integration platform that puts XML, XSL Transformations (XSLT), and remoting to work.

Chapter 13, "Understanding .NET Security and Cryptography," exposes the security and cryptography services provided by the .NET Framework. You will use these services to implement user-level and code-level security within an application. A detailed look at encryption reveals methods for scrambling data into an unreadable format that is secure for transmission over the Internet.

Chapter 14, "Installing .NET Applications," wraps up the development of an enterprise application by presenting the deployment project. Deploying Web, desktop, and mobile applications is made significantly easier with the help of the Visual Studio .NET environment. A functional and user-friendly application setup adds a polished and professional look to an application and helps ensure that user configurations are consistent.

Each chapter describes the technology as it relates to the .NET Framework and provides examples for applying it within the scope of an enterprise application. Although the examples are applied to the IssueTracker sample application, they are flexible enough to be applied to just about any business application.

A Personal Note

On a personal note, I have been charged up about Microsoft's .NET initiative from the get-go. My professional development experience comes from a mix of languages and platforms, including C++ and Java. Since Microsoft's first .NET announcement, I have followed its evolution into the robust framework it is today.

For the past several years, Java gained a lot of momentum as the preferred platform for server-side development, while C++ remained the preferred platform for desktop development. The .NET Framework has changed all of that. Sophisticated .NET applications can be quickly produced to run on or run from enterprise-wide servers and meet increasing scalability demands. I am still impressed with the myriad of capabilities .NET offers, ranging from building mobile device applications to creating code that dynamically generates new code. Overall, the .NET platform holds a lot for the future of computing.

Introducing .NET and Enterprise Architecture

AN *ENTERPRISE APPLICATION* is one that supports any multidivisional organization with data and services that enable business-specific functions. Such applications typically integrate multiple technologies, such as database access, directory services, mail services, business processes, and more. This chapter defines the components of an enterprise application and then explores the technologies involved in creating one.

Finally, the chapter introduces IssueTracker, the fully functional enterprise application that this book builds with each subsequent chapter. The IssueTracker example application will serve as a central repository for issues within an enterprise, such sales requests, support issues, development bugs, and executive status. As an enterprise-wide application, IssueTracker will interact with multiple server-side resources, such as databases, e-mail servers, process management engines, directory services, Web services, reporting services, and mobile services. Starting with this chapter, each chapter outlines the best practices that yield maximum performance, reliability, and scalability.

Defining Enterprise Applications

An *enterprise* represents a corporate entity with several interacting departments, each managing different types of data and performing different functions. Figure 1-1 models a typical enterprise. It is composed of several departments including Sales, Marketing, Human Resources, Development, Customer Support, and Information Technology. Each department operates independently but shares specific data or services. For example, the Sales department tracks the names and contact details of customers. The Support department refers to the customer information to help customers experiencing problems with the company's product and to enter customer problem information. The Development department reviews the customer problem information to improve the product and update the status of the problem. Finally, the company's management monitors the customer and problem information captured in an effort to improve the company's operations.

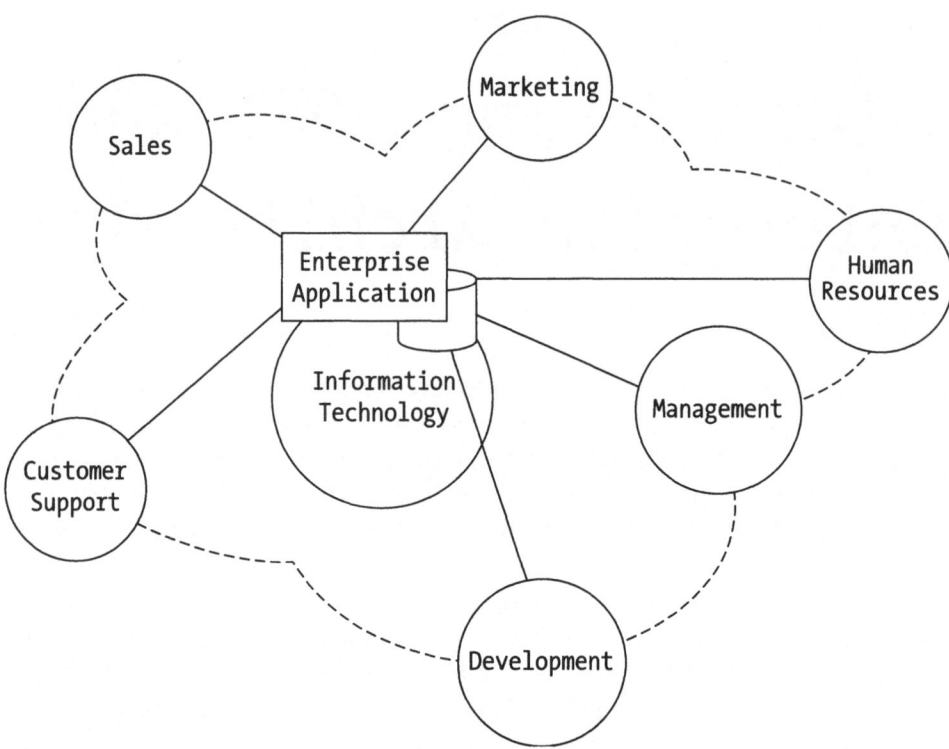

Figure 1-1. Department relationships within a typical enterprise organization

For an enterprise application to support different departments, it needs to manage two important company assets: business data and business processes.

Introducing Business Data

Business data is any data that helps a business operate more effectively. It typically needs to be accessed by different departments within an organization. Business data needs to be reliably accessible, scalable, and secure.

Accessibility refers to the capability of multiple users operating on a variety of platforms and devices being able to interact with the business data. Flexible enterprise applications will have more than one form of user interface. In most cases, one primary user interface client will be developed, and one or more additional clients will be developed. This scenario might include a primary Web-based client and supporting clients in the form of a Windows application, a Pocket PC application, or a cellular phone application. All clients are accessibility tools that help users interact with business data and services.

Scalability refers to the capability of increasing the number of system resources, such as servers, to support an increase in the number of connected users without impacting performance. Typically, smaller database applications, such as Microsoft Access or Microsoft Visual FoxPro, can reliably support large amounts of data storage but with only a handful of concurrent connections. An enterprise database, such as Microsoft SQL Server, Oracle, or MySQL, has built-in support for handling larger volumes of data with hundreds of concurrent connections, as well as transaction and backup services. However, such databases are significantly more expensive and require specialized maintenance.

To *secure* business data, you offer data access to specific users privileged to access that data. There are many different levels of security. For example, you could fundamentally grant access to employees and block everyone who does not work at the company. Then, within a company, you could grant access to department team members and block everyone else. Finally, you could grant access to certain levels of management and block everyone else. In this scenario, you need to look at the data closely to determine which employee should access which data. Also, you need to determine the type of data access: read-only, read-write, or no access.

Introducing Business Processes

A *business process*, or workflow, is a series of steps that accomplishes a specific business goal. Business processes are typically either internal or external. Internal processes might span multiple departments, and external processes usually span multiple enterprises. Both process types might combine automated tasks with human interaction tasks.

An example of an internal business process is an employee new-hire process. When the Human Resources department enters a new employee's personal data, that data is validated for completeness. Then, the Information Technology (IT) department is notified to create a new user account, create a new telephone account, create a new e-mail account, assign a computer, and then notify the Human Resources department when completed.

An example of an external business process is a supply-chain process. When one company orders merchandise from another, the supplier inventory is checked. If the item being purchased is out of stock, then the supplier orders from the distributor. If the distributor is also out of stock, the product is ordered from the manufacturer.

Business process automation solutions implement processes that combine automated and human interaction tasks and that provide a user interface for graphical modeling.

Introducing the Enterprise Application Components

Developing an enterprise application requires interactions with many components, including data access, business rules, and the user interface. Figure 1-2 illustrates a typical enterprise application architecture and its software components.

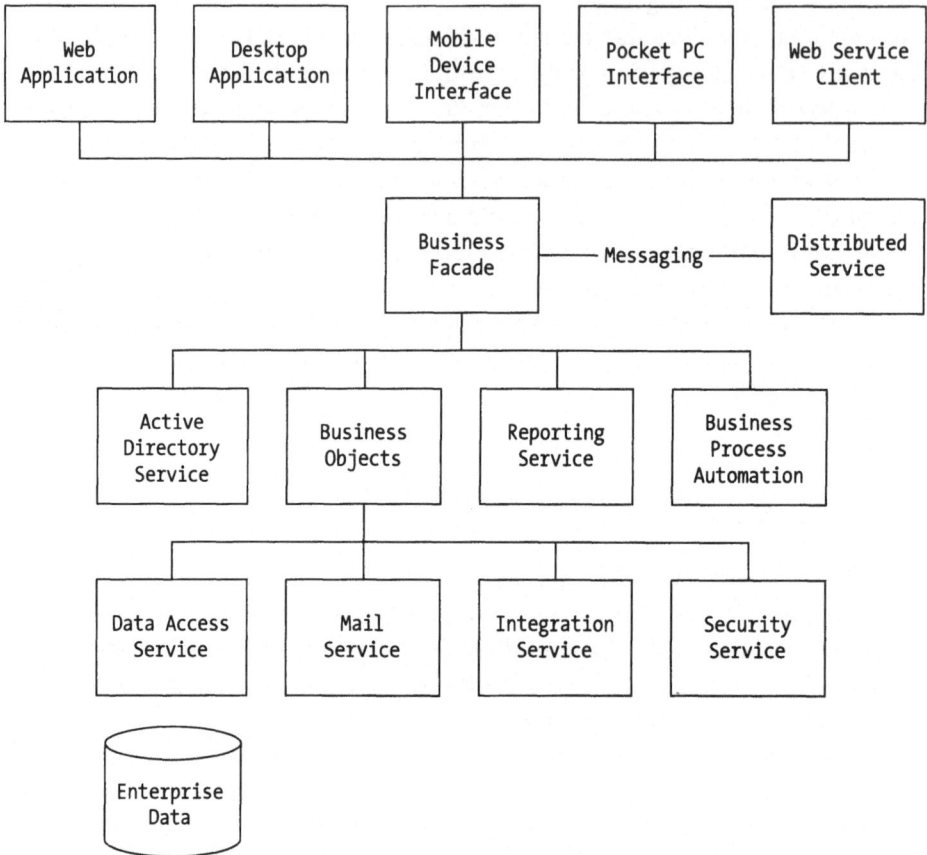

Figure 1-2. Enterprise application components

As Figure 1-2 illustrates, multiple technologies work together to implement an enterprise application:

Database access services: Database access technology is fundamental to any application regardless of whether it is an enterprise application. The purpose of any application is to interact with data by storing, retrieving, and searching for specific values. The .NET Framework provides the Active Data Objects (ADO) framework as the primary toolset for reading from and writing to databases. As explained in Chapter 2, "Accessing Data in ADO.NET," ADO.NET provides different data access mechanisms optimized for different types of data sources.

Directory services: Directory services provide a single point of entry into a networked application. With Active Directory, users can be validated and then access networked resources such as directories, printers, and so on from a single login. Applications can leverage directory services to search the network for system resources, such as files and printers. Active Directory also supports third-party directory service solutions found in many enterprises, such as the Novell Directory System (NDS) and the Netscape Directory Server. Chapter 3, "Using Networking and Directory Services," covers directory services and their role in an enterprise application.

Messaging services: Messaging services provide a mechanism by which applications can reliably send and receive messages between applications within the enterprise or across multiple enterprises. Message content can vary between applications and can initiate a process on another system. Messages are also reliable in that if they fail to reach their destination, they are queued and resent when the destination is accessible again. Chapter 4, "Applying Reliable Messaging," covers messaging services and the Microsoft Message Queue (MSMQ).

Mail services: Mail services enable applications to send and receive standard e-mail messages between applications. Because many enterprise applications link multiple users together, e-mail-based notification systems can be an effective means of notifying users when a server-side process ends or when human interaction is necessary to complete a workflow. Support for mail services is undoubtedly a cornerstone technology that helps an enterprise application tightly integrate into the organization. Chapter 5, "Integrating Mail Services," covers integrating mail services into the application framework.

Business process automation: Business process automation enables users to define a series of repeatable tasks that helps accomplish a specific business goal. You can start these processes by hand, by an application-triggered event, or by the presence of a document within a specified location. Processes can combine automated tasks, such as routing documents from one place to another, and human interactive tasks, such as setting a manager's approval. Business processes are valuable to enterprise applications in that they streamline business operations so that tasks are accomplished faster and with fewer resources. They also help link different parts of the enterprise. Chapter 6, "Automating Business Processes," covers how to define business processes and incorporate them into an enterprise application.

Web applications: Web applications are software solutions that reside largely on a remote server. Users interact with these remote servers with a thin client, such as a Web browser. Although Web applications are easily deployable to multiple operating system platforms, the result is a simple user interface that offers slower performance. For many enterprise developers, choosing to develop a thick desktop client vs. a thin Web client is a difficult decision. Chapter 7, "Building Web Applications," covers developing Web applications that tap into core business functionality.

Desktop applications: Desktop applications reside largely on each user's computer. All application logic executes locally but typically connects to a remote database. Desktop applications often have a much richer user interface than their thin Web application counterparts. Desktop applications also execute much faster in terms of screen refreshing. Chapter 8, "Developing Desktop Applications," covers building deployable desktop applications that integrate core business functionality.

Web services: Web services provide a framework for platform-independent data exchange based on published open standards. Web services implement or wrap specific business functionality and return platform-independent documents structured in the Extensible Markup Language (XML) format. Web services are ideal for building inter-enterprise application integration solutions. Some think of a Web service as a Web site without the user interface. Chapter 9, "Using XML and Web Services," includes a detailed look at Web services and how they can enhance accessibility in an enterprise application.

Reporting services: Reporting services provide a mechanism for generating structured reports in tabular or graphical format. Reports communicate status or statistical information relating to the enterprise application's data. Although you can also implement reporting within a dynamic Web page or a dynamically rendered Windows form, using a reporting technology such as Crystal Reports streamlines the report-building process and makes it easier to create and deploy new reports. Chapter 10, "Integrating Reporting Services," covers building a reporting layer that integrates with an enterprise application.

Wireless services: Wireless services expose enterprise application data and services to mobile devices, such as Personal Digital Assistants (PDAs) or Web browser–enabled cellular phones. Wireless services help extend an enterprise application's reach to employees outside of the office, such as a field service representative who is at a customer's site and needs to check back with the office. Enterprise applications supporting wireless extensions offer additional value to customers in need of application data access anywhere and anytime. Chapter 11, "Deploying .NET Applications on Wireless Devices," covers building a wireless application layer that targets PDAs and Web-enabled cellular phones.

Integration services: Application integration binds different applications together to work as a single application that solves a single problem. There are many different techniques for accomplishing application integration that depend on the type of applications being integrated. Chapter 12, "Integrating .NET Applications," outlines different approaches as well as the advantages and disadvantages to each approach.

Security services: Securing enterprise data and services is an increasing concern to most consumers of enterprise applications. Chapter 13, "Understanding .NET Security and Cryptography," explores potential security holes within an enterprise application and outlines implementation strategies to ensure that an application is designed and built with security in mind.

Deploying an enterprise application into a customer environment might be the last step, but you should not take it lightly. The deployment process is often the first impression that an application makes to its user. If that process is too lengthy, too complicated, or requires too much user involvement, users might be turned off to the application before they even use it. Chapter 14, "Installing .NET Applications," dives into the details and best practices for building easy-to-use deployment projects.

Leveraging the .NET Servers

In some respect, you can think of Microsoft's .NET platform as the next generation of Windows DNA, an earlier platform for developing enterprise applications. Windows DNA included many foundation technologies still found within the .NET Framework, such as Microsoft Transaction Server (MTS), COM+, MSMQ, and Microsoft SQL Server. The .NET Framework incorporates these technologies and adds a Web service framework around them.

The .NET servers offer developers the flexibility to develop scalable enterprise applications. Enterprise applications can leverage the .NET servers to build scalable applications quickly and reliably. The .NET servers include the following:

- **Application Center Server:** This server manages and monitors clusters of application servers and is primarily for managing application scalability.

- **Application Center Test Server:** This server tests and measures the scalability of enterprise applications by scripting and simulating concurrent connections and measuring response times.

- **BizTalk Server:** This server integrates applications and enterprises by graphically modeling business processes. Processes can trigger system resources and integrated applications or wait for human interaction.

- **Commerce Server:** This server supports the development of e-commerce applications with tools and templates for building Web components and services.

- **Exchange Server:** This server offers messaging and collaboration services that include sending and receiving e-mail, scheduling appointments, managing tasks, and keeping journals.

- **Host Integration Server:** This server offers integration with legacy applications, such as SAP, PeopleSoft, and Siebel Systems, with specialized data adapters.

- **Internet Information Server:** This Web server distributes static and dynamic Web content and services to remote Web-based clients.

- **Internet Security and Acceleration Server:** This server offers firewall and Web caching services.

- **Microsoft Message Queue Server:** This server manages and routes messages between applications within and between enterprises.

- **SharePoint Portal Server:** This server provides a functional portal supporting content management, search, and crawling, along with subscription management.

- **SQL Server:** This server manages enterprise data and accessibility to that data with support for caching, indexing, transactions, stored procedures, and backup/restore services.

Understanding the Enterprise Development Process

The success of any enterprise application depends upon how well its development can follow a rigid process. This process typically maps into six specific steps: capturing the requirements, prototyping, designing, developing, testing, and releasing the application.

Capturing the Requirements

The most critical step in the development process is capturing the requirements. Product managers need to listen closely to customer needs and expectations. They need to document these requirements with clear descriptions of what data is entered, what data is returned, and how the data is processed. In addition to application requirements, product managers should discuss any type of printed reports expected by the customer. Specifics include the type of report, formatting and graphic preferences, and performance expectations.

Prototyping the Application

Prototyping essentially helps an enterprise developer validate their understanding of the product requirements. Typically, a prototype will be a lightweight and featureless version of the application. With the help of Visual Studio .NET, you can build rich user interfaces for desktops as well as Web applications fairly quickly. You often present these prototypes to key customers for feedback to ensure that the customer needs are fulfilled. Committing a long development effort to a product that doesn't meet customer expectations will be nearly impossible to sell. Prototypes also help to better estimate the total development effort and, in turn, the total cost of development.

Designing the Application

The design step should be the longest in the development process. You cannot build an enterprise application ad-hoc with a general concept in mind. You need to have detailed discussions about security, performance, and scalability. The first step is to outline the high-level framework, as illustrated earlier in Figure 1-2. Next, determine which elements you can purchase and which components you need to build. Then, looking at the product requirements, you need to design the database schema—one that can capture the necessary application data with flexibility for expansion. Finally, you need to address a component-level design, identifying which classes you will need to create, what their public and private interfaces will be, what inheritance relationship they will have to each other, and what data members will be private and public. When you have clearly defined the application from a high-level picture down to a database schema and class definition, it is time for development.

Developing the Application

Application development should be one of the shortest stages of the entire process. This is largely because the design phase should clearly spell out everything that needs to be coded. Also, the application framework should provide enough templates that trivial and repetitive development tasks are minimized. The requirements have already been captured and translated into a complete design. All that is necessary is to translate design drawings and class definitions into code. In addition to application development, you also need to create the installation and configuration code. Although the .NET Framework supports multiple development languages to coexist within a single solution, it is ideal to select one language and work with it exclusively. This helps build internal skills with a specific language and keeps maintenance costs lower.

Testing the Application

Like the design step, the testing step should be one of the longest in the development process. Ensuring application quality should come first with all application development. If application development begins slipping past schedule, it is a smarter strategy to drop a handful of product requirements than to trim back testing time. Customers have repeatedly communicated that they can live with a product that falls short of expectations much more easily than a product filled with software bugs.

During this step, you should also develop product documentation, such as user and administrative guides. In some cases, documentation occurs during the development step. However, it is far too common for functional changes, labeling changes, or even flow changes to occur, which forces rewrites of the product documentation. Also, keeping the documentation effort in parallel with the testing effort helps ensure a longer testing stage. Ideally, you should write product documentation with a tool that easily generates online help as well as printed documentation. Some enterprise providers attempt to produce only online help and then find that corporate IT managers insist on printed documentation.

Deploying the Application

The final step in the enterprise application development process is packaging the application and labeling the CD. You need to include all printed documentation, including license agreements. An organized release package often sends a strong message to enterprise customers. This message expresses that the application has been well organized and professionally developed, stemming from a solid enterprise application design.

Understanding Enterprise Application Design

As mentioned earlier, the application design step is essential to the success of the application's development. This step requires creating a high-level framework, which includes determining what components will be bought vs. built, creating a database schema, and creating a component-level design.

Understanding Multitier Architectures

The most common enterprise application design revolves around a multitier architecture. A *multitier* architecture distributes core functionality across different servers to maximize overall application performance. The four major components of any application include presentation, workflow, business logic, and data access. The presentation layer captures user input and displays the functional output. The workflow layer typically manages the flow of execution from one block of code to another. The business logic implements specific functionality that acts upon input data. The data access keeps user input persistent by reading from and writing to a database.

As Figure 1-3 illustrates, classical desktop applications typically package all four application layers into a single binary file, the .exe file. A two-tier application separates the data access layer to a different process. This allows for greater scalability because you can introduce an additional server to offload work. A three-tier application separates the business logic layer, as well as the data access layer, to different processes. And in an n-tier application, all major application layers are separated into their own processes for the greatest scalability.

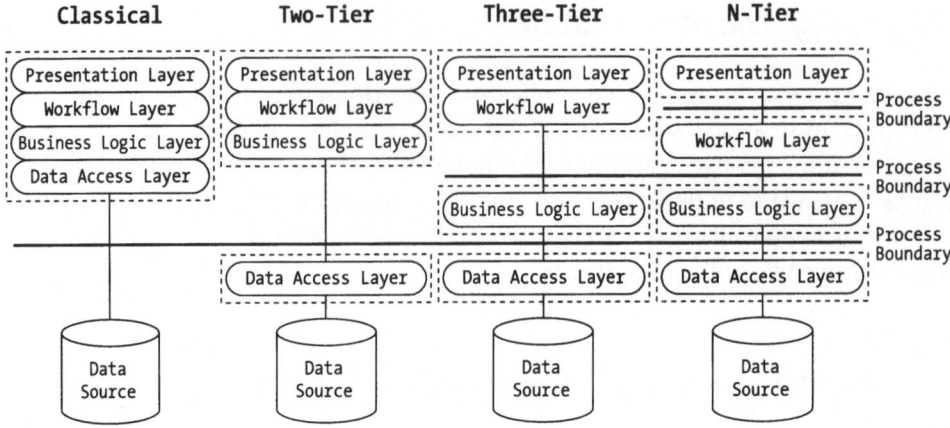

Figure 1-3. Multitier architectures distribute work to different servers.

Determining Buy vs. Build

Most developers would enjoy the opportunity to develop an enterprise application completely from the ground up. However, this may not be very cost effective. It terms of dollars, it is likely to cost more in developing and testing than to purchase a third-party solution. In many cases, such as database services, process automation, messaging, and directory services, the decision to leverage existing software solutions should be easy.

Licensing Microsoft solutions such as SQL Server, BizTalk Server, MSMQ, and Active Directory can be more cost effective than building equivalent systems from scratch. However, other solutions, such as document management, are not as obvious because you can develop a lightweight version relatively quickly. Figure 1-4 illustrates an enterprise architecture with the purchased technologies shaded. The blocks that are not shaded need to be developed internally. You need to investigate early on and decide whether to buy or build specific application components. This includes evaluating the effort required to integrate the component as well as the features it supports.

Defining the User Interface

The user interface definition is an important starting point in the application design process and results in the creation of the user interface definition document. Two levels of detail make up this document: the user interface mockup and the user interface details.

The user interface mockup can vary from hand-drawn representations of Windows forms and Web pages to screen captures of a semifunctional prototype. Its primary purpose is to represent how the finished application will look and broadly define what functions the application will perform.

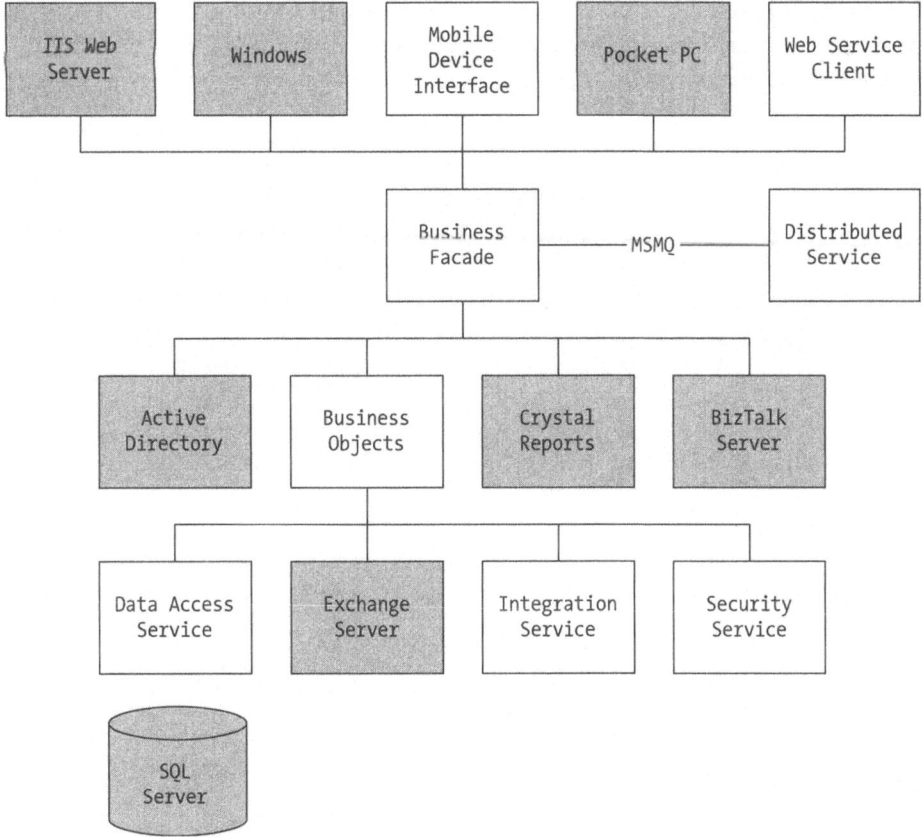

Figure 1-4. Architectural diagram with the purchased components shaded

The user interface details provide the next level of technical information. This specifies exactly what user controls will be displayed within each Windows form or Web page. This specification also includes additional details for each control, such as what events each control responds to and what business functionality is executed. Finally, the specification indicates data formatting and data validation. Data formatting outlines how a label or textbox should represent data, such as percentages vs. currency. Data validation outlines the acceptable ranges for textbox controls, such as restricting letters from a number entry field.

Creating a Database Schema

The database schema is one of the most important elements of the enterprise application design. The difference between a good schema and a bad one can determine the scalability and performance of the application. It is important to structure the schema for extensibility because new features will certainly work their way into the product. However, abstracting data into too many tables will result in poor performance because all the tables will then need to be joined. Figure 1-5 illustrates the IssueTracker data schema.

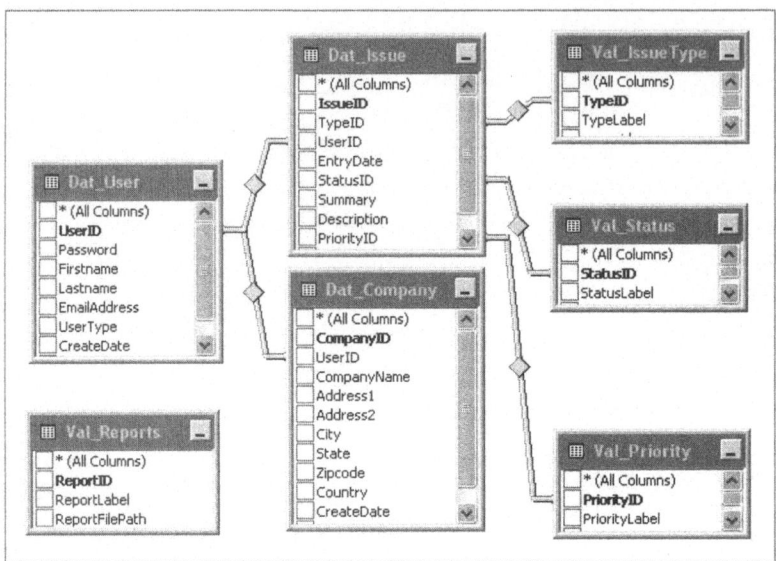

Figure 1-5. The IssueTracker database schema

The person responsible for the schema design needs to understand what the application does and how it will access the data. This includes knowing which tables will be accessed most and how often data will be accessed. During development, the schema designer will also be responsible for creating primary keys, indexes, and stored procedures. There will always be minor changes to the database schema; however, you should complete the overall schema design before the component-level design begins.

Creating the Component-Level Design

The component-level design is where most of the real design time goes. Starting with the high-level architecture, you need to expand each block into detailed class definitions. Each class definition will have private and public data as well as private and public methods. Implementing the principles of object-oriented design will improve overall reusability and extensibility.

Establishing an Application Development Framework

An application development framework is very important to the success of any large-scale development project. By nature, enterprise application development requires multiple full-time developers working on various implementation tasks. Ensuring quality and consistency across the entire application can be nearly impossible without a well-defined and well-structured application framework.

The application development framework outlined in this book relies heavily upon clear design documentation and foundation design patterns. The design documentation includes those items previously described: the user interface definition, a database schema, and a component-level design. The foundation design patterns include uniform data access, interface definitions for business objects, templates for differently behaving forms, style sheets, and reusable user controls. Pulled together, an application framework can significantly accelerate the speed of development, ensure user interface consistency, reduce the potential for bugs, enhance overall security, and apply best practices for functionality reuse.

The most difficult aspect of establishing an application development framework is determining how much functionality should go into it and how much should be implemented in application-specific code. In general, you should probably add any functionality to the framework that you expect to be used in at least 80 percent of the applications. If there is no clear use of a specific technology beyond a specific project, then you should implement that functionality only for that application. Otherwise, time will tend to clutter the application framework and make it less useful and less robust. Determining whether specific functionality should be implemented within the application framework or within a specific project will be a constant challenge for enterprise developers, and it deserves careful thought and planning.

The application development framework in this book is flexible enough to be applied to multiple domains and is composed of design patterns reflected across all application tiers. As Figure 1-6 illustrates, the framework begins with a collection of stored procedures optimized for quick and secure data access. These stored procedures interact with a middle tier that manages a DataSet for cached validation data as well as business objects that manage in-memory representations of interactive data. These business objects implement framework interfaces that define how the data is interacted with, especially for data storage and retrieval, data value validation, and help descriptions. These business objects leverage data binding to populate Windows forms or Web pages that render the application user interface to the user. Windows forms inherit from predefined form classes, and Web pages are laid out based on predefined Hypertext Markup Language (HTML) page layouts. Style sheets also provide predefined visual characteristics, such as fonts and colors, for Web pages. Finally, a *collection of* predefined user controls provide common functionality, such as page headers and footers, role-based menus, and common event handling, such as save and cancel functions.

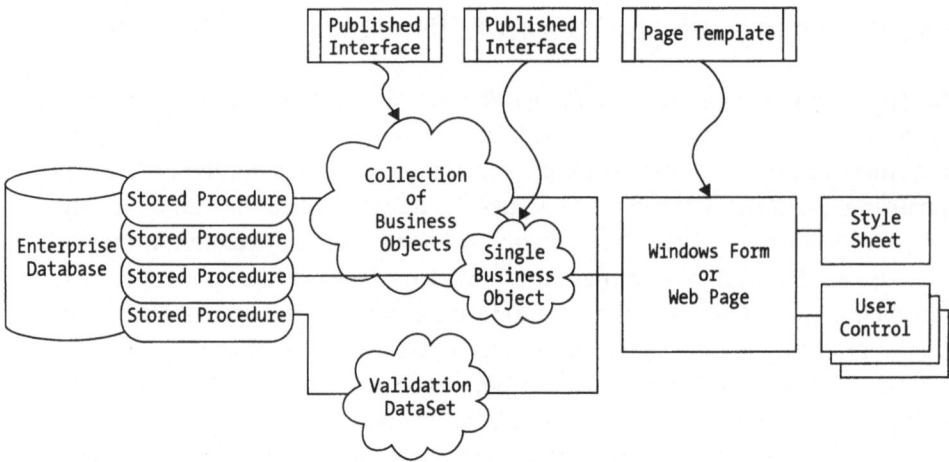

Figure 1-6. A flexible application framework composed of interfaces and templates

Each of the following chapters focuses on and develops a specific part of the framework as it fits into the IssueTracker application. You can leverage the best-practice design patterns from these examples and build a variety of enterprise applications including supply-chain solutions, e-commerce solutions, and enterprise resource planning systems.

Getting Started with Visual Studio .NET

Three different versions of Visual Studio .NET 2003 are available: Enterprise Architect, Enterprise Developer, and Professional. The examples and templates in this book require Visual Studio .NET Enterprise Architect or Enterprise Developer. Most concepts and examples work with the Professional version but will be incomplete.

Exploring the New Solution Options

In Visual Studio .NET, application source code is grouped into two entities: projects and solutions. *Projects* implement a specific business function, and *solutions* are collections of projects (similar to the workspace concept in Visual Studio 6.0). As each chapter progresses, you will implement a small piece of the overall enterprise application. The source code for each chapter will be packaged as projects within the IssueTracker solution.

To begin, start Visual Studio .NET 2003 and click the New Project button in the Projects tab. The New Project dialog box presents several templates related to creating an enterprise application. Expand the Other Projects tree node and select the Enterprise Template Projects node (see Figure 1-7).

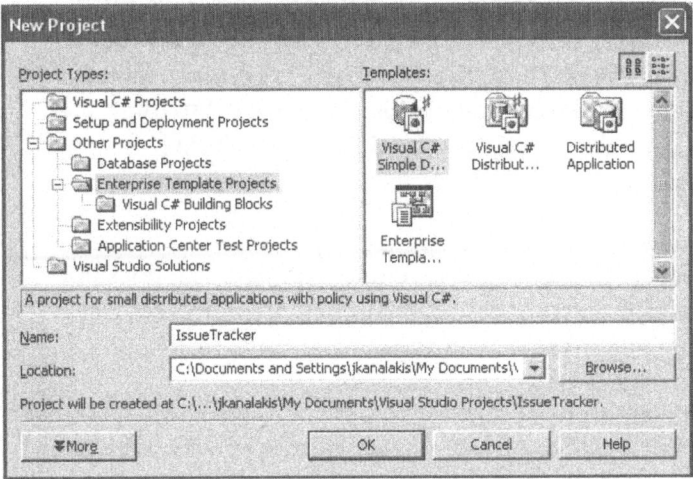

Figure 1-7. The New Project dialog box

The following project templates become available:

Visual C# Distributed Application: This template creates a C# version of the standard Distributed Application solution. This template consists of seven layers, allowing for multiple projects of different programming languages within each layer of the application. This creates either a Windows application or a Web application.

Visual C# Simple Distributed Application: This template is a simpler version of the standard Distributed Application template. This template creates applications that have a simpler structure than the Visual C# Distributed Application template. Each application layer has only a single language project. This creates both a Windows application and a Web application.

Visual Basic Distributed Application: This template is a Visual Basic version of the standard Distributed Application template. This template consists of seven layers, allowing for multiple projects of different programming languages within each area of the application. It includes both a project that produces a Windows user interface and a project that produces a Web user interface.

Visual Basic Simple Distributed Application: This template is a simpler version of the standard Distributed Application template. This template creates applications that have a simpler structure than the Visual Basic Distributed Application template. Each application layer has only a single language project. This template includes a project that produces a Windows user interface and a project that produces a Web user interface.

Distributed Application: This template provides the same structure as the C# and Visual Basic Distributed Application templates but without the initial language projects. This template creates large-scale, mixed-language applications by adding building blocks (projects) to each layer. Conversely, when you select the C# or Visual Basic Distributed Application template, each layer already includes a C# or Visual Basic project.

Enterprise Templates Project: This is an empty template that does not include any language projects or associated policy. Architects can use it to create their own templates.

As mentioned, each enterprise project is composed of multiple layers. Each layer is implemented as a separate project that abstracts a specific enterprise function. These layers include the following:

Business Facade: This project is often used to provide a consistent interface to the underlying business objects and to isolate the client from changes to the underlying business logic. It lives either between the client and the business logic or between the Web service projects and the business logic layers. You abstract application functionality into high-level methods exposed within this layer.

Business Rules: This project contains the business objects themselves and the rules applied to them. They implement the business entities or objects of the system. The business rules of the system are coded within these objects; however, some of the business rules might actually be coded in the database within stored procedures and triggers.

Data Access: This project performs the function of retrieving data from and sending data to the database. It accomplishes this using ADO.NET data access objects and SQL Server stored procedures.

System Frameworks: This project manages the parts of the application that provide system service, system infrastructure functionality, or other shared functionality. This functionality might not be specific to any given application.

ASP.NET Web Service: The Web Service project provides public Web interfaces that are accessible to Web service clients. It can be present independent of the type of user interface (such as a Web client or a Windows client), if any, used in your application. It is one of the ways of remoting application servers. This project is similar to the Business Facade layer except that other Web service clients access its methods, which means it is not limited to being accessed by other parts of the application.

WebUI: This project implements a Web application that renders Web pages to present data, capture user input, perform data validation, provide task guidance to users, send user input to the Business Facade project, and receive results from the Business Facade project.

WinUI: This project implements a Windows form application that renders a user interface to present data, capture user input, perform data validation, provide task guidance to users, send user input to the Business Facade project, and receive results from the Business Facade project.

Implementing the Solution

Select Enterprise Template Projects from the Project Types list box. Next, select Visual C# Simple Distributed Application from the Templates list. Finally, enter *IssueTracker* in the Name box (as shown previously in Figure 1-7), and click the OK button. Visual Studio .NET will prompt you for a Uniform Resource Locator (URL) that points to an Internet Information Server (IIS) location, as illustrated in Figure 1-8. In most cases, the default localhost setting is fine.

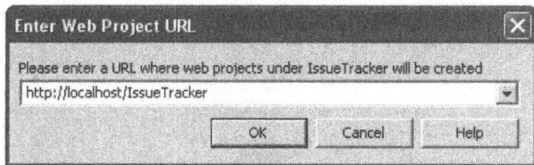

Figure 1-8. Visual Studio .NET can store Web projects on any accessible IIS Web server.

Visual Studio .NET will quickly generate the new solution in different locations. The bulk of the source code will appear within the following location:

```
\My Documents\Visual Studio Projects\IssueTracker
```

The generated Web service project code will appear within the following location:

```
\inetpub\wwwroot\IssueTracker\IssueTracker_WebService
```

The generated Web application project code will appear within the following location:

`\inetpub\wwwroot\IssueTracker\IssueTracker_WebUI`

The IssueTracker solution contains seven projects that implement the business facade, business rules, data access, system framework access, Web user interface, and desktop user interface. As the development of the IssueTracker application continues, new projects will appear within the same solution. Visual Studio .NET displays each project in the Solution Explorer, as illustrated in Figure 1-9.

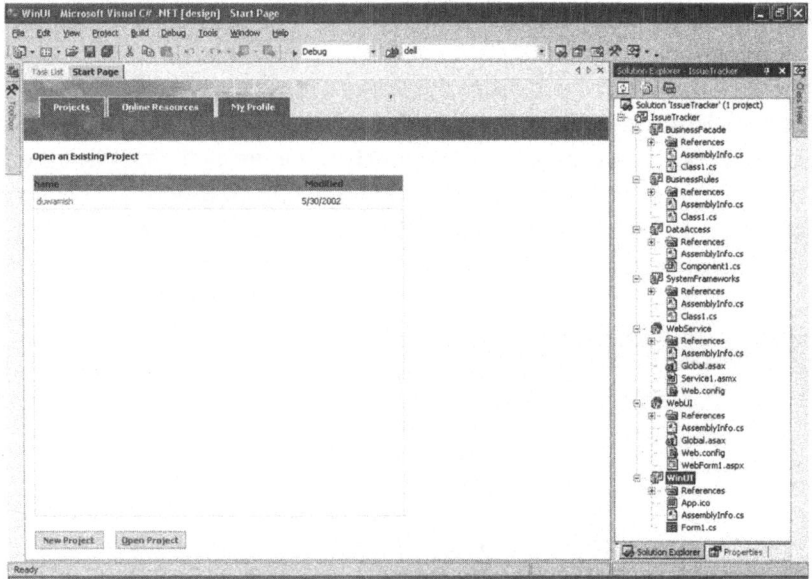

Figure 1-9. The empty enterprise solution in Visual Studio .NET

Once the solution has been created, development of the IssueTracker enterprise application can begin. Over the next few chapters, you will fill in the individual projects under this solution that handle database access, directory services accessibility, messaging, business process automation, e-mail support, and the user interface. Each project will be complete with source code and a test utility.

Summary

As long as there are large businesses, there will always be a need for enterprise applications. This chapter started by defining an enterprise application. Next it described some of the technologies involved in building an enterprise application, such as database access, directory services, messaging services, mail services, process automation, reporting, and user interfacing. The chapter also explained how enterprise applications are designed and how you can use Microsoft's .NET Framework to support rapid development. Finally, the chapter introduced the IssueTracker enterprise application that you will incrementally develop with each chapter of this book.

In the next chapter, you will be exposed to the data services of a .NET enterprise application. You will learn how a structured data access framework can accelerate the development time of data-centric applications. You will also see how you can use certain .NET characteristics—such as properties, collections, and reflection—to implement business objects and an intelligent business object manager.

CHAPTER 2

Accessing Data
in ADO.NET

THIS CHAPTER LAUNCHES your enterprise application development by diving into the heart of any enterprise application, the database. Because the database is indisputably the most important element of any enterprise application, it serves as an ideal starting point for development. This chapter begins by defining the application data access framework and showing how to architect it. Next, the chapter reviews ADO.NET and describes how it fits into the data access framework. It breaks the framework down into its key elements, such as the data access component, the business objects, the business object manager, and the reference data. All examples outline the steps for building the IssueTracker enterprise application, which can translate to just about any enterprise domain.

Building a Data Access Framework

As mentioned in the prior chapter, applying an application framework is important to the success of an enterprise application. A data access framework can ensure scalability, guarantee consistency, and reduce development time in an application. When application developers adopt a uniform framework for data access, they simplify ongoing maintenance and minimize bugs. Figure 2-1 illustrates the data access framework implemented by the IssueTracker enterprise application.

As illustrated, the data access framework has three logical tiers: the data tier, the business tier, and the presentation tier. The data tier represents the physical database, its tables, and rows of data. You expose this data through stored procedures only.

The business tier manages business objects, or in-memory representations of the underlying data. Figure 2-1 divides the business tier into two categories: application business objects and a DataSet. The business objects, defined within the application, represent business-specific entities, such as an Issue or a User.

The DataSet, however, is an ADO.NET-cached collection of tables and rows representing reference data, such as IssueTypes or IssuePriorities.

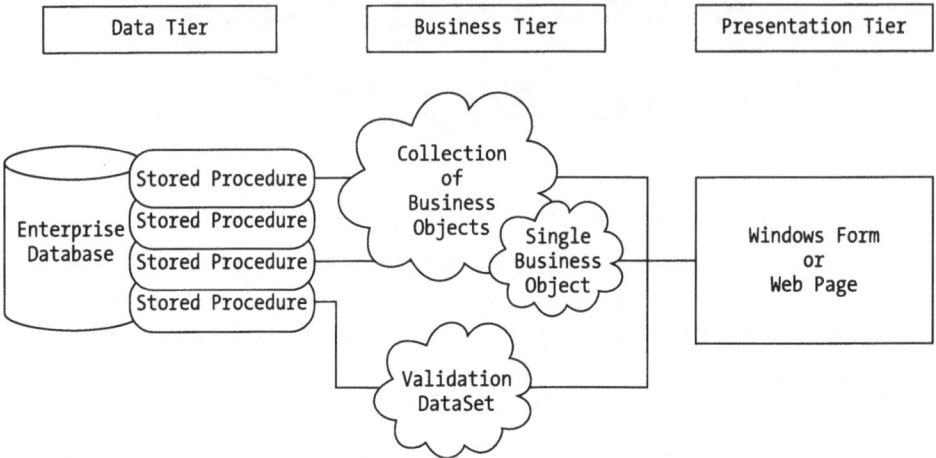

Figure 2-1. Data access framework composed of three functional tiers

The presentation tier interacts with the application data through the business objects only. It is completely disconnected from the underlying database. As a result, the underlying database system can switch from Microsoft SQL Server to Oracle to MySQL without changes to the user interface. Similarly, multiple clients may consistently interact with the underlying data—including Web pages, Web services, Windows forms, and mobile clients—simply by interacting with business objects.

Understanding the ADO.NET Architecture

ADO.NET has been designed specifically for multitier enterprise development. In other words, an enterprise application can scale with support for thousands of connecting users without slowing down significantly because its major elements run on different servers. ADO.NET provides flexibility to multitier environments by providing both direct and disconnected data access.

Direct data access and disconnected data access offer different advantages to an enterprise application. *Direct data access* allows an application to read from and write to a database directly and immediately. This offers the fastest response time to an application. *Disconnected data access* allows an application to read from and write to a memory image of the database, not the database itself. The memory image of the database is complete with separate tables, columns, and relationships between the tables. This offers the advantage of freeing valuable database connections while performing extensive processing on data or while binding user interface elements directly to values within the database. The application later commits the changes in memory back to the database.

ADO.NET abstracts direct and disconnected data access with two foundation objects in the System.Data namespace: the DataProvider object and the DataSet object. Both objects contain additional supporting objects that help round out their functionality. A DataProvider object abstracts direct data access and contains the Connection, Command, DataReader, and DataAdapter objects. The DataSet object abstracts disconnected data access and contains DataTables and DataRelations. A DataTable object contains the DataColumn, DataRow, and Constraint objects. Figure 2-2 illustrates these object relationships as defined by the ADO.NET framework.

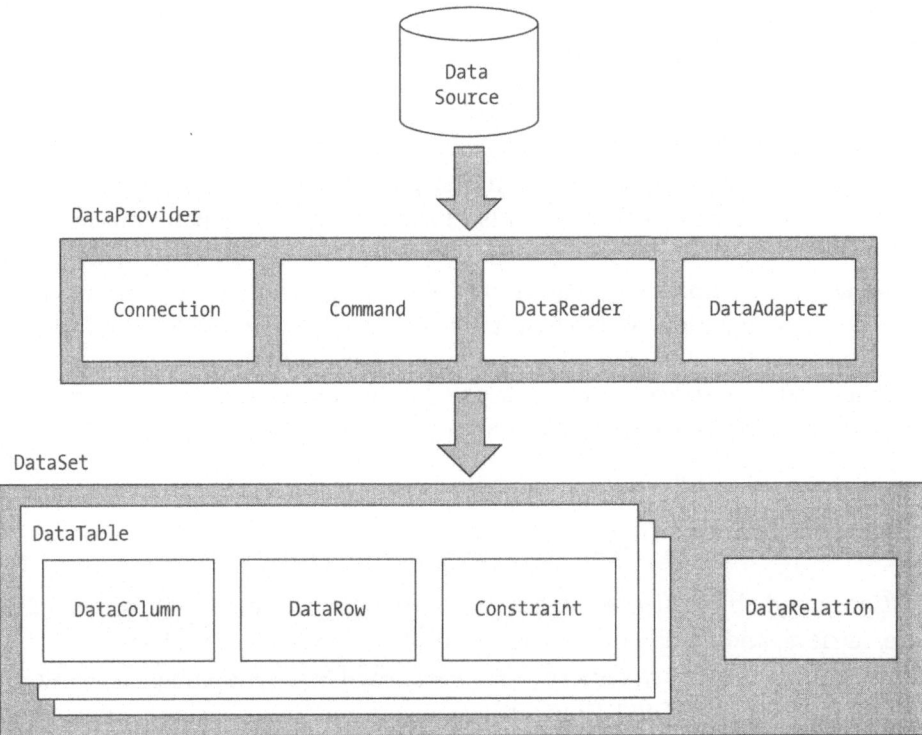

Figure 2-2. ADO.NET data access objects and their relationships

Using the DataProvider Object

The ADO.NET DataProvider object establishes direct database connections and executes commands that store and retrieve application data. You can build and optimize data providers, also known as *managed providers*, for maximum performance on a specific database platform. ADO.NET provides two managed providers, one optimized for SQL Server database connectivity and another that connects to Object Linking and Embedding (OLE) databases, such as Microsoft Access. Vendors, such as DB/2 and Sybase, can create and distribute customized DataProvider objects that optimize performance for their database engines. As shown in Figure 2-2, the DataProvider object comprises four principal objects: Connection, Command, DataReader, and DataAdapter. Each object within a DataProvider has been optimized for performance with a specific database platform. You can download an Oracle DataProvider directly from the Oracle Technology Network site at `http://otn.oracle.com/tech/windows/odpnet/content.html`. You can download data providers for other database solutions from the respective vendor Web sites.

Using the Connection Object

The Connection object provides the basic connectivity to a database. When an application establishes a direct database connection, this is where the application begins. The three most significant methods this object offers are its constructor, the Open method, and the Close method. The constructor initializes the Connection object with connection details passed as an argument, known as a *connection string*. The connection string includes a username, password, database location, and default table name. The Open method establishes the connection to the database and manages a handle to that connection. Subsequent database access methods use that handle, which is eventually released when the Close method disconnects the database connection.

Using the Command Object

The Command object invokes database commands and stored procedures that store, retrieve, and modify data residing within the database. Database commands, known as *query statements*, follow standard SQL syntax such as SELECT, INSERT, UPDATE, and DELETE to retrieve, insert, modify, or delete records (respectively). The query string passes to the Command object along with a reference to the database connection.

The SqlCommand object contains four methods that execute commands to the database: ExecuteNonQuery, ExecuteReader, ExecuteScalar, and ExecuteXmlReader. Each serves a different purpose depending upon the expected response from the database.

The ExecuteNonQuery method is for executing commands that do not return any rows of data but, rather, that return the number of records affected by the command. Typically, commands that modify the database, such as INSERT, UPDATE, or DELETE commands, use the ExecuteNonQuery method.

The ExecuteReader method is for executing commands that return multiple rows of data. Typically, commands that retrieve data, such as the SELECT command, use the ExecuteReader method. This method returns a SqlDataReader object that provides forward-only and read-only access to the command results. An application can traverse the records by retrieving them one at a time but cannot view previous records already read.

The ExecuteScalar method is for executing commands that return only a single column of data from a single row. Typically, this method is for executing an aggregate function, such as COUNT, SUM, or MAX.

The ExecuteXmlReader method is for executing commands that return data intended for Extensible Markup Language (XML) document formatting. Typically, commands that retrieve data and specify FOR XML AUTO in their command clauses use the ExecuteXmlReader method.

Using the DataReader Object

The DataReader object provides the fastest means of data access by sending forward-only and read-only data access to an application. The DataReader object works closely with the ExecuteReader method to provide an application with the results of a data retrieval command. There is cost associated with its fast data access, however. Specifically, the DataReader object is resource intensive in that it maintains an open connection to the database. This can adversely affect the scalability of an application because multiple data requests by multiple users force the database to run out of available connections. Using the DataReader object should be limited to fast-executing queries that do not tie up valuable connections for any length of time.

A number of data access methods are available to retrieve record values based on the different column types. The most common methods used include GetInt16, GetInt32, GetString, and GetBoolean. Each method requires a zero-based column identifier. Each time you call the Read method, the application returns the next row of data. When a database command first initializes a DataReader object, the DataReader always points just before the first row. To access the first row of data, you must invoke the Read method.

Because the DataReader object is resource intensive, it is also often useful to construct batch queries and use multiple result sets. This allows an application to retrieve the results of multiple queries with a single request to the database. You can accomplish this by assigning the SqlCommand object to multiple SQL queries by a semicolon or to a Transact-SQL stored procedure. After invoking the ExecuteReader method, you can retrieve data using the data access methods previously described. Finally, to point to the next batched result set, invoke the DataReader object's NextResult method.

Using the DataAdapter Object

Although the Connection, Command, and DataReader objects provide applications with all that they need to accomplish direct database connectivity and interactivity, the DataAdapter object rounds out the DataProvider object's functionality by providing a bridge to the memory image of the database. That memory image is the DataSet object, as shown in Figure 2-2. The DataAdapter fills the DataSet object with records from the database and later commits changes in the DataSet back to the database.

Using the DataSet Object

The ADO.NET DataSet object manages a disconnected memory representation of the database. Applications can quickly execute commands that store and retrieve data from this memory image, which is periodically synchronized with the actual database. See the "Understanding the DataSet Object" section to see how the IssueTracker application uses it to manage the cached reference data.

Creating the Data Access Component

The data access component exists within the data tier and serves as the middle-man between the underlying database and the business objects. It is responsible for filling the business object with data from database records as well as creating or updating records based upon changes within the business objects.

Implementing the DataAccess Project

The Visual C# Simple Distributed Application solution template (created in Chapter 1, "Introducing .NET and Enterprise Architecture") provides a DataAccess project, as shown in Figure 2-3. Initially, this project contains a single source file that implements the DataComponent object.

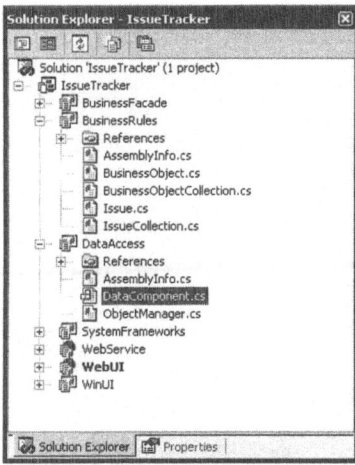

Figure 2-3. The DataAccess project for the IssueTracker solution

Creating the Application Database

The IssueTracker enterprise application will consist of eight tables, three containing application data records and five containing reference data records. You can create the tables manually using the table designer within the SQL Server Enterprise Manager or by using the SQL Server Query Analyzer to execute the setup scripts defined in Appendix A, "Building the IssueTracker Database."

Using the SQL Server Enterprise Manager

The SQL Server Enterprise Manager provides an interface for administering the entire SQL Server database. Services include creating and managing database instances, connections, users, stored procedures, tables, and constraints. The built-in table designer offers the fastest and easiest way to create new database tables.

The IssueTracker enterprise application will require a database, such as SQL Server, to store its application data. From the SQL Server Enterprise Manager, expand the local server tree node, as shown in Figure 2-4. Next, click the node labeled *Databases* and then select Action ➤ New Database from the menu. Enter **IssueTracker** for the database name, as shown in Figure 2-5, and click OK to create the database.

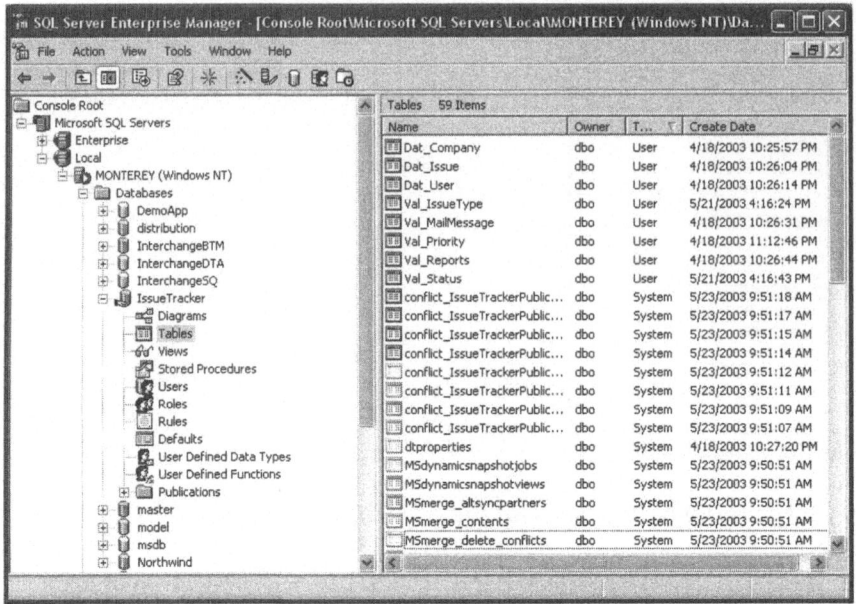

Figure 2-4. The SQL Server Enterprise Manager

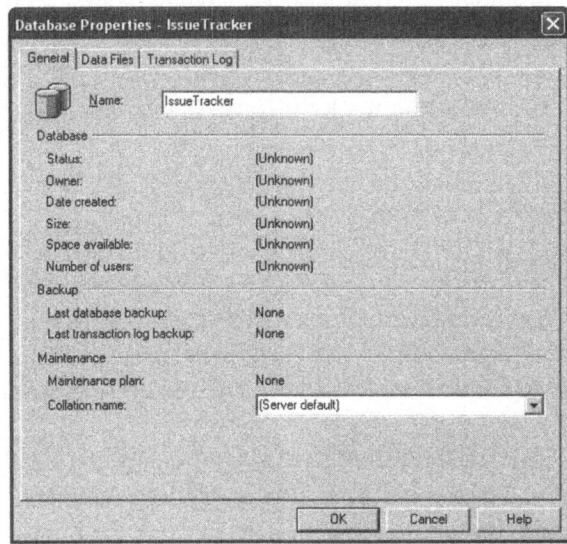

Figure 2-5. Creating a new database in SQL Server

Once you have created the database, you can add new tables with the help
of the table designer. First, select Action ➤ New ➤ Table from the SQL Server
Enterprise Manager menu. In the table designer, enter the column name, the
data type, and the data type characteristics for each column to match the

IssueTracker table creation scripts as specified in Appendix A, "Building the IssueTracker Database."

Using the SQL Server Query Analyzer

The SQL Server Query Analyzer is another helpful database tool that provides an interface for executing SQL statements and viewing the results. This tool helps test SQL statements before you embed them within the application. Another approach to creating tables is to build SQL statements that build each table, as shown in Figure 2-6. Typically, applications provide database setup scripts with many lines of SQL instructions that build a database schema required by an application. You can customize these scripts for a target database platform that might offer features not available from other databases.

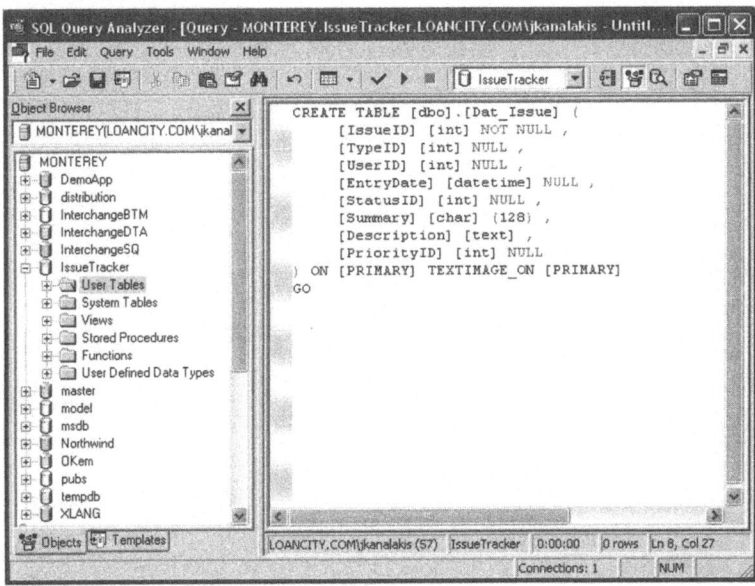

Figure 2-6. The SQL Server Query Analyzer

Creating Stored Procedures

Stored procedures are fast-executing routines that are coded and compiled on the database server. You can use stored procedures for all forms of data access, including select, insert, update, delete, and validation commands. Visual Studio .NET provides a helpful approach to quickly create stored procedures.

To create a stored procedure, begin by displaying the data access component in its design view. Right-click the sqlDataAdapter control and select Configure Data Adapter from its context menu. This launches the Data Adapter Configuration Wizard, as shown in Figure 2-7.

Click Next to advance from the wizard's start page. Next, create a connection to the database by clicking the New Connection button and entering the connection details in the Data Link Properties dialog box, as shown in Figure 2-8.

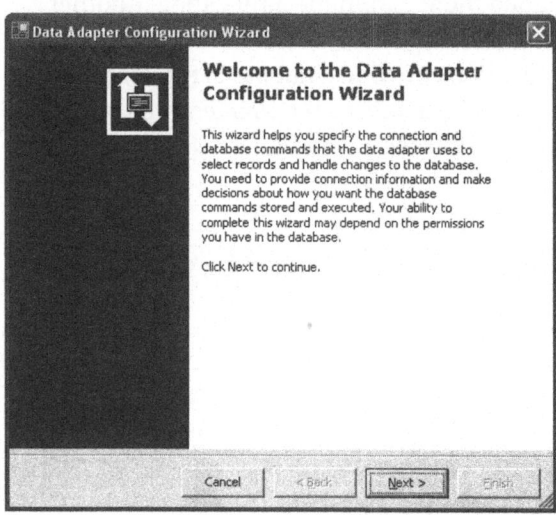

Figure 2-7. The Data Adapter Configuration Wizard start page

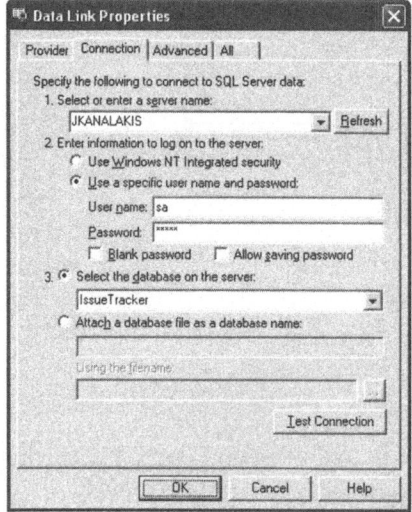

Figure 2-8. Data Link Properties dialog box used to create new database connections

Click Next to continue and click the Create New Stored Procedures radio button. Click Next to continue to the Generate Stored Procedures page. Click the Query Builder button to choose a table with which to work. In the Add Table dialog box, select only the table relating to the business object being worked on—in this case, the Dat_Issue table—and then click the Close button. The Query Builder window displays, as shown in Figure 2-9.

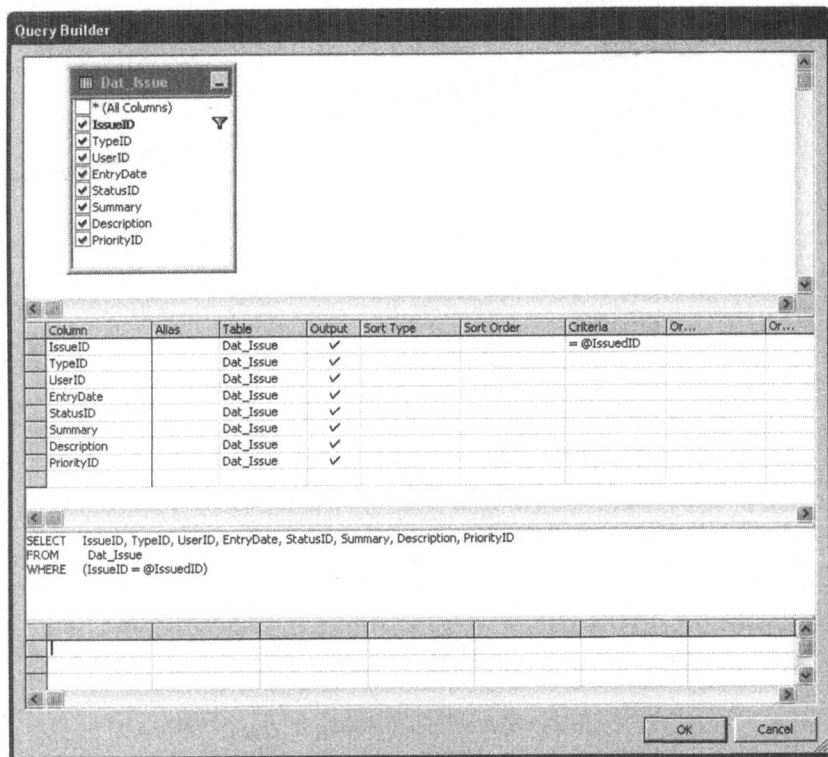

Figure 2-9. The ADO.NET Query Builder

Individually select each column name that will be used to fill the business object and click the OK button. For stored procedures relating to a single business object, enter a criteria field associated with the primary key column. In the case of the app_IssueSelect stored procedure, enter a criteria of **= @IssueID**. Before advancing, click the Advanced Options button, disable the Use Optimistic Concurrency and Refresh the DataSet options, and click the OK button. Click the Next button to display the Create the Stored Procedures page. It is important to enter the stored procedure names consistently in the naming convention specified by the data access framework:

```
app_[object][action]
```

Figure 2-10 illustrates the stored procedure naming convention as it is applied to the Issue object. From here, you can view the stored procedure creation scripts by clicking the Preview SQL Script button. The wizard also provides an option to automatically create the stored procedures within SQL Server. Click the Finish button to finalize the process.

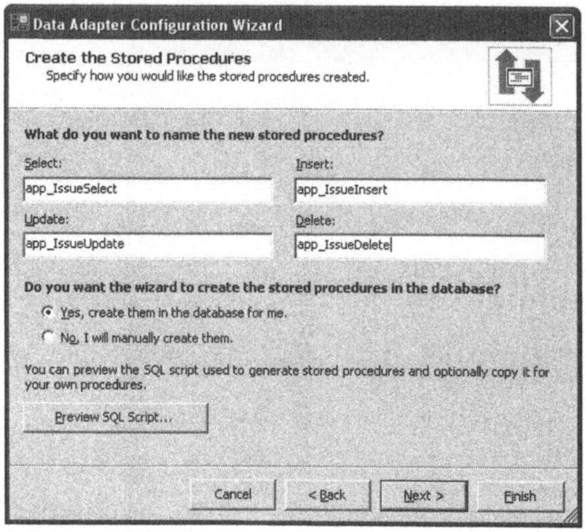

Figure 2-10. Naming the auto-created stored procedures

The wizard produces the stored procedures shown in Listing 2-1 and may optionally create the stored procedures in the connected database.

Listing 2-1. Auto-Generated Stored Procedures for the Dat_Issue Table

```
CREATE PROCEDURE [dbo].[app_IssueSelectAll]
AS SET NOCOUNT ON;
SELECT IssueID, TypeID, UserID, EntryDate, StatusID, Summary, Description,
PriorityID FROM Dat_Issue
GO


CREATE PROCEDURE [dbo].[app_IssueSelect]
(
    @IssueID int
)
AS SET NOCOUNT ON;
SELECT IssueID, TypeID, UserID, EntryDate, StatusID, Summary, Description,
PriorityID FROM Dat_Issue WHERE (IssueID = @IssueID);
GO
```

```
CREATE PROCEDURE [dbo].[app_IssueInsert]
(
    @IssueID int,
    @TypeID int,
    @UserID int,
    @EntryDate datetime,
    @StatusID int,
    @Summary char(128),
    @Description text,
    @PriorityID int,
    @ModifiedDate datetime
)
AS SET NOCOUNT OFF;
INSERT INTO Dat_Issue(IssueID, TypeID, UserID, EntryDate, StatusID, Summary,
Description, PriorityID, ModifiedDate) VALUES (@IssueID, @TypeID, @UserID,
@EntryDate, @StatusID, @Summary, @Description, @PriorityID, @ModifiedDate);
GO


CREATE PROCEDURE [dbo].[app_IssueUpdate]
(
    @IssueID int,
    @TypeID int,
    @UserID int,
    @EntryDate datetime,
    @StatusID int,
    @Summary char(128),
    @Description text,
    @PriorityID int,
    @ModifiedDate datetime,
    @Original_IssueID int,
    @Original_ModifiedDate datetime
)
AS SET NOCOUNT OFF;
UPDATE Dat_Issue SET IssueID = @IssueID, TypeID = @TypeID, UserID = @UserID,
EntryDate = @EntryDate, StatusID = @StatusID, Summary = @Summary, Description =
@Description, PriorityID = @PriorityID, ModifiedDate = @ModifiedDate WHERE
(IssueID = @Original_IssueID) AND (ModifiedDate = @Original_ModifiedDate);

IF @@ROWCOUNT=0
    RAISERROR ('Optimistic concurrency failed.', 10, 1)
GO


CREATE PROCEDURE [dbo].[app_IssueDelete]
```

```
(
    @Original_IssueID int,
    @Original_ModifiedDate datetime
)
AS SET NOCOUNT OFF;
DELETE FROM Dat_Issue WHERE (IssueID = @Original_IssueID) AND
(ModifiedDate = @Original_ModifiedDate);
GO
```

The process of creating stored procedures can be time consuming. Four stored procedures should exist for every business object. In the IssueTracker application, this means you need four stored procedures for the Issue, User, and Company objects. You must create an additional stored procedure for each collection of objects as well.

You need to modify the stored procedures produced by Visual Studio .NET to better support concurrency. In any enterprise application, the possibility exists that a row of data will be accessed and possibly modified by more than one user. Adopting a concurrency model defines how the application reacts to such a situation. The three common models for handling concurrency are the last-in-wins, optimistic, and pessimistic models.

The least dependable approach to handling concurrency is to take no action. As multiple users view and edit the same record, the last user to update the row ends up with the stored values. This is known as a *last-in-wins* scenario because it does not matter which user begins editing row data first. The last user to update the row keeps the changes.

An alternative approach is to implement optimistic concurrency. *Optimistic concurrency* locks a row from other users while an update operation is in progress. If it is detected that an existing row has already been claimed for change by another object, then the update fails and the user is prompted to refresh the data. This approach adds a slight performance overhead for update operations but adds to the overall data integrity. Optimistic concurrency is the preferred model for managing concurrency within disconnected data.

Another alternative to handling concurrency is to completely lock the row from the moment the data is initially read, a process known as *pessimistic concurrency*. This adds a tremendous performance overhead because rows that may not be intended for updates still perform expensive record locks. If an application is not concerned about accommodating concurrent updates, then no action is necessary. If concurrency handling is necessary, then optimistic concurrency performs best for data that rarely encounters user conflicts during update and delete operations. Records that are often shared and updated concurrently by multiple users should rely upon pessimistic concurrency for better performance.

By default, DataSet objects handle optimistic concurrency by comparing all original row values to the values that currently exist within the database.

If the values are the same, it is assumed that another user did not change the row and the new values may be committed to the database. In Listing 2-1, the app_IssueUpdate stored procedure has been modified to evaluate a time stamp, identified as ModifiedDate. The code that invokes this stored procedure supplies values that indicate when the record was originally read. If the time stamp of the row is more recent than that provided by the code, then the code is working with out-of-date data. In this case, the RAISERROR statement throws an exception.

> **NOTE** *Alternatively, another approach to managing concurrency is to replace the DateTime column with a Globally Unique Identifier (GUID) column. This permits the same row version comparison in the WHERE clause, but it offers the added performance benefit of applying a nonclustered index.*

You can handle optimistic concurrency violations in many ways. In most cases, the application notifies the user that their changes cannot be saved and offers to reload the relevant data. A rich user interface could also track the user interface form fields that changed and, if they are not affected by the reload, automatically reapply the user edits. You should consistently apply the approach you choose to all concurrency situations.

Setting Up Database Security

Because enterprise applications manage business data and services, security must be a part of the application from the beginning. In the data tier, there are three areas of security: stored procedures, Windows Authentication, and nonpersisted security information.

Working with Stored Procedures

Stored procedures are much more than compiled scripts that efficiently execute SQL statements. They are a first line of defense against intrusive attacks upon the application. Any time a SQL command is created dynamically based upon user input, it is at risk of being hijacked by a malicious user. The most common example is a simple query:

```
SELECT IssueID, Summary from Dat_Issue WHERE PriorityID = ?
```

Assuming that the question mark (?) identifies a user-inputted value, it is possible for a malicious user to enter a value that results in the following query instead:

```
SELECT IssueID, Summary from Dat_Issue WHERE PriorityID = 1; DROP Dat_Issue;
```

The result of the query would return the appropriate records and then immediately delete the entire Dat_Issue table. Limiting the user interface entry field helps, but accepting only parameterized values in a stored procedure is better. This is part of the reason that the data access framework relies upon stored procedures for all data management.

Working with Windows Authentication

SQL Server supports two different approaches to user authentication: Windows Authentication and Mixed Mode Authentication. By relying upon Windows Authentication, you avoid the need to build a connection string that embeds the database password.

Also, because typical enterprise data is read from significantly more than written to, you should create two separate accounts with separate permissions to read and write. This reduces the risk of damage if someone compromises the read-access password.

Avoiding Persisted Security Information

Set `persist security info` to false to avoid security-sensitive details, such as the password, from being returned by means of the ConnectionString property of the SqlConnection or OleDbConnection object. Append the following statement to the connection string:

```
persist security info=False;
```

Enabling Connection Pooling

When several users are connecting to a database, opening and closing a connection for each user can add overhead that eventually brings the database to a crawl. *Connection pooling* enables an application to work with a number of already-open connections that are passed between processes rather than constantly opened and closed. Most languages require extra code or a third-party library to enable connection pooling. However, with ADO.NET, the connection pooling is already in the Connection object. The following code implicitly creates a new connection pool when the Open method is invoked using a different connection string:

```
SqlConnection connection1 = new SqlConnection();
connection1.ConnectionString = "Initial Catalog=IssueTracker";
connection1.Open();
//connection pool 1 is created

SqlConnection connection2 = new SqlConnection();
connection2.ConnectionString = "Initial Catalog=CustomerDatabase";
connection2.Open();
//connection pool 2 is created because the connection strings differ

SqlConnection connection3 = new SqlConnection();
connection3.ConnectionString = "Initial Catalog=IssueTracker";
connection3.Open();
//connection comes from pool 1 because connection string matches
```

When a SqlConnection object requests a connection, it obtains that connection from the connection pool until the maximum pool size is reached. If the maximum pool size is reached, the SqlConnection object queues that request until the connection pool has an available connection. This is why it is important to always close a database connection. If several connections are made and the connection pool reaches its capacity, any remaining connections will be queued. Any queued connection requests that reach their Connect Timeout property value will return as an error. You can set the connection pool characteristics by appending to the connection string. To override the default connection pool settings and set a new maximum pool size of 250 connections, include the following connection string:

```
//example
SqlConnection connection;
connection = new SqlConnection( "user id=sa;password=;" +
    "Data Source=localhost;Initial Catalog=IssueTracker;" +
    "Max Pool Size=250");
connection.Open();
```

Using Transactions

Transactions are a series of commands that all need to be executed successfully for the whole series to be successful. If any of the commands within a series fails, then all of the commands within the series fail. You can accomplish transactions in ADO.NET with three methods: BeginTransaction, Commit, and RollBack. The following example creates a SqlTransaction object and assigns it to a SqlCommand object. One or more queries execute within the transaction, and the SqlTransaction object's Commit method commits all changes. If any exceptions are thrown within the try/catch block, the RollBack method undoes the changes:

```
SqlTransaction transaction = connection.BeginTransaction();
command.Transaction = transaction;

try
{
    command.CommandText = "UPDATE Dat_Issue SET StatusID = 0";
    command.ExecuteNonQuery();
    command.CommandText = "UPDATE Dat_Issue SET TypeID = 1";
    command.ExecuteNonQuery();
    transaction.Commit();
}
catch( SqlException exception )
{
    transaction.RollBack();
}
```

Building Application Framework Objects

Application framework objects are memory structures that closely resemble parts of the database schema. They temporarily hold information that is passed between the database and the user interface. The two foundation entities are business objects and business object collections.

Working with Business Objects

Within the application framework, you implement business objects within a public class that inherits from the BusinessObject class. They have properties that match fields within a corresponding database table. Business objects are more functional than simple DataRow objects in that they may also provide object-specific functionality, such as data validation. Listing 2-2 presents the BusinessObject base class.

Listing 2-2. The Abstract Base Class for All Business Objects

```
public abstract class BusinessObject
{
    private DateTime _RowModified;

    public BusinessObject()
    {
        return;
    }
    public bool Select()
    {
        return false;
    }
    public bool Insert()
    {
        return false;
    }
    public bool Update()
    {
        return false;
    }
    public bool Delete()
    {
        return false;
    }
    public bool Validate()
    {
        return false;
    }

    public DateTime RowModified
    {
        set
        {
            _RowModified = value;
        }
        get
        {
            return _RowModified;
        }
    }
}
```

The BusinessObject class is abstract and cannot be instantiated itself. Application business objects, such as Issue and User, must inherit from this to participate within the application framework. The BusinessObject class defines the methods that must be implemented in the inherited class. Listing 2-3 outlines the implementation of the Issue business object.

Listing 2-3. The Issue Business Object Definition

```
public class Issue : BusinessObject
{
    private int _IssueID;
    private int _TypeID;
    private int _UserID;
    private int _StatusID;
    private int _PriorityID;
    private string _Summary;
    private string _Description;
    private DateTime _EntryDate;

    //property accessor implementation
    public int IssueID
    {
        get { return _IssueID; }
        set { _IssueID = value; }
    }

    public int TypeID
    {
        get { return _TypeID; }
        set { _TypeID = value; }
    }

    public int UserID
    {
        get { return _UserID; }
        set { _UserID = value; }
    }

    public DateTime EntryDate
    {
        get { return _EntryDate; }
        set { _EntryDate = value; }
    }
```

```
    public int StatusID
    {
        get { return _StatusID; }
        set { _StatusID = value; }
    }

    public String Summary
    {
        get { return _Summary; }
        set { _Summary = value; }
    }

    public String Description
    {
        get { return _Description; }
        set { _Description = value; }
    }

    public int Priority
    {
        get { return _PriorityID; }
        set { _PriorityID = value; }
    }
}
```

The Issue business object begins by inheriting from the BusinessObject base class. The object properties are defined as they appear in the database table definition, and the resulting stored procedure should comply with a specific naming convention. For example, the object name *Issue* should match its relative data table name of *Dat_Issue*.

Most traditional classes have private data members and public access methods. Although public get and set methods are easy to create, the C# language preference is to define property accessors for each data element. This way, an application can set the value of a data member on the right side of an equals operator rather than as a parameter to a set method. Given the object definition for the Issue class, an application can quickly and easily set data members without the need for public access methods:

```
Issue issue = new Issue();
issue.Summary = "Unable to print.";
issue.Description = "Everytime I print, an error message appears.";
issue.Priority = 1;
```

When implementing the property accessors, it is important that the public accessor name matches its relative column name in the database table. For example, the property name of *IssueID* should match the column name of *Dat_Issue.IssueID*. The private data member name, however, can be just about anything. The User and Company entities require that additional business objects be created.

Working with Business Object Collections

Enumerators are another C# utility that help provide structure to application code. Rather than managing an array of Issue objects and then iterating through the list, the user interface logic can use the foreach statement to cycle through a list of Issue objects. First, define the Issue class to be Enumerable. Next, create an enumerator class that owns the responsibility of cycling through the Issue objects within an array. Implementing a custom collection class has advantages over using simple DataRow objects because you can create custom validation code and interobject mappings. Listing 2-4 shows the abstract base class for all framework business object collections, and Listing 2-5 shows how that class is inherited to implement the IssueCollection.

Listing 2-4. The Abstract Base Class for All Business Object Collections

```
public abstract class BusinessObjectCollection
{
    //manage business objects within an ArrayList with a default size of 25
    ArrayList _Objects = new ArrayList(25);

    //force derived classes to implement the New method
    public abstract BusinessObject New();

    //add a new business object to the collection
    public void Add( BusinessObject argObject )
    {
        _Objects.Add( argObject );
    }

    //return the number of contained business objects
    public int Count
    {
        get
        {
            return( _Objects.Count );
        }
```

```
    }

    //internally validate if an array index is valid
    private void CheckIndex(int argIndex)
    {
        if( argIndex >= _Objects.Count )
            throw new ArgumentOutOfRangeException( "Index out of range" );
    }

    //return a business object by array index reference
    public BusinessObject this[int argIndex]
    {
        get
        {
            CheckIndex(argIndex);
            return (BusinessObject)_Objects[argIndex];
        }
        set
        {
            CheckIndex(argIndex);
            _Objects[argIndex] = value;
        }
    }

    //return the associated enumerator object
    public IEnumerator GetEnumerator()
    {
        return( new BusinessObjectCollectionEnumerator(this) );
    }
}



class BusinessObjectCollectionEnumerator: IEnumerator
{
    BusinessObjectCollection _Collection;
    int _Index;

    //initialize the enumerator with the collection
    internal BusinessObjectCollectionEnumerator(
        BusinessObjectCollection argCollection)
    {
        _Collection = argCollection;
        Reset();
```

```
        }

        //advance the current position to the next element
        public bool MoveNext()
        {
            _Index++;
            if( _Index >= _Collection.Count )
                return( false );

            else
                return( true );
        }

        //return the current business object
        public object Current
        {
            get
            {
                return( _Collection[ _Index ]);
            }
        }

        //reset the enumerator
        public void Reset()
        {
            _Index = -1;
        }

    }
```

Listing 2-5. The IssueCollection Business Object Collection

```
public class IssueCollection : BusinessObjectCollection
{
    public IssueCollection()
    {
        return;
    }

    //create a new instance of the Issue object
    public override BusinessObject New()
```

```
    {
        return new Issue();
    }
}
```

The BusinessObjectCollection class is an abstract base class from which framework business object collections should be derived. By inheriting business object collections, such as IssueCollection, from this class, they will behave consistently and benefit from the filling capability of the business object manager. Inherited objects will have the same base properties, such as Count, and the same base methods, such as New. Listing 2-6 demonstrates a variation of the IssueCollection that includes a method that can be applied to a group of Issue objects.

Listing 2-6. IssueCollection Implementation with an Optional Group Action Method

```
public class IssueCollection : BusinessObjectCollection
{
    public IssueCollection()
    {
        return;
    }

    public override BusinessObject New()
    {
        return new Issue();
    }

    public void MyCustomGroupAction()
    {
        return;
    }
}
```

The IssueCollection class must implement the abstract base method New. This method simply creates an instance of the object it collects and is largely needed by the business object manager. The MyCustomGroupAction method merely demonstrates the ability to implement a collection-level method, specific to this object type. This derived class will also benefit from an enumerator object that can return individual business objects in a foreach statement. Not only will inherited collections benefit from the batch loading of business objects provided by the business object manager, but they may also implement custom functionality that performs unique validation:

```
IssueCollection myIssues = new IssueCollection();
DataAccess.ObjectManager objManager = new DataAccess.ObjectManager();
objManager.SelectAll( myIssues );

foreach( Issue myIssue in myIssues )
{
    System.Diagnostics.Debug.WriteLine( myIssue.Summary );
}
```

Creating the Business Object Manager

The business object manager is responsible for managing the relationship of data between the business objects and the underlying database. This includes filling the business objects from records within the database as well as inserting, updating, and deleting database records based on values within the business objects.

Creating a business object manager can significantly accelerate application development. Rather than implementing specialized code for every business object that selects, inserts, updates, deletes, and validates data, you can create one utility that manages all of these interactions consistently. The tradeoff, however, is flexibility. For a business object to be properly managed, it must adhere to specific naming requirements that allow the reflection code to function properly.

Creating the SelectOne Method

The SelectOne method loads a single identified business object from the database using a dynamically specified stored procedure. Listing 2-7 implements the SelectOne method, which populates a single business object with values stored in a specific database record.

Listing 2-7. The SelectOne Method That Populates a Single Business Object

```
public bool SelectOne( BusinessObject objSource, int intObjectID )
{
    bool boolStatus = false;
    string strObject;
    string strStoredProc;
    SqlParameter parameter;
```

```
SqlCommand command;

try
{
    //get the object name
    Type objType = objSource.GetType();
    strObject = objType.FullName.Substring( objType.FullName.IndexOf(".")+1);

    //get the stored procedure name
    strStoredProc = "app_";
    strStoredProc += strObject;
    strStoredProc += "Select";

    //initialize the command
    command = new SqlCommand( strStoredProc, dataComponent.Connection );
    command.CommandType = CommandType.StoredProcedure;

    //add the ID parameter
    parameter = new SqlParameter( "@" + strObject + "ID", SqlDbType.Int );
    parameter.Direction = ParameterDirection.Input;
    parameter.Value = intObjectID;
    command.Parameters.Add( parameter );

    //open the connection and execute query
    dataComponent.Connection.Open();
    SqlDataReader reader = command.ExecuteReader();

    if( reader.Read() )
    {
        //examine results and set business object, set return code to true
        for( int intIndex = 0; intIndex < reader.FieldCount; intIndex++ )
        {
            string strColName = reader.GetName( intIndex );
            PropertyInfo field = objType.GetProperty( strColName );
            field.SetValue( objSource, reader.GetValue( intIndex ), null );
        }

        boolStatus = true;
    }
}
catch( Exception exception )
{
    EventLog systemLog = new EventLog();
```

```
        systemLog.Source = "IssueTracker";
        systemLog.WriteEntry( exception.Message, EventLogEntryType.Error, 0 );
    }
    finally
    {
        dataComponent.Connection.Close();
    }

    return boolStatus;
}
```

This method populates a single business object that must derive from the BusinessObject abstract class. Let's assume that this method populates an Issue business object. The method begins by receiving an Issue object and an Issue ID that identifies the specific row in the Dat_Issue table. The Type object captures the named object type, which is trimmed down to the specific class name of *Issue*. Next, the method dynamically creates the stored procedure name to look like *app_IssueSelect*. Framework standards dictate that a stored procedure with a matching name must exist. Next, a local SqlCommand object initializes with the name of the stored procedure and a valid SqlConnection. The CommandType is set to expect a stored procedure. Next, because only a single Issue object is expected, a SqlParameter object is defined. Again, standards require the parameter be named *@IssueID* and be of type Int. The parameter is set to the ID originally supplied to the method. The connection opens, the query executes, and a SqlDataReader receives the results. Next, each column of the resulting row is examined with the GetName method. The reflection FieldInfo object peeks into the passed Issue business object to seek out a property that matches the column name. Again, standards dictate that the business object has data properties that match the corresponding table's columns. Next, the FieldInfo object's SetValue method sets the appropriate business object property to the corresponding column data. This process repeats for each column of the resulting row, returning a success or fail status.

Creating the SelectAll Method

The SelectAll method loads all database records that apply to a specified business object type. This is typically for list pages within the application. The stored procedure looks nearly identical. When creating the script using the Data Adapter Configuration Wizard, all criteria fields are left empty and the new SELECT stored procedure is app_IssueSelectAll. Listing 2-8 implements the SelectAll method to populate a collection of business objects with values stored in the database.

Listing 2-8. The SelectAll Method That Populates a Business Object Collection

```csharp
public bool SelectAll( BusinessObjectCollection objSource )
{
    bool boolStatus = false;
    string strObject;
    string strStoredProc;
    SqlParameter parameter;
    SqlCommand command;

    try
    {
        //get the object name
        Type objType = objSource.GetType();
        strObject = objType.FullName.Substring( objType.FullName.IndexOf(".")+1);
        strObject = strObject.Replace( "Collection", "" );

        //get the stored procedure name
        strStoredProc = "app_";
        strStoredProc += strObject;
        strStoredProc += "SelectAll";

        //initialize the command
        command = new SqlCommand( strStoredProc, dataComponent.Connection );
        command.CommandType = CommandType.StoredProcedure;

        //open the connection and execute query
        dataComponent.Connection.Open();
        SqlDataReader reader = command.ExecuteReader();

        while( reader.Read() )
        {
            BusinessObject newObject = objSource.New();
            objType = newObject.GetType();

            for( int intIndex = 0; intIndex < reader.FieldCount; intIndex++ )
            {
                string strColName = reader.GetName( intIndex );
                PropertyInfo field = objType.GetProperty( strColName );
                field.SetValue( objSource, reader.GetValue( intIndex ), null );
            }

            objSource.Add( newObject );
```

```
        }

        boolStatus = true;
    }
    catch( Exception exception )
    {
        EventLog systemLog = new EventLog();
        systemLog.Source = "IssueTracker";
        systemLog.WriteEntry( exception.Message, EventLogEntryType.Error, 0 );
    }
    finally
    {
        dataComponent.Connection.Close();
    }

    return boolStatus;
}
```

The SelectAll method functions nearly identically to the SelectOne method. There are only a few subtle differences. The object being passed into the method is an empty business object collection. The stored procedure requires a different name and no parameters. After the query executes, the SqlDataReader object expects multiple rows of data. For each row, the business object collection needs to provide a new business object appropriate to its container type by invoking its New method. The remaining code functions almost the same way as the SelectOne method by applying reflection to determine and fill the business object properties.

Creating the Insert Method

The Insert method performs the opposite task from the SelectOne method. Its purpose is to take a filled business object and insert a new row into the database. Listing 2-9 shows how to use reflection to take values stored in a business object, map them into stored procedure parameters, and insert those values into the database.

Listing 2-9. The Insert Method That Writes a Filled Business Object to the Database

```
public bool Insert( BusinessObject objSource )
{
    bool boolStatus = false;
    string strObject;
    string strStoredProc;
```

```
SqlParameter parameter;
SqlCommand command;

try
{
    //get the object name
    Type objType = objSource.GetType();
    strObject = objType.FullName.Substring( objType.FullName.IndexOf(".")+1);

    //get the stored procedure name
    strStoredProc = "app_";
    strStoredProc += strObject;
    strStoredProc += "Insert";

    //initialize the command
    command = new SqlCommand( strStoredProc, dataComponent.Connection );
    command.CommandType = CommandType.StoredProcedure;

    //add the parameters
    parameter = new SqlParameter( "@RETURN_VALUE", SqlDbType.Int );
    parameter.Direction = ParameterDirection.ReturnValue;
    command.Parameters.Add( parameter );

    PropertyInfo[] fields = objType.GetProperties();

    for( int intIndex = 0; intIndex < fields.Length; intIndex++ )
    {
        parameter = new SqlParameter( "@" + fields[intIndex].Name,
            fields[intIndex].PropertyType );

        parameter.Direction = ParameterDirection.Input;
        parameter.Value = fields[intIndex].GetValue( objSource, null );
        command.Parameters.Add( parameter );
    }

    //open the connection and execute query
    dataComponent.Connection.Open();
    command.ExecuteNonQuery();

    //return the results of the procedure
    if( (Int32)command.Parameters["@RETURN_VALUE"].Value == 0 )
        boolStatus = true;
}
catch( SqlException exception )
```

```
    {
        EventLog systemLog = new EventLog();
        systemLog.Source = "IssueTracker";
        systemLog.WriteEntry( exception.Message, EventLogEntryType.Error, 0 );
    }
    catch( Exception exception )
    {
        EventLog systemLog = new EventLog();
        systemLog.Source = "IssueTracker";
        systemLog.WriteEntry( exception.Message, EventLogEntryType.Error, 0 );
    }
    finally
    {
        dataComponent.Connection.Close();
    }

    return boolStatus;
}
```

The method begins by determining the incoming object type and creating an appropriate stored procedure name. Next, the method creates a stored procedure parameter named *@RETURN_VALUE* and adds it to the SqlCommand object. Then, a series of dynamically generated SqlParameter objects follow. You create each SqlParameter object by dissecting the passed business object using the reflection services. First, the business object's GetFields method returns an array of FieldInfo objects that represent all of the business object properties. Second, that array of fields iterates to dynamically create stored procedure parameters based on the property name, data type, and value. This adds all the created SqlParameter objects to the SqlCommand object. The query executes, and the resulting value evaluates to determine if the operation was successful.

Creating the Update Method

The Update method also receives a filled business object and attempts to update its corresponding row in the database (see Listing 2-10).

Listing 2-10. The Update Method That Replaces a Filled Business Object in the Database

```
public bool Update( BusinessObject objSource )
{
    bool boolStatus = false;
    string strObject;
```

```csharp
string strStoredProc;
SqlParameter parameter;
SqlCommand command;

try
{
    //get the object name
    Type objType = objSource.GetType();
    strObject = objType.FullName.Substring( objType.FullName.IndexOf(".")+1);

    //get the stored procedure name
    strStoredProc = "app_";
    strStoredProc += strObject;
    strStoredProc += "Update";

    //initialize the command
    command = new SqlCommand( strStoredProc, dataComponent.Connection );
    command.CommandType = CommandType.StoredProcedure;

    //add the parameters
    parameter = new SqlParameter( "@RETURN_VALUE", SqlDbType.Int );
    parameter.Direction = ParameterDirection.ReturnValue;
    command.Parameters.Add( parameter );

    //add the original id parameter
    parameter = new SqlParameter( "@Original_" + strObject + "ID",
        SqlDbType.Int );
    parameter.Direction = ParameterDirection.Input;
    FieldInfo field = objType.GetField( strObject + "ID" );
    parameter.Value = (int)field.GetValue( objSource );
    command.Parameters.Add( parameter );

    //original modified date parameter for concurrency check
    parameter = new SqlParameter( "@Original_ModifiedDate",
        SqlDbType.DateTime );
    parameter.Direction = ParameterDirection.Input;
    field = objType.GetField( "RowModified" );
    parameter.Value = (int)field.GetValue( objSource );
    command.Parameters.Add( parameter );

    //update the modified date
    objSource.RowModified = DateTime.Now;
```

```
            PropertyInfo[] fields = objType.GetProperties();

            for( int intIndex = 0; intIndex < fields.Length; intIndex++ )
            {                                    .
                parameter = new SqlParameter( "@" + fields[intIndex].Name,
                    fields[intIndex].PropertyType );

                parameter.Direction = ParameterDirection.Input;
                parameter.Value = fields[intIndex].GetValue( objSource, null );
                command.Parameters.Add( parameter );
            }

            //open the connection and execute query
            dataComponent.Connection.Open();
            command.ExecuteNonQuery();

            //return the results of the procedure
            if( (Int32)command.Parameters["@RETURN_VALUE"].Value == 0 )
                boolStatus = true;
        }
        catch( SqlException exception )
        {
            EventLog systemLog = new EventLog();
            systemLog.Source = "IssueTracker";
            systemLog.WriteEntry( exception.Message, EventLogEntryType.Error, 0 );
        }
        catch( Exception exception )
        {
            EventLog systemLog = new EventLog();
            systemLog.Source = "IssueTracker";
            systemLog.WriteEntry( exception.Message, EventLogEntryType.Error, 0 );
        }
        finally
        {
            dataComponent.Connection.Close();
        }

        return boolStatus;
    }
```

The Update method functions almost exactly as the Insert method. Aside from a different stored procedure name, the only other difference is an additional SqlParameter that supplies the original business object identifier. The update method also checks for data concurrency. Each row in the database is time stamped. Before updating any row in the database, the time stamp is checked to see if the values within the User object are out of date. If the object data is out of date, an exception is thrown and the object data is not committed.

Creating the Delete Method

The Delete method accepts a filled business object and removes its corresponding row from the database. It is common for enterprise applications to not literally delete rows from a database because there are typically many cross-dependencies between tables. Rather, it is common for each entity data table to include an IsDeleted column or something similar. When an entity is marked for deletion, a stored procedure that looks more like *app_IssueUpdate* updates this value from false to true. Listing 2-11 shows how to delete a database record based on values stored in a business object.

Listing 2-11. The Delete Method That Removes a Matching Business Object from the Database

```
public bool Delete( BusinessObject objSource )
{
    bool boolStatus = false;
    string strObject;
    string strStoredProc;
    SqlParameter parameter;
    SqlCommand command;

    try
    {
        //get the object name
        Type objType = objSource.GetType();
        strObject = objType.FullName.Substring( objType.FullName.IndexOf(".")+1);

        //get the stored procedure name
        strStoredProc = "app_";
        strStoredProc += strObject;
        strStoredProc += "Delete";

        //initialize the command
        command = new SqlCommand( strStoredProc, dataComponent.Connection );
        command.CommandType = CommandType.StoredProcedure;

        //add the parameters
        parameter = new SqlParameter( "@RETURN_VALUE", SqlDbType.Int );
```

```
                parameter.Direction = ParameterDirection.ReturnValue;
                command.Parameters.Add( parameter );

                //add the ID parameter
                parameter = new SqlParameter( "@Original_" + strObject + "ID",
                    SqlDbType.Int );
                parameter.Direction = ParameterDirection.Input;
                PropertyInfo field = objType.GetProperty( strObject + "ID" );
                parameter.Value = (int)field.GetValue( objSource, null );
                command.Parameters.Add( parameter );

                //original modified date parameter for concurrency check
                sqlParameter = new SqlParameter( "@Original_ModifiedDate",
                    SqlDbType.DateTime );
                sqlParameter.Direction = ParameterDirection.Input;
                field = objType.GetField( "RowModified" );
                sqlParameter.Value = (int)field.GetValue( objSource );
                sqlCommand.Parameters.Add( sqlParameter );

                //update the modified date
                objSource.RowModified = DateTime.Now;

                //open the connection and execute query
                dataComponent.Connection.Open();
                command.ExecuteNonQuery();

                //return the results of the procedure
                if( (Int32)command.Parameters["@RETURN_VALUE"].Value == 0 )
                    boolStatus = true;
            }
            catch( SqlException exception )
            {
                EventLog systemLog = new EventLog();
                systemLog.Source = "IssueTracker";
                systemLog.WriteEntry( exception.Message, EventLogEntryType.Error, 0 );
            }
            catch( Exception exception )
            {
                EventLog systemLog = new EventLog();
                systemLog.Source = "IssueTracker";
                systemLog.WriteEntry( exception.Message, EventLogEntryType.Error, 0 );
            }
            finally
```

```
    {
        dataComponent.Connection.Close();
    }

    return boolStatus;
}
```

The Delete method functions almost exactly like the Update method does. Instead of the full parameter list, it requires only the return value and unique row identifier. The query executes and the resulting parameter determines whether the operation was successful. Concurrency rules are applied to the Delete method just in case a user decides to delete a record based on stale data.

Managing Reference Data

In an enterprise application, reference data typically does not change. It represents fairly constant values that are displayed in selection lists within the user interface. In the IssueTracker application, this includes values that represent issue types, priority levels, and status codes. Although these values may also be managed as application business objects, their static nature lends themselves well to the cached hierarchical support that the DataSet object offers.

Understanding the DataSet Object

The ADO.NET DataSet is for disconnected database interactions against a memory image of a database. Applications can execute commands that store and retrieve data from this memory image, which is periodically synchronized with the actual database.

You can create a DataSet object by invoking the DataSet constructor, specifying an optional name, or accepting the default DataSet name of *NewDataSet*. You can also create a new instance by cloning an existing DataSet instance as an exact copy, with or without its data. The following example creates a DataSet object and assigns it the name *IssueTrackerReference*:

```
DataSet dataset = new DataSet("IssueTrackerReference");
```

As Figure 2-2 illustrated, the DataSet object comprises five principal objects: DataTable, DataColumn, DataRow, Constraint, and DataRelation. Each of these objects has properties and methods that mimic the behavior of actual database elements.

Working with DataTables

The DataSet object maintains a collection of objects that represent database tables. As in the case of databases, each DataTable object comprises column, row, and constraint information. You can create a DataTable object by using the DataTable constructor or by invoking the Add method of the Tables property within the DataSet object.

Once you have added a DataTable to the collection, you cannot add it to any other DataSet Tables collection. Also, when creating a DataTable object, it does not require the TableName property. You can specify the name can be specified later or leave its default value, Table*n*, where *n* represents an incrementing number beginning with zero. All references to names of DataSet tables and relations are case sensitive.

Working with DataColumns

When a DataTable is first created, it does not have any table structure. To define a schema, you must create and add DataColumn objects to the columns collection of the DataTable. Each column represents a piece of data that is captured and identified by a column name and column data type.

For performance gains, every database table should have at least one primary key designated. A *primary key* is a column that contains a unique value for each row within the table. This is normally an identifier that helps an application find a specific record. For a column to serve as a primary key, it must be unique and it must not be null. You can insert DataRows into the table as long as the table's primary key column is not null and does not already exist.

Working with DataRows

Once you have defined a schema for a DataTable object, you can insert the actual data. You insert data one row at a time using the DataRow object. To add a new row of data to a table, begin by creating a new DataRow object and initializing it by invoking the NewRow method provided by the DataTable object. Next, set the column values. Finally, invoke the Add method and provide the new DataRow object as a parameter:

```
DataRow row = table.NewRow();
row["ID"] = 100;
row["Name"] = "Simon West";
row["Active"] = true;

//when working with a DataSet object
```

```
dataset.Tables.["Employees"].Rows.Add(row);

//when working directly with a DataTable object
table.Rows.Add(row);
```

To edit a row of data already existing with a table, begin by invoking the BeginEdit method and putting the DataRow object into edit mode. When in edit mode, events are suspended and applications are free to make multiple edits without triggering any validation rules. Next, set values to the different columns. Finally, invoke the EndEdit method to end editing. Alternatively, if an application needs to revert to the DataRow's original state before editing, invoke the CancelEdit method to clear all changes:

```
row.BeginEdit();
row["Name"] = "Simon West";
row.EndEdit();
```

To delete a row of data from a table, identify the row to be deleted by its zero-based array index. Next, invoke the Delete method to mark the row for deletion. Finally, invoke the AcceptChanges method provided by the table object to commit the deletion. Alternatively, to unmark a row for deletion, invoke the RejectChanges method instead of the AcceptChanges method:

```
table.Rows[intRowID].Delete();
table.AcceptChanges();
```

A DataRow object exists in one of five states as defined by the DataRowState enumeration. Knowing which rows are in which state provides an application with more control over how data can be processed. For example, when an application is about to close, it can lose all records that have changed and prompt the user to either save or discard them. Obtain the state value by checking the RowState property of a DataRow. Table 2-1 describes these DataRow states.

Table 2-1. DataRow States

DATAROWSTATE	DESCRIPTION
Deleted	This row has been deleted and no longer exists.
Detached	This row has been created but not associated with any DataTable.
Modified	This row has been modified, but the changes have not been accepted.
New	This row has been associated with a table.
Unchanged	This row has not been changed since last accepted.

Another approach to reading from or writing to a DataRow object is to work with the ItemArray property. This approach lets the application set and get values within a DataRow object based upon column positions rather than column names.

Working with DataRelations

A DataRelation defines the relationship between multiple DataTable objects within a single DataSet object. An application can use a DataRelation to navigate from one table to the next and to return parent or child rows from a related table. Typically, relationships bind a DataTable object with a validation lookup table. To create a new DataRelation, all that is required is a name for the relation and a list of columns that will be bound together. Once a relation is added to a DataSet object, a UniqueConstraint is associated with the parent table and a ForeignKeyConstraint is automatically associated to the child table:

```
dataset.Relations.Add( "IssueType",
    custDS.Tables["Dat_Issue"].Columns["TypeID"],
    custDS.Tables["Val_IssueType"].Columns["TypeID"] );
```

In this case, the code created a new relation, named *IssueType*, to bind the Val_IssueType table to the Dat_Issue table. The Val_IssueType table is the parent table, and the Dat_Issue table is the child table. Both tables are bound by the TypeID column. When a relationship between parent and child tables is defined, invoking GetChildRows will return all child rows based on a specific column value:

```
DataRelation relation = dataset.Relations.Add( "IssueType",
    custDS.Tables["Dat_Issue"].Columns["TypeID"],
    custDS.Tables["Val_IssueType"].Columns["TypeID"] );

foreach( DataRow row in dataset.Tables["Dat_Issue"].Rows )
{
    Console.WriteLine( row["TypeID"] );

    foreach( DataRow childrow in row.GetChildRows( relation ) )
        Console.WriteLine( childrow["TypeID"] );
}
```

Creating Stored Procedures

Implementing the reference DataSet object begins with creating the stored procedures. The process for creating them is the same as described earlier. The only difference should be in the naming convention. It is important to enter the stored procedure names consistently in the naming convention specified by the data access framework:

```
ref_[table_types][action]
```

This can apply to the Val_IssueType table by defining a query stored procedure named *ref_IssueTypeSelect*.

Creating a DataSet Object

With the database tables defined and the stored procedures in place, it is time to create the DataSet object. From the design view of the data access component, select the sqlDataAdepter object or add one from the Toolbox if one does not exist. Next, select Generate Dataset from its context menu. The Generate Dataset dialog box appears, as shown in Figure 2-11.

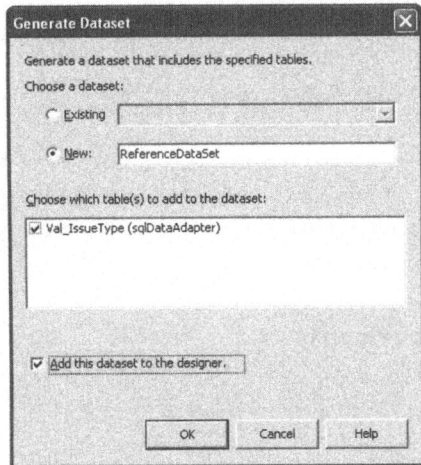

Figure 2-11. The Generate Dataset dialog box

Select the New radio button and enter **ReferenceDataSet** as its new name. Select all reference tables that should be added to the DataSet object. Select the option to add the DataSet to the designer and click the OK button. A new object representing the DataSet object, named *referenceDataSet1*, appears in the designer. For clarity and consistency, rename this DataSet object to *_IssueTrackerReference*.

Filling a DataSet Object

You fill a DataSet object with structure and values from the database with the help of a DataProvider object. Each DataProvider includes a DataAdapter object with a Fill method that defines a table schema and populates a DataSet. You can replace the data access component's default constructor with one that uses a DataAdapter object to fill the DataSet object using multiple stored procedures:

```
public DataComponent()
{
    string strStoredProc;
    SqlCommand command;
    SqlDataAdapter adapter;

    InitializeComponent();

    //load IssueType types
    strStoredProc = "ref_IssueTypeSelect";
    command = new SqlCommand( strStoredProc, Connection );
    command.CommandType = CommandType.StoredProcedure;
    adapter = new SqlDataAdapter( command );
    adapter.Fill( _IssueTrackerReference, "Val_IssueType" );

    //load Priority types
    strStoredProc = "ref_PrioritySelect";
    command = new SqlCommand( strStoredProc, Connection );
    command.CommandType = CommandType.StoredProcedure;
    adapter = new SqlDataAdapter( command );
    adapter.Fill( _IssueTrackerReference, "Val_Priority" );

    //load Status types
    strStoredProc = "ref_StatusSelect";
    command = new SqlCommand( strStoredProc, Connection );
    command.CommandType = CommandType.StoredProcedure;
    adapter = new SqlDataAdapter( command );
    adapter.Fill( _IssueTrackerReference, "Val_Status" );

    //load MailMessage types
    strStoredProc = "ref_MailMessageSelect";
```

```
command = new SqlCommand( strStoredProc, Connection );
command.CommandType = CommandType.StoredProcedure;
adapter = new SqlDataAdapter( command );
adapter.Fill( _IssueTrackerReference, "Val_MailMessage" );

//load Report types
strStoredProc = "ref_ReportsSelect";
command = new SqlCommand( strStoredProc, Connection );
command.CommandType = CommandType.StoredProcedure;
adapter = new SqlDataAdapter( command );
adapter.Fill( _IssueTrackerReference, "Val_Reports" );

return;
}
```

The DataComponent object constructor begins by initializing the component's connections, commands, and adapters. Next, it specifies each stored procedure that ties to reference data and associates each with a SqlCommand object. The SqlCommand object is supplied to the DataAdapter object, which invokes the appropriate stored procedure to load records into the DataSet object. The only remaining detail is an accessor method that returns the ReferenceDataSet object to a data component client:

```
public ReferenceDataSet ReferenceDataSet
{
    get
    {
        return _IssueTrackerReference;
    }
}
```

Connecting to Databases Other Than SQL Server

As mentioned earlier, ADO.NET connects to databases through direct or disconnected data access with the assistance of data providers. Data providers are essentially ADO.NET adapters that optimize data storage and retrieval for a specific database platform. Most of the examples in this chapter used the Microsoft SQL Server database and therefore used the SQL Server data provider. Until database vendors such as Oracle, Sybase, and Informix produce data providers that optimize access to their products, application developers need to connect via the Open Database Connectivity (ODBC) managed provider.

Connecting to MySQL

One of the most popular databases servers connected to the Internet today is
MySQL. MySQL is an open-source database implementation that is publicly
available from the Downloads section of the MySQL Web site
(http://www.mysql.com/downloads).

ODBC is an interface that describes connection points between databases
and the host operating system. ODBC drivers allow different database systems to
communicate in a uniform way to different applications running on different
operating systems. To facilitate this, database vendors offer ODBC drivers that
bridge their product to different operating systems. In the case of the MySQL
database, you can download an ODBC driver for the Microsoft Windows operating system from http://www.mysql.com/downloads/api-myodbc-2.50.html.

After downloading and installing the driver, create a system ODBC data
source pointing to the online MySQL database. From the Windows Desktop, click
Start ➤ Control Panel ➤ Administrative Tools ➤ Data Sources (ODBC). The
ODBC Administrator will display, as shown in Figure 2-12.

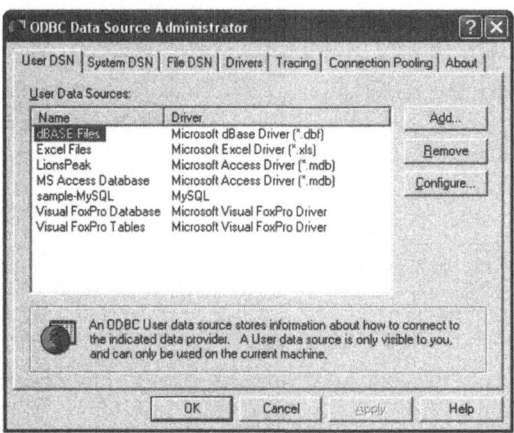

Figure 2-12. The ODBC Data Source Administrator

Next, select the System DSN tab and click the Add button. A list of installed
ODBC drivers displays. Scroll to the end of the list and select the MySQL driver.
The new MySQL data source form will display, as shown in Figure 2-13. Enter a
name for your data source and the connection information.

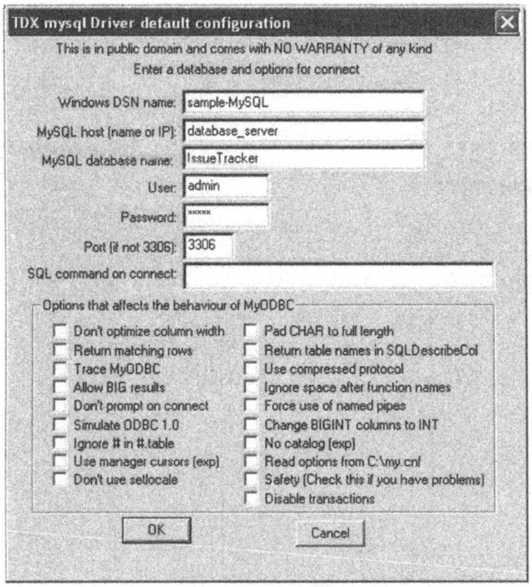

Figure 2-13. The new MySQL data source interface

In addition to the ODBC managed provider, you need to download the
Microsoft Data Access Components (MDAC) package version 2.6 and higher. The
MDAC package contains a collection of updated ODBC drivers and is available for
download from Microsoft at http://www.microsoft.com/data/download_270RTM.htm.

After restarting Visual Studio, the ODBC managed provider is available for
use. Set the reference to its namespace with the following statement:

```
using System.Data.Odbc;
```

You can use the ODBC managed provider objects to connect to and interact
with the database just as you would with the SqlClient objects:

```
public void TestConnection()
{
    string strConnection;
    OdbcConnection connection;

    try
    {
        strConnection = "DSN=IssueTracker;UID=sys;PWD=syst3m";
        connection = new OdbcConnection( strConnection );
        connection.Open();
```

```
            //perform data access functions
    }
    catch( OdbcException exception )
    {
        EventLog systemLog = new EventLog();
        systemLog.Source = "IssueTracker";
        systemLog.WriteEntry( exception.Message, EventLogEntryType.Error, 0 );
    }
    finally
    {
        connection.Close();
    }

    return;
}
```

Connecting to Microsoft Access

Microsoft Access has proven itself well as a small and reliable application database. Although it does not offer the performance or reliability that is needed by an enterprise application, stand-alone desktop applications can make good use of Windows' built-in driver support.

Connecting to a Microsoft Access database is similar to connecting to a MySQL database because both rely on the ODBC interface and ADO.NET's OLE data provider. The namespace reference looks more like this, though:

```
using System.Data.OleDb;
```

The only real difference is the connection string passed to the OleDbConnection object's constructor:

```
public void TestConnection()
{
    string strConnection;
    OleDbConnection connection;

    try
    {
        strConnection = "Provider=Microsoft.JET.OLEDB.4.0;" +
            @"Data Source=C:\Program Files\IssueTracker\Data\IssueTracker.mdb"
```

```
        connection = new OleDbConnection( strConnection );
        connection.Open();

        //perform data access functions
    }
    catch( OleDbException exception )
    {
        EventLog systemLog = new EventLog();
        systemLog.Source = "IssueTracker";
        systemLog.WriteEntry( exception.Message, EventLogEntryType.Error, 0 );
    }
    finally
    {
        connection.Close();
    }

    return;
}
```

Once you have established a connection with the database, you can store and retrieve data just as with the MySQL and SQL Server databases.

Summary

This chapter implemented the foundation for the enterprise application: the data access layer. To support accelerated application development, minimize bugs, and enforce consistency, the chapter created a structured data access framework. Although the framework does place stricter requirements upon the developer, the additional security and maintainability make it worth the cost. This chapter also explored some of the ADO.NET architecture and its two foundation objects, DataProviders and DataSets. Additionally, the chapter laid the foundation for the enterprise application, IssueTracker, by defining its database schema, building its structure within the database, implementing stored procedures, and developing the data access framework. Finally, the chapter reviewed various issues and solutions that relate to typical enterprise application development.

In the next chapter, you will learn about directory services, how they work, and how corporate enterprises use them to manage user accounts. You will also interact with Active Directory, Microsoft's directory service solution, to build out a directory services business service that fits cleanly into the application framework and interacts with application business objects.

CHAPTER 3

Using Networking Directory Services

ENTERPRISE APPLICATIONS EXPECTING TO be installed in top-tier corporations, such as Cisco Systems, IBM, and Hewlett-Packard, can expect integration with directory services to be a requirement. This chapter introduces directory services and how Active Directory manages information about networked objects. This chapter also demonstrates how you use .NET Framework objects to integrate an enterprise application with Active Directory. Finally, this chapter provides a close look at how to interact with directory services and expand the IssueTracker application to retrieve user information.

Exploring Directory Services

In a networked environment, applications should be able to store and retrieve information about users, other machines, other applications, and networked services. Applications should also be able to interact with users differently based on the role of the user. Finally, enterprise applications should be able to find networked resources, such as printers and files.

Directory services are central locations for storing information about networked objects. You can make this information available to users, administrators, and other networked applications based on security permissions. Directory services bundle access to network resources into a single network login and provide a single point of administration for network administrators. Administrators can create one user account in one place, allowing users to access different network resources. Directory services also serve as an organized naming service for looking up resources within the network. Enabling support for directory services within enterprise applications increases the sales potential for the enterprise application developer.

Furthermore, applications supporting directory services are often more aware of their deployment environment, and they are capable of adapting to changes and sharing information about themselves with other applications.

Enterprise applications can also take advantage of information already stored within directory services by other applications. Many corporate enterprises deploy an Enterprise Resource Planner (ERP) to manage human resources information. An ERP application stores a lot of business data, including employee names and organizational relationships. Such user attributes may be accessible to other enterprise applications capable of retrieving values from Active Directory.

Examining the Lightweight Directory Access Protocol Specification

The Lightweight Directory Access Protocol (LDAP) specification is the dominant directory service protocol based on the X.500 specification. It specifies how to organize attribute-based data into a hierarchical tree structure. It is also based upon the belief that directory service data is generally read from more than written to and is therefore designed for fast data retrieval at the cost of slow data storage. There is no specification for transactional processing or rollback handling. It simply defines a central repository for hierarchically storing data and a structured syntax for searching and retrieving entries.

Understanding the Directory Information Tree

The hierarchical representation of data in LDAP is a Directory Information Tree (DIT). It specifies the packaging of information in the form of objects that represent networked resources such as individual users, groups, and computers. These objects comprise customizable attributes that describe an object, such as a first name, last name, or password. Objects can be grouped into containers that represent collections of related objects just as a file server groups related files into subdirectories. Figure 3-1 illustrates the hierarchical relationships between networked objects in a DIT.

A namespace, or *path*, is a named reference to a specific object in the hierarchy. The path refers to an object's location relative to the top of the tree. It is used to traverse, search, and modify the object tree as well as read and write an object's properties. All tree nodes also have a Globally Unique Identifier (GUID) that uniquely identifies each node in the hierarchy throughout the domain. A node's GUID remains constant, even if a node moves from one location to another.

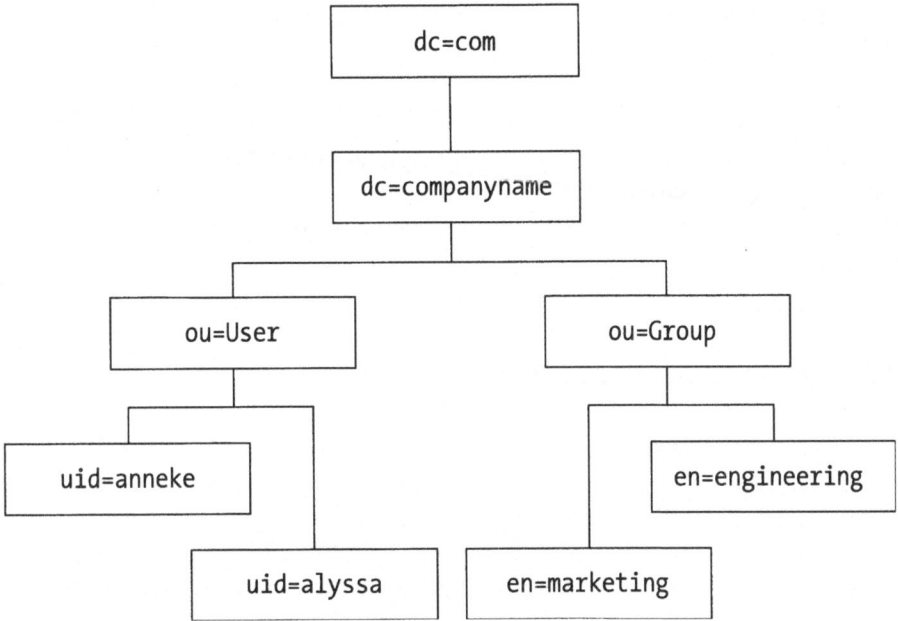

Figure 3-1. A sample DIT describing networked objects

Understanding the LDAP Schema

A *schema* is an object map that describes all objects, object classes, and their attributes. This object map makes up the directory service repository and defines the rules for describing how data must be stored. The schema helps to maintain the consistency and quality of the data while minimizing data duplication. Schema rules are defined by object class attributes, and they specify how the rules must be applied. A complete schema contains required attributes, custom attributes, rules for comparing attributes, and limits on what the attributes can store. It is always important to fully understand the underlying schema of a directory service before planning an integration project.

Understanding the LDAP Search Filter

Search filters specify what data should be returned from a directory service to the calling client. You create search filters using logical expressions that combine attributes, operators, and criteria values. Attributes and values combine with operators to complete the syntax for a search filter. Any number of expressions can join together to narrow down a search to a single object:

```
(&(objectClass=User)(cn="Bill Bruchs"))
```

The most significant part of any directory service integration is identifying a search filter that returns the desired information with the least performance impact. Often, a number of different search filters need to be written and performance tested to find the one that provides the best results. The LDAP specification is flexible and is a time-tested standard for many directory service solutions. Microsoft's Active Directory solution also implements the LDAP specification, bringing the power and flexibility of directory services to Windows users and .NET applications.

Examining Active Directory

Active Directory is a directory service solution deployed with Microsoft .NET Server and Windows 2000 Server. It provides a secure repository of information relating to networked objects within the enterprise, including users, computers, and services. Active Directory provides access to multiple resources through a single login and provides network administrators with an intuitive view of the entire network.

In addition to being secure, Active Directory is also distributed and replicated to ensure data integrity and reliability. Furthermore, it is scalable to support any size of deployment—from a single server with hundreds of objects to hundreds of servers with thousands of objects. Although Active Directory is deployed with .NET Server and Windows 2000, client-side platforms can include Windows NT 4.0, Windows 9*x*, Windows XP, and Unix. Depending upon permissions, clients can have full access to networked resources within the domain. Figure 3-2 shows the Active Directory manager on the Windows Server 2003.

Understanding Active Directory Services

Active Directory offers three primary functions: network administration, search, and developer support. The administrative functions of Active Directory enable a network administrator to manage multiple user accounts, groups, and access permissions from a single application. You can enable or disable access to different applications, files, and printers without requiring client-side configuration. As a result, the directory service becomes the hub around which a large enterprise grows.

The search functions of Active Directory enable administrators, users, and applications to track down networked resources when they do not know the exact name or path of the objects in which they are interested. If you know one or more object attributes, you can search the directory service to return a list of possible matches.

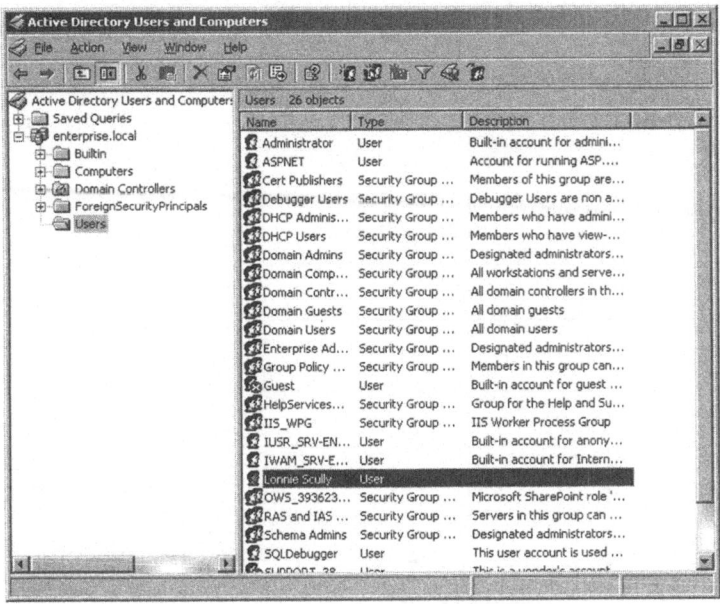

Figure 3-2. Active Directory manager in .NET Server

The developer functions of Active Directory are exposed through the Active Directory Services Interfaces (ADSI), a set of open interfaces that abstract the directory services. Applications can use ADSI to manage resources in a directory service, regardless of which network environment manages the resource. ADSI addresses the issue of enabling a single login for desktop clients and interacts with multiple directory service providers for searching. ADSI enables applications to interact with different directory service implementations through a single interface layer. You can create applications to perform common tasks, such as backing up databases, accessing printers, and administering user accounts. Figure 3-3 illustrates how a .NET enterprise application integrates with the underlying directory service platforms.

Because Active Directory implements the LDAP specification, it is also capable of performing integrated searches against other directory service servers that also implement the LDAP 2 specification. These additional servers include the following:

- Microsoft Windows Server 2003 Active Directory

- Microsoft Windows 2000 Server Active Directory

- Netscape Directory Server 1.0

- Microsoft Exchange Server 5.0

- Novell LDAP-enabled NetWare Directory Service (NDS)

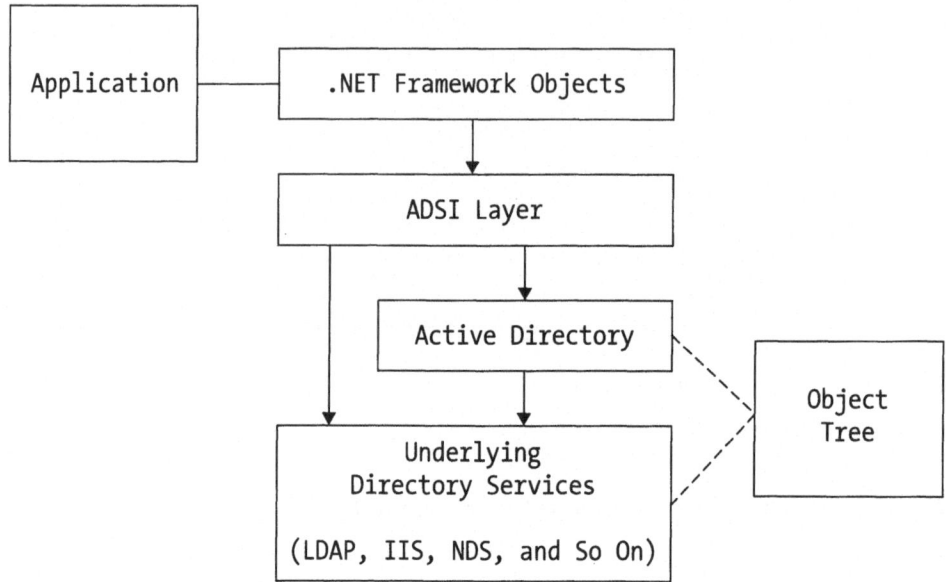

Figure 3-3. Directory service layers

Understanding Active Directory Object Attributes

The Active Directory object schema is flexible and can change to accommodate application-specific needs. As Figure 3-1 illustrated, the directory service tree comprises multiple objects. Each object has multiple attributes that are either required or optional. The object definitions are maintained by object class definitions within the directory schema. The schema already defines objects, such as User, with multiple properties, such as first name, last name, and e-mail address. If an additional attribute is necessary, the schema will need to be changed.

Changes to the Active Directory schema are irreversible and must be carefully planned. In Windows Server 2003, you can modify the schema definition with the Active Directory Schema Editor snap-in component for the Microsoft Management Console (MMC). For security reasons, the Active Directory Schema Editor is not initially installed. To activate it, select Start ➤ Run and enter *regsvr32.exe schmmgmt.dll*. Next, start the MMC by selecting Start ➤ Run and enter *mmc /a*. From the empty MMC view, select Console ➤ Add/Remove Snap-in to display the snap-in manager. Next, click the Add button and select the Active Directory Schema snap-in, as shown in Figure 3-4.

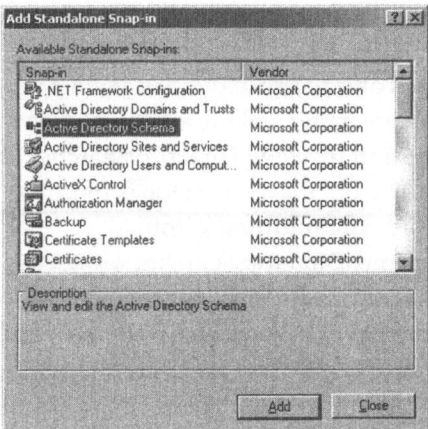

Figure 3-4. Adding the Active Directory Schema snap-in for the MMC

Now the MMC is capable of displaying the Active Directory object schema and accepting changes to objects and attributes. You will use the Active Directory Schema Editor later to add a custom attribute to the default user definition.

Leveraging .NET Framework Objects

The .NET Framework provides the System.DirectoryServices namespace to interact with directory services. It comprises two primary objects and a number of supporting objects. The DirectoryEntry and DirectorySearcher objects both interact directly with the underlying ADSI services. They are not limited to interaction with only Active Directory; custom providers can also enable interaction with other directory service solutions, such as Internet Information Services (IIS), LDAP, and Novell NDS.

Using the DirectoryEntry Object

The DirectoryEntry object abstracts a specific networked resource object in the directory service hierarchy. This object is primarily used for binding directly to such objects, retrieving properties, and updating properties. This object is largely a data storage object rich with properties but limited on functionality. The DirectoryEntry object provides support for life-cycle management and navigation methods, including creating, deleting, renaming, and moving a child node. Properties are largely divided into three areas: validation, node description, and schema related.

Using the DirectorySearcher Object

You use the DirectorySearcher object to search and perform queries against an Active Directory hierarchy. An administrator can create, delete, and edit objects within the hierarchy. A search of the object hierarchy using DirectorySearcher returns an instance of a SearchResult object. If more than one value is returned as a result of the search, then multiple instances are returned within a SearchResultCollection object. Setting the various DirectorySearcher properties affects how the directory services will be searched and how the results will be returned. When an instance of the DirectorySearcher object is created, the SearchRoot property can specify where in the hierarchy tree the search should begin. When searching any object tree, it is important to start the search as close as possible to the target node to minimize the search time.

Using the SearchResult Object

The SearchResult object abstracts an entry node in the directory service hierarchy. An instance of a SearchResult object is similar to an instance of the DirectoryEntry object. The most obvious difference is that the DirectoryEntry object is populated each time a new object is accessed. Conversely, a SearchResult object is populated as result of a DirectorySearcher query. Only those properties specified through the DirectorySearcher.PropertiesToLoad property's collection in your query will be available from SearchResult.

Applying Directory Services

Because the IssueTracker application is intended for deployment in large corporate enterprises, supporting directory services will be essential. You will now extend the IssueTracker application to leverage an existing Active Directory system to manage user information. You will accomplish this by implementing the User and UserCollection business objects. Rather than relying upon the standard business object manager developed in Chapter 2, "Accessing Data in ADO.NET," you will create a specialized business object manager to manage user data maintained within an Active Directory system. Figure 3-5 illustrates how this new object manager relates to the standard business object manager.

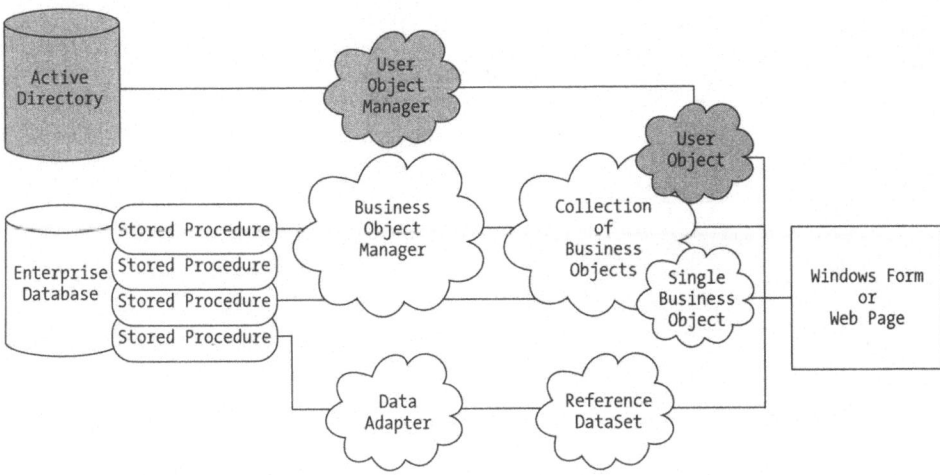

Figure 3-5. Extending the application framework to support directory services

Adding Active Directory User Attributes

As mentioned, you can add custom object attributes to any Active Directory entity, including its user definition. The IssueTracker application can benefit from this by tightly integrating its application security with an enterprise's Active Directory deployment. Instead of managing its own application login accounts, IssueTracker can validate user credentials against an existing Active Directory deployment. This way, as new employee accounts are created within the enterprise, access to the IssueTracker application can more easily be configured. Furthermore, Active Directory can have attributes added to its user definition that maintain additional user information specific to the IssueTracker application, such as a unique user identifier and a user role.

To add the unique identifier and user role attributes to the user definition, open the Active Directory Schema Editor snap-in created earlier. Select the Attributes folder in the left pane to display a complete list of available object attributes in the right pane. Next, select Action ➤ Create New Attribute from the menu to display the Create New Attribute dialog box. Enter the custom object attribute as illustrated in Figure 3-6, paying close attention to the values entered.

Again, you must perform this step with care because changes to the Active Directory schema are permanent. The Common Name field is the readable label for the attribute, whereas the LDAP Display Name field is the internal label that will be later queried. The X.500 OID value is a unique identifier, ideally assigned by the ANSI organization. Finally, the Syntax field identifies the attribute's underlying data type. In the case of IssueTrackerRole, the Syntax field is Integer. This value relates to a numeric identifier that in turn relates to a specific IssueTracker user role. Click OK to permanently save the attribute to the Active Directory schema.

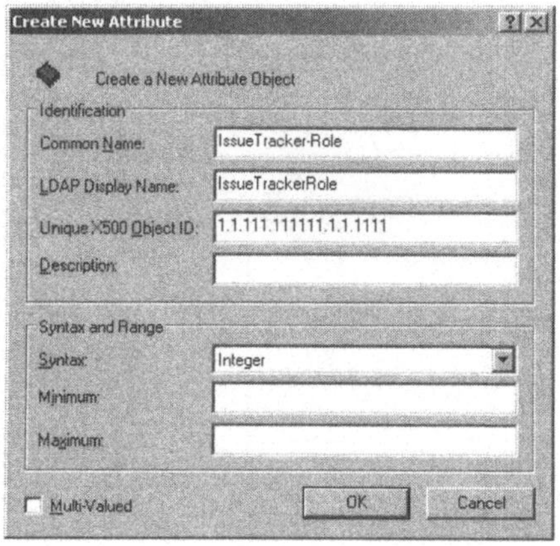

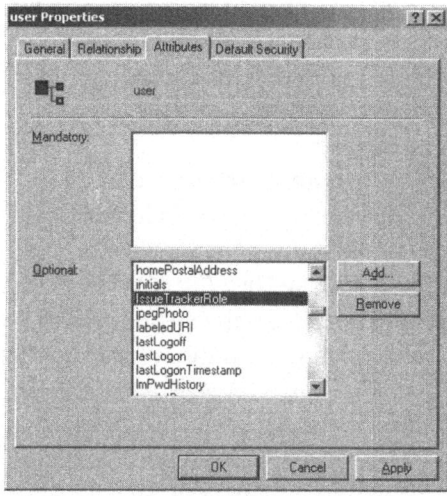

Figure 3-6. Creating a new custom attribute

To add the new custom attribute to the existing user definition, return to the Active Directory Schema Editor. Expand the Classes folder and select the user node in the left pane. All associated attributes are populated in the right pane. Next, select Action ➤ Properties from the menu to display the user Properties dialog box. Select the Attributes tab to display the existing mandatory and optional user attributes. Next, click the Add button and select the IssueTrackerRole attribute from the pop-up dialog box and click OK. The user Properties dialog box updates to include the new attribute, as shown in Figure 3-7.

Figure 3-7. The updated user definition displaying a new application attribute

Creating the Application User Object

The User object is the next major application business object to be implemented. It must also inherit from the BusinessObject abstract base class and implement a supporting collection class. All supporting data elements should also be present, including its data table and stored procedures. However, instead of being managed by the business object manager, like any other business object, the User object will be managed by a new specialized object manager tied into Active Directory. Listing 3-1 outlines the code that implements the User business object.

Listing 3-1. The User Business Object Class

```
public class User : BusinessObject
{
    private int _UserID = 0;
    private string _Password = "";
    private string _Firstname = "";
    private string _Lastname = "";
    private string _EmailAddress = "";
    private int _UserRole = 0;
    private DateTime _CreateDate = DateTime.Now;


    public enum UserRoleType
    {
        Guest = 0,
        TypicalUser = 1,
        Manager = 2,
        Administrator = 3
    }

    public User()
    {
    }

    public User( string strFirstname, string strLastname )
    {
        _Firstname = strFirstname;
        _Lastname = strLastname;
    }

    public User(string strFirstname, string strLastname, string strEmailAddress)
```

```
    {
        _Firstname = strFirstname;
        _Lastname = strLastname;
        _EmailAddress = strEmailAddress;
    }

    public int UserID
    {
        set
        {
            _UserID = value;
        }
        get
        {
            return _UserID;
        }
    }

    public string Password
    {
        set
        {
            _Password = value;
        }
        get
        {
            return _Password;
        }
    }

    public string Firstname
    {
        set
        {
            _Firstname = value;
        }
        get
        {
            return _Firstname;
        }
    }
```

```
public string Lastname
{
    set
    {
        _Lastname = value;
    }
    get
    {
        return _Lastname;
    }
}

public string EmailAddress
{
    set
    {
        _EmailAddress = value;
    }
    get
    {
        return _EmailAddress;
    }
}

public int UserRole
{
    set
    {
        _UserRole = value;
    }
    get
    {
        return _UserRole;
    }
}

public DateTime CreateDate
{
    set
    {
        _CreateDate = value;
    }
```

```
        get
        {
            return _CreateDate;
        }
    }

    public bool ValidateLogin()
    {
        return false;
    }

}
```

Again, the User business object adheres to the framework's style and naming conventions for implementing a business object. Unlike the Issue object, the User object also includes an enumerated type definition that identifies the user as a guest, typical user, manager, or administrator.

Creating the UserObjectManager Object

UserObjectManager will be responsible for validating user credentials against Active Directory and returning a populated User business object. For environments that do not have Active Directory installed, the existing business object manager can still be used. Because the UserObjectManager extends the existing business object manager functionality, it can be implemented in the DataAccess project within this solution. Select the DataAccess project within the Solution Explorer. To access the .NET Framework support for directory services, a new reference will need to be added. Select Add Reference from the project's context menu and include the System.DirectoryServices.dll component, as shown in Figure 3-8.

Although an enterprise can access information about any networked resource, the IssueTracker application leverages Active Directory only to manage user information within the network domain.

Validating a User Login

You can add a small method to the application that quickly evaluates if user-supplied credentials are valid. This validation is performed against the Active Directory repository using the DirectoryEntry and DirectorySearcher objects provided by the .NET Framework (see Listing 3-2). This method is only intended to be used by the application for quick validation. A separate method will actually extract the user profile.

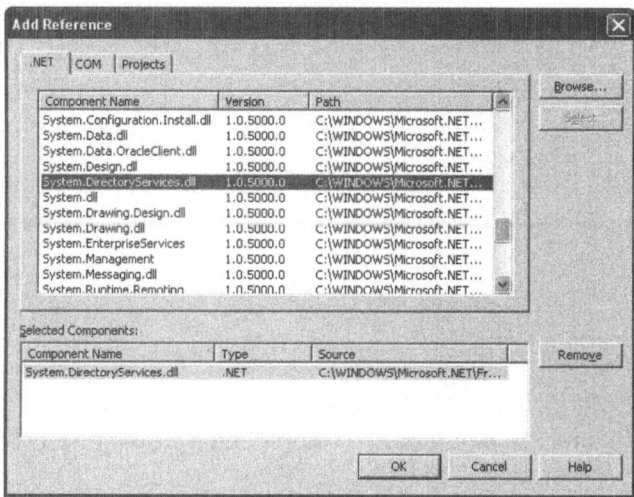

Figure 3-8. Adding a new reference to the directory service namespace

Listing 3-2. Validating a User Login Against Active Directory

```
public DirectoryEntry ValidateLogin( string strUsername, string strPassword )
{
    DirectoryEntry dirResult = null;

    try
    {
        //initialize the root search object
        DirectoryEntry dirEntry = new DirectoryEntry( "LDAP://srv-enterprise",
            strUsername, strPassword );

        //initialize the search object
        DirectorySearcher dirSearcher = new DirectorySearcher( dirEntry );

        //set the filter to retrieve the specific user
        dirSearcher.Filter = "(&(objectClass=user)(mail=" +strUsername+ "))";
        dirSearcher.SearchScope = SearchScope.Subtree;

        //execute the search
        SearchResult searchResult = dirSearcher.FindOne();
        dirResult = searchResult.GetDirectoryEntry();

    }
```

```
catch( Exception x )
{
    EventLog systemLog = new EventLog();
    systemLog.Source = "IssueTracker";
    systemLog.WriteEntry( x.Message + " for user " + strUsername,
        EventLogEntryType.Error, 0 );
}

return dirResult;
}
```

The result of this method is a DirectoryEntry object that is either valid or null, rather than a boolean value of true or false. This approach is in the interest of application performance. Although this quick login validation method is helpful, it will often need to be followed up with a method call to retrieve the user profile. Rather than having the GetUserProfile method begin its search from the top of the directory tree, supplying it with the returned DirectoryEntry object gives it a significant head start.

Evaluating a User Profile

Validating a user login against Active Directory is a good start to application security. In many cases, however, that might not be enough. It might be necessary to know more about a logged-in user, such as their full name, e-mail address, and designated role within the application. You can capture all of this into a single user profile maintained by Active Directory. Of all these different application attributes, the user role is of significant interest. There are two different approaches to storing and retrieving the user in Active Directory: by group membership and by custom attribute.

In the case of group membership, application roles are defined as Active Directory groups, of which any added user can be a member. Figure 3-9 shows the three newly added groups: IssueTrackerUser, IssueTrackerManager, and IssueTrackerAdministrator.

In Listing 3-3, the User object is populated with an application role value that comes from one of the default Active Directory user attributes, memberOf. Based on the value of this attribute, the User object is assigned a role value during application use.

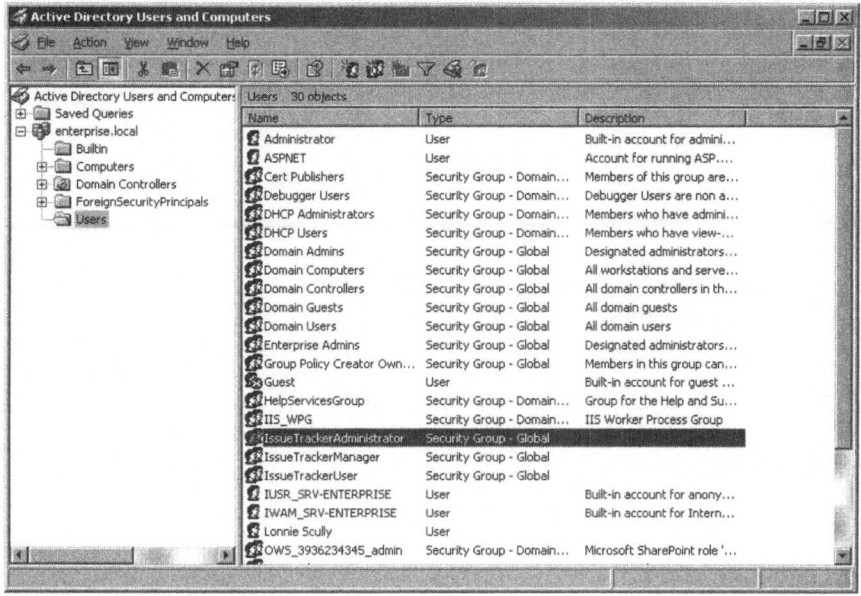

Figure 3-9. Specifying application user roles with Active Directory groups

Listing 3-3. Evaluating the User Profile Against Active Directory Values

```
public User GetUserProfile( DirectoryEntry entryUser )
{
    User objUser = new User();

    try
    {
        //extract default user attributes
        objUser.Firstname = entryUser.Properties["givenName"][0].ToString();
        objUser.Lastname = entryUser.Properties["sn"][0].ToString();
        objUser.EmailAddress = entryUser.Properties["mail"][0].ToString();

        //extract application specific user attribute
        if( entryUser.Properties["memberOf"][0].ToString().IndexOf(
            "IssueTrackerUser" ) >= 0 )
            objUser.UserRole = (int)User.UserRoleType.TypicalUser;

        if( entryUser.Properties["memberOf"][0].ToString().IndexOf(
            "IssueTrackerManager" ) >= 0 )
            objUser.UserRole = (int)User.UserRoleType.Manager;
```

```
            if( entryUser.Properties["memberOf"][0].ToString().IndexOf(
                "IssueTrackerAdministrator" ) >= 0 )
                objUser.UserRole = (int)User.UserRoleType.Administrator;

        }
        catch( Exception x )
        {
            EventLog systemLog = new EventLog();
            systemLog.Source = "IssueTracker";
            systemLog.WriteEntry( x.Message, EventLogEntryType.Error, 0 );
        }
        finally
        {
        }

        return objUser;
}
```

This method begins with a DirectoryEntry key as a starting point that resulted from the ValidateLogin method defined in Listing 3-2. This helps reduce the time-consuming overhead in searching out this User object within the Active Directory object tree. Next, specific properties are retrieved and assigned to related attributes of the application's User object. One of the more important attributes, IssueTrackerUserRole, will become more significant when implementing the application user interface. This attribute will define what functions a user is capable of performing as role-based security comes into light. The populated User object is returned to the caller while thrown exceptions are logged.

Listing 3-4 takes a different approach to retrieving the user role value. Rather than infer the user role value based on group membership, the role value can be retrieved from the custom user attribute defined earlier.

Listing 3-4. Evaluating the User Profile Against Active Directory Values

```
public User GetUserProfile( DirectoryEntry entryUser )
{
    User objUser = new User();

    try
    {
        //extract default user attributes
        objUser.Firstname = entryUser.Properties["givenName"][0].ToString();
        objUser.Lastname = entryUser.Properties["sn"][0].ToString();
        objUser.EmailAddress = entryUser.Properties["mail"][0].ToString();
```

```
        //extract application specific user attribute
        objUser.UserRole = (int)entryUser.Properties["IssueTrackerRole"][0];

    }
    catch( Exception x )
    {
        EventLog systemLog = new EventLog();
        systemLog.Source = "IssueTracker";
        systemLog.WriteEntry( x.Message, EventLogEntryType.Error, 0 );
    }

    return objUser;
}
```

This method demonstrates an alternative approach to capturing user role information. In this case, the user role is stored as an integer value within the IssueTrackerRole custom attribute. You can quickly modify this alternative approach to implementing the GetUserProfile method in order to retrieve any other application setting stored as a custom user attribute. Again, this approach includes an element of risk in that any modifications to the Active Directory schema are permanent.

Improving Directory Service Performance

Although directory services store a wealth of useful information, the volumes of data they contain can easily result in slow search performance. A slow directory service gives an overall impression that the application is slow. Although most directory service solutions, such as Active Directory, are scalable and improve as additional hardware is added, improvements to the search parameters can more easily address the problem. The following guidelines can significantly improve the performance of a search and, as a result, the application.

Selecting the Base Object

Improving the performance of a search has a lot to do with choosing the optimal starting point for the search. This starting point can be either the root of the hierarchy, an object entry, or a container. One-level searches on a container are faster than subtree searches over the entire hierarchy. When you know the name of the container where the object is, use the name of the container and perform a one-level search. After you find the object, bind to the object using its name to access its attributes:

```
public void ConnectToSpecificUser()
{
    //connect as close as possible to target object
    String strConnection = "LDAP://srv-enterprise/CN=User/UID=alyssa";
    DirectoryEntry dirEntry = new DirectoryEntry( strConnection );

    return;
}
```

Specifying Search Scope

The scope of a search also impacts performance. You can select three scopes for a search: base, one level, and subtree. The base scope is the fastest scope to use for retrieving a single object. The one-level scope is the fastest way to retrieve multiple objects. When the objects are located in a single known container, you should use the one-level scope to return the attributes for one or more objects. The subtree scope retrieves data from multiple containers. When you need to return the attributes for one or more objects contained in multiple containers in the same hierarchy, you should use the subtree scope

Querying Only the Attributes Needed

When performing a search, specify only the attributes needed in the returned results. By default, all attributes associated with an object are returned. The fewer attributes that need to be loaded, the faster the results can be built and returned. This is where the PropertiesToLoad property becomes handy. In this example, only the givenname and sn attributes are necessary to build a user list. To increase performance, only those properties are requested:

```
public void RetrieveSpecificData()
{
    String strConnection = "LDAP://srv-enterprise/CN=User";

    //establish connection to base object
    DirectoryEntry dirEntry = new DirectoryEntry( strConnection );
    DirectorySearcher dirSearcher = new DirectorySearcher( dirEntry );

    //search for the specific user
    dirSearcher.Filter = "(&(objectClass=User)(cn=\"Lonnie Scully\"))";
    dirSearcher.SearchScope = SearchScope.Subtree;
```

```
//specify the data to retrieve
dirSearcher.PropertyNamesOnly = true;
dirSearcher.PropertiesToLoad.Add( "givenname" );
dirSearcher.PropertiesToLoad.Add( "sn" );

//perform the search
SearchResult searchResult = dirSearcher.FindOne();

return;
}
```

Minimizing Partial String Searches

Although the directory service has powerful support for partial string matches, it is time consuming. If partial matches are necessary, place the wildcard character at the end of the search string, rather than the beginning. A query, such as (cn=alyssa*) performs much faster than (cn=*lyss*) or (cn=*lyssa).

Querying Objects Once

When reading attributes from a directory service object, such as a User object, load all attributes at once and store them locally. This way, you can retrieve attributes more quickly than retrieving a number of attributes from the directory service a little at a time:

```
class UserData
{
    string _Lastname = "";
    string _Firstname = "";

    public void GetUserFullName()
    {
        String strConnection = "LDAP://srv-enterprise/CN=User";

        //establish connection to base object
        DirectoryEntry dirEntry = new DirectoryEntry( strConnection );
        DirectorySearcher dirSearcher = new DirectorySearcher( dirEntry );

        //search for the specific user
        dirSearcher.Filter = "(&(objectClass=User)(cn=\"Lonnie Scully\"))";
        dirSearcher.SearchScope = SearchScope.Subtree;
```

```
            SearchResult searchResult = dirSearcher.FindOne();

            //retrieve and store the user data
            DirectoryEntry dirResult = searchResult.GetDirectoryEntry();

            _Firstname = dirResult.Properties["givenname"].Value.ToString();
            _Lastname = dirResult.Properties["sn"].Value.ToString();

            return;
        }
}
```

Referencing Objects by GUID

Because directory searches can take time, applications should perform only an initial search for an object. Once found, the application should store the unique identifier, or GUID, for that object. If another connection in the future is necessary, it is faster to connect directly to the object based on its GUID rather than perform another search for the same object:

```
public string RetrieveNodeGuid()
{
    String strConnection = "LDAP://srv-enterprise/CN=User";

    //establish connection to base object
    DirectoryEntry dirEntry = new DirectoryEntry( strConnection );
    DirectorySearcher dirSearcher = new DirectorySearcher( dirEntry );

    //search for the specific user
    dirSearcher.Filter = "(&(objectClass=User)(cn=\"Lonnie Scully\"))";
    dirSearcher.SearchScope = SearchScope.Subtree;
    SearchResult result = dirSearcher.FindOne();

    //return the object's GUID for later binding
    return result.GetDirectoryEntry().NativeGuid;
}

public void ConnectByGuid( string strGuid )
{
    //bind to the object by its native guid
    DirectoryEntry dirEntry = new DirectoryEntry( strGuid );
```

```
//interact with bound object's properties
string strFirstname = dirEntry.Properties["givenname"].Value.ToString();
string strLastname = dirEntry.Properties["sn"].Value.ToString();

    return;
}
```

Using Timeouts

Because the operational status of a directory service is unknown, it can be difficult to determine if a directory service is performing a long search or is simply
not available. If a directory service is not available, then using timeouts enables
searches to simply time out rather than never returning at all:

```
public SearchResult SearchWithTimeout()
{
    String strConnection = "LDAP://srv-enterprise/CN=User";

    //establish connection to base object
    DirectoryEntry dirEntry = new DirectoryEntry( strConnection );
    DirectorySearcher dirSearcher = new DirectorySearcher( dirEntry );

    //set the timeout to one minute
    dirSearcher.ClientTimeout = new TimeSpan( 0, 1, 0 );

    //set the filter to retrieve the specific user
    dirSearcher.Filter = "(&(objectClass=User)(cn=\"Lonnie Scully\"))";
    dirSearcher.SearchScope = SearchScope.Subtree;

    //execute the search
    return dirSearcher.FindOne();
}
```

Summary

Many large enterprises realize the value of directory services because of they can
simplify user and machine management in a network environment. Storing
information about users and machines hierarchically in a directory allows
administrators to delegate management responsibilities to individuals within
departments and groups, leaving administrators to focus on other tasks and give
more control to users. By deploying enterprise applications that integrate with

directory services, companies are able to simplify management, enhance network services, provide greater application functionality, and seamlessly integrate with the host networking environment.

This chapter explored the world of directory services and how the .NET Framework integrates with Microsoft's Active Directory. After an introduction to directory services and Microsoft's Active Directory, it reviewed the related .NET Framework classes and showed how to leverage them to expand the IssueTracker enterprise application to include user validation and profile retrieval functionality. Finally, the chapter examined methods for improving directory services–related performance.

In the next chapter, you will learn about real-time messaging services and see how you can leverage them to build out a scalable business tier based on asynchronous communication. This includes creating messages and queues that implement a framework for building out a sample distributed analysis engine.

CHAPTER 4

Applying Reliable Messaging

MESSAGING PROVIDES AN INFRASTRUCTURE that binds distributed enterprise components together. Components, such as reporting services and analytical services, might reside on different computers at different locations. Messaging services provide a way to support reliable communication that binds all components together. Messaging also supports an open development framework that allows an enterprise solution to easily integrate new functionality produced after an enterprise product has shipped.

This chapter closely looks at messaging within the .NET Framework and how this vital communication mechanism can tie together a scalable enterprise application. The chapter begins by looking at how messaging systems work and showing how to configure a messaging environment. Next, it introduces the messaging-supported classes within the .NET Framework and shows how to implement an application messaging framework. The chapter concludes by implementing a sample distributed service.

Introducing Messaging Systems

Messaging binds distributed components together. If a distributed component becomes unavailable, the process requesting the services is not immediately impacted. Suppose an application requires the services of a reporting engine. If the reporting engine is integrated by direct method invocation, the requesting application fails when the reporting engine is disconnected. However, if message binding integrates the two, then the application requesting the reporting services would simply post a request and move on to other activities. When the reporting engine is available, it processes the request and performs its function.

Many successful enterprise applications, such as PeopleSoft, count on messaging for flexibility. Essentially, the application is organized into discrete modules that accomplish specific tasks. Messages sent between the modules define the behavior of the application. For example, when a user enters information into a form, the functional code behind the form formats that information into a message that is then sent to a data access component, which commits the information to the database. At first, this might sound like an unnecessarily complex way to process information. However, the benefits outweigh the costs. It requires little effort later to add a new user interface component that seamlessly replaces the outdated one by sending and receiving the same messages. Even a new component can intercept the message, validate the submitted information, and then forward the message to the data access component.

If building applications purely on messaging sounds familiar, it probably should. This is essentially how all Internet applications work. Client code, packaged within a Web browser, sends messages using the Hypertext Transfer Protocol (HTTP). The messages contain a header and a body as defined by the protocol. The messages are received by a Web server, which shares many characteristics of a message queue. The server either processes the data contained within the body of the message or forwards the message to another process.

Messaging services offer a number of advantages over direct method calls between components. Messages are much more robust than direct method calls in that the invoking process is more insulated from failures within the referenced component. Also, messages can have varying priorities so that specific functions can be accomplished sooner. Messages can also have transactional characteristics if several related messages are grouped together. This ensures that the series of messages are received only once and in the intended order. Finally, messaging leverages the sophisticated security model built into the underlying operating system with support for auditing, encrypting, and authenticating messages.

Messaging systems share a lot of similarity with e-mail systems. Both operate using three fundamental components: messages, queues, and a managing server. *Messages* communicate specific information between a sender and recipient. They are sent from one point to another and are held within *message queues* until read. *Message servers*, such as Microsoft Message Queue (MSMQ), are responsible for managing message queues, encrypting messages, sending and receiving messages, authenticating, and routing messages to their final destination.

Understanding Messages

Messages are discrete packages of information with a distinct sender and recipient. In most cases, messages are composed of a label, which describes the subject of the message, and a body, which communicates the actual information. Message labels are usually human-readable text descriptions; the body might vary from simple text to images to compiled code.

Defining the Message Label

A *message label* is similar to the subject line of a typical e-mail message. The label provides the message a means to describe its contents, which in turn allows multiple listening applications to determine if it should be interested in the message. Typically, the message header will contain a word or phrase for which an application is looking. If the word appears in the message label, the application reads the message body and processes its contents. Otherwise, the application ignores the message entirely.

Defining the Message Body

The *message body* contains the information that needs to be communicated from one process to another. The message body can contain any type of data including a simple text message, a selection of spreadsheet cells, and a graphic file. There are different methods available for accessing and processing the message body.

Defining Transactional Messages

A message-driven process can bind several related messages into a single *transactional message*, ensuring that the messages are delivered in order, are delivered only once, and are successfully retrieved from their destination queue. If any errors occur, the entire transaction is cancelled.

Understanding Message Queues

Message queues hold messages until they are read by messaging clients. When a client reads a message, the messaging system removes the message from a queue. The queue is also responsible for ensuring the integrity of a message. When a server hosting a message queue goes down, it is expected that the message queue is restored to its original state when the server becomes available again. There are two fundamental types of message queues: user queues and system queues.

User queues maintain messages used by installed applications. They are divided into two different classifications: public queues and private queues. A *public queue* is available to all clients and servers within a domain. Other messaging systems within a network are able to post messages to a locally managed public queue. A *private queue* is only available to locally installed applications. Some operating systems, primarily workstation platforms, are unable to create public message queues for security reasons.

System queues exist whether public or private message queues are available. These queues manage two basic types of system messages: journal messages and dead-letter messages. *Journal messages* are duplicates of outgoing nontransactional messages created when a sent message reaches its destination. Journal messages are disabled by default because copies of outgoing messages quickly drain system resources. *Dead-letter messages* are undeliverable, expired nontransactional messages that are stored for future reference. Messages are considered undeliverable when the destination queue is unknown, the maximum number of hops is exceeded, the destination queue is filled, or a transactional message is sent to a nontransactional queue.

Message systems also adopt one or more of the following three messaging models: point-to-point, publish-subscribe, and request-reply.

Defining Point-to-Point

Point-to-point messaging enables one process to send messages to and receive messages from another specific process. In this model, messages are targeted at a single specific receiver. Other message handlers within the enterprise application should not process them. Point-to-point typically requires a message queue that the receiver monitors.

Defining Publish-Subscribe

Publish-subscribe messaging enables multiple processes to receive any given message. This model is based on the concept of a message topic. Usually, topics are broadly defined events that multiple processes listen for and act upon. This messaging model is essentially what is at the core of the Microsoft Windows operating system. Every keystroke and mouse click generates an event that the operating system handles. At the same time, the active application receives the same system messages and might decide to act upon them. Even the form controls, such as buttons and list boxes, receive the same event messages. Although MSMQ does not specifically support this methodology, you can accomplish the effect by having connected clients peek into a shared message queue containing messages marked with an expiration.

Defining Request-Reply

Request-reply messaging ensures that a process that sends a message will receive a message in response. Minimally, this might represent an acknowledgment that the message was received. In most cases, the request-reply model applies to transactions that send a request message and suspend activity until a reply is returned.

Understanding a Message Server

The message server manages one or more message queues and ensures that messages either arrive at the destination or return with a notification. Message servers maintain information about message delivery, including how many stops (referred to as *hops*) a message makes before reaching its destination. Each hop represents a message queue on a server closer to the destination where individual messages can be evaluated and routed to the next hop. If a message does not reach its destination within a specified number of hops, the server holds on to the message until the destination is available. The message server also preserves the state of its message queues. When a server is brought down and later restarted, its original state will be returned.

Using Microsoft Message Queue

MSMQ offers reliable messaging infrastructure closely integrated with the Microsoft Windows platform. MSMQ configurations vary from heavyweight transactional services on the server platforms to simple routing services on the workstation platforms.

MSMQ is normally installed as an extra operating system service option. In the case of most workstation platforms, it is not installed by default. This seriously affects the enterprise application developer. If your solution requires messaging services on at the client side, you need to determine if it is installed. Ideally, you will do this when you install your client software. Minimally, you should provide a compatibility test application to check if a client computer is ready to support your application.

Managing Message Queues

You can create message queues manually or programmatically. To create a message queue manually, first check to ensure that MSMQ is installed locally by opening the Control Panel, opening Add or Remove Programs, selecting Add/Remove Windows Components, and validating that the Message Queuing component is checked. If installed, open the Computer Management console by selecting Start ➤ Control Panel ➤ Administrative Tools ➤ Computer Management. Expand the Services and Applications tree node and then expand the Message Queuing tree node. You should see a list of public, private, and system message queues. To create a new private message queue, right-click the Private Queues tree node and select New ➤ Private Queue from the context menu. A prompt for the message queue name appears, as shown in Figure 4-1. Once you enter a name and the dialog box closes, the queue is available.

With the appropriate access rights, deleting message queues requires about the same effort as creating them. You can delete message queues manually from the Computer Management console by highlighting the message queue and pressing the Delete key.

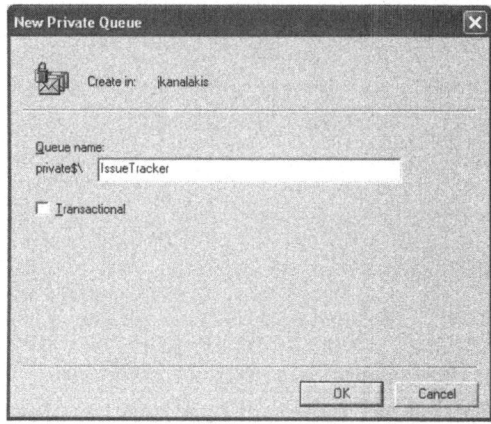

Figure 4-1. Creating a new MSMQ private message queue

Understanding the Limitations of Servers and Workstations

MSMQ supports the creation of public and private message queues. However, depending upon which operating system your application runs on, you might be able to create and access only certain types of message queues.

On Windows servers—including Windows NT, 2000, and 2003 Server—both a user and an application are capable of creating public message queues. Public message queues can receive and route messages from any other application within the network. Workstation computers—such as Windows 95, 98, and Millennium Edition—support only the creation of private message queues. Private message queues support only messages sent from one application on the local computer to another application on the local computer. Also, workstation computers behave differently whether they operate as stand-alone computers or within a domain. When operating within a domain, they disable support for journal and dead-letter message queues. Finally, Windows XP is able to create public and private message queues. When developing applications that implement a messaging framework, bear in mind which platform the product will be installed on so that the installation program is able to create a public or private message queue as needed.

Working with .NET Messaging Services

In the .NET Framework, messaging services reside within the System.Messaging namespace. Three fundamental classes accomplish most messaging functionality: Message, MessageQueue, and MessageQueueException.

The Message class abstracts individual messages and enables you to specify properties such as label, body, priority, authentication, and so on. This class also offers methods supporting data encryption, tracing, and expirations.

The MessageQueue class abstracts an individual message queue and enables you to create and delete queues. You can also use this class to send simple and complex messages, delete all messages from the message queue, read posted messages, or peek into the queue to find a specific message.

The MessageQueueException class provides detailed information about exceptions thrown while attempting messaging-related activities. When any messaging task fails to succeed, this exception is thrown, and it provides a description of the problem, an error code, and stack trace information.

Creating a Messaging Framework

A messaging framework can bring consistency to how queues and messages are managed within an application. The enterprise application and the extended distributed service can use the framework.

Begin by selecting the SystemFrameworks project within the IssueTracker solution. Next, it is important to add a project-level reference to the messaging namespace within Visual Studio .NET. From the menu, select Project ➤ Add Reference. Then, select the System.Messaging.dll component, as shown in Figure 4-2.

The MessagingFramework object provides a uniform method for managing message queues and for managing the sending and receiving of messages. Both the application and distributed services connected to the application use this object by means of messaging. Listing 4-1 outlines the basic MessagingFramework object code.

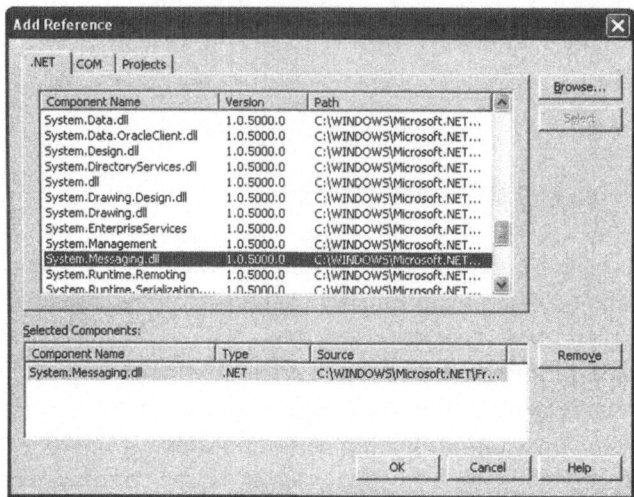

Figure 4-2. Selecting the project reference in Visual Studio .NET

Listing 4-1. The MessagingFramework Class

```
public class MessagingFramework
{
    private string _ProcessName = "";
    private string _QueueInboxName = "";
    private string _QueueOutboxName = "";
    private string _QueueErrorsName = "";

    public enum QueueType
    {
        Inbox = 1,
        Outbox = 2,
        Errors = 3
    }

    public MessagingFramework()
    {
        _ProcessName = "Undefined";
        _QueueInboxName = ".\\private$\\" + _ProcessName + "Inbox";
        _QueueOutboxName = ".\\private$\\" + _ProcessName + "Outbox";
        _QueueErrorsName = ".\\private$\\" + _ProcessName + "Errors";
```

```
        return;
    }

    public MessagingFramework( string strProcessName )
    {
        _ProcessName = strProcessName;
        _QueueInboxName = ".\\private$\\" + _ProcessName + "Inbox";
        _QueueOutboxName = ".\\private$\\" + _ProcessName + "Outbox";
        _QueueErrorsName = ".\\private$\\" + _ProcessName + "Errors";

        return;
    }

    public string ProcessName
    {
        get
        {
            return _ProcessName;
        }
        set
        {
            _ProcessName = value;
            _QueueInboxName = ".\\private$\\" + _ProcessName + "Inbox";
            _QueueOutboxName = ".\\private$\\" + _ProcessName + "Outbox";
            _QueueErrorsName = ".\\private$\\" + _ProcessName + "Errors";
        }
    }
}
```

The first element of the path identifies the target server. Because you are creating a message queue locally, you use a dot in place of a server name. The next element designates which type of queue to create. To create a private message queue, you use the private$ identifier. To create a public message queue, the path appears the same but without the private$ identifier.

Within this application framework, each messaging client should keep a single instance of the MessagingFramework class. MessagingFramework maintains the fully qualified name of Inbox, Outbox, and Errors message queues as well as the name of the process (or client) managing it. The code also defines an enumerated type that identifies the three application message queue types. All variables are set within the two available constructors or within an accessor method.

Creating Message Queues

Although creating a message queue using the Computer Management console seems easy enough, you cannot expect the average enterprise customer to handle it. To create a message queue programmatically, as in an installation program, only a single method call to the MessageQueue object is necessary. Listing 4-2 demonstrates how the Create method creates public and private message queues.

Listing 4-2. Creating a New Message Queue

```
public void CreateQueues()
{
    try
    {
        //create the inbox queue
        if( ! MessageQueue.Exists( _QueueInboxName ) )
            MessageQueue.Create( _QueueInboxName );

        //create the outbox queue
        if( ! MessageQueue.Exists( _QueueOutboxName ) )
            MessageQueue.Create( _QueueOutboxName );

        //create the errors queue
        if( ! MessageQueue.Exists( _QueueErrorsName ) )
            MessageQueue.Create( _QueueErrorsName );

    }
    catch( MessageQueueException exception )
    {
        EventLog systemLog = new EventLog();
        systemLog.Source = "IssueTracker";
        systemLog.WriteEntry( exception.Message, EventLogEntryType.Error, 0 );
    }

    return;
}
```

The Create method creates three new message queues. Before the application creates each queue, it checks to see that they do not already exist. This code catches any exceptions that are thrown and writes them to the Windows Event Viewer.

Deleting Message Queues

You can also delete message queues programmatically. To delete a message queue, as in an uninstall program, only a single method call to the MessageQueue object is necessary. Listing 4-3 demonstrates how the Delete method removes all three application message queues.

Listing 4-3. Deleting an Existing Message Queue

```
public void DeleteQueues()
{
    try
    {
        //delete the inbox queue
        if( ! MessageQueue.Exists( _QueueInboxName ) )
            MessageQueue.Delete( _QueueInboxName );

        //delete the outbox queue
        if( ! MessageQueue.Exists( _QueueOutboxName ) )
            MessageQueue.Delete( _QueueOutboxName );

        //delete the errors queue
        if( ! MessageQueue.Exists( _QueueErrorsName ) )
            MessageQueue.Delete( _QueueErrorsName );

    }
    catch( MessageQueueException exception )
    {
        EventLog systemLog = new EventLog();
        systemLog.Source = "IssueTracker";
        systemLog.WriteEntry( exception.Message, EventLogEntryType.Error, 0 );
    }

    return;
}
```

The Delete method functions similarly to the Create method. It deletes all three message queues after checking to ensure they actually exist. If permissions do not allow the deletion of a queue or the queue does not exist, then a MessageQueueException exception will be thrown. Although it is permissible to delete a message queue while unread messages are still present, it is much cleaner to purge a queue first.

Sending Simple Messages

You can send simple messages from one process to another with the help of the System.Messaging namespace objects. Essentially, an application only needs to connect to a message queue (assuming that the queue already exists), specify a message label and body, and then send the message. Listing 4-4 implements the SendMessage method within the messaging framework. An application uses this method to specify a target process, a subject, and a message body.

Listing 4-4. MessageComposer Test Application

```
public void SendMessage( string strTargetProcess, string strSubject,
    string strBody )
{
    MessageQueue queue = null;
    string strTargetQueueName;

    try
    {
        strTargetQueueName = ".\\private$\\" + strTargetProcess + "Inbox";

        if( MessageQueue.Exists( strTargetQueueName ) )
        {
            queue = new MessageQueue( strTargetQueueName );
            queue.Send( strSubject, strBody );
        }
    }
    catch( MessageQueueException exception )
    {
        EventLog systemLog = new EventLog();
        systemLog.Source = "IssueTracker";
        systemLog.WriteEntry( exception.Message, EventLogEntryType.Error, 0 );
    }
    finally
    {
        queue.Close();
    }

    return;
}
```

Listing 4-4 begins by declaring working variables. Next, it specifies the fully qualified path to the destination Inbox message queue. The code then checks the target message queue to ensure it exists. If the queue exists, then the method connects to the queue and sends the message using the subject and body values supplied to the method. If the named message queue does not exist or the message fails to send, an exception is thrown. The exception handler traps all MessageQueueExceptions and writes the message to the Windows Event Viewer. Otherwise, the message is sent successfully. From the Computer Management console, you can view the list of posted messages within the IssueTracker private message queue. The message remains in the queue until it is read.

Receiving Simple Messages

Receiving simple messages from another process is also consistently packaged into the application messaging framework. Essentially, the messaging framework points to the same message queue to receive the message. Listing 4-5 implements the ReceiveMessage method to query a message queue for a new message.

Listing 4-5. MessageConsole Test Application

```
public Message ReceiveMessage()
{
    MessageQueue queue = null;
    Message message = null;

    try
    {
        MessageQueue queue = new MessageQueue( _QueueInboxName );

        //retrieve message from the queue
        message = queue.Receive();
    }
    catch( Exception exception )
    {
        EventLog systemLog = new EventLog();
        systemLog.Source = "IssueTracker";
        systemLog.WriteEntry( exception.Message, EventLogEntryType.Error, 0 );
    }
    finally
    {
        queue.Close();
    }

    return message;
}
```

Listing 4-5 begins by establishing a connection to the object owner's Inbox message queue. Next, the queue's Receive method returns a single message. The message returned is the latest message entered into the queue. If any exceptions are thrown, they are handled and written to the Windows Event Viewer. In any case, the queue closes and the received message returns to the calling process.

Peeking into Messages

Each time the Receive method is invoked, the received message is permanently removed from the message queue. The Peek method lets you preview the message labels and decide if you want to read it. This is helpful because a message within a shared queue might be intended for another application and removing it from the queue could cause problems. Listing 4-6 demonstrates how you change the application messaging framework to peek at message labels rather than receive the entire message.

Listing 4-6. MessageConsole Application with Message Peeking

```
public Message PeekMessages( string strLookFor )
{
    MessageQueue queue = null;
    Message message = null;

    try
    {
        MessageQueue queue = new MessageQueue( _QueueInboxName );
        message = queue.Peek();

        string[] types = { "System.String" };
        message.Formatter = new XmlMessageFormatter( types );

        if( message.Label.IndexOf( strLookFor ) >= 0 )
            return message;
    }
    catch( Exception exception )
    {
        EventLog systemLog = new EventLog();
        systemLog.Source = "IssueTracker";
        systemLog.WriteEntry( exception.Message, EventLogEntryType.Error, 0 );
    }
```

```
    finally
    {
        queue.Close();
    }

    return message;
}
```

The method begins by invoking the Peek method and assigning its results to a new Message object. Next, a string array specifies the target data type as a String. The method also defines a message formatter to be applied to the message queue. Regardless of what content is entered for the body, its internal representation is persistent in Extensible Markup Language (XML). Because the message body is natively persistent in XML, it is necessary to apply a message formatter to convert the body into a readable message. The XmlMessageFormatter class offers services that serialize and deserialize objects from the body of a message. To use this class, the target type needs to tell the formatter what schemas to attempt to match when deserializing a message. In this case, set the target type to System.String, instructing the formatter to convert the body of a message into a readable string.

After the message label has been read and the data has been converted, regular expressions can be applied to the message. The method searches for a match to the string parameter provided. If there is a match, the entire message is returned to the calling process. The problem with the Peek method is that it only sees the first message in the queue; some applications might find this limiting. Fortunately, there are other methods that enable an application to view multiple messages within a queue.

Receiving Multiple Messages

You can retrieve a dynamic list of messages using the MessageEnumerator. The messages within the enumerator appear in the same order as within the queue: by message priority. The enumerator serves as a cursor and allows an application to advance from the first message in the queue to the next by invoking the MoveNext method. The enumerator is only able to advance and cannot step backward through the messages. If a new message is added to the queue with a higher priority than the message being read, then it will not be accessed. To return to the top of the queue, invoke the Reset method. Listing 4-7 shows how to display multiple messages within a message queue.

Listing 4-7. Displaying Multiple Messages Within a Message Queue

```
public MessageEnumerator ReceiveAllMessages()
{
    MessageQueue queue = null;
    MessageEnumerator enumerator = null;

    try
    {
        queue = new MessageQueue( _QueueInboxName );

        //retrieve all messages from the queue
        enumerator = (MessageEnumerator)(queue.GetEnumerator());
    }
    catch( Exception exception )
    {
        EventLog systemLog = new EventLog();
        systemLog.Source = "IssueTracker";
        systemLog.WriteEntry( exception.Message, EventLogEntryType.Error, 0 );
    }
    finally
    {
        queue.Close();
    }

    return enumerator;
}
```

In Listing 4-7, the GetEnumerator method retrieves a dynamic list of the messages within the queue. Like a DataReader object, MessageEnumerator advances through the list of messages in a forward-only read by invoking the MoveNext method.

 NOTE *If the message queue is instantiated with the DenyShareReceived attribute set to true, then no other applications can modify messages within the enumerator while the connection is open.*

Understanding Additional Message Queue Interaction

In addition to basic message queue manipulation such as creating and deleting message queues, a number of other method functionality is available. Such functionality includes retrieving a list of all available queues, searching for a specific queue, and purging all messages within a queue.

Listing Available Queues

Enterprise applications that implement a messaging framework often interact with multiple message queues on multiple computers. There are several occasions when it is necessary to build a list of available message queues. This often occurs in a messaging management interface where the system administrator configuring your enterprise application can create, modify, and delete message queues. Listing 4-8 presents an additional method that lists all available message queues.

Listing 4-8. Outputting All Available Message Queues

```
public ArrayList ListAllQueues()
{
    ArrayList arrayQueues = new ArrayList();

    try
    {
        arrayQueues.AddRange( MessageQueue.GetPrivateQueuesByMachine( "." ) );
    }
    catch( MessageQueueException exception )
    {
        EventLog systemLog = new EventLog();
        systemLog.Source = "IssueTracker";
        systemLog.WriteEntry( exception.Message, EventLogEntryType.Error, 0 );
    }

    return arrayQueues;
}
```

In Listing 4-8, the GetPrivateQueuesByMachine method lists all private message queues on the local computer. To list all available public message queues, substitute GetPublicQueuesByMachine for this method. You can also specify the computer name to search for all message queues on that computer. The resulting list is stored in an ArrayList object for easier iteration within the application.

Searching for a Queue

In enterprise environments, it is easy to end up with multiple message queues processing information from different systems. Returning a list of all available message queues is helpful, but being able to search for a specific message queue is invaluable. Listing 4-9 demonstrates how to define search criteria to return a list of message queues that match the specified criteria.

Listing 4-9. Specifying a Message Queue by Criteria

```
public ArrayList ListApplicationQueues()
{
    ArrayList arrayQueues = new ArrayList();

    try
    {
        arrayQueues.AddRange(
            MessageQueue.GetPublicQueuesByLabel( _QueueInboxName ) );

        arrayQueues.AddRange(
            MessageQueue.GetPublicQueuesByLabel( _QueueOutboxName ) );

        arrayQueues.AddRange(
            MessageQueue.GetPublicQueuesByLabel( _QueueErrorsName ) );
    }
    catch( MessageQueueException exception )
    {
        EventLog systemLog = new EventLog();
        systemLog.Source = "IssueTracker";
        systemLog.WriteEntry( exception.Message, EventLogEntryType.Error, 0 );
    }

    return arrayQueues;
}
```

Listing 4-9 creates an array of message queues that is populated by the GetQueuesByLabel method. It passes a string argument to this method to filter the list of message queues down to those whose label matches. In addition to filtering message queues by label, you can use other methods to filter by category or machine name.

Determining If a Queue Exists

Applications can easily determine if a specific message queue exists. The MessageQueue class provides a test method called Exists that takes a parameter indicating the qualified path to the message queue. Listing 4-10 checks to see if a specific message queue exists before attempting to delete it.

Listing 4-10. Checking to See If a Message Queue Exists

```
public void DeleteQueues()
{
    try
    {
        //delete the inbox queue
        if( ! MessageQueue.Exists( _QueueInboxName ) )
            MessageQueue.Delete( _QueueInboxName );

        //delete the outbox queue
        if( ! MessageQueue.Exists( _QueueOutboxName ) )
            MessageQueue.Delete( _QueueOutboxName );

        //delete the errors queue
        if( ! MessageQueue.Exists( _QueueErrorsName ) )
            MessageQueue.Delete( _QueueErrorsName );
    }
    catch( MessageQueueException exception )
    {
        EventLog systemLog = new EventLog();
        systemLog.Source = "IssueTracker";
        systemLog.WriteEntry( exception.Message, EventLogEntryType.Error, 0 );
    }

    return;
}
```

Purging a Queue

It is not often that you want to completely clear out a message queue. However, if you need to empty a message queue, the MessageQueue class provides the Purge method. This method internally sets the queue modification flag, which in turn updates its LastModifyTime property. Listing 4-11 defines a simple method that clears out all messages within the specified application message queue.

Listing 4-11. Purging All Messages from a Queue

```
public void EmptyQueue( MessagingFramework.QueueType queueType )
{
    MessageQueue queue = null;

    try
    {
        switch( queueType )
        {
            case QueueType.Inbox:
                queue = new MessageQueue( _QueueInboxName );
                break;

            case QueueType.Outbox:
                queue = new MessageQueue( _QueueOutboxName );
                break;

            case QueueType.Errors:
                queue = new MessageQueue( _QueueErrorsName );
                break;
        }

        queue.Purge();
    }
    catch( MessageQueueException exception )
    {
        EventLog systemLog = new EventLog();
        systemLog.Source = "IssueTracker";
        systemLog.WriteEntry( exception.Message, EventLogEntryType.Error, 0 );
    }

    return;
}
```

The Purge method deletes all messages within the specified queue without sending a copy of the message to the dead-letter queue or the journal queue. Once purged, the messages cannot be recovered.

Returning Failed Message Acknowledgments

You can enable message queues to return acknowledgment messages that indicate whether a message was successfully delivered. There are two types of acknowledgments. *Positive acknowledgment messages* indicate that a message was delivered to its destination message queue. *Negative acknowledgment messages* indicate that a message failed to reach its destination message queue. Both acknowledgments are system-generated messages sent from the original destination queue to a specially designated administration queue. Aside from being system generated, the most significant difference from other messages is that acknowledgment messages have no message body; instead, they have only a message label. Otherwise, acknowledgment messages are read from the administrative message queue just like any other message. Listing 4-12 demonstrates how you can designate an administrative message queue to receive negative acknowledgments when a message expires.

Listing 4-12. Designating an Administration Queue for Acknowledgment Messages

```
public void SendMessage( string strTargetProcess, string strSubject,
    string strBody, int intMaxWaitSeconds )
{
    string strTargetQueueName;
    string strTargetErrorsQueueName;

    try
    {
        strTargetQueueName = ".\\private$\\" + strTargetProcess + "Inbox";
        strTargetErrorsQueueName = ".\\private$\\" + strTargetProcess + "Errors";

        if( MessageQueue.Exists( strTargetQueueName ) )
        {
            MessageQueue queue = new MessageQueue( strTargetQueueName );
            MessageQueue queueErrors =
                new MessageQueue( strTargetErrorsQueueName );

            Message message = new Message();
            message.Label = strSubject;
            message.Body = strBody;
            message.TimeToBeReceived = new TimeSpan( 0, 0, intMaxWaitSeconds );

            message.AdministrationQueue = queueErrors;
            message.AcknowledgeType = AcknowledgeTypes.NegativeReceive;

            queue.Send( message );
        }
    }
    catch( MessageQueueException exception )
    {
```

```
        EventLog systemLog = new EventLog();
        systemLog.Source = "IssueTracker";
        systemLog.WriteEntry( exception.Message, EventLogEntryType.Error, 0 );
    }


    return;
}
```

Listing 4-12 designates an administration queue to receive a negative acknowledgment message if the outgoing message fails to reach its destination. First, two message queue objects are instantiated: the original destination queue where the outgoing message is posted to and an administration message queue where system-generated acknowledgment messages appear. Next, you create the outgoing message. Set the AdministrationQueue property to point to your administration queue. Set the AcknowledgementType property to NegativeReceive to indicate that you are only interested in receiving negative acknowledgment messages. The TimeToBeReceived property identifies the expiration time of the outgoing message. With the help of the TimeSpan class, you can force the outgoing message to expire after 15 seconds. When your method is invoked, a message with the label "Test Message Label" appears in the IssueTracker message queue. After 15 seconds, the message expires and is removed from the Inbox queue, and an acknowledgment message is sent to the Errors administration queue. Additionally, the acknowledgment message includes a class description stating, "The time-to-be-received has elapsed."

Resending Failed Messages

Acknowledgment messages and administration queues can work together to resend messages that have failed to reach their destinations. Listing 4-13 presents an approach to reading messages stored in the administration queue and resending them to their intended destinations.

Listing 4-13. Resending Failed Messages

```
public void ResendMessage()
{
    MessageQueue queueErrors = null;
    MessageQueue queueDestination = null;
    ArrayList messagesArray = new ArrayList();

    try
```

```
    {
        queueErrors = new MessageQueue( _QueueErrorsName );
        messagesArray.AddRange( queueErrors.GetAllMessages() );

        foreach( Message message in messagesArray )
        {
            queueDestination = message.ResponseQueue;
            queueDestination.Send( message );
        }

        queueErrors.Purge();
    }
    catch( MessageQueueException exception )
    {
        EventLog systemLog = new EventLog();
        systemLog.Source = "IssueTracker";
        systemLog.WriteEntry( exception.Message, EventLogEntryType.Error, 0 );
    }
    finally
    {
        queueErrors.Close();
        queueDestination.Close();
    }

    return;
}
```

In Listing 4-13, any messages that expire and trigger an acknowledgment message will be resent. The listing begins by specifying the administration message queue as IssueTrackerErrors. Next, your method reads the administration queue like any other message queue—by invoking GetAllMessages. Next, you loop through the messages within the queue. For each acknowledgment message within the queue, you set its new destination queue to the original message's destination queue. You can do this by assigning the destination queue to the acknowledgment message's ResponseQueue property. With the destination queue changed, the message can be resent to its original destination with one significant difference. The TimeToBeReceived property has been lost. The expiration property is gone because you are now working with the acknowledgment message, not the original. Unfortunately, the acknowledgment message maintains a limited subset of the original message's properties. To work with a true copy of the message, you need to work with the system journal queue.

Working with the Journal Message Queue

Resending messages from an administration queue works, but it certainly has some limitations. The problem is that the acknowledgment message that appears in the administration queue is not a true copy of the original message sent. Journal message queues actually store copies of the original outgoing message. Journal queues are meant to store critical messages that might need to be resent if they fail to reach their destinations.

Journal messages work well with acknowledgment messages. In addition to including the reason that an outgoing message has failed, acknowledgment messages also contain a CorrelationId. This property maps to the original message copied to the journal message queue. When an acknowledgment message comes in, you can match the CorrelationId to the original message and resend the original message.

By default, outgoing messages are not copied to the journal queue. Both messages and message queue objects have a UseJournalQueue property. When this property is true for a message queue, all messages tied to that queue are copied to the journal queue. When this property is true for an individual message, then only the specified message is copied. Typically, only transactional messages are important enough to copy into the journal queue. If a transactional message fails, then a number of other related business functions might be impacted. Working with the acknowledgment messages and the journal queue, the original transactional message can be resent quickly and accurately.

 NOTE *Journal queues have a maximum capacity determined by available disk space. When this capacity is reached, new messages are not copied and no notifications to the application are made. Thus, it is important to periodically purge the journal queue.*

Understanding Message Serialization

Message *serialization* is the process of breaking down objects into a portable state that can be transported from one message queue to another. When objects are serialized, essentially their data members are stored and transported. The receiving component *deserializes* an object by reading the saved state information and instantiating the same object with the saved state. Figure 4-3 illustrates the message serialization and deserialization process.

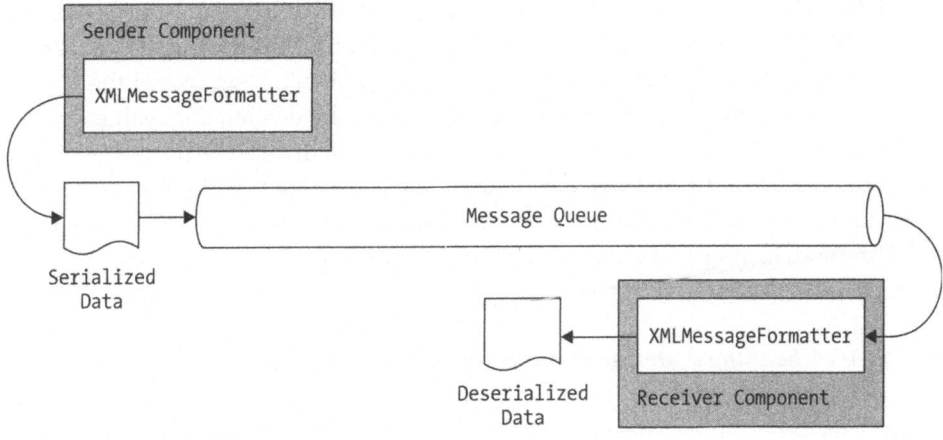

Figure 4-3. The message serialization/deserialization process

The function of serializing and deserializing an object is the responsibility of a message formatter. When a data object is sent to a message queue, the message formatter serializes the object into a stream. When that message is later read from the message queue, another message formatter deserializes the stream into the Body property of a Message object. There are three different message formatters available with Visual Studio .NET: XmlMessageFormatter, BinaryMessageFormatter, and ActiveXMessageFormatter.

XmlMessageFormatter is the default formatter used for all messages. Data objects and primitive data types are structured as a collection of human-readable XML tags and attributes. Without any extra coding, any message will be serialized using this formatter when a MessageQueue object's Send method is invoked.

The BinaryMessageFormatter and ActiveXMessageFormatter formatters both convert data objects and primitive data types into a non-human-readable binary stream. ActiveXMessageFormatter is used specifically for compatibility with the MSMQ ActiveX component typically found in earlier Visual Basic applications.

For a complex data object to be properly serialized by BinaryMessageFormatter, the object's class declaration must apply the Serializable attribute. For example, to stream the Issue business object defined in Chapter 2, "Accessing Data in ADO.NET," modify the class declaration and its abstract base class definition to include the Serializable attribute:

```
[Serializable]
public class Issue : BusinessObject
```

With a serializable object available to stream, modify the SendMessage method to use BinaryMessageFormatter, rather than its default XmlMessageFormatter. Begin by instantiating the BinaryMessageFormatter object. Next, assign the object to the Formatter property of the Message object. Set the desired data values in the serializable object—in this case, the Issue object. Next, invoke the formatter's Write method to perform the process of serializing the Issue object to the Body property of the Message object. Finally, send the message to its destination queue using the Send method. Listing 4-14 shows how to send a message containing a serialized object.

Listing 4-14. Sending a Message Containing a Serialized Object

```
public void SendBusinessObject( string strTargetProcess, string strSubject,
    BusinessObject objSource )
{
    string strTargetQueueName;
    MessageQueue queue = null;

    try
    {
        strTargetQueueName = ".\\private$\\" + strTargetProcess + "Inbox";

        queue = new MessageQueue( strTargetQueueName );
        Message message = new Message();

        //specify the message formatter
        BinaryMessageFormatter formatter = new BinaryMessageFormatter();
        message.Formatter = formatter;

        //set the message properties
        message.Label = strSubject;
        formatter.Write( message, objSource );

        //send the binary serialized message
        queue.Send( message );
    }
    catch( MessageQueueException exception )
    {
        EventLog systemLog = new EventLog();
        systemLog.Source = "IssueTracker";
        systemLog.WriteEntry( exception.Message, EventLogEntryType.Error, 0 );
    }
    finally
```

```
    {
        queue.Close();
    }

    return;
}
```

Deserializing an object from a message is just as easy. Again, establish a connection to a message queue. Next, create a Message object and assign it to the data returned from the MessageQueue object's Receive method. Instantiate a new BinaryMessageFormatter object and assign it to the Message object's Formatter property. Finally, create an instance of the serializable Issue object and assign it to the Body property of the retrieved message. The local Issue object will contain all data deserialized from the message body. Listing 4-15 shows how to receive a message containing a serialized object.

Listing 4-15. Receiving a Message Containing a Serialized Object

```
public BusinessObject ReceiveBusinessObject()
{
    MessageQueue queue = null;
    BusinessObject objReceived = null;

    try
    {
        queue = new MessageQueue( _QueueInboxName );

        //retrieve message from the queue
        Message message = queue.Receive();

        //specify the message formatter
        message.Formatter = new BinaryMessageFormatter();

        //display retrieved object data
        objReceived = (BusinessObject)message.Body;
    }
    catch( MessageQueueException exception )
    {
        EventLog systemLog = new EventLog();
        systemLog.Source = "IssueTracker";
        systemLog.WriteEntry( exception.Message, EventLogEntryType.Error, 0 );
    }
    finally
```

```
{
    queue.Close();
}

return objReceived;
}
```

The difference between an XML-formatted message and a binary-formatted message is visually apparent. You can view the difference in the Computer Management console by selecting any of the application message queues, selecting a message, and viewing its properties, as shown in Figure 4-4.

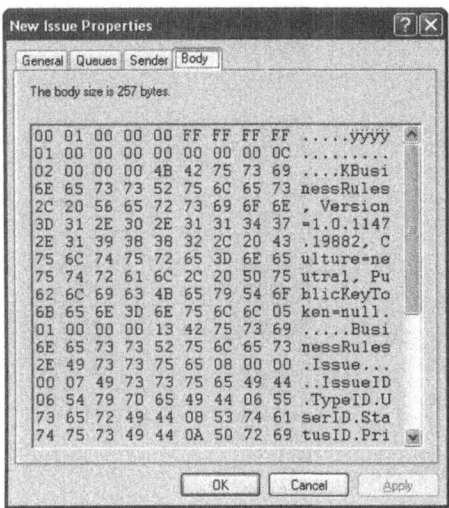

Figure 4-4. Message properties displaying a binary-serialized message body

The decision between using XML formatting and using binary formatting is an important one to make early in the design process. XML formatting is more open and flexible to integrate with other client components. Binary formatting is faster and easier to implement when other client components are internally developed from the same code base and have access to the same business objects.

Working with Transactions

As mentioned, message queues can process messages in a transactional behavior. Transactions ensure that a series of messages are delivered in order, are delivered only once, and are successfully retrieved. When a transaction is processed, all messages are either committed or aborted. In the event of a failure in delivery, a transactional message queue can be rolled back to its original state.

To support transactional messages, create a message queue as transactional. As with regular message queues, you can create transactional message queues manually or programmatically. Figure 4-5 illustrates the creation of a transactional message queue using the Computer Management console.

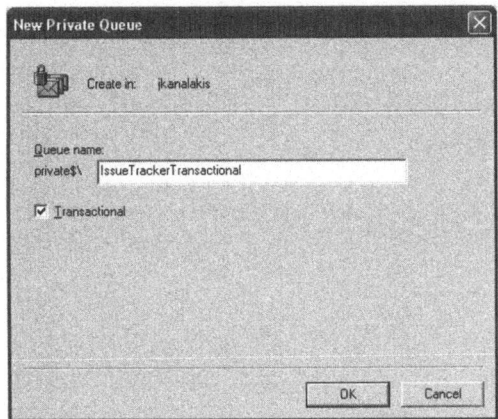

Figure 4-5. Creating a transactional message queue

Behavioral rules regarding messages and message queues are fairly clear. Nontransactional message queues are unable to process messages that are part of a transaction. However, if a nontransactional message is sent to a transactional message queue, the message is converted into a single-message transaction. Listing 4-16 shows how to send a series of messages as a transaction.

Listing 4-16. Sending a Series of Messages as a Transaction

```
public void SendTransactionMessages( string strTargetProcess,
    ArrayList arrayMessages )
{
    string strTargetQueueName;
    MessageQueueTransaction queueTransaction = new MessageQueueTransaction();
    MessageQueue queue = null;

    try
    {
        strTargetQueueName = ".\\private$\\" + strTargetProcess + "Inbox";
        queue = new MessageQueue( strTargetQueueName );

        queueTransaction.Begin();
```

```
            foreach( Message message in arrayMessages )
            {
                queue.Send( message, queueTransaction );
            }

            queueTransaction.Commit();
    }
    catch( Exception exception )
    {
        queueTransaction.Abort();

        EventLog systemLog = new EventLog();
        systemLog.Source = "IssueTracker";
        systemLog.WriteEntry( exception.Message, EventLogEntryType.Error, 0 );
    }
    finally
    {
        queue.Close();
    }


    return;
}
```

To execute a message-based transaction, instantiate a MessageQueueTransaction object. Next, instantiate a MessageQueue object and point it to the destination transactional message queue. Invoke the Begin method belonging to the MessageQueueTransaction object to mark the starting point of the messaging transaction. This sends each message, passing the MessageQueueTransaction object as a parameter to the Send method. Finally, invoke the Commit method to mark the end of the transaction. In the exception-handling block, the Abort method rolls back the entire transaction, including all messages sent or received.

Listing 4-17 creates a receive method to retrieve messages from a transactional message queue. If any exceptions are thrown during the message retrieval process, all read messages removed from the transactional message queue are restored as if they were never read. The message queue then returns to its original state marked by the Begin method.

Listing 4-17. Receiving a Message Within a Transaction

```
public Message ReceiveTransactionMessage()
{
    MessageQueueTransaction queueTransaction = new MessageQueueTransaction();
    Message message = null;
```

```
MessageQueue queue = null;

try
{
    queue = new MessageQueue( _QueueInboxName );

    queueTransaction.Begin();
    message = queue.Receive( queueTransaction );
    queueTransaction.Commit();
}
catch( Exception exception )
{
    queueTransaction.Abort();

    EventLog systemLog = new EventLog();
    systemLog.Source = "IssueTracker";
    systemLog.WriteEntry( exception.Message, EventLogEntryType.Error, 0 );
}
finally
{
    queue.Close();
}

return message;
}
```

Receiving messages from a transactional message queue is similar to receiving normal messages. Begin by creating a MessageQueueTransaction object. Invoke its Begin method to mark the beginning of the retrieval transaction. Next, retrieve individual messages by invoking the MessageQueue object's Receive method, passing MessageQueueTransaction as a parameter. Once all messages within the transaction are received and processed, invoke the Abort method to mark the end of the retrieval transaction and close the message queue connection.

Implementing a Distributed Service

The MessagingFramework object binds two different application elements through messaging services. On the application side, the client can be a business service, a Windows form, or a Web form. On the distributed service side, the client is likely to be a Windows service that performs a specialized, and probably lengthy, operation.

The following sections implement an analytical service. This service might include functionality that is notified of incoming messages and that performs a lengthy analysis to help determine trends in the issues filed. Because this analytical process is likely to run a long time, it makes sense to offload that functionality to a separate process running on a separate server. For the purpose of this example, messaging is the form of communication. Remoting is another viable option, but for the sake of this example, assume that the incoming issues are mission critical and need to be persisted in case of hardware failure.

Adding the Project

The first step in implementing AnalysisService is to create a new Windows Service project and add it to the IssueTracker solution. Figure 4-6 illustrates the process of creating a new service within the Add New Project dialog box.

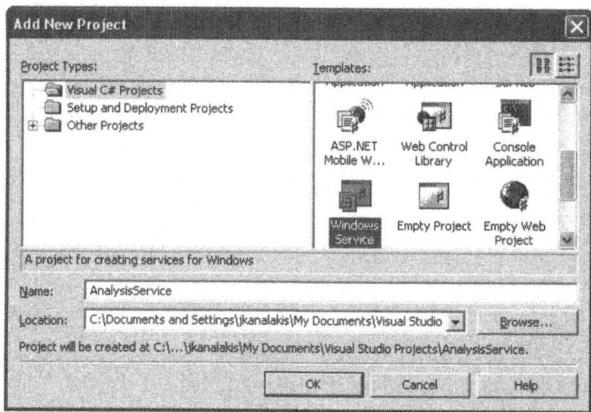

Figure 4-6. Creating a transactional message queue

Implementing the Service

Once you have named the project and clicked OK, Visual Studio .NET creates the project and adds it to the solution. To access the messaging services, you need to add the references to the System.Messaging and the local SystemFrameworks namespaces. The source code also needs to include the appropriate using statements. Listing 4-18 outlines additional methods that you need to add to the service code.

Listing 4-18. AnalysisService Implementation

```
protected override void OnStart(string[] args)
{
    Thread listeningThread = new Thread( new ThreadStart(MessageListener) );
    listeningThread.Start();

    return;
}

public static void MessageListener()
{
    Issue objIssue = null;

    MessagingFramework messagingServices = new MessagingFramework();
    messagingServices.ProcessName = "AnalysisService";
    messagingServices.CreateQueues();

    while( true )
    {
        objIssue = (Issue)messagingServices.ReceiveBusinessObject();
        //perform analysis on issue object

        Thread.Sleep(1000);
    }

    return;
}
```

In this code, you fill in the OnStart method to start a new thread of execution. This new thread will be responsible for executing the lengthy analytical processing. The processing itself is implemented in the MessageListener method. This method uses the MessagingFramework object to create the application message queues and continuously listen for new incoming messages. When a message is received, the analytical services go to work and perform their function. After processing, the thread is suspended briefly to yield processing time to other services.

Summary

Messaging is an essential part of an enterprise framework and complements other technologies described within this book. Although messaging does not solve all problems related to distributed computing, it offers many advantages including the ability to decouple application components. Unfortunately, there is a cost attached to this flexibility. Messages are greater in size than their body and can contain overhead needed to support the messaging framework. Also, because messages are often routed by servers, they can be slower than direct connections. However, in the end, the benefits outweigh the costs to achieve reliable messaging.

In the next chapter, you will learn about e-mail services within the .NET Framework. You will learn how they work, how enterprises applications use them, and how they can facilitate online collaboration between the users and the application. You will also interact with the Collaboration Data Objects, Microsoft's solution for building e-mail-based services. You will put these elements together to implement a messaging service that fits cleanly into the application framework and interacts with application business objects.

Integrating Mail Services

THIS CHAPTER DIVES INTO the e-mail services available to the .NET Framework. First, it introduces the key concepts and protocols related to mail services. Next, it looks at sending and receiving mail messages programmatically. The chapter also shows how to incorporate Hypertext Markup Language (HTML) into mail messages as a means to streamline collaborative communication within the enterprise. Finally, it puts all of these elements to work as you build out the mail services layer in the IssueTracker application.

Understanding E-Mail Concepts

Sending and receiving e-mail messages across the Internet means interacting with countless variations of messaging clients and mail servers, each running on various operating system platforms. You can only successfully achieve this through well-defined protocols that specify how a message is encoded, sent, and received. As Figure 5-1 illustrates, these protocols work together to relay e-mail messages from the original sender to the final recipient.

Exploring the Exchange Protocols

In an electronic world filled with mixed technologies, the only way to exchange common information, such as e-mail, is through open communication standards. These open standards include exchange protocols for packaging, sending, and receiving e-mail.

Using the Simple Mail Transport Protocol

The Simple Mail Transport Protocol (SMTP) is a protocol generally used to send messages from a mail client to a mail server. Most e-mail systems that send mail over the Internet use SMTP to send messages from one server to another.

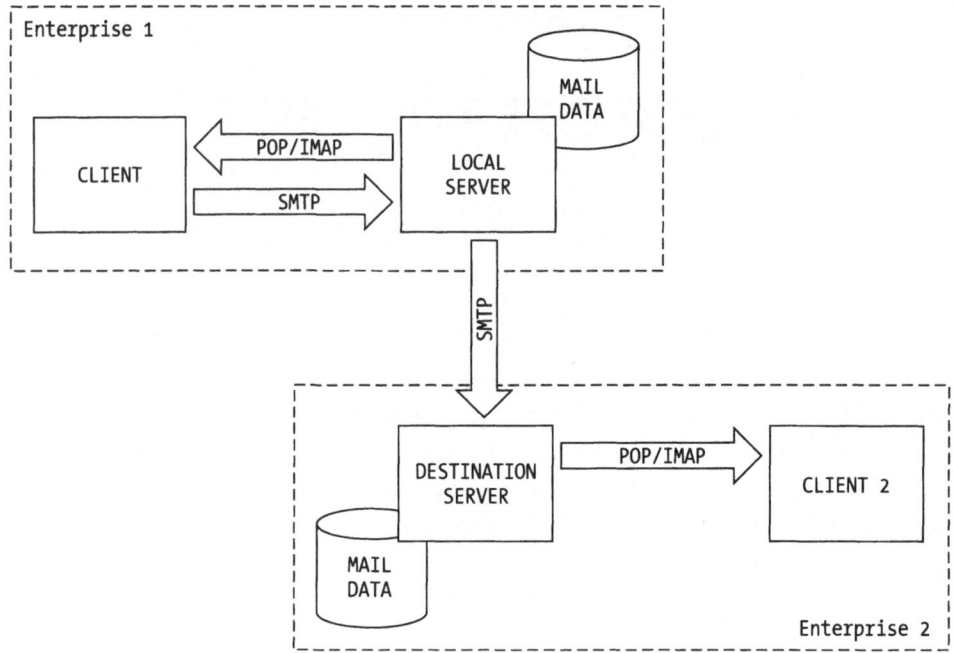

Figure 5-1. Relationship between e-mail clients, servers, and binding protocols

Using the Post Office Protocol

When e-mail messages are exchanged, they are queued in message stores. The Post Office Protocol (POP) is used to retrieve mail messages that are queued in a mailbox. With POP, messages are removed from the mailbox after they have been transferred to the client. This enables mail clients to read messages offline. There are two versions of POP. POP2 is an older standard that requires SMTP to send messages. You can use the newer POP3 with or without SMTP.

Using the Internet Message Access Protocol

The Internet Message Access Protocol (IMAP) is also a protocol for retrieving e-mail messages. With IMAP, the message store keeps the messages for the clients. Each time the mail client reads the message, it downloads from the mail server. This enables multiple clients in multiple locations to access the same message, such as in Microsoft Hotmail. IMAP4 is similar to POP3 but supports some additional features including a keyword search through e-mail messages while they are still on the mail server. Also, users can select specific messages for download to the client instead of downloading all the messages. This lets the e-mail client respond faster because it can first download only the message subject and then later download the entire message body.

Using Multipurpose Internet Mail Extensions

Multipurpose Internet Mail Extensions (MIME) is a specification for formatting non-ASCII messages so that they can travel over the Internet. MIME enables the sending and receiving of rich media, such as graphics, audio, and video files. In addition to e-mail applications, Web browsers also support various MIME types to display or output files that are not in HTML format. A new version of MIME, called S/MIME, is also available and supports encrypted messages.

Exploring E-Mail Body Formats

The body format of e-mail messages can either be plain text or be HTML. Both formats are in common use today by enterprise applications, and each offers different advantages and disadvantages.

Using Plain-Text Messages

Plain-text messages have existed since the beginning of e-mail and are natively supported by all e-mail clients. HTML, however, is relatively new with support existing in most e-mail clients, but not all. Part of the resistance to HTML messages comes from Internet-enabled consumer devices, such as cellular phones, pagers, and Personal Digital Assistants (PDAs) that are hindered by low bandwidth as well as minimal message display areas. Another downside to HTML messages is that they have been widely adopted by the spam-sending community. As a result, many corporate e-mail filters are configured to block e-mail messages that use HTML formatting and stick with plain-text messages. Figure 5-2 illustrates how a plain-text e-mail message appears in a typical user's e-mail client.

Using HTML Messages

HTML messages offer a level of richness that significantly improves the readability and usability of an e-mail message. This richness can include specialized text formatting, embedded graphics, and audio clips. Figure 5-3 illustrates the same plain text e-mail message, enhanced with HTML formatting.

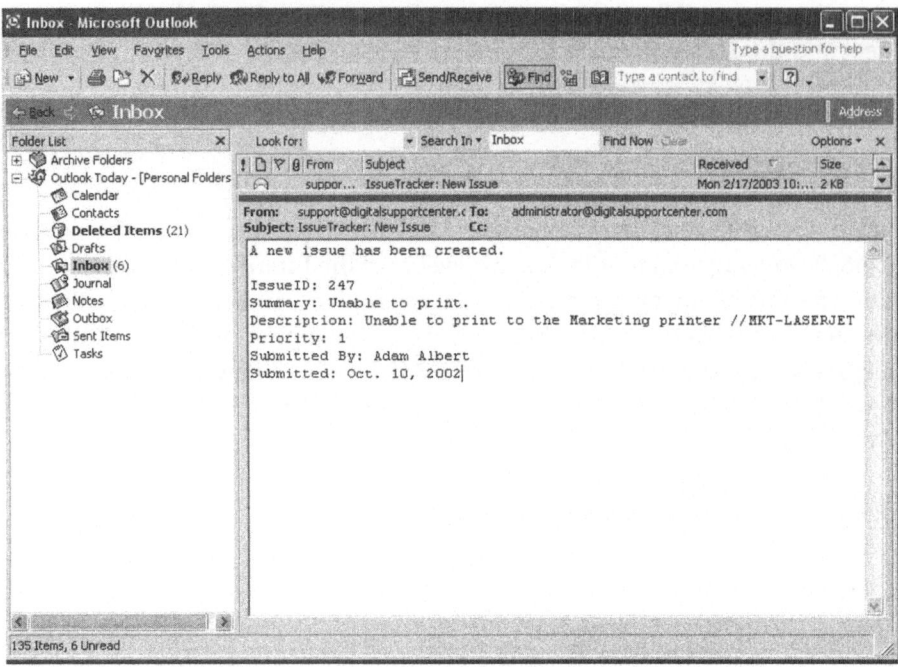

Figure 5-2. Plain-text e-mail message in Microsoft Outlook

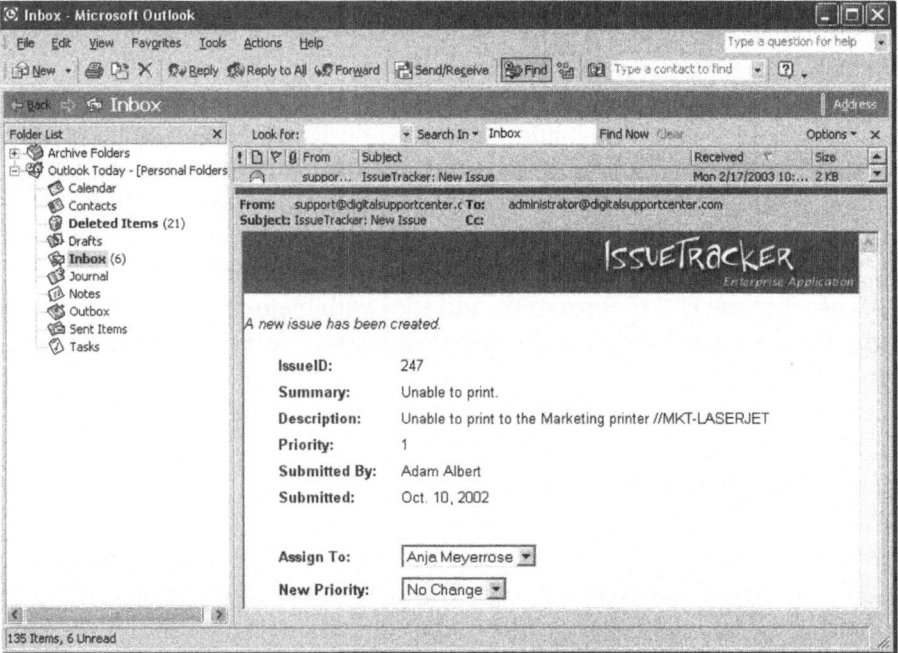

Figure 5-3. HTML e-mail message in Microsoft Outlook

The message body has been formatted with a different font in a variety of sizes. The message also contains page breaks and an embedded image. The message depicted in Figure 5-3 is more readable than its plain-text counterpart. When message sizes grow to multiple pages, ensuring good readability encourages the user to continue reading to the end.

In addition to enhanced message formatting, HTML messages also have the ability to include Web forms. HTML forms embedded within an e-mail message function as they do within any Web page. Form fields can include textboxes, check boxes, list boxes, option buttons, and push buttons. Form controls can be formatted and positioned with tables just as in Web pages.

To create HTML messages, set the BodyFormat property of the MailMessage object to HTML. Next, set the UrlContentBase property. This property designates the starting point for all relative Uniform Resource Locators (URLs) defined within the Web form, similar to the <BASEREF> tag in HTML. When the mail recipient clicks the Send button, the action specified in the <FORM> tag will execute. Furthermore, the click can take a POST action, sending the posted values to an .aspx file for processing. An example of such a <FORM> tag follows:

```
<form
    action="http://127.0.0.1/IssueTracker/IssueTracker_WebUI/ProcessSubmit.aspx"
>
```

In this case, the button form control triggers the POST action to submit all form data to the ProcessSubmit.aspx page. Chapter 7, "Building Web Applications," goes deeper into building Web forms that process user input. In an enterprise application, the URL specified in the action attribute should point to the deployed domain or subdomain of the server. Also, authentication is necessary to ensure that the person filling in the e-mail form is authorized to do so. You can implement this through Forms Authentication, which is detailed in Chapter 13, "Understanding .NET Security and Cryptography."

Exploring Platform E-Mail Services

On the Microsoft operating system platforms, the underlying Collaboration Data Objects (CDO) performs the messaging between the client and the server. CDO is a Component Object Model (COM) object library that exposes the interfaces of the Messaging Application Programming Interface (MAPI). CDO has evolved over the years and has taken many different names. In Exchange Server 4.0, it was termed *OLE Messaging*, and in Exchange Server 5.0, it was termed *Active Messaging*. With the release of Exchange Server 5.5, the library was renamed to *CDO* to describe its services as more than just messaging functionality. All applications using previous versions of CDO, from Exchange Server 4.0, are compatible with the latest version of the library.

Exploring .NET E-Mail Services

The .NET Framework provides limited support for e-mail manipulation within an application. The System.Web.Mail namespace defines a MailMessage object. This object abstracts a normal e-mail message with attributes, such as Subject, Body, and Priority. This namespace also provides the SmtpMail object with static methods, such as Send, used to deliver e-mail messages.

Unfortunately, the .NET Framework does not offer any capability to read messages directly from the mail server. Receiving e-mail messages is an important part of an enterprise solution, which can still be accomplished by interacting directly with the CDO library.

Receiving messages from a mail server is typically important to the enterprise developer because e-mail communication has become the dominant form of enterprise communication. An example use of mail receiving services includes embedding an e-mail client within a corporate portal. Another example might require an application to monitor customer postings and ensure that someone responds to them in a reasonable amount of time. This functionality is typical of Customer Relationship Management (CRM) applications. An automated response will let a customer know that their message was received. However, ensuring that a real customer support representative responds to the user is even more important for customer retention.

The CDO library is packaged as a COM component designed to simplify writing programs that create or manipulate e-mail messages. CDO is one in a suite of collaborative COM components referred to collectively as CDO and is an integral part of the Windows operating system. CDO is designed for creating applications that create and manage messages formatted and sent using Internet standards such as MIME. The CDO component supports sending messages using both the SMTP and the Network News Transport Protocol (NNTP), as well as through a local SMTP/NNTP service pickup directory.

Exploring Application Business Services

Chapter 2, "Accessing Data in ADO.NET," described application framework objects as memory structures that closely resemble parts of the database schema. They temporarily hold information that is passed between the database and the user interface. Application framework services, however, interact with the framework objects to accomplish specific business functions. Figure 5-4 illustrates the relationship between business objects and business services.

Within the application framework, business services are implemented within the Business Facade project. They are implemented as public classes that inherit from the abstract BusinessService class. They have methods that match specific business functions that need to be accomplished. Listing 5-1 presents the BusinessService base class.

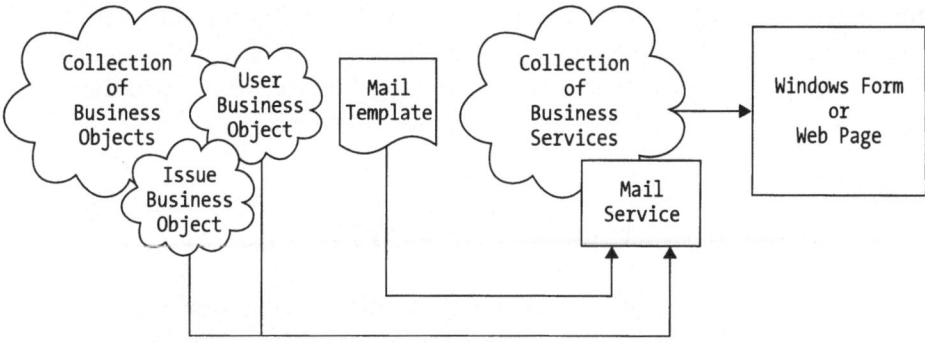

Figure 5-4. Relationship between the mail service and existing business objects

Listing 5-1. The BusinessService Abstract Class Definition

```
public abstract class BusinessService
{
    EventLog _SystemLog = new EventLog();

    public BusinessService()
    {
    }

    public void LogEvent( string strMessage )
    {
        try
        {
            _SystemLog.Source = "IssueTracker";
            _SystemLog.WriteEntry( strMessage, EventLogEntryType.Error, 0 );
        }
        catch( Exception x )
        {
            Debug.WriteLine( "Unable to write to Event Log." );
            Debug.WriteLine( "Event Massage:" + strMessage );
        }
        return;
    }
}
```

The BusinessService class defines a specification for how business services must be implemented within the application framework. It also implements a more robust approach to application error logging. Although output to the console is useful during application debugging, it offers little help when the application is running in a deployed environment. The System.Diagnostics namespace also provides the EventLog object, which enables applications to write messages to the Windows system event log. Messages written to the event log are persisted, even if the server shuts down or restarts.

Building an E-Mail Business Service

Building a mail services layer for an enterprise application requires interaction with the presentation layer clients, internal business objects, the database, and the underlying mail system.

The purpose of the mail services layer is to provide a high-level interface for mail sending functions. For example, when a new issue is entered, IssueTracker might be configured to notify a specific team member. In this case, the New Issue user interface invokes a method within the mail services layer. This method accesses the database to obtain the destination user's e-mail address, the configurable message text, and the application's mail settings.

To implement the e-mail business service, open the IssueTracker project in Visual Studio .NET and select the Business Facade project in the Solution Explorer. From the menu, choose Project ➤ Add Class and enter *EmailService.cs* as the item name. Visual Studio .NET will create a new source file for the EmailService class.

The process of programmatically sending messages happens in three parts: creating the message, appending attachments, and sending. The .NET Framework packages e-mail sending functionality into the System.Web.Mail namespace. Listing 5-2 shows the e-mail business service definition.

Listing 5-2. The E-Mail Business Service Definition

```
public class EmailService : BusinessService
{
    private User _UserFrom = new User();
    private User _UserTo = new User();
    private User _UserCc = new User();
    private User _UserBcc = new User();
    private MailMessage _OutgoingMessage = new MailMessage();
    private ArrayList _IncomingMessages = new ArrayList();

    public EmailService()
    {
    }
}
```

Because the EmailService class is going to access the .NET Framework's
e-mail classes, you will need to add a reference to the System.Web namespace.
Therefore, select the Business Facade project in the Solution Explorer and choose
Project ➤ Add Reference from the menu. The Add Reference dialog box will
appear, as shown in Figure 5-5. In the .NET tab, select System.Web.dll from the
component list and click Select, then OK. A reference will be added under the
Business Facade References folder.

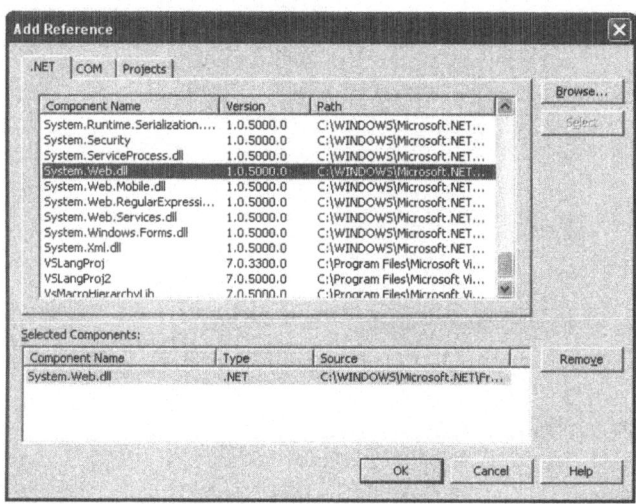

Figure 5-5. Adding the assembly reference to the System.Web namespace

After you have added the reference to the Business Facade project, add the
namespace reference to the top of the EmailService class definition:

```
using System.Web.Mail;
```

Sending Messages

After you have created a message, you need to send it. The message can be delivered either through the SMTP mail service built into Microsoft Windows 2000 or
through a designated SMTP server. The .NET Framework abstracts the SMTP mail
server with the SmtpMail object. This object interacts with the underlying mail
services to process the outgoing message. In most cases, this requires a system-
level interaction with the Collaboration Data Objects for Windows 2000 (CDOSYS)
message component.

To send messages with the SmtpMail object, first designate the location of
the SMTP mail server. By default, mail is queued on a Windows 2000 system,

ensuring that the calling program does not block network traffic. If you set the
SmtpServer property, you deliver the mail directly to the specified server.

The final step in the mail sending process is to call the SmtpMail object's
Send method. This method takes a single parameter that represents the initialized MailMessage object complete with content and attachments. The resulting
code appears in Listing 5-3.

Listing 5-3. The SendMessage Method Implemented in the EmailService Object

```
public void SendMessage()
{
    try
    {
        //assign 'to' user
        _OutgoingMessage.To = _UserTo.EmailAddress;

        //assign 'cc' user
        _OutgoingMessage.Cc = _UserCc.EmailAddress;

        //assign 'bcc' user
        _OutgoingMessage.Bcc = _UserBcc.EmailAddress;

        //assign the 'from' user
        _OutgoingMessage.From = _UserFrom.EmailAddress;

        SmtpMail.SmtpServer = "127.0.0.1";
        SmtpMail.Send( _OutgoingMessage );
    }
    catch( Exception x )
    {
        LogEvent( x.Message );
    }

    return;
}
```

The MailMessage object abstracts all aspects of a message including its
addressing, content, and attachments. Sending an e-mail message begins by setting the message destination and origination values of the message with the To,
Cc, Bcc, and From properties. These properties accept one or more e-mail
addresses separated by a semicolon.

Next, set the e-mail message attributes such as encoding, format, and priority. The encoding should be one of the System.Text.Encoding enumerated types
that define the target character set. You must define the format of the message

as either plain text or as HTML. The MailPriority enumeration indicates the urgency of the message as Low, Normal, or High. With the message attributes well defined, you are ready to add the content of the message. Two properties define the message content: the subject and the body. The subject is summary text that identifies what the message is about, and the body is the full detail of the message.

In the application code, the task of sending an e-mail message has been simplified by the .NET Framework services. Listing 5-4 outlines the application code.

Listing 5-4. EmailService Client Code

```
private void SendAlertToUser()
{
    User userTo = new User();
    userTo.EmailAddress = "sendto@something.com";

    User userFrom = new User();
    userFrom.EmailAddress =  "sentfrom@something.com";

    User userCc = new User();
    userCc.EmailAddress = "copyto@something.com";

    User userBcc = new User();
    userBcc.EmailAddress =  "blindcopyto@something.com";

    MailMessage message = new MailMessage();
    message.Subject = "IssueTracker Alert";
    message.Body = "A new issue has been assigned to you.";

    EmailService mail = new EmailService();
    mail.SendTo = userTo;
    mail.SendCc = userCc;
    mail.SendBcc = userBcc;
    mail.SentFrom = userFrom;
    mail.OutgoingMessage = message;

    mail.SendMessage();

    return;
}
```

First, the application code must include the System.Web.Mail namespace to reference the MailMessage object. Second, the User objects are instantiated to capture the To, From, Cc, and Bcc e-mail addresses. Next, the MailMessage object is instantiated, and the User objects are assigned to it. Next, the message formatting is set to a plain-text message with Normal delivery priority. The message subject and body are also set to the parameters supplied to this method. Finally, the SendMessage method is called to send the message to its destination.

Appending Attachments

E-mail message sent through the .NET Framework can have any number of file attachments. There is no restriction on the file type or size of message attachments. These files typically range from small text files or documents to large images or even compressed packages of files.

To programmatically associate a file attachment to an outgoing e-mail message, begin by creating and initializing the MailMessage object. Next, create and initialize a MailAttachment object, passing a logical file path to the source document:

```
MailAttachment attachment = new MailAttachment( "c:\\IssueTracker\\sample.txt" );
```

Alternatively, you can supply the attachment filename as a property value of the MailAttachment object:

```
attachment.Filename = "c:\\IssueTracker\\sample.txt";
```

Next, specify the encoding of the message attachment. Encoding converts binary data into a series of ASCII characters that can be transmitted over the Internet. The two most common specifications for attachment encoding are UUEncode and Base64. UUEncode originally stood for *Unix-to-Unix Encode*, but it has become a universal protocol used to transfer files between different platforms such as Unix, Windows, and Macintosh. UUEncode converts data into a series of 7-bit characters that can be transmitted over the Internet. Base64 encoding converts data into a series of 6-bit characters, consistently keeping encoded data about 33 percent larger than the original data. By default, Base64 encoding is used for attachment encoding:

```
attachment.Encoding = System.Web.Mail.MailEncoding.Base64;
```

After you have created the MailAttachment object, pointed it to the source file, and encoded it, you can finally bind it to the MailMessage object. Invoke the Add method in the Attachments collection:

```
mail.Attachments.Add( attachment );
```

You can add any number of attachments to the MailMessage object by changing the filename and calling the Add method. When the message is sent, the .NET Framework will locate the referenced files, encode them as specified, and transmit them along with the outgoing message. Listing 5-5 shows the EmailService client code that sends an attachment with the message.

Listing 5-5. EmailService Client Code with an Attachment

```
private void SendAlertToUser()
{
    User userTo = new User();
    userTo.EmailAddress = "sendto@something.com";

    User userFrom = new User();
    userFrom.EmailAddress =  "sentfrom@something.com";

    User userCc = new User();
    userCc.EmailAddress = "copyto@something.com";

    User userBcc = new User();
    userBcc.EmailAddress =  "blindcopyto@something.com";

    MailMessage message = new MailMessage();
    message.Subject = "IssueTracker Alert";
    message.Body = "A new issue has been assigned to you.";

    EmailService mail = new EmailService();
    mail.SendTo = userTo;
    mail.SendCc = userCc;
    mail.SendBcc = userBcc;
    mail.SentFrom = userFrom;
    mail.OutgoingMessage = message;

    MailAttachment attachment = new MailAttachment();
    attachment.Filename = "c:\\IssueTracker\\sample.txt";
    attachment.Encoding = System.Web.Mail.MailEncoding.Base64;
    mail.Attachments.Add( attachment );

    mail.SendMessage();

    return;
}
```

Sending an Object-Driven Message

In addition to sending messages from one user to another, the EmailService class will support automated messages that require only a recipient e-mail address and message template. The message template will represent a specific automated message stored in the database. The message subject, body, type, delivery type will all come from the database to build a message that is automatically sent to another user when certain conditions are met. Storing automated message information in a database helps keep the messages maintainable and easier for future translation into foreign languages. A typical use for this method is for an automated message that is sent to an administrator each time a new issue is entered. Listing 5-6 shows the MailMessageTemplate business object.

Listing 5-6. The MailMessageTemplate Business Object

```
public class MailMessageTemplate : BusinessObject
{
    public MailMessageTemplate()
    {
    }

    public int MailMessageID = 0;
    public int Format = 0;
    public int Priority = 0;
    public string Subject = "";
    public string Body = "";
}
```

Now that the basic User and MailMessageTemplate business objects exist, you must add property accessor methods to the EmailService object (see Listing 5-7).

Listing 5-7. Adding Property Accessors to the EmailService Object

```
public User SendTo
{
    get
    {
        return _UserTo;
    }
    set
    {
        _UserTo = value;
    }
```

```
}

public User SendCc
{
    get
    {
        return _UserCc;
    }
    set
    {
        _UserCc = value;
    }
}

public User SendBcc
{
    get
    {
        return _UserBcc;
    }
    set
    {
        _UserBcc = value;
    }
}

public User SentFrom
{
    get
    {
        return _UserFrom;
    }
    set
    {
        _UserFrom = value;
    }
}

public MailMessage OutgoingMessage
{
    get
    {
        return _OutgoingMessage;
```

```
    }
    set
    {
        _OutgoingMessage = value;
    }
}
```

Another implementation of the SendMessage method is an object-driven version that accepts a MailMessageTemplate object and an Issue object. Because this method depends upon reflection objects, you must specify the System.Reflection namespace in the code. Listing 5-8 shows a sample template for an object-driven message.

Listing 5-8. Sample E-Mail Template for an Object-Driven Message

```
Dear Administrator,

Issue # <Issue.IssueID> was filed on <Issue.Date>.
The description of the new Issue is:

<Issue.Summary>
_____

<Issue.Description>

Sincerely,

IssueTracker Auto-mailer
```

Listing 5-9 shows how to implement the object-driven SendMessage method within EmailService.

Listing 5-9. Implementing the Object-Driven SendMessage Method within EmailService

```
public void SendMessage( MailMessageTemplate argTemplate, Issue argIssue )
{
    int intStart = 0;
    int intEnd = 0;
    string strField = "";
    string strValue = "";
    string strSource = "";

    Type objType;
    FieldInfo field;
```

```
try
{
    //fill the message template
    strSource = argTemplate.Body;

    while( intStart >= 0 )
    {
        //find the start
        intStart = strSource.IndexOf( "<Issue.", intStart ) + 7;

        //find the end
        intEnd = strSource.IndexOf( ">", intStart );

        //get the field name
        strField = strSource.Substring( intStart, intEnd - intStart );

        objType = argIssue.GetType();
        field = objType.GetField( strField );

        strValue = field.GetValue( objType ).ToString();

        strSource = strSource.Replace( "<Issue." + strField + ">", strValue);
    };

    //set the outgoing message
    MailMessage _OutgoingMessage = new MailMessage();
    _OutgoingMessage.To = _UserTo.EmailAddress;
    _OutgoingMessage.Cc = _UserCc.EmailAddress;
    _OutgoingMessage.Bcc = _UserBcc.EmailAddress;
    _OutgoingMessage.From = _UserFrom.EmailAddress;
    _OutgoingMessage.Subject = argTemplate.Subject;
    _OutgoingMessage.Body = strSource;

    //send the messsage
    SmtpMail.SmtpServer = "localhost";
    SmtpMail.Send( _OutgoingMessage );
}
catch( Exception x )
{
    LogEvent( x.Message );
}

return;
}
```

This method begins by retrieving the message details from the message template. Next, the user information is retrieved from the attached EmailService User objects. Once the message and user information is available, the rest of the method works similarly to the SendSimpleMessage method. The MailMessage object is created and assigned properties such as From, To, BodyFormat, Priority, Subject, and Body. Finally, the Send method in the SmtpMail object is called to send the message to its destination.

This method implements a simple parser to replace tokens in the mail message template with business object values. Although this solution meets basic needs, a more flexible solution would be to leverage XSL Transformations (XSLT) to accommodate the replacements. Chapter 9, "Using XML and Web Services," takes a close look at Extensible Markup Language (XML) and its related technologies, such as XSLT.

Retrieving E-Mail Messages

As mentioned earlier, the .NET Framework does not natively support the ability of reading e-mail messages from a mail server. Therefore, this method will use the CDO object library to check the mail server for customer messages. The mail messages that IssueTracker will listen for are those with a specific destination address created for IssueTracker to use. Later, IssueTracker will provide a link on a Web page for customer support questions. This link will be a mailto link that triggers the customer's e-mail client to open with the addressee and subject lines filled in:

```
<a href="mailto:issuetracker@company.com?subject=IssueTracker Submission...">
Send message to customer support.</a>
```

This link displays the text *Send message to customer support* in the Web page. When clicked, a new e-mail message form is displayed with the default addressee set to issuetracker@company.com and the default subject line set to IssueTracker Submission....

Begin by adding a project reference. With the Business Facade project in the Solution Explorer selected, choose Project ➤ Add Reference from the Visual Studio .NET menu. Select the COM tab. In the Windows XP environment, find the Microsoft CDO for Exchange 2000 Library component, click Select, and then click OK (see Figure 5-6). In the Windows 2000 environment, the component name will be Microsoft Outlook 9.0 Object Library. A reference to CDO and Outlook will appear in the Solution Explorer, and the CDO services will become accessible.

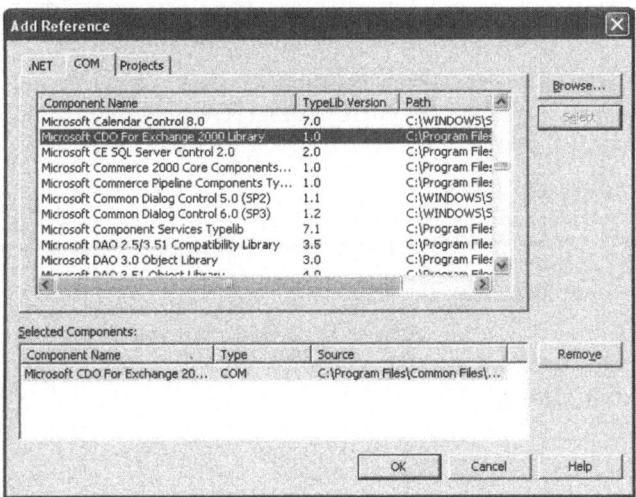

Figure 5-6. Adding the COM component reference to the Microsoft CDO object library

Once you have added the CDO and Outlook references, you can implement the functional code to scan the Inbox and return a collection of messages. This method begins with local variable declarations. Listing 5-10 shows how to implement the GetMail method in the EmailService Object.

Listing 5-10. Implementing the GetMail Method in the EmailService Object

```csharp
public ArrayList GetMail()
{
    MailMessage message;
    Outlook.MailItem msgInbox;
    ArrayList arrayMessages = null;
    Outlook.ApplicationClass appOutlook = null;

    try
    {
        arrayMessages = new ArrayList();

        //connect to the CDO library
        appOutlook = new Outlook.ApplicationClass();
        Outlook.NameSpace appNamespace = appOutlook.GetNamespace("MAPI");
        appNamespace.Logon( "jkanalakis", "jkanalakis", false, false );

        //navigate to the inbox folder
        Outlook.Explorer exp = appOutlook.Explorers.Item(1);
```

```
        for( int intIdx = 1; intIdx <= exp.CurrentFolder.Items.Count; intIdx++ )
        {
            //retrieve the next message from the inbox
            msgInbox = (Outlook.MailItem)exp.CurrentFolder.Items.Item(intIdx);

            //convert data into MailMessage
            message = new MailMessage();
            message.Subject = msgInbox.Subject;
            message.Body = msgInbox.Body;

            //add MailMessage to the ArrayList
            arrayMessages.Add( message );
        }
    }
    catch( Exception exception )
    {
        LogEvent( x.Message );
    }
    finally
    {
        Marshal.ReleaseComObject( appOutlook );
    }

    return arrayMessages;
}
```

Because this method returns an ArrayList containing MailMessage objects, you must include the System.Collections namespace. Next, you connect to the CDO object by creating an ApplicationClass object. Next, you create a NamespaceClass object and point it to the MAPI namespace. Then, you can log into the Outlook session by supplying a username and password. After logging in, an Explorer object is created to help navigate the CDO object hierarchy and point to the Inbox folder. Once pointed to the Inbox, you can iterate through the Items array. Because all CDO e-mail messages are represented by a MailItem data type, this method performs a mapping of data fields into a MailMessage object. The assembled MailMessage object is then added to the ArrayList collection. Any exceptions thrown during execution are caught and logged for future reference. Finally, the ReleaseComObject method forces the runtime-callable wrapper to release the COM object reference, and the filled array of MailMessage objects returns to the calling application.

This method provides an easy approach for an application to scan an Inbox and return a collection of MailMessage objects. The application can then iterate through the message collection for display or keyword search.

Summary

This chapter explored the mail services provided by the .NET Framework. It reviewed key concepts and protocols related to mail services, such as SMTP, POP, and IMAP. It reviewed sending mail messages with attachments programmatically. The chapter also looked at building server forms as a means to streamline collaborative communication within the enterprise. Because the .NET Framework offers functionality only for sending and not receiving messages, the chapter looked into using the CDO object library to tap into Outlook services. Finally, you put all of these elements to work to build out the mail services infrastructure in the IssueTracker application.

The next chapter takes a close look at business process automation and how you can quickly add it to an enterprise application with the help of Microsoft BizTalk Server. BizTalk Server provides tools that simplify process definitions that span across multiple applications and execute for weeks. You can implement these processes using either the built-in BizTalk Server tools or the .NET managed code that is plugged in as an integration component.

CHAPTER 6

Automating Business Processes

THIS CHAPTER EXPLORES the benefits of externalized business process automation and how the .NET Framework leverages Microsoft's BizTalk Server as a flexible and scalable solution. This chapter begins with an introduction to externalized business process automation and describes how enterprise applications can benefit from it. Next, the chapter describes BizTalk Server and its components and then describes how BizTalk Server addresses the need for scalable and reliable business process automation. Finally, the chapter shows a practical example that automatically routes information throughout the enterprise based on specific business rules.

Enabling Business Process Automation

Business process automation, also known as *workflow automation*, streamlines or automates the human involvement in standardized processes. Process automation is most widely found in Supply-Chain Management (SCM) projects, where customer demand is linked to the retailer, which is linked to the distributor, which is linked to the manufacturer. A collection of business rules and methods automatically manages the billing, accounting, and shipping activities.

Business process automation is important to the enterprise to function as efficiently as possible. Business processes can span multiple applications on multiple platforms, Internet services, extranets, and Business-to-Business (B2B) exchanges. Business process automation also needs to support existing technology infrastructure, which might include legacy systems, Electronic Data Interchange (EDI), and X12 networks. Even outside of B2B environments, business process automation can cut out excessive duplicate data entry into multiple systems.

Just about every business application supports some sort of business process, even if it is a simple one. When information needs to be routed from one person to another, or when an automatic alert needs to be generated, business rules need to be in place. A process automation engine always executes these business rules, and some sort of action then takes place. In the IssueTracker enterprise application, when a new issue is created, business rules need to be in place to notify the administrator via e-mail if a high-priority ticket is in the queue and to possibly replicate the details of that ticket into another system.

Exploring BizTalk Server

BizTalk Server provides a scalable solution for the organization and management of business processes. It can define document formats, map how documents are transformed, and specify how documents are exchanged between applications. BizTalk Server also includes the ability to execute transactions that run as long as weeks or months and enable monitoring and event logging. BizTalk Server was originally intended for document routing, such as product catalogs and shipping orders exchanged between companies and their trading partners. Also, BizTalk Server can send and receive documents across the Internet and ensure data integrity, delivery, and security.

BizTalk Server comprises different applications with different specialties, including document editing, document mapping, messaging and routing management, process definition, process implementation, and process execution. Each application integrates to complete the BizTalk Server process automation solution illustrated in Figure 6-1.

Understanding the Orchestration Services

BizTalk Orchestration enables the creation of detailed business processes within a visual design environment based on Microsoft Visio. When an organization's business process changes, a business analyst can use the BizTalk Orchestration Designer to specify matching changes (see Figure 6-2). Traditionally, the process definition phase and the process implementation phase happen separately with different tools. In BizTalk Orchestration, both phases happen within the same design environment.

Because business processes are defined and implemented side by side, changes to a process definition can easily trigger changes to the implementation. BizTalk Orchestration also provides several other important features to solve tasks that otherwise are hard to accomplish. This includes the ability to create process definitions that branch out into multiple activities at the same time and the ability to create long-running business processes that span different applications, platforms, and organizations.

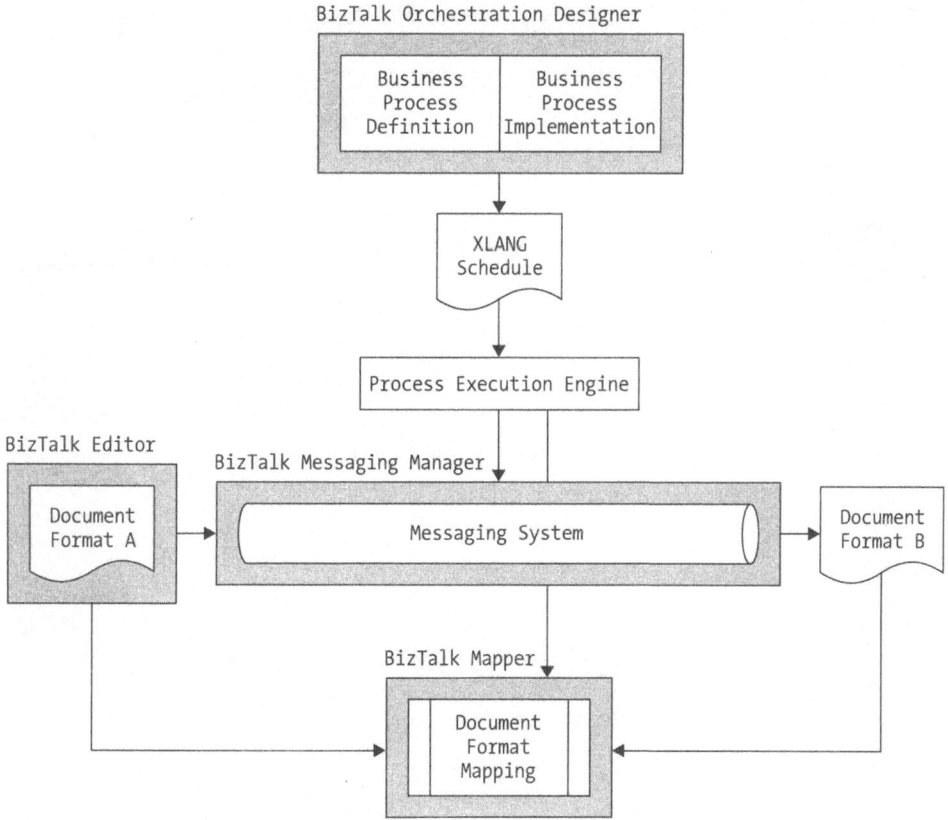

Figure 6-1. BizTalk Server's application components

Understanding the Messaging Services

BizTalk Messaging provides the ability to send and receive business-related documents securely and reliably. An example of such a document could include issue data. BizTalk Messaging is able to pass documents between internal applications and external business partners. This includes defining how documents are received, processed, and delivered to their destinations. It also performs document validation, uses digital signatures, encrypts documents, and guarantees delivery over unreliable transports, such as Hypertext Transfer Protocol (HTTP), Hypertext Transfer Protocol Secure (HTTPS), and Simple Mail Transfer Protocol (SMTP).

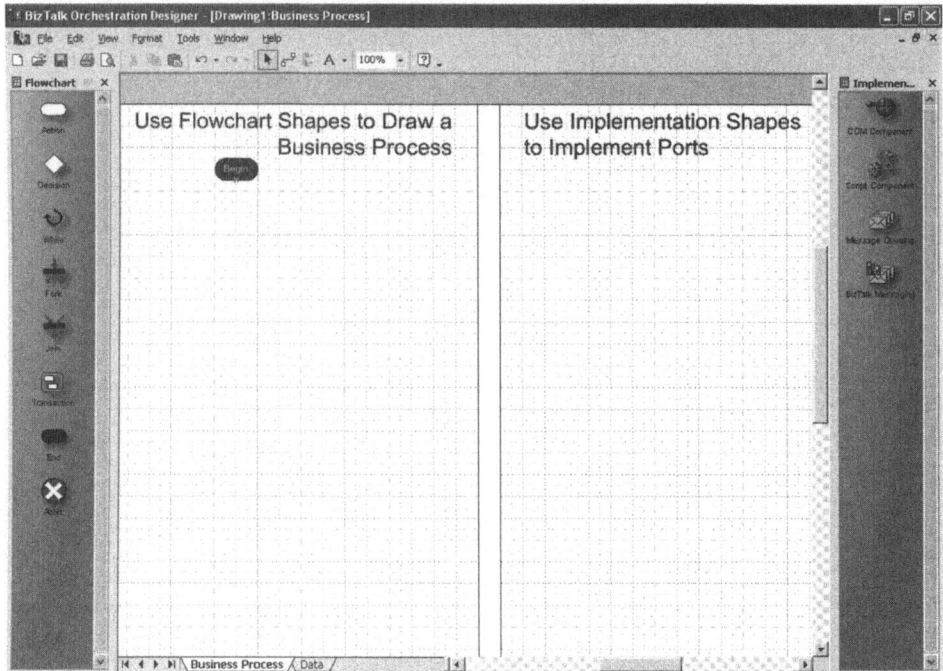

Figure 6-2. The BizTalk Orchestration Designer

Understanding the XML Source Documents

For businesses to exchange documents in an environment where neither side wants to depend on the technology the other side is using, businesses need a universal language in which to write these documents. This universal language has evolved into Extensible Markup Language (XML), a flexible language for document exchange. You can view or edit a business document written in XML with the BizTalk Editor. In the following example, information about a new, high-priority issue appears in an XML document:

```
<Issue>
    <Header issueNumber="809" issueStatus="New" issuePriority="High"
            dateCreated="2003-05-01" timeCreated="13:17:00" />
    <Author>
        Peter Frassmann
    </Author>
    <PriorityID>
        1
    </PriorityID>
    <Summary>
```

```
        Unable to print.
    </Summary>
    <Description>
        I am unable to print to the //LJ-MARKETING printer from my
            notebook computer. The problem just started acting up recently.
    </Description>
</Issue>
```

Although this document appears somewhat unusual, it is still fairly easy to read. The text strictly follows a specific document definition, called a *schema*. A schema is another XML document that describes the format of an XML data document. A schema does not contain any data itself. It only defines rules for what might appear in an XML data document. Chapter 9, "Using XML and Web Services," goes into deeper detail about XML and how you can apply it.

BizTalk Server natively exchanges XML documents between business partners because data fields are clearly identified and easy to find. BizTalk Server can also create or edit XML documents as an Orchestration schedule is processing.

In addition to XML documents, BizTalk Server can also exchange plain-text documents for applications that only import or export data in fixed-positioned or Comma-Separated Values (CSV) documents. Finally, BizTalk Orchestration provides additional tools that map areas of such text documents into an XML schema for easier integration.

Understanding the XLANG Schedule

After a business analyst has drawn a process diagram in BizTalk Orchestration and the developer has completed the implementation of the process diagram, they compile everything into a single document referred to as an *XLANG schedule*. The XLANG schedule is a file written in XLANG, which is also based on XML. XLANG describes the logical sequencing of activities that make up business processes, as well as the implementation of business processes, by using various components and technologies.

Extending .NET Applications with BizTalk Server

BizTalk Server is a flexible solution for exchanging documents and defining structured business processes. Although these services work well alone and between trading partners, they also make great add-on services to enterprise applications. Enterprise applications that need to have business processes defined outside of the application can benefit from the rich process definition environment that BizTalk Server offers. Conversely, you can write custom .NET code to add new functionality to any BizTalk Server schedule. This enables BizTalk Server solutions to benefit from reusable application services that are implemented within an enterprise application. Figure 6-3 illustrates how an application can externalize business processes into a BizTalk Server schedule. This schedule can also include any number of components that implement .NET code written in any of the supported Common Language Runtime (CLR) languages.

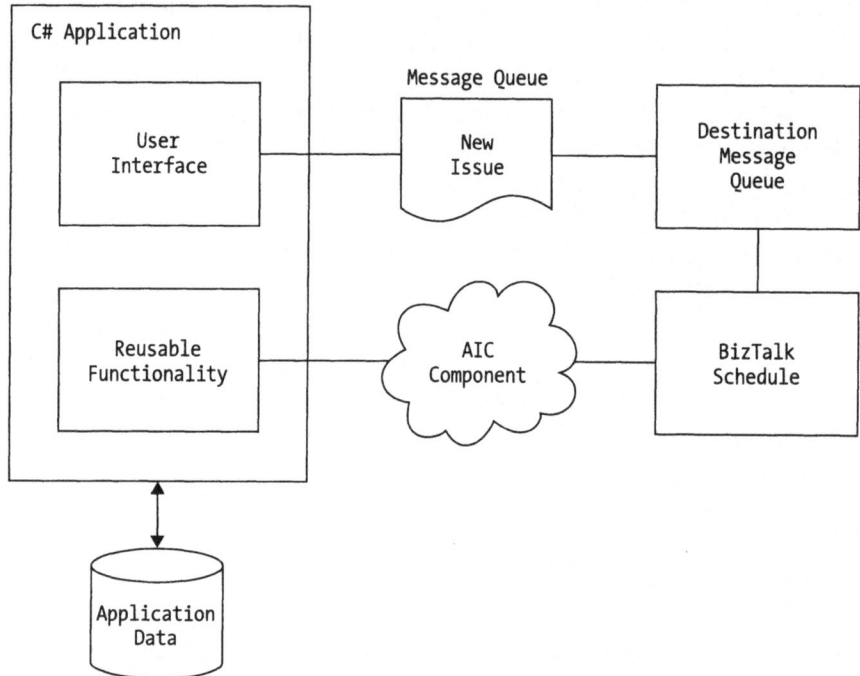

Figure 6-3. The relationships between C# applications and BizTalk Server

Externalizing Business Processes to BizTalk Server

There is good reason to externalize business processes from the application into an external engine, such as BizTalk Server. In many cases, business processes change on a regular basis. If these processes are hard-coded into the application, then every change requires you to rebuild the application. You could also accomplish externalization with other technologies, such as XML and XSL Transformations (XSLT). Changes made to an external file would be loaded and parsed by the application when it starts. The only problem with this approach is that XSLT comes with a steep learning curve for the application user. This is where BizTalk Server comes into play. Internally, the logic is maintained in XML format according to BizTalk Server's XLANG specification. Externally, the business user sees a Visio-like user interface and interacts with business process steps in the form of a block diagram.

Exposing Developed .NET Services to BizTalk Server

Just as an enterprise application can leverage BizTalk Server as an externalized business process engine, a modular application can include multiple components that can be packaged for use by a BizTalk Server schedule. One example of this is the e-mail service created in Chapter 5, "Integrating Mail Services." The e-mail service created for the IssueTracker application can be wrapped and used within an Orchestration schedule. You implement this integration between BizTalk Server and .NET Framework components with Application Integration Components (AICs).

Developing Application Integration Components

AICs are extensions to the BizTalk Server solution that implement custom logic. You can include these components within a process implementation diagram or directly bind them to a messaging port to process a document. Because BizTalk Server does not include built-in support for the .NET CLR or managed code, AICs must be implemented as COM+ components. Code written in C# inherits from ServicedComponent and implements a specific BizTalk Server integration interface method. These components are registered and bound to a destination messaging port in BizTalk Server. The "Creating the AIC Project and Class" section later in this chapter walks through the details of creating an AIC.

Defining the Business Process

Designing and implementing a business process with BizTalk Server involves several steps. These typical steps require collaboration between the business analyst and the implementing developer:

1. **Define the data document**: Carefully design and store the data that enters and exits the business process as an XML template. Document definitions validate documents before processing.

2. **Draw the business process diagram**: Draw all the necessary business processes, including decisions and exceptions. Each process comprises multiple actions that are graphically drawn and linked together to complete a process.

3. **Implement the business process**: The business process diagram must be implemented by placing functional objects, such as COM and script components that implement business logic, into the Orchestration diagram.

4. **Bind the business process to the implementation**: Establish the connection between the process diagram and the implementation shapes that provide the business logic.

5. **Perform data flow mapping**: Specify the flow of data and transformations from the source document throughout the business process to an end document.

6. **Compile the schedule**: Translate the business process diagram into an XML file representation that can be interpreted by the process engine.

7. **Create the message port**: Define the entry and exit points for business documents entering and exiting the business process.

8. **Create the message channel**: Define the data document path from initial discovery through delivery to the message port and any encryption or transformation needed in between.

BizTalk Server includes the tools that work together to accomplish these business process development steps.

Defining the Data Document

As mentioned earlier, it is important for businesses to use the same language for describing the documents passed between them. In today's enterprises, this common language is XML. Although XML documents are stored in a text format and can be opened with any text editor, creating or modifying them manually is a tedious and error-prone process. The BizTalk Editor, shown in Figure 6-4, helps to simplify this step.

The BizTalk Editor provides a way to visualize a document's layout, define data types for individual elements and attributes, and define whether data fields are required or optional. Although the schema representation in the BizTalk Editor looks similar to EDI and flat-file schemas, it is still an XML editor that produces structured XML documents.

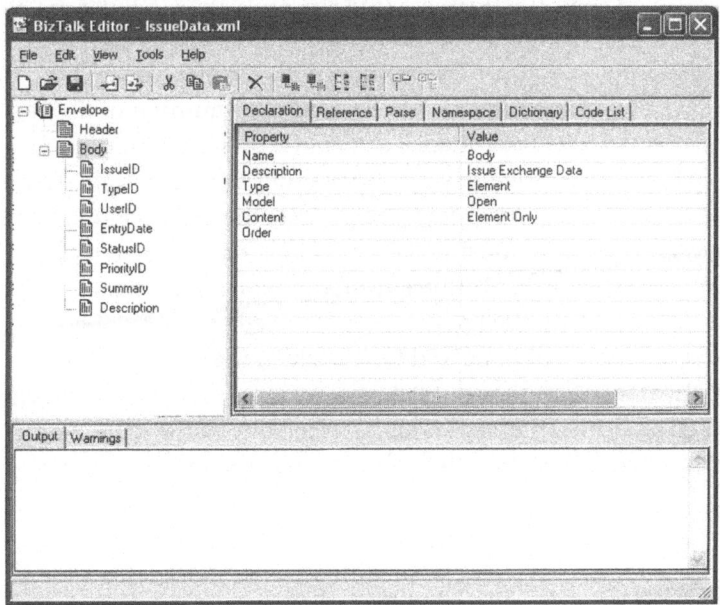

Figure 6-4. The BizTalk Editor used for XML document definition

Using the WebDAV Repository

BizTalk Messaging expects a document's structure to remain generally unchanged and located in the same place. BizTalk Messaging interacts mostly with documents stored in a central document repository that is compliant with World Wide Web Distributed Authoring and Versioning (WebDAV). WebDAV is the Internet Engineering Task Force (IETF) standard for collaborative authoring on the Web, and it supports collaborative editing and file management between users. Although the BizTalk Editor can read and write files anywhere in the file system, completed documents should be stored in the WebDAV repository.

To store documents within the WebDAV repository, use the BizTalk Editor to create the document. Next, choose File ➤ Store to WebDAV to save completed documents into the WebDAV repository. Enter *NewIssue.xml* as the filename. You can create multiple document definitions based on the same schema document, and you can optionally define global document tracking options for each document definition.

Diagramming with Orchestration

The next step in the business process development is to define and diagram the specific business process activities. A business analyst or domain expert using BizTalk Orchestration typically performs this diagramming.

The business analyst defines the business process using basic shapes, such as Action, Decision, and While shapes. The business analyst is not required to think in terms of documents, specifications, components, or messages. The developer addresses these implementation details later. Any number of the steps can appear in a business process. Fork shapes can split a process into multiple concurrent paths, such as requesting the same price quote from multiple suppliers. Later, these paths can reunite with a Join shape. Also, the Transaction shape can encapsulate several steps of the business process into a single activity.

Figure 6-5 shows the IssueTracker business process, which might be described as follows: First, a new issue document is received by the business process. Next, this document is validated and forwarded to the next step. The issuePriority field of the document is evaluated by a business rule. If issuePriority evaluates to High, then an e-mail message is sent to the administrator. In any case, the resulting document is logged into the IssueTracker database and the process ends.

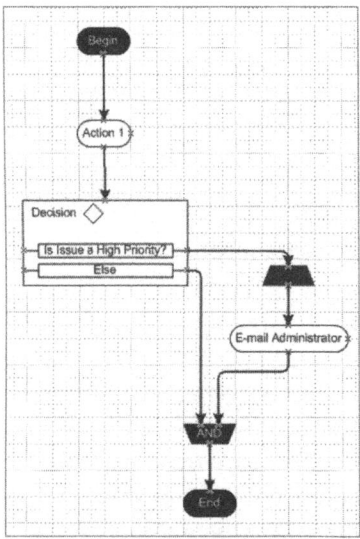

Figure 6-5. Diagramming a business process with the BizTalk Orchestration Designer

Because BizTalk Orchestration supports long-running business processes, they may need to be suspended and saved to conserve computing resources and provide extra reliability. BizTalk Server later restarts these sleeping processes from the exact point they were suspended. If the server running BizTalk Server is switched off, the suspended processes are restarted when the system is eventually restored.

Adding Business Rules

The Decision shape implements the business rules. After placing a Decision shape in the process diagram, right-click the Add Rule pop-up menu item. Select Create New Rule and enter the business rule definition, as shown in Figure 6-6.

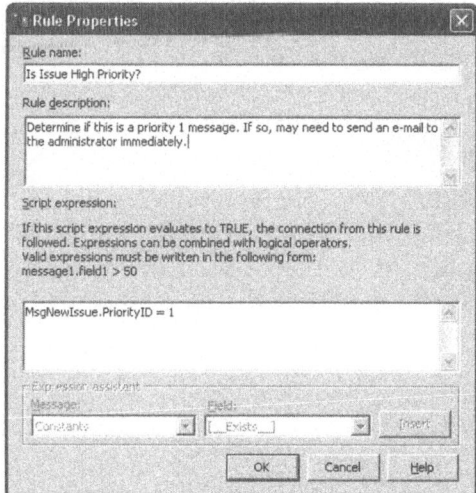

Figure 6-6. Applying business rules based on properties within the document

To add a specific script expression, select a message item from the Message list and a field item from the Field list. Click the Insert button to insert the specific data field to the script expression textbox. From the script expression textbox, you can include additional constants or expression code to complete the rule. For IssueTracker, this rule evaluates the PriorityID for the IncomingMessage and compares it to the condition of 1. If the expression is true, the process diagram will continue with additional steps.

Implementing the Business Process

Developers interact with BizTalk Orchestration differently than business analysts do. After the business analyst defines the business process, developers implement it by mapping out how BizTalk Server must perform each task. BizTalk Orchestration does most of the work, so the amount of actual coding left is minimal. A developer completes the diagram by adding a combination of BizTalk Messaging shapes, COM Component shapes, and Message Queuing shapes. Code is not written to bind the individual steps together. Rather, coding is applied to the individual components that provide specialized business logic.

By dragging the BizTalk Messaging shape into the implementation section of the drawing, the BizTalk Messaging Binding Wizard starts, as shown in Figure 6-7. This wizard steps through a series of pages that define how the messaging port is associated with an implementation shape. A messaging port is simply an access point into or out of a process implementation diagram and is associated with a collection of properties. Enter *IncomingIssue* for the port name. The message port name must match the port name specified in the BizTalk Messaging Manager. Set the communication direction to receive and enable the XLANG schedule activation. Finally, click the Finish button to complete the wizard.

Figure 6-7. Binding BizTalk Server to messaging services

If you indicate that a port will send documents from the XLANG schedule to BizTalk Messaging rather than receive them, the BizTalk Messaging Binding Wizard requires the name of a channel that will receive these documents. This channel does not have to exist at the time that the XLANG schedule drawing is being created, but it must exist when the schedule is executed.

Another way to receive a document in an XLANG schedule is to use the Message Queuing shape. When you add this shape to the drawing, the Message Queuing Binding Wizard starts, and you must specify the name of a private or public message queue that will send or receive documents. This is how the IssueTracker application will submit data, using the message queues created in Chapter 4, "Applying Reliable Messaging."

In addition to the Microsoft Message Queue (MSMQ) and BizTalk Messaging ports, a business process can be exposed to other ports where specialized business logic is implemented by the enterprise application. These other ports include script components and COM components. Script components implement simple tasks and are created with a scripting language such as Microsoft

Visual Basic Scripting Edition (VBScript). COM components implement specialized tasks, such as access to databases or other system and application resources. COM components can also wrap C# code, as shown in Figure 6-8.

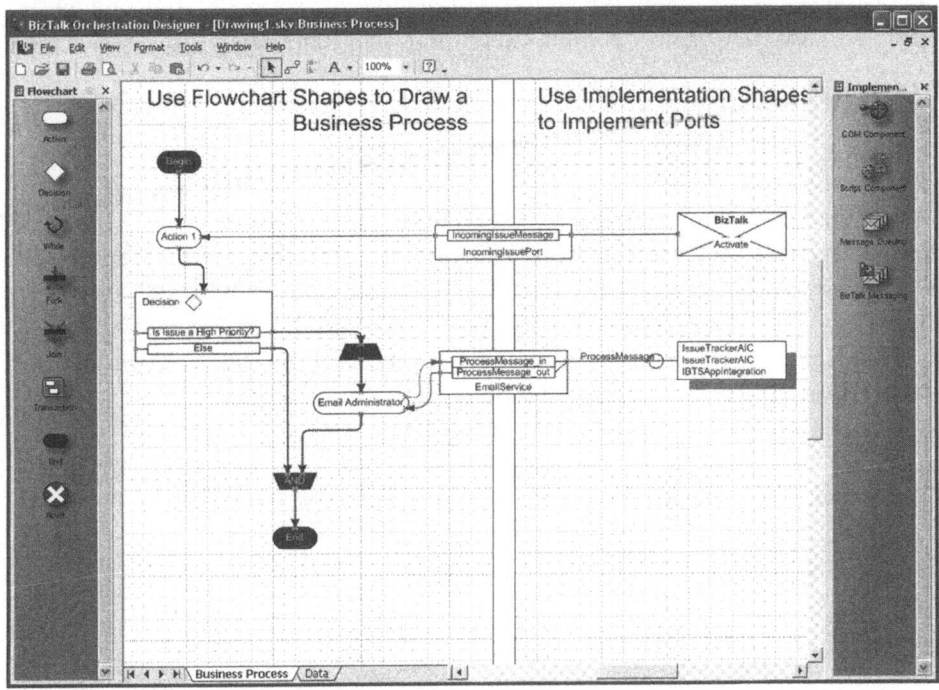

Figure 6-8. Completing the business process with implementation objects

After an XLANG schedule processes data, the next step is to send out the resulting data. To send the document back to BizTalk Messaging, add a BizTalk Messaging shape to the right side of the drawing and specify the name of the channel to which the document must be sent. After the Orchestration port is created, connect an Action shape to this port and in the XML Communication Wizard specify whether the document is sent as XML or as a string, specify the message type information, and specify an optional XML specification to validate the document, which is similar to the receive document messaging port described earlier.

You can also send out documents from an XLANG schedule by using Message Queuing. In this case, instead of specifying the name of a channel, specify a name of a private or public queue, where the document will be posted. Again, this is how the IssueTracker application expects to receive responses from the business process.

Creating an Application Integration Component in C#

To expose any .NET application functionality to BizTalk Server, you need to create a new AIC that wraps the functionality. Implementing an AIC requires the following key steps: create the wrapper project and class, create a strong name, build and register the component, and bind it to a schedule.

Creating the AIC Project and Class

To implement the AIC, create a new class library project named *IssueTrackerAIC* under the IssueTracker solution. Next, add a .NET reference to System.EnterpriseServices and a COM reference of Microsoft BizTalk Server Application Interface Component 1.0 Type Library to the project. Rename the Class1 declaration to *IssueTrackerAIC*. Finally, modify the class declaration to inherit from the ServicedComponent class and implement the IBTSAppIntegration interface as in Listing 6-1.

Listing 6-1. The Application Integration Component Skeleton Class

```
public class IssueTrackerAIC : ServicedComponent, IBTSAppIntegration
{
    public IssueTrackerAIC()
    {
    }

    string IBTSAppIntegration.ProcessMessage( string strDocument )
    {
        return "Welcome to BizTalk!";
    }
}
```

This skeleton class implements the minimal code that completes an AIC. The only required interface method to implement is ProcessMessage. This is the method invoked by BizTalk Messaging. The method parameter is a single string that contains the contents of the document being edited. The intention is that the AIC will work on this document and send a modified version back to the caller as a return value. Once inside this method, any application-specific or .NET-related functionality can occur. The incoming document can be written to a file, stored to a database, delivered elsewhere via File Transfer Protocol (FTP) or SMTP, or it can be processed in any other way specific to your business needs.

Creating and Applying a Strong Name

Because the AIC is implemented as an enterprise service and will be registered as a COM+ application, you need to create a strong name key and associate it with the IssueTrackerAIC assembly. Create a strong name key at the command line using the sn.exe application as follows:

```
sn.exe -k sharedkey.snk
```

After you create the strong name key file, copy it to the project directory and then add the file to the project. Finally, you need to associate the shared key file with the IssueTrackerAIC assembly. Select the IssueTrackerAIC project node in the Solution Explorer and open its properties. In the Common Properties' General section, enter *sharedkey.snk* for the Wrapper Assembly Key File value. Next, add the strong name key reference to the AssemblyInfo.cs file by replacing the following statement:

```
[assembly: AssemblyKeyFile(@"..\..\sharedkey.snk")]
```

The file path specified is relative to the project output directory. Lastly, you must recompile and register the project.

 NOTE *The Visual Basic .NET Integrated Development Environment (IDE) is not able to generate strongly named COM wrapper classes. Developers must use the tlbimp.exe utility from the command line rather than simply providing an AssemblyKeyFile attribute.*

Registering an Application Integration Component

To register AIC as a COM+ application that BizTalk Server recognizes, begin by opening Start ➤ Control Panel ➤ Administrative Tools ➤ Component Services. From the console root, click Computers ➤ My Computer ➤ COM+ Applications. This displays all registered COM+ applications. To add a new one, select Action ➤ New ➤ Application from the menu. This starts the COM+ Application Installation Wizard. Step through the wizard and click the Create an Empty Application button. Next, enter *IssueTrackerAIC* for the application name, as shown in Figure 6-9.

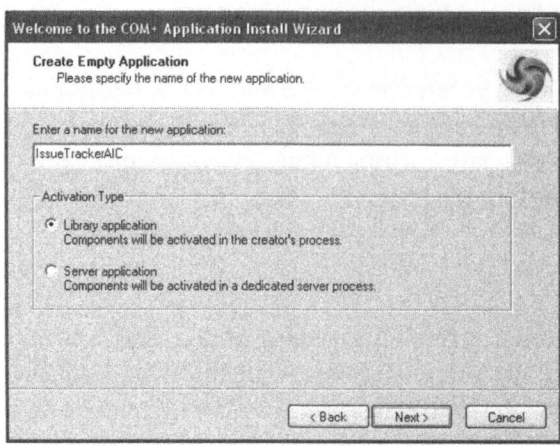

Figure 6-9. Registering an AIC as a COM+ service

Select Library Application as the Activation Type and complete the wizard. This creates an empty application container. In the component tree, select the newly created IssueTrackerAIC entry and click New ➤ Component from its context menu. Step through the wizard and click the Install New Component(s) button. Browse to the new AIC's project output directory and select IssueTrackerAIC.dll. The new AIC should appear in the Components Found list. After completing the wizard, the new AIC should appear in the components list—ready for BizTalk Server use.

Binding an Orchestration Diagram

After drawing the process diagram and defining the implementation ports in BizTalk Orchestration, you need to link the two drawings together. Each flowchart shape drawn by a business analyst and each implementation shape drawn by a developer have a connection point on its side. Using familiar Visio techniques, an Action shape on the left connects to an implementation shape on the right by simply drawing a line between their handles. Each time you make a connection, the XML Communication Wizard starts to capture how the communication between these shapes will occur.

The first binding you need to create is the one that begins the entire automation process. First, connect the Receive Issue Item process step defined by the business analyst to the IncomingIssue port defined by the developer. Bind the two together by clicking the process step, selecting the yellow grab handle on its right, and dragging a connection to the IncomingIssue port. This action triggers the XML Communication Wizard, as shown in Figure 6-10.

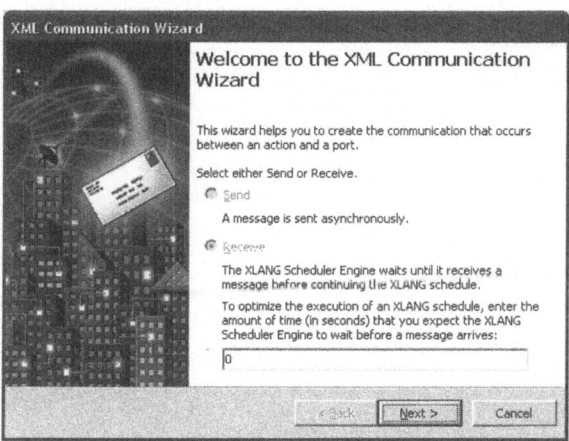

Figure 6-10. Identifying incoming documents

The XML Communication Wizard goes through the process of creating a message that will carry the source document through the business process. Label the new message *IncomingMessage*. Specify to receive XML from the message queue. If the document is not formatted as XML, the XLANG Schedule Engine must "wrap" the document in the engine's standard XML wrapper. After that, the wizard prompts you for a message type. Use the same document definition used to configure the messaging port that delivered this document to the XLANG schedule or enter the name of the root element from the document schema. Set the message type label to *IncomingIssue*. Choose the message specification by browsing to and selecting the NewIssue.xml file. BizTalk Orchestration will validate each document against this specification prior to processing it. Click the Add button to display the Field Selection dialog box. The NewIssue schema will appear. Expand the header node and select the issuePriority field, as shown in Figure 6-11. You can browse individual fields from the original schema document by using a standard XML query language called *XPath*. XPath is a standard XML query language used for addressing parts of an XML document. A blue line will appear that connects the IncomingMessage port to the Receive Issue Item process step.

Next, the process definition needs to bind the E-mail Administrator process step with the NotifyAdministrator script object. Drag a link from the E-mail Administrator action object to the SendMessage_in node of the NotifyAdministrator port. This action launches the Method Communication Wizard. Select the Initiate a Synchronous Method Call option and click Next. Then, select the Create a New Message option and click Next. Finally, select the message specification for the communication and click Finish.

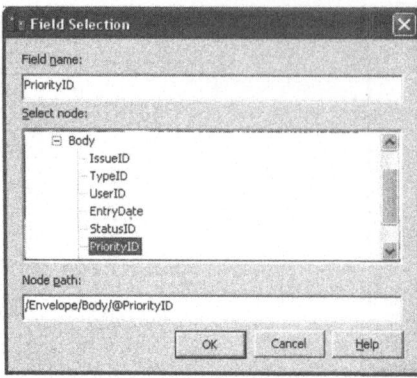

Figure 6-11. Selecting specific document fields to act upon

Defining the Data Flow

When all of the business process steps have been connected to all of the implementation shapes, all that remains is the underlying data flow. The data view defines how business documents pass from one process step to the next. In BizTalk Orchestration, open the data view by clicking the Data tab at the bottom of the screen. The process data view appears as shown in Figure 6-12. Several groups of fields will display. Each group is named after the message that carries the document to or from an Orchestration port.

Earlier, you used the XML Communication Wizard to define a message and indicate which XML specification represented the document being received. In the process data view, values of individual fields inside the document are mapped to implementation objects, such as COM or script components. The Document fields represent an entire document passed into the XLANG schedule.

The document received from BizTalk Messaging by IncomingMessage needs to be passed on to the SendMessage_in and InsertIssue_in messages, which will later submit the document to script components. The NotifyAdministrator script component will return the same document to BizTalk Messaging via the SendMessage_out message. You can reposition the message objects on this page to make the drawing easier to read. Figure 6-13 shows the resulting page.

After you have connected all the message fields in the process data view, you can save and compile the diagram into an XLANG schedule file.

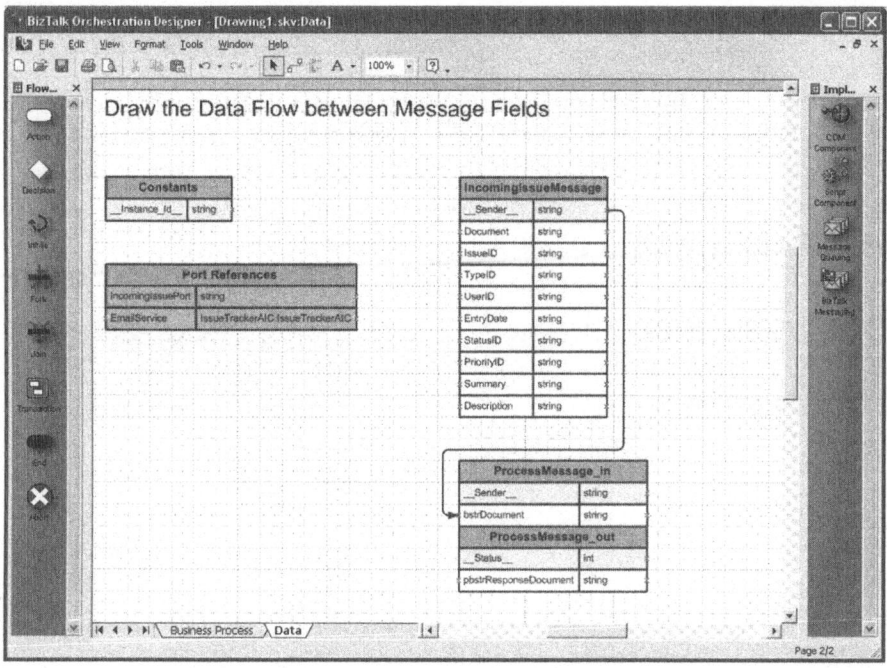

Figure 6-12. Viewing the flow of data within a document by individual fields

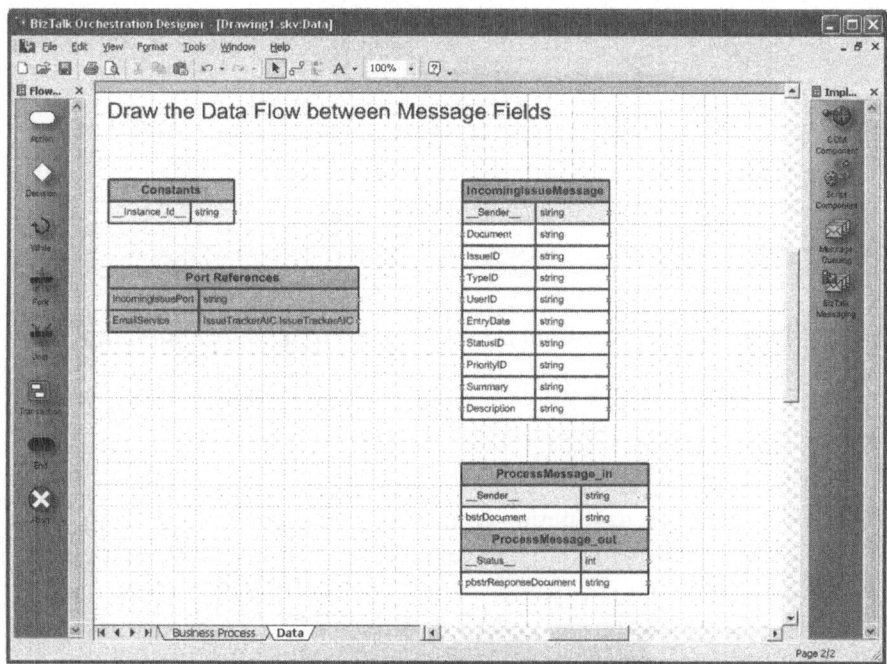

Figure 6-13. Specifying document field mappings

Mapping the Data Document

To have BizTalk Messaging accept an incoming document and route it as an
outgoing document, you need to define document mapping (see Figure 6-14).
BizTalk Mapping provides an interface for mapping data fields from a source
document to a destination document. Document mapping can also apply transformation methods that reshape the data as necessary.

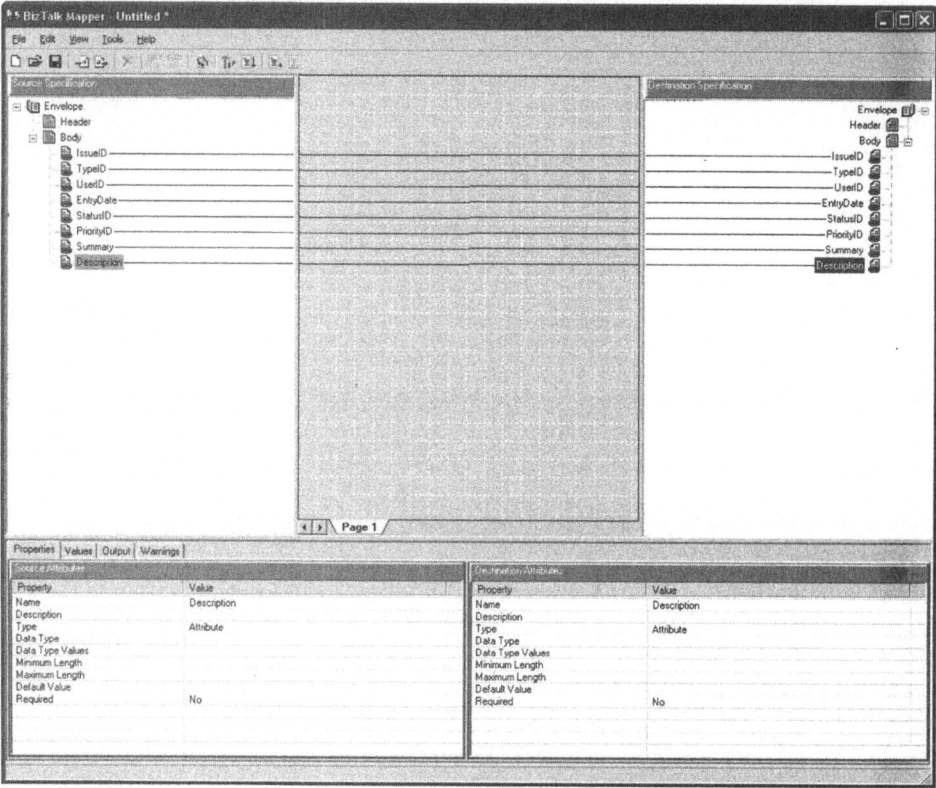

Figure 6-14. Applying transformation functions to document field mappings

Defining Messaging Ports

To deliver a document to a destination, you must define the destination in
BizTalk Messaging. Destinations are known in BizTalk Messaging as *messaging
ports*. A messaging port also contains a set of properties that define how documents are secured and transported to their destination. You can group messaging
ports into distribution lists to have the same document sent to several different
destinations.

From the BizTalk Messaging Manager, open the Messaging ports view. Next, select File ➤ New ➤ Messaging Port ➤ To an Application from the menu. Enter *New Issue* for the messaging port name and click the Next button. In the next page, select New XLANG Schedule as the destination for this port and IncomingMessage for the port name to receive the notification, as shown in Figure 6-15. No special envelope or encoding is necessary. When finished, the wizard creates the messaging port and starts the Channel Definition Wizard.

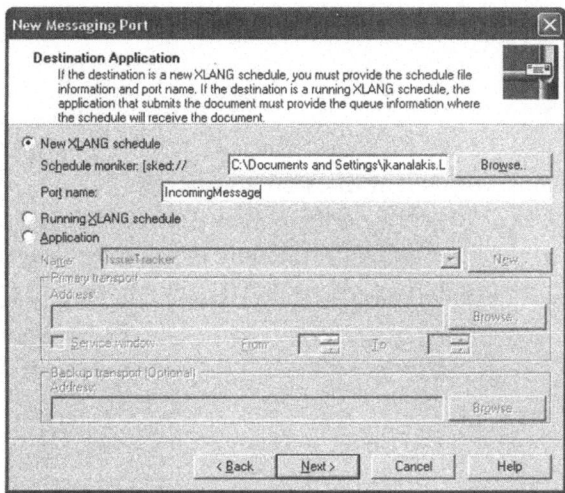

Figure 6-15. Configuring BizTalk Server messaging ports

Instead of delivering a document to BizTalk Orchestration or a file, you can configure a messaging port to deliver documents using any of the supported protocols, including HTTP(S), SMTP, and Message Queuing. You can also configure a messaging port with extra security features that optionally encrypt documents and/or include digital signatures.

Binding an Application Integration Component to a Message Port

Binding a new messaging port to an AIC is similar to binding to a new XLANG schedule. In the New Messaging Port Wizard, click the Application radio button as the port destination. Enter the destination application name by clicking the New button and adding a new logical application name, such as *IssueTracker*. Next, specify the primary transport by clicking the Browse button and then selecting Application Integration Component in the Primary Transport dialog box. Specify the component name by clicking the Browse button and selecting

IssueTrackerAIC.IssueTrackerAIC in the Component Selection dialog box. Finally, complete the remaining wizard steps to create the AIC new message port.

 NOTE *If the IssueTrackerAIC component does not appear in the list, make sure it has been properly deployed as a COM+ application. The most common reason for a registration failure is that an assembly does not have a strong name.*

Defining Channels

A channel contains a set of properties, which identifies the source that has sent the document and defines the specific steps performed by BizTalk Server before the document is delivered to the messaging port. Figure 6-16 shows the relationship between the receive functions, channels, and messaging ports.

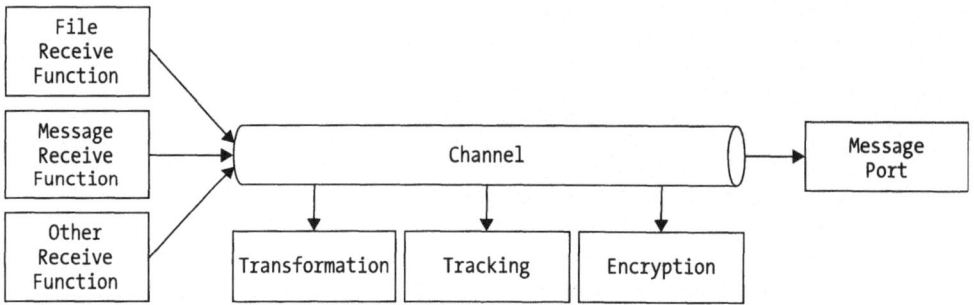

Figure 6-16. The relationship between the receive functions, channels, and messaging ports

After the New Messaging Port Wizard completes in BizTalk Messaging, the New Channel Wizard begins. You can also start the New Channel Wizard by selecting the message ports view and selecting the message port that needs to be associated with a channel. Next, select File ➤ New ➤ Channel ➤ From an Application from the menu. In the New Channel Wizard, enter *New Issue* as the channel name. Select Next and specify Application as the information source for this channel. Select New and enter *IssueTracker* for the application name, as shown in Figure 6-17. Later, this name will be associated with a receive function that polls for new documents. Select the default organization identifier and click the Next button. Specify the Inbound document format as New Issue and the Outbound document format as Recorded Issue.

Click Finish to complete the wizard. This creates a new channel definition that defines the documents to be processed, defines they will originate from the IssueTracker application, and defines these documents will be in a format described by the document definition New Issue.

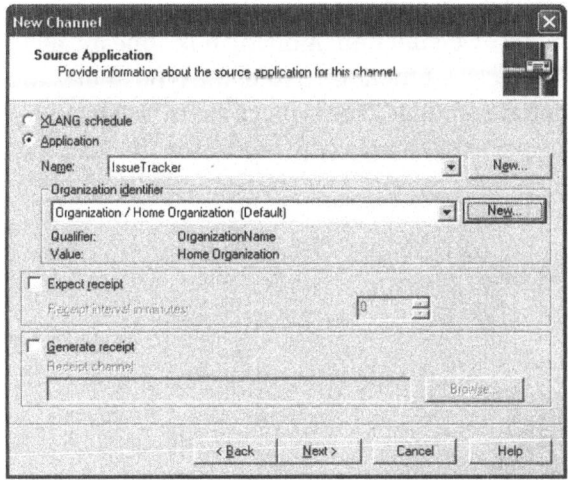

Figure 6-17. Creating a new channel in the BizTalk Messaging Manager

You can instruct a channel to translate a document from one document format into another. Channels can also specify which information must be logged for tracking purposes as the channel delivers a document.

Defining Receive Functions

If BizTalk Server needs to process a file created by an internal application, it uses a file receive function. A file receive function polls a specific directory for the existence of a specific file. If the file is discovered, it is read into an XML document, passed into BizTalk Messaging, and removed from the directory.

One advantage of working with an output file is that an internal business application that creates this file does not need to know anything about BizTalk Server. It simply creates a file containing the document somewhere on a file system, and BizTalk Server instantly picks it up.

File receive functions introduce an element of asynchronous execution into the business process. Asynchronous execution is important in a distributed environment because it allows each part in the solution to stand by itself without being affected by the temporary unavailability of another part. If a brief network failure arises, the overall business process is not affected because the documents produced would simply accumulate on the hard drive. Once the network is available again, BizTalk Server picks up and processes all the files it finds in its source directory. Also, you can add and configure additional BizTalk Servers to process documents from the same directory to scale up performance.

To create a file receive function, start the BizTalk Server Administrator. Expand the BizTalk Server Group tree node and select the Receive Functions node. Select Action ➤ New ➤ File Receive Function. A dialog box appears, as shown in Figure 6-18. Enter the file receive function's name, the type of files to poll for, and the directory that should be polled. The type of file to poll for can either be a complete filename or a partial filename with wildcards, such as *Issue.xml.

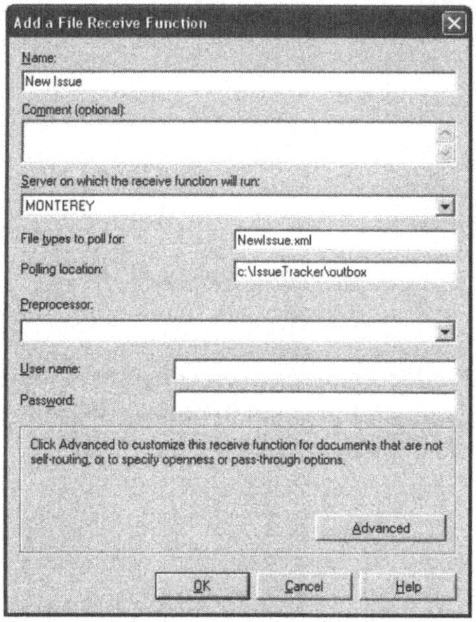

Figure 6-18. BizTalk Server components

File receive functions are not the only way to submit documents to BizTalk Server. BizTalk Server can also receive documents from Message Queuing, through SMTP e-mail, from HTTP(S) Web pages, and from COM components within an application.

The IssueTracker application interacts with external business processes through message queuing. This requires a new message queuing receive function to be added. Create a new receive function as specified earlier; however, specify a new message queuing receive function instead of a file receive function. Enter a name for the function and point the polling location to the message queue created in Chapter 4, "Applying Reliable Messaging." In the Advanced options, select the IssueTrackerChannel and close both dialog boxes to create the receive function.

Compiling the XLANG Schedule

When the business process definition is completed by the business analyst and the process implementation is completed by the developer and both diagrams are bound together, work with BizTalk Orchestration is complete. Next, the process diagram needs to be compiled into a file with which the BizTalk Server process engine can work.

As mentioned earlier, an XLANG schedule is a plain-text document that is coded in XML. This document contains the sequence of activities, rules, and components that were mapped in the BizTalk Orchestration Designer.

To create an XLANG schedule, open the process diagram in BizTalk Orchestration and select File ➤ Make XLANG. This command translates the Orchestration diagram saved as a *.skv file and produces the *.skx XLANG file.

Executing the Business Process

To understand how all the BizTalk Server components work together, the picture looks like this: The file receive function picks up a data file and delivers it to a messaging port through a specific channel. The channel validates the document against an XML specification. The messaging port is tied to an XLANG schedule that begins by processing the source file. With the document inside the XLANG schedule, various business components are called to pass the document as one of their parameters. These components address a variety of business rules, access enterprise databases and legacy systems, send e-mail messages, and generally do anything necessary to accomplish a business process. Components also modify the source document and return these changes back to the XLANG schedule to be passed on to the next action. Finally, the schedule produces an output file that is deposited in a specified output directory.

Summary

This chapter explored the complexities of business process automation and how the .NET Framework leverages Microsoft's BizTalk Server as a flexible and scalable solution. This chapter started with an introduction to business process automation and described how enterprise applications benefit from it. Then, this chapter described BizTalk Server and its components and how it addresses the need for scalable and reliable business process automation. Then, this chapter defined a business process for the IssueTracker enterprise application and leveraged BizTalk Server to implement process automation services that automatically route information throughout the enterprise based on specific business rules.

The next chapter implements the application's presentation layer with the use of Web forms, reflection, and data binding. The presentation layer finally adds the user interface to all of the services covered so far and relies upon templates and user controls to reduce errors and encourage reusability.

CHAPTER 7

Building Web Applications

THIS CHAPTER EXPLORES ASP.NET and shows how to use this powerful technology to build enterprise Web applications. Although ASP.NET is derived from its ASP predecessor, ASP.NET has evolved with a new framework specifically designed for building complex, scalable, and robust Web applications. Two fundamental framework components of ASP.NET include Web forms and Web services. This chapter provides some background into Web forms, including how forms are processed and how events are handled. It also examines how to construct Web forms, use server and user controls, and accomplish important application functions, such as form validation, browser detection, and page redirection. From the examples presented, you will continue to build the IssueTracker enterprise application.

Standardizing Web Forms with Templates

When multiple developers are working together to build an enterprise solution, many unexpected problems tend to surface. The most common problems include code replication and user interface inconsistencies. Code replication occurs when a user interface element or client-side function is needed in one or more regions of the application. Different developers working on those different regions often implement the same element differently rather than using a single shared element. User interface inconsistencies occur when different developers implement application forms that are similar but execute certain details slightly different, such as font selection, positioning, or alignment.

The simplest solution to these problems is to use templates. User interface templates for common application elements can go a long way to add consistency and reduce errors in an application. To determine how many or what type of templates you need, build a map of the entire Web application, form by form. Then, look for common patterns. In the IssueTracker Web application, there are three different types of Web forms: static content forms, list forms, and data entry forms. A more complex application will have even more refined template pages than the three mentioned. Before implementing Web form templates, it is important to have a clear understanding of how you present Web forms using page layouts.

Exploring Page Layout Options

A layout mechanism determines how controls are placed within a Web page. Web forms support two basic page layout mechanisms: flow layout and grid layout. Developers with a strong background in Web application development will best relate to the flow layout because its top-to-bottom relative positioning of controls closely resembles Hypertext Markup Language (HTML). Conversely, developers with a strong background in desktop application development will best relate to the grid layout because the absolute positioning of the controls closely resembles traditional Visual Studio form building. Each layout mechanism has its own unique benefits, and selecting the appropriate one depends upon your project's requirements.

Choosing the Flow Layout

The flow layout works best for Web applications that are targeted for a wide range of clients. Because you place controls in a relative position, it is easier to build an application capable of sizing itself to fit in any size Web browser window. As Figure 7-1 demonstrates, you lay out server controls from left to right and from top to bottom. If a server control does not fit on a line, it wraps around to the next line. As a browser window narrows, the server controls continue to shift, moving down the page.

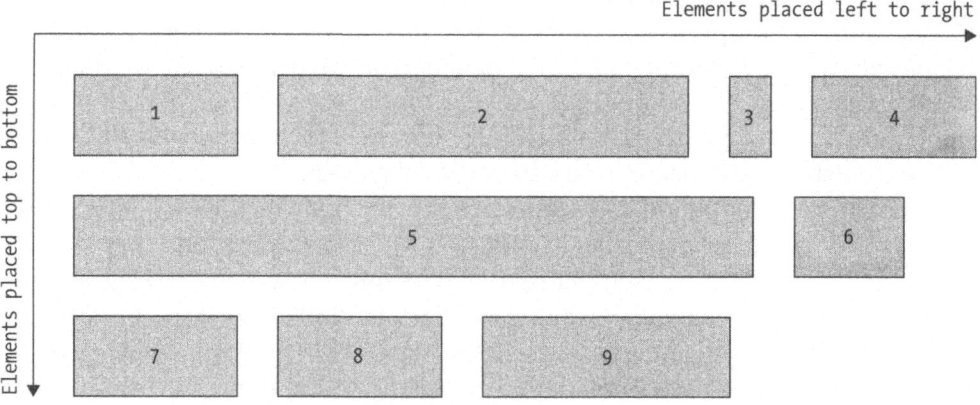

Figure 7-1. A representation of the flow layout

With this method, users operating at different screen resolutions can view the application differently. At higher resolutions, users see more content within a single view, and at lower resolutions, users can avoid horizontal scrolling.

Web applications rely heavily upon the HTML table control to help with page formatting. Because you can specify the width and height properties of a table control, you can effectively accomplish absolute positioning of form controls even when applying the flow layout to a Web form.

Choosing the Grid Layout

The grid layout works best for Web applications that want to enforce consistency among all users. Because controls placed within a page using the grid layout remain in a fixed position, each user, regardless of Web browser version or screen resolution, will see the same user interface. Users with lower resolution screens may need to scroll around to see the entire application, but the position of the controls remains constant. This is especially useful when trying to keep a data entry user interface consistent with the printed form. Listing 7-1 demonstrates the same login page using the grid layout.

Listing 7-1. Login Page Implemented Using the Grid Layout

```
<%@ Page language="c#" Codebehind="login_enter.aspx.cs"
    Inherits="IssueTracker.LoginForm" %>
<!DOCTYPE HTML PUBLIC "-//W3C//DTD HTML 4.0 Transitional//EN" >
<HTML>
    <body MS_POSITIONING="GridLayout">
    <FORM id="LoginForm" method="post" runat="server">

    <DIV style="DISPLAY: inline; Z-INDEX: 101; LEFT: 240px; WIDTH: 70px;
        POSITION: absolute; TOP: 24px; HEIGHT: 15px"
        ms_positioning="FlowLayout">Username:</DIV>

    <INPUT style="Z-INDEX: 102; LEFT: 328px; POSITION: absolute; TOP: 24px"
        type="text" name="edtUsername">

    <DIV style="DISPLAY: inline; Z-INDEX: 103; LEFT: 240px; WIDTH: 70px;
        POSITION: absolute; TOP: 56px; HEIGHT: 15px"
        ms_positioning="FlowLayout">Password:</DIV>

    <INPUT style="Z-INDEX: 104; LEFT: 328px; POSITION: absolute; TOP: 64px"
        type="password" name="edtPassword">

    <INPUT style="Z-INDEX: 105; LEFT: 328px; POSITION: absolute; TOP: 96px"
        type="button" value="  OK  " name="btnOK">
```

```
<INPUT style="Z-INDEX: 106; LEFT: 400px; POSITION: absolute; TOP: 96px"
    type="button" value="Cancel" name="btnCancel"></FORM>

    </FORM>
    </body>
</HTML>
```

Controls placed into a Web form using the grid layout only look slightly different in HTML. The type, name, and size attributes of the input tag remain the same, but a lengthy style attribute has been added. The z-index value refers to the layering order of controls placed within a Web form. Web forms can layer controls over each other and partially cover each other. A higher z-index value puts a control on top of those with lower values. Figure 7-2 demonstrates how two overlapping controls appear in a Web form.

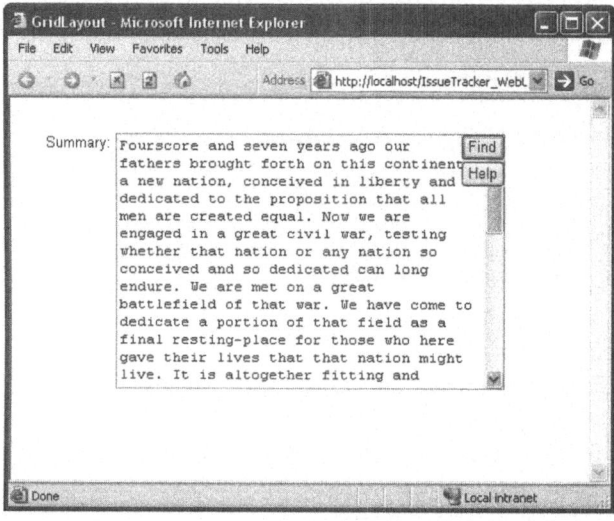

Figure 7-2. A Web form with overlapping button controls

The left and top values identify the horizontal and vertical position of a control, respectively. The position value identifies how the control should be placed when rendered: static, absolute, or relative. A static value places the control according to the natural flow of the page, ignoring the left and top values. A relative value also places the control according to the natural flow of the page, but it is influenced by the left and top values. An absolute value places the control exactly where it is specified as defined by the left and top values.

The grid layout depends heavily upon the style attribute within HTML. The problem is that the only Web browsers that support it are Microsoft Internet Explorer 4.0 and higher. Web forms include a targetSchema property that identifies the Web browser and optimize the rendering. To support older Web browsers, ASP.NET can render HTML pages by placing controls within tables to achieve the grid layout positioning specified. Listing 7-2 outlines the HTML code produced by the ASP.NET engine when the targetSchema form property is set to Netscape Navigator 4.0. The produced code uses HTML table formatting to approximate the exact control positioning specified in the form designer.

Listing 7-2. Login Page Target for Netscape Navigator 4.0

```
<!DOCTYPE HTML PUBLIC "-//W3C//DTD HTML 4.0 Transitional//EN" >
<HTML>
    <HEAD>
        <title>GridLayout</title>
        <meta name="GENERATOR" Content="Microsoft Visual Studio .NET 7.1">
        <meta name="CODE_LANGUAGE" Content="C#">
        <meta name="vs_defaultClientScript" content="JavaScript">
        <meta name="vs_targetSchema"
            content="http://schemas.microsoft.com/intellisense/nav4-0">
    </HEAD>
<body MS_POSITIONING="GridLayout">
<TABLE height="377" cellSpacing="0" cellPadding="0" width="218" border="1"
    ms_2d_layout="TRUE">
    <TR vAlign="top">
    <TD width="218" height="377">
        <form name="Form1" method="post" action="GridLayout.aspx" id="Form1">
            <input type="hidden" name="__VIEWSTATE"
                value="dDwtMTMxMzA2ODI5ODs7PmyeHStznlqmkTbO90NU3FrpXTeC" />
            <TABLE height="201" cellSpacing="0" cellPadding="0" width="365"
                border="1" ms_2d_layout="TRUE">
                <TR vAlign="top">
                    <TD width="96" height="96"></TD>
                    <TD width="112"></TD>
                    <TD width="157" rowSpan="2"></TD>
                </TR>
                <TR vAlign="top">
                    <TD height="8"></TD>
                    <TD rowSpan="2">
                    <span id="Label1">E-mail Address:</span></TD>
                </TR>
                <TR vAlign="top">
                    <TD height="32"></TD>
                    <TD>
                    <input name="TextBox1" type="text" id="TextBox1" /></TD>
                </TR>
                <TR vAlign="top">
```

```
                        <TD height="40"></TD>
                        <TD>
                        <span id="Label2">Password:</span></TD>
                        <TD>
                        <input name="TextBox2" type="text" id="TextBox2" /></TD>
                    </TR>
                    <TR vAlign="top">
                        <TD colSpan="2" height="25"></TD>
                        <TD>
                        <input type="submit" name="Button1" value="   OK   "
                            id="Button1" /></TD>
                    </TR>
                </TABLE>
            </form>
        </TD>
        </TR>
        </TABLE>
    </body>
</HTML>
```

This code has been altered to make the tables visible, revealing how the ASP.NET engine accomplishes absolute control positioning in HTML. Figure 7-3 illustrates the login page with the border size set to 1.

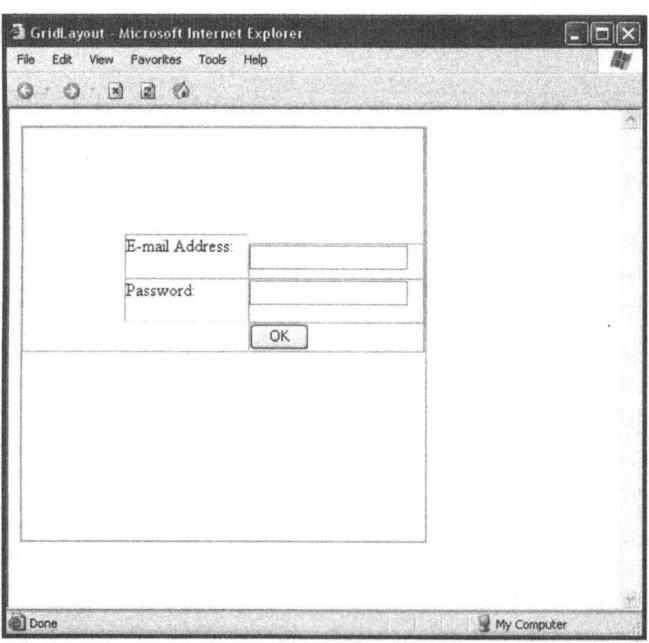

Figure 7-3. A Web form using HTML tables to position controls in a grid layout

With a better understanding of Web form layout options, it is time to implement Web form templates.

Creating a Cascading Style Sheet

A Cascading Style Sheet (CSS) broadly sets the look and feel of a Web application by creating styles of text formatting and applying them to different HTML user interface elements. CSS values replace the need to hard-code font settings for each HTML element. This brings consistency to the application's look and feel and further accelerates application development time.

To create a CSS document, create a styles folder under the WebUI project. Next, select the styles folder and select Add ➤ Add New Item. In the Add New Item dialog box, select the Style Sheet template and assign its name to match the application name, such as *issuetracker.css* for the IssueTracker application. Next, fill in the style details for the various HTML elements:

```
body
{
    font-size: 12px;
    font-family: verdana, arial, helvetica, sans-serif;
    color: #000000;
}
A:Hover
{
    font-size: 11px;
    font-family: verdana, arial, helvetica, sans-serif;
    background: transparent;
    text-decoration: underline;
    color: #FF6600;
}
A:Link,
A:Visited,
A:Active
{
    font-size: 11px;
    font-family: verdana, arial, helvetica, sans-serif;
    background: transparent;
    text-decoration: none;
    color: #000000;
}
```

In this case, you can set a style for all unformatted HTML body text to display a 12-point Verdana font in black. Also, hyperlinks should only appear underlined when the mouse hovers over them, and they should appear the same whether active, inactive, or visited.

To reference CSS files within Web forms, place the following statement into the <HEAD> section of each Web form's HTML:

```
<LINK href="../styles/issuetracker.css" type="text/css" rel="stylesheet">
```

Once each Web form includes a reference to a style sheet, you can update the entire application to use different font settings by changing only the referenced CSS file.

Creating a Static Content Template

Begin creating Web form templates by organizing the Web application project into folders. From the Visual Studio .NET Solution Explorer, select the Web application project and choose Add ➤ New Folder from the context menu. Create the following folders:

- **controls**: Contains custom developed user controls that can be easily reused between Web forms

- **images**: Contains all application image files

- **pages**: Contains all application Web forms

- **static**: Contains all static content related to the Web application

- **styles**: Contains all CSS files related to the application

- **templates**: Contains all application Web form templates

After you have created the folders, select the templates folder and choose Add ➤ Add HTML Page from the context menu. In the Add New Item dialog box, enter *StaticTemplate.html* for the filename. When the new blank page appears, select Table ➤ Insert ➤ Table from the menu. In the Insert Table dialog box, specify a new table that has one column, four rows, 100-percent width, and a 0 border size. Next, insert some placeholder text, such as *$$PAGE_HEADER$$*, where form elements should appear. These placeholders should indicate where to place the page header, footer, menu, title, and so on. You can apply row shading and colors to match the company's or product's color scheme. Also, if any of the rows should apply custom fonts or formatting, you should also specify it within the template. Figure 7-4 illustrates the static content template that applies to the IssueTracker application. It might look simple, but it will go a long way to reduce the time needed to build the entire Web application.

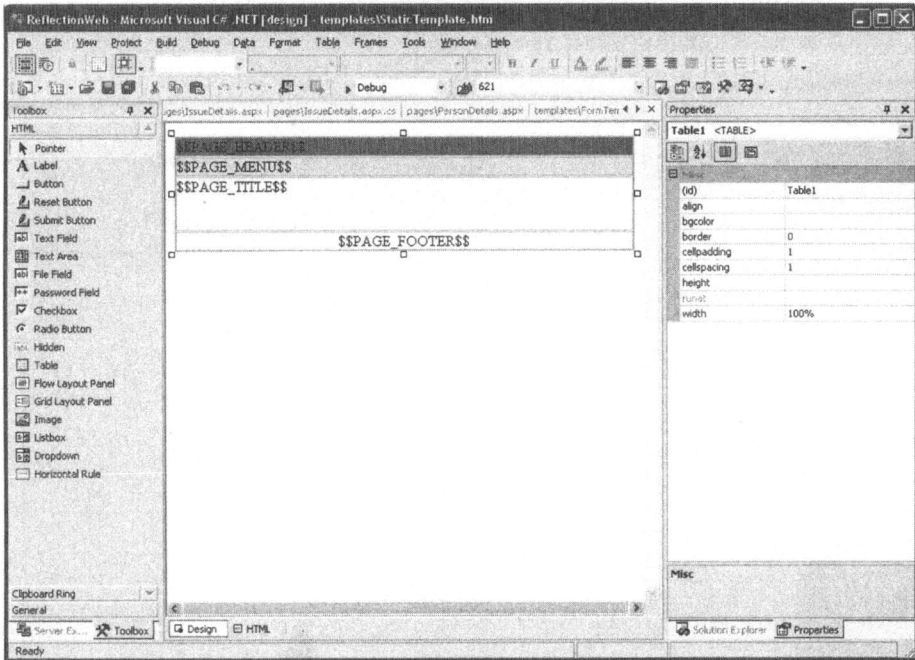

Figure 7-4. Creating the static content template

The static content template is always simple. Its principal purpose is to display static text, such as online help or corporate messaging. It can also act as a starting point for building the remaining templates.

In any Web application, the real advantage of a template comes when you want more complicated formatting, custom menus, mixed fonts, and so on. When you create a new Web form, for instance, you can open the HTML view and paste the contents of the template's HTML view. The result is a new Web form with a consistent starting point for adding specialized user interface elements.

Creating a Data Entry Template

The data entry Web form template does not add too much more to the existing static content template. Create a new HTML page named *FormTemplate.htm*. The only item really added is another nested table within the center of the static content space. This new table has the following properties: two columns, three rows, 80-percent width, and a 0 border size. The two columns will contain the field labels and data entry controls, so add two additional placeholders to the first row. The specific dimensions of the inserted table are completely arbitrary and should be consistent with your corporate Web site's formatting. Figure 7-5 shows the data entry template created for the IssueTracker application.

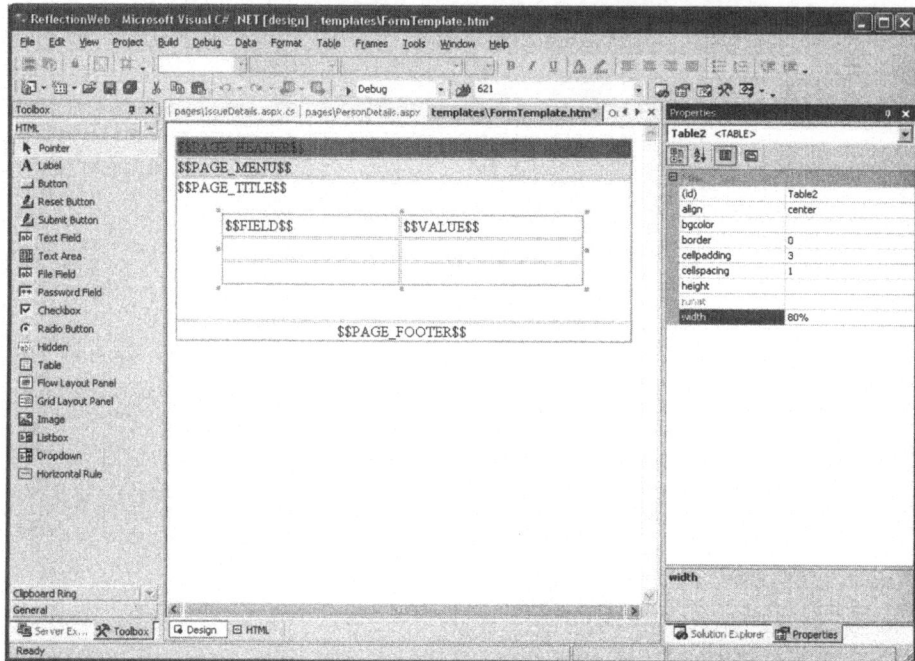

Figure 7-5. Creating the data entry template

Creating a Web Form from a Template

After producing the foundation form templates, it is time to put them into action and create application Web forms. In the Solution Explorer, select the pages folder under the IssueTracker_WebUI project. Select Add ➤ Add Web Form from the context menu. Enter *IssueDetails.aspx* as the new filename. When the empty Web form appears in the Visual Studio .NET form designer, click the HTML tab at the bottom.

To apply an existing template pattern, open the FormTemplate.html file and click the HTML tab button at the bottom. Select the entire HTML text from top

to bottom and copy it to the Clipboard. Return to the new IssueDetails.aspx
HTML view and paste the Clipboard contents to replace all the HTML beginning
with (and including) the following line:

```
<!DOCTYPE HTML PUBLIC "-//W3C//DTD HTML 4.0 Transitional//EN" >
```

Next, return to the design view of the IssueDetails.aspx Web form. The new
Web form should appear just as the data entry template. With the Web form
structure now in place, begin adding controls associated with Issue business
object. Table 7-1 summarizes what data entry controls should appear down the
right column of the Web form and their related control IDs.

Table 7-1. User Interface Controls in the IssueDetails.aspx Page

MATCHING LABEL	CONTROL TYPE	CONTROL ID
Entry Date:	TextBox	Issue_EntryDate
Issue ID:	TextBox	Issue_IssueID
Type:	DropDownList	Issue_TypeID
Status:	DropDownList	Issue_StatusID
Priority:	DropDownList	Issue_PriorityID
Summary:	TextBox	Issue_Summary
Description:	TextBox	Issue_Description
OK	Button	btnOK
Cancel	Button	btnCancel

You should name the control IDs consistently. Because these controls will
be later bound to the Issue business object, each data entry control ID should be
prefixed with *Issue_*. The sizes of the data entry controls should also match the
expected data. Figure 7-6 shows the resulting Web form.

To test this page, select it as the start page for IssueTracker_WebUI. Next,
select this project as the startup project for the entire solution and then start the
debugger. The new IssueDetails Web form should appear without any real functionality. The next step is to enable this form to display and capture dynamic data.

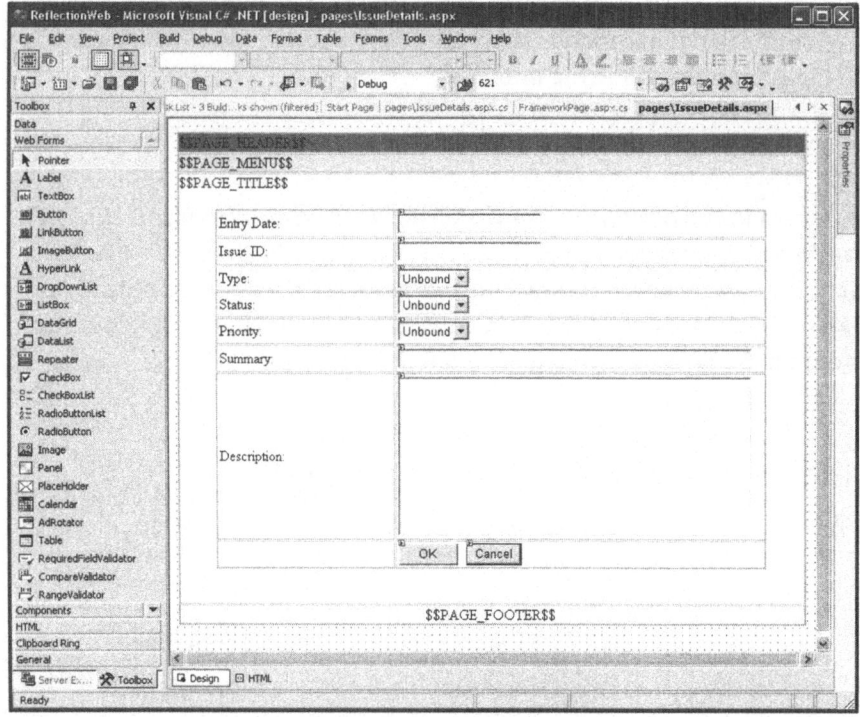

Figure 7-6. The completed IssueDetails.aspx Web form

Adding Dynamic Data to Web Forms

Web forms are dynamic Web pages that are compiled on the server and that return HTML code to the requesting client Web browser. Several Web forms with controls and dynamic content that interact with a user make up a Web application. Web forms are divided into two separate code entities: presentation code and functional code. The presentation code implements the visual aspect of a Web form, such as where text, images, and controls are placed within a form and how they are formatted. The functional code implements the functional aspect of the Web form, such as how controls interact with the user and each other. Understanding both code entities is essential to building successful .NET enterprise applications.

Exposing the Business Facade Project

The Visual C# Simple Distributed Application solution created in Chapter 1, "Introducing .NET and Enterprise Architecture," includes a Business Facade project. The purpose of the Business Facade project is to abstract the underlying business and data services. The presentation layer of an application should not include any references to the Data Access, System Frameworks, or any business process–related projects. Rather, the presentation layer should only reference the Business Rules and Business Facade projects. Applications need to access the Business Rules project to access the business objects definitions. Applications need to access the Business Facade project to access the underlying data, system, and business services.

The reason for the abstraction via the Business Facade project is two-fold. First, insulating the application from its implementation allows for greater flexibility in changes. Significant changes to the Data Access component can occur without significant impact to the application. Of course, there are limitations. Renaming or drastically changing data structures used in data binding operations will break application functionality. However, low-level changes to the database and table structure in most cases will not impact the application. Another reason for such abstraction is application flexibility. Keeping the Business Facade project presentation agnostic allows for easy migration to different applications. Desktop and mobile applications can access underlying services just as easily as Web applications. To accomplish this, it is important to not include any presentation-specific information in the Business Facade project, including references to a Web session or Registry settings.

The IssueTracker application implements three classes that serve as middle ground between the application and the underlying functionality: IssueManager, UserManager, and ReferenceDataManager.

The IssueManager class is a simple interface that prevents the application— whether it is a Web, desktop, or mobile application—from knowing where the Issue data resides initially. It simply provides methods to get one or more Issue objects or to save a new Issue object. The IssueManager class includes the necessary namespace references to the Data Access project and interacts with the BusinessObjectManager to get or set data. Listing 7-3 shows the implementation of the IssueManager class and its member methods. All methods interact with the BusinessObjectManager, which sets and gets data from the database with the help of stored procedures.

Listing 7-3. Abstracting Issue Set and Get Functions with the IssueManager Class

```
public class IssueManager
{
    private BusinessObjectManager _ObjectManager = new BusinessObjectManager();

    public IssueManager()
    {
    }

    public void SaveIssue( Issue argIssue )
```

```
    {
        _ObjectManager.Insert( argIssue );
    }

    public Issue GetIssue( int intIssueID )
    {
            Issue objIssue = new Issue();

            _ObjectManager.SelectOne( objIssue, intIssueID );
            return objIssue;
    }

    public IssueCollection GetAllIssues()
    {
        IssueCollection objIssueCollection = new IssueCollection();

        _ObjectManager.SelectAll( objIssueCollection );
        return objIssueCollection;
    }
}
```

The UserManager class performs a similar task but for the User object. Its only public method, GetUser, takes basic information about a person, validates their credentials, and returns a populated User object. You can change the underlying UserObjectManager class to validate credentials against values in the database rather than within Active Directory. Such a drastic change in implementation has no impact upon the application as long as the User business object was not altered. Listing 7-4 shows the implementation of the UserManager class and its member methods. A single method is exposed, GetUser, that takes a username and a password as parameters, validates them, and returns a populated User object.

Listing 7-4. Abstracting User Set and Get Methods with the UserManager Class

```
public class UserManager
{
    private UserObjectManager _ObjectManager = new UserObjectManager();

    public UserManager()
    {
    }

    public User GetUser( string strEmailAddress, string strPassword )
    {
```

```
        User objUser = null;

        objUser = _ObjectManager.ValidateLoginWithProfile( strEmailAddress,
            strPassword );

        return objUser;
    }
}
```

Finally, the ReferenceDataManager initializes and exposes parts of the DataComponent object. Three methods expose DataTable structures that are populated by the DataComponent object, making them available for data binding functions. Listing 7-5 shows the implementation of the ReferenceDataManager class. All get methods return DataTables that can be bound between the Web form controls and the DataComponent object.

Listing 7-5. Abstracting Reference Data Retrieval with the ReferenceDataManager Class

```
public class ReferenceDataManager
{
    DataComponent _AppDataComponent;

    public ReferenceDataManager()
    {
        _AppDataComponent = new DataComponent();
    }

    public DataTable GetIssueTypes()
    {
        return _AppDataComponent.ReferenceDataSet.Val_IssueType;
    }

    public DataTable GetPriorities()
    {
        return _AppDataComponent.ReferenceDataSet.Val_Priority;
    }

    public DataTable GetStatuses()
    {
        return _AppDataComponent.ReferenceDataSet.Val_Status;
    }
}
```

Applying Standard Data Binding

Data binding is a mechanism within the .NET Framework that enables form fields to establish a connection with any data collection. A form control, such as a DropDownList, can reference a data collection, such as a DataSet object, and auto-populate the control with the values within the collection. This frees the developer from implementing code that first retrieves the values from a collection, iterates through them, and then individually inserts them to the DropDownList control.

Adding Reference Data Binding

Adding data binding to a Web form requires changes to the code-behind page for the Web form. To set the connection between the DropDownList control within the Web form and the reference data, specify the DataSource, DataTextField, and DataValueField properties. Then, invoke the DataBind method to establish the connection. Listing 7-6 shows the code behind the IssueDetails.aspx page. A class member points to the ReferenceDataManager object. Next, the Page_Load method uses that object reference to establish data bindings to three different form controls. For each control, three properties are set. First, the DataSource property points to the data collection. Next, the DataTextField points to display values within the data collection. Finally, the DataValueField property points to the values within the data collection that match the display values. Once all properties are set, the DataBind method triggers the binding process.

Listing 7-6. Binding Web Form Controls to Reference DataTable Objects

```
public class IssueDetails : System.Web.UI.Page
{
    ReferenceDataManager _DataManager = new ReferenceDataManager();

    private void Page_Load(object sender, System.EventArgs e)
    {
        Issue_TypeID.DataSource = _DataManager.GetIssueTypes();
        Issue_TypeID.DataTextField = "TypeLabel";
        Issue_TypeID.DataValueField = "TypeID";

        Issue_StatusID.DataSource = _DataManager.GetStatuses();
        Issue_StatusID.DataTextField = "StatusLabel";
        Issue_StatusID.DataValueField = "StatusID";

        Issue_PriorityID.DataSource = _DataManager.GetPriorities();
        Issue_PriorityID.DataTextField = "PriorityLabel";
```

```
        Issue_PriorityID.DataValueField = "PriorityID";

        Page.DataBind();

        return;
    }
}
```

At runtime, the Web form will initialize and the Page_Load method will establish the data binding. The result is that the three specified DropDownList controls will automatically fill with data from the bound table. Given the relative ease involved in binding list-related controls to data tables, enterprise applications should make the greatest effort to externalize all list data within the database rather than hard-coded within the Web form itself. The result will pay off in terms of greater customization and possible localization.

Adding Application Data Binding

In the case of reference data binding, DropDownList controls were bound to DataTable objects that were populated by the DataAccess project and exposed by the Business Facade project. You can also establish data binding between more complex user interface elements, such as a DataGrid control and a business object collection. In Listing 7-7, the IssueSummary.aspx page populates a DataGrid control with Issue objects retrieved by the BusinessObjectManager class.

Listing 7-7. Data Binding a DataGrid to a Custom Business Object Collection

```
public class IssueSummary : System.Web.UI.Page
{
    protected System.Web.UI.WebControls.DataGrid gridIssues;

    private IssueManager _Issues = new IssueManager();

    private void Page_Load(object sender, System.EventArgs e)
    {
        gridIssues.DataSource = _Issues.GetAllIssues();
        gridIssues.DataBind();

        return;
    }
}
```

The Page_Load method populates the DataGrid control with the contents of an object inheriting from the BusinessObjectCollection class. In this case, the control displays all Issue objects stored in the Dat_Issue table. The BusinessObjectCollection class makes this possible because it implements the IEnumerable interface. The only problem remaining is that the DataGrid control is not properly formatted, and all Issue object fields are displayed. The next step is to apply formatting within the form designer. Open the IssueSummary.aspx, select the DataGrid control, and select PropertyBuilder from its context menu. The PropertyBuilder will display. First, select the Columns tab page on the left. Next, uncheck the Create Columns Automatically at Run Time option. Finally, format the DataGrid by adding Bound Column from the Available Columns list to the Selected Columns list. For each column, specify a column header for the grid and a data field from which to load. In Figure 7-7, the first column added is a Bound Column with an Issue ID header label. The actual row data for this column will be pulled from the IssueID property of the business object. You can do more formatting, such as alternating row colors and custom fonts, within the other tab pages.

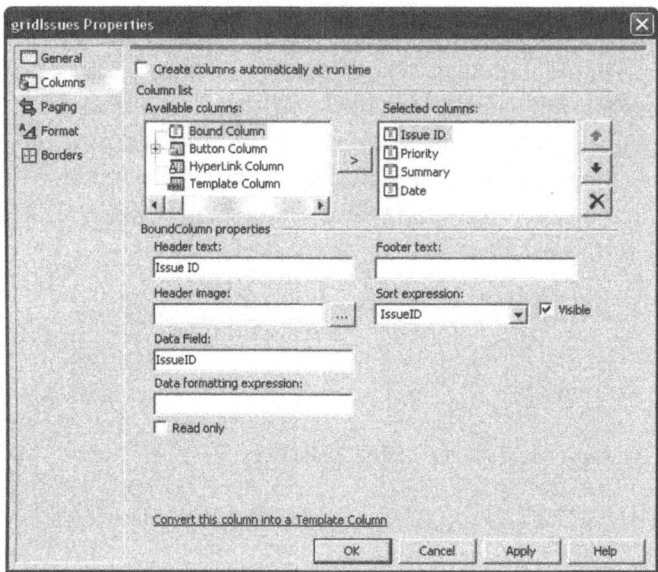

Figure 7-7. Setting DataGrid properties within the form designer

The result is a properly formatted DataGrid control that is bound to a custom business object collection. Figure 7-8 shows the completed IssueSummary.aspx Web form. It has additional formatting, such as row alignment and fonts, to blend with the rest of the Web application.

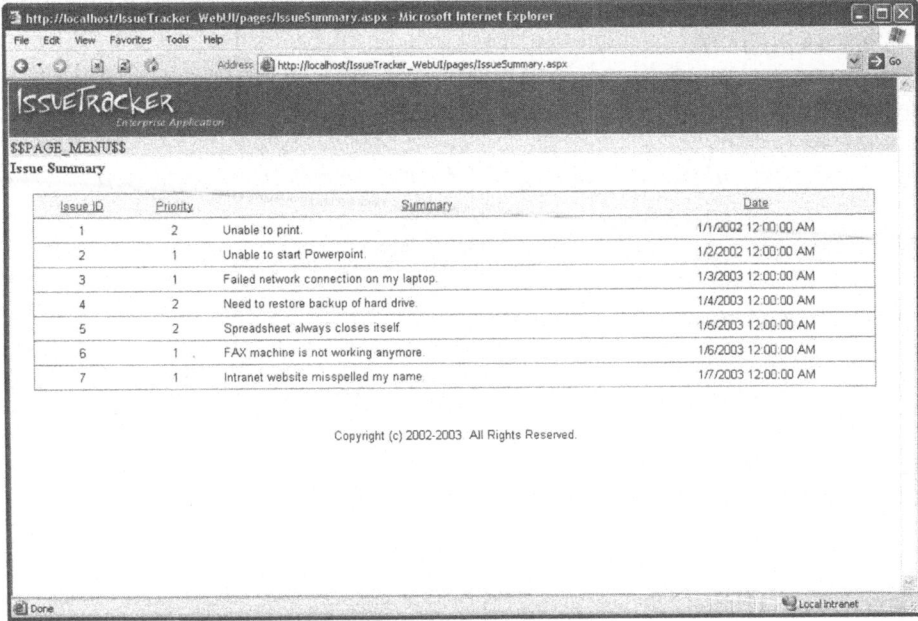

Figure 7-8. Displaying dynamic data in a DataGrid control using data binding

Applying Business Object Reflection

Another option for displaying dynamic data within a Web form is to implement a reflection-based data binding system. This approach works by using reflection methods to examine a specific business object and set form controls with matching IDs. Implementing reflection-based data binding is a two-step process. First, you must implement the functionality that examines a business object and sets control values. Second, you create and modify Web forms to use this functionality.

Creating the Reflection Page

There are many different ways to implement reflection-based data binding. The IssueTracker application implements this in the new object ReflectionPage. ReflectionPage inherits from the System.Web.UI.Page class and is able to easily interact with all child controls placed into any derived child pages.

To begin, add a new class file named *ReflectionPage.cs* to the WebUI project. The new class file will require a namespace reference to the Business Rules project as well as System.Reflection, System.Web.UI, and System.Web.UI.WebControls. There are three different parts to the ReflectionPage object. First, a private

BusinessObject variable serves as the source of reflection data. Second, a property accessor method exposes that business object. Third, the ReflectBusinessObject sets form control values based upon business object values. Listing 7-8 outlines the complete class.

Listing 7-8. Dynamically Populating Web Form Controls Using Reflection

```
public class ReflectionPage : System.Web.UI.Page
{
    private BusinessObject _SourceObject;

    public BusinessObject BusinessObject
    {
        get { return _SourceObject; }
        set { _SourceObject = value; }
    }

    public void ReflectBusinessObject()
    {
        string strObjectPrefix;
        string strObjectValue;
        string strFieldName;
        Type objType;
        Type controlType;
        PropertyInfo propObject;

        try
        {
            objType = _SourceObject.GetType();
            strObjectPrefix = objType.FullName.Substring(
                objType.FullName.IndexOf(".") + 1 ) + "_";

            //iterate through all controls on the page
            foreach( Control controlChild in Page.Controls[1].Controls )
            {
                if( controlChild.ClientID != null )
                {
                    if( controlChild.ClientID.StartsWith( strObjectPrefix ) )
                    {
                        //get the property value matching the control name
                        controlType = controlChild.GetType();

                        //get the field name
```

```
            strFieldName = controlChild.ClientID.Substring(
                controlChild.ClientID.IndexOf( "_" ) + 1 );

            //get the text value
            propObject = objType.GetProperty( strFieldName );
            strObjectValue = propObject.GetValue( _SourceObject,
                null ).ToString();

            //set the textbox control

            if( controlType.Name.CompareTo( "TextBox" ) == 0 )
            {
                ((TextBox)controlChild).Text = strObjectValue;
            }

            if( controlType.Name.CompareTo( "DropDownList" ) == 0
)

            {
                ((DropDownList)controlChild).SelectedIndex =
                    int.Parse(strObjectValue);
            }
            }
            }
            }
        }
        catch( Exception x )
        {
        }

        return;
    }
}
```

The ReflectBusinessObject method does all of the real work. It begins by retrieving information about the business object (specifically, its data type). Next, the method iterates through all of the child controls on the Web form. If a form control has a valid ID, then it is examined more closely. The control ID must have a prefix that matches the business object's data type. From there, the control ID suffix tries to match specific attributes defined within the business object. If it finds a match, then it examines the form control's type to set its display value appropriately. TextBox controls have their Text properties assigned while DropDownList controls have their SelectedIndex property assigned.

NOTE *Because naming conventions insist that form controls have IDs that match the business object name and attributes, the method runs quickly. Without such naming conventions, this method could also access a collection of business object and study each one until a match is found. The cost would be a tremendous performance impact.*

Turning Web Forms into Reflection Pages

Because the ReflectionPage object inherits from the Page object, just as any other Web form does, any new or existing Web form can become a reflected page by simply changing its class definition to inherit from ReflectionPage rather than Page. Listing 7-9 tests the IssueDetails.aspx page by changing the Web form into a reflection page and setting its business object to a test Issue object.

Listing 7-9. Inheriting from ReflectionPage Instead of the Page Base Class

```
public class IssueDetails : ReflectionPage //System.Web.UI.Page
{
    private void Page_Load(object sender, System.EventArgs e)
    {
        Issue myIssue = new Issue();
        myIssue.Summary = "This is test summary text.";
        myIssue.Description = "This is a detailed test description.";
        myIssue.EntryDate = new DateTime();
        myIssue.Priority = 3;
        myIssue.TypeID = 3;

        BusinessObject = myIssue;

        ReflectBusinessObject();
    }
}
```

By changing the base class of the Web form to the new ReflectionPage class and specifying a new Issue business object to populate from, the IssueDetails.aspx page renders itself, as shown in Figure 7-9.

There are many approaches for displaying dynamic data in a Web form. Integrated data binding and reflection both have their own advantages. Selecting the appropriate implementation depends upon the purpose of the form.

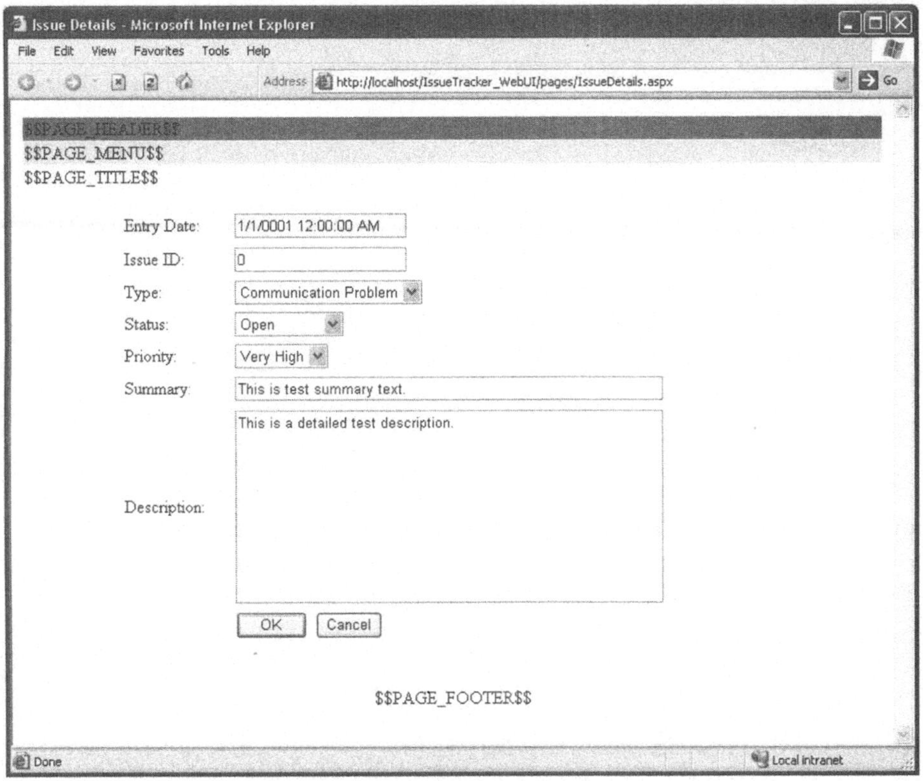

Figure 7-9. Displaying dynamic Web form data using reflection

Managing User Session Data

The session stores temporary application variables that need to be shared between different Web forms within an application. Because the server stores a separate instance of session data for each user connection, it is important to store information in the session selectively. As more data is stored into the session, its footprint grows, slowing down the performance of the Web server.

Writing Values to the Session

Any type of data object can be stored in the session by one Web form and accessed by another. The only limitation is that the object stored has a Serializable attribute. In Listing 7-10, you can modify the Business Facade layer that validates user login against Active Directory to take the returned User object and save it as session data. When the user enters their credentials and clicks the OK button, the user invokes the btnOK_Click method.

Listing 7-10. Storing a User Object to the Session

```
private void btnOK_Click(object sender, System.EventArgs e)
{
    User objUser = new User();

    objUser = UserManager.GetUser( txtEmailAddress.Text, txtPassword.Text );
    Session.Add( "USER_OBJECT", objUser );

    Response.Redirect( "IssueSummary.aspx", true );

    return;
}
```

This method invokes the GetUser method, passing the user's entered credentials. If the login is successful, the UserManager class returns a User object filled with various user details. This User object is stored into the session for later reference. At any time, another page can access the session and immediately access the user's profile.

Reading Values from the Session

Reading data saved to the application session is as easy as storing it. As Listing 7-11 outlines, the Page_Load method of any other Web form can create a new User object and assign it to a value pulled from the session. Then, the User object is used as needed (in this case, to display a greeting).

Listing 7-11. Retrieving a User Object from the Session

```
private void Page_Load(object sender, System.EventArgs e)
{
    try
    {
        User objUser = (User)Session["USER_OBJECT"];
        lblGreeting.Text = "Welcome to IssueTracker, " + objUser.Firstname;
    }
    catch( Exception x )
    {
    }

    return;
}
```

Validating User Data Entry

You cannot assume that the application user will enter data into form fields as expected. In nearly every case, you will need to perform some field validation against every user entry field. The remaining question is where and when that validation occurs.

Client-side scripting languages, such as JavaScript and VBScript, have gained popularity for their ability to execute field validation code on the client side within the Web browser. This offers instant data validation as data is entered. Events that validate user entry trigger the moment that focus switches from one form field to the next. The only problem is that a variety of Web browser providers implement their scripting support differently, almost ensuring that script code targeted for one browser will not work in another.

The question then becomes, why must field validation be performed on the client side? When it works properly, it is nice to have that instant field-level validation. However, the client side might not be the right place for that. This is where postbacks are helpful.

Validating Data in Web Form Postbacks

Web form postbacks validate field data as it is entered—on the server side. You can enable form field postback by setting a control's AutoPostBack property to true. When enabled, any change in a control's value results in a postback event handled by the Page_Load method.

The benefit is that client-side scripting does not need to target one or more Web browser platforms because it is completely avoided. Although validation is occurring on the server, it appears to the user that it is occurring locally and presents the appearance of a more interactive user interface.

The cost is performance and flexibility. If a trip to the Web server is necessary for each field to be validated, then a dozen validated fields means a dozen requests from the server. This additional processing load to the server did not exist before. Also, the busier the server becomes, the slower the page will appear to the application user. Also, because the Page_Load method handles the postbacks, it is important to separate the logic that initializes the page from the logic that validates a form field; otherwise, page initialization logic might be called in every case. The IsPostBack is an important property to check while handling page loads:

```
private void Page_Load(object sender, System.EventArgs e)
{
    if( IsPostBack )
    {
        //perform page validation logic
```

```
    }
    else
    {
        //perform page initialization logic
    }
    return;
}
```

Although Web form postbacks keep validation code on the server, where it should be, it is still not in the best place. You should place validation code within the business object that internally represents the data.

Validating Data in Business Objects

The optimal location for field validation logic is within the business objects that are filled in response to user input. Rather than validate field by field, all validation should occur at once when the user submits the page for processing. The page's submit handler should instantiate a new business object, populate it with the user-supplied data, and then invoke its Validate method. Listing 7-12 outlines this process by implementing an event handler for the OK button in the new Issue form. If any error messages are generated, then they are displayed within a Label control in red. Otherwise, the data is committed and the user is redirected to another page.

Listing 7-12. Web Form Values Assigned to a Matching Business Object

```
private void btnOK_Click(object sender, System.EventArgs e)
{
    Issue objIssue = new Issue();

    //assign business object properties
    objIssue.Description = Issue_Description.Text;
    objIssue.EntryDate = Issue_EntryDate.Text;
    objIssue.PriorityID = Issue_PriorityID.SelectedValue;
    objIssue.StatusID = Issue_StatusID.SelectedValue;
    objIssue.Summary = Issue_Summary.Text;
    objIssue.TypeID = Issue_TypeID.SelectedValue;

    //validate business object
    lblError.Text = objIssue.Validate();
    if( lblError.Text.Length == 0 )
        Response.Redirect( "IssueSummary.aspx", true );
```

```
    return;
}
```

The business object's Validate method, outlined in Listing 7-13, performs field-by-field validation of its properties. A string that appends all discovered errors is returned to the caller.

Listing 7-13. The Business Object Implementing a Validate Method That Checks the Values

```
public string Validate()
{
    string strErrorMessage = "";

    if( _TypeID == 0 )
        strErrorMessage += "Issue Type is not set. ";

    if( _StatusID == 0 )
        strErrorMessage += "Issue Status is not set. ";

    if( _PriorityID == 0 )
        strErrorMessage += "Issue Priority is not set. ";

    if( _Summary.Length == 0 )
        strErrorMessage += "Issue Summary has no value. ";
    if( _Summary.Length > 64 )
        strErrorMessage += "Issue Summary is too long. ";

    if( _Description.Length == 0 )
        strErrorMessage += "Issue Description has no value. ";
    if( _Description.Length > 64 )
        strErrorMessage += "Issue Description is too long. ";

    return strErrorMessage;
}
```

The reason for placing validation logic within the business object is to minimize errors and maximize reuse. Because the business object becomes a central location for validating data, multiple Web forms do not need to implement it separately. This reduces errors in that all pages capturing this data will apply the same validation logic. Also, because validation is performed in the business logic and not the Web form code-behind page, it can be reused by other non-Web applications targeting the desktop and mobile platforms.

Applying Web User Controls

Another component of accelerated enterprise application development is the reuse of user interface elements. User interface reuse also yields the same benefits that come from using templates: consistency, reduction of errors, and faster development. Begin by looking at the application's User Interface Specification (UIS). A properly designed enterprise application will include a UIS that sketches or "mocks up" the entire application. It should include every form control on every Web form. It should describe the form controls in good detail, such as control names, types, labels, valid values, actions, and behavior when interacting with various roles. The IssueTracker enterprise application implements both static and dynamic Web user controls.

Packaging Static Content

Examples of packaging static content into Web user controls include the application header and footer. These two user interface elements will appear within every page of the Web application. These two items could easily be coded into the Web form itself. If the application name or version number changes, then there is a likely possibility that every Web form will need to change in response.

To address this possibility, open the Solution Explorer and navigate to the controls folder within the WebUI project. Select Add ➤ Add Web User Control from the context menu. Enter *AppHeader.ascx* for the filename and click OK. The form designer displays an empty Web form. For the IssueTracker application, just a simple graphic is sufficient for the application header. After creating and saving the header image as a GIF file, drag an Image control from the Toolbox and drop it into the AppHeader.ascx page. Then, point its ImageUrl property to the location of the new GIF file. The result looks something like Figure 7-10.

After you create the application header's user control, you can compile and use it. Rebuild the WebUI project and then open the IssueDetails.aspx Web form. Drag the AppHeader Web user control straight from the Solution Explorer and drop it into the Web form, replacing the $$PAGE_HEADER$$ marker. In the form designer, the new header appears as a plain box marked as *User Control—AppHeader1*. To see the new header in action, start the project and point to the IssueDetails.aspx page. Figure 7-11 illustrates the IssueDetails.aspx page with its new header control in place.

The same steps implement the footer control. A new file, AppFooter.aspx, implements static text as a Web user control. Web user controls nicely package any static content needed in multiple Web forms. As functional and useful as they are, Web user controls are even more beneficial for reused dynamic functionality.

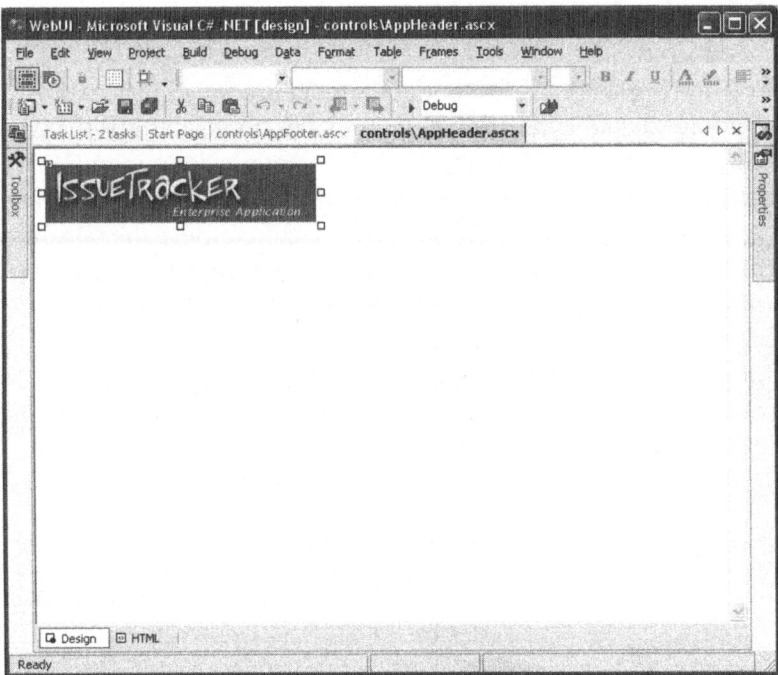

Figure 7-10. Creating the application header user control

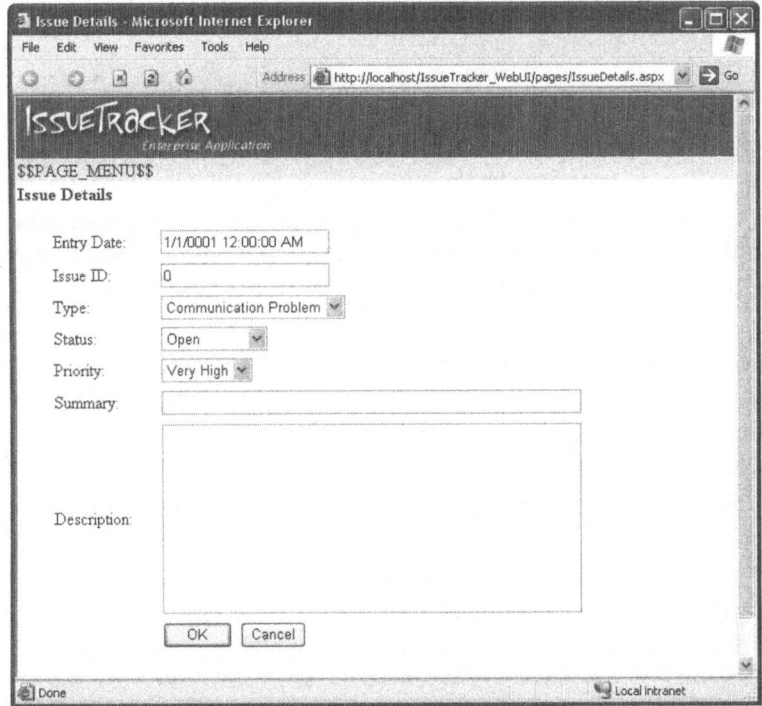

Figure 7-11. The IssueDetails.aspx page displaying its new header Web user control

Packaging Dynamic Functionality

Just as Web user controls package static content for reuse among multiple Web forms, they also package dynamic functionality. A great example of this is the Web application's menu. Because the .NET Framework does not provide a menu Web control, you need to implement one as a Web user control. To make things more interesting, this menu will also tap into the Session object to retrieve the person's role and enable only functions enabled for that role. Chapter 13, "Understanding .NET Security and Cryptography," goes into much deeper detail about handling user roles at the application level and the code level.

Begin by adding a new Web user control, AppMenu.ascx, to the controls folder within the WebUI project. In the empty form designer, place six LinkButton controls with the properties shown in Table 7-2.

Table 7-2. Properties of LinkButton Controls Placed into AppMenu.ascx

TEXT	ID	ENABLED
View Issue	lnkViewIssue	False
New Issue	lnkNewIssue	False
Edit Issue	lnkEditIssue	False
Delete Issue	lnkDeleteIssue	False
Help	lnkHelp	True
Logout	lnkLogout	True

After adding the controls outlined in Table 7-2, the AppMenu.ascx Web user control should look like Figure 7-12. For extra cosmetics, the figure shows a simple label control displaying the pipe character (|) between the LinkButton controls.

Next, you need to enable the AppMenu.asc Web user control. Open the code-behind document for the control to edit its Page_Load event handler. As Listing 7-14 outlines, the first step is to create a new User object instance and assign it to the values saved in the application's session. Next, the User object's role is evaluated. For added safety, the C# language does not permit automatic fall-through from one case to another. An explicit goto case must actively specify a fall-through. The reason for the case fall-through is that the IssueTracker security model defines roles with incremental permissions. In each case, the role with access to certain functionality simply enables the matching LinkButton control.

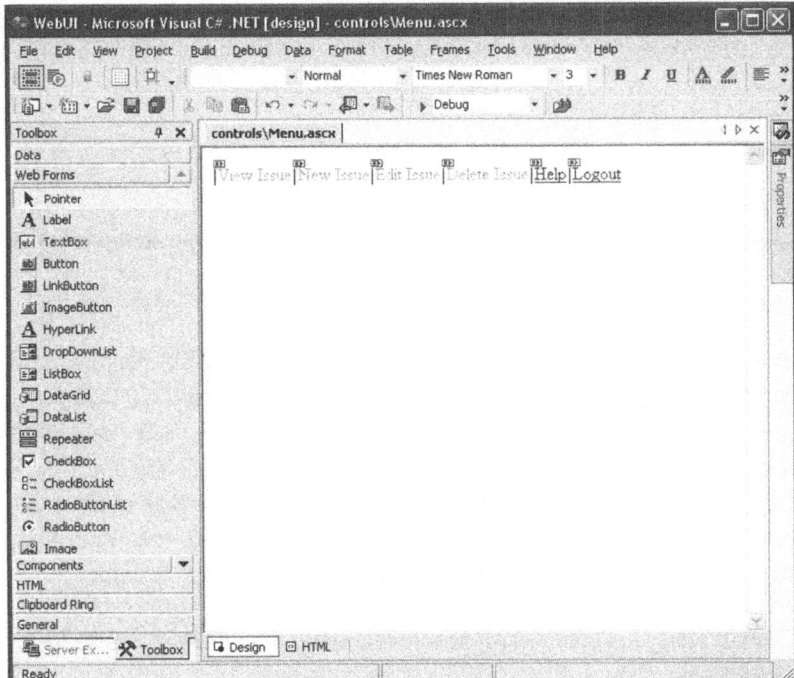

Figure 7-12. Implementing a role-based menu that dynamically enables options

Listing 7-14. Implementing the Page_Load Method of the AppMenu.ascx Control

```csharp
private void Page_Load(object sender, System.EventArgs e)
{
    // Put user code to initialize the page here
    User objUser = (User)Session["USER_OBJECT"];

    switch( objUser.UserRole )
    {
        case (int)User.UserRoleType.Administrator:
            lnkDeleteIssue.Enabled = true;
            goto case (int)User.UserRoleType.Manager;

        case (int)User.UserRoleType.Manager:
            lnkEditIssue.Enabled = true;
            goto case (int)User.UserRoleType.TypicalUser;

        case (int)User.UserRoleType.TypicalUser:
            lnkNewIssue.Enabled = true;
```

```
                lnkViewIssue.Enabled = true;
                goto case (int)User.UserRoleType.Guest;

            case (int)User.UserRoleType.Guest:
                break;
        }


    return;
}
```

Tying everything together, Listing 7-15 implements the btnOK_Click event handler for the AppLogin.aspx page. This method replaces Listing 7-12 and populates a new User object with data retrieved from the Business Facade project's UserManager class rather than the hard-coded sample data. As Listing 7-4 described earlier, the UserManager class works with other underlying classes to validate a person's credentials. When the User object is populated, it is added to the session and the Web form redirects to the IssueSummary.aspx page.

Listing 7-15. A New Event Handler to Validate Credentials and Save to the Session

```
private void btnOK_Click(object sender, System.EventArgs e)
{
    User objUser = new User();

    objUser = UserManager.GetUser( txtEmailAddress.Text, txtPassword.Text );
    Session.Add( "USER_OBJECT", objUser );
    Response.Redirect( "IssueSummary.aspx", true );

    return;
}
```

Figure 7-13 shows the completed IssueSummary.aspx page, complete with a header, footer, data-bound list, and role-based menu. The menu only displays links enabled by the role of the logged-in user. That role was assigned during application login in Listing 7-15 and validated when the menu control was loaded in Listing 7-14.

You can create any number of Web user controls to add to a project. The goal is to identify reuse of content and functionality across the entire Web application. Doing so immediately reduces the time it takes to build the application, reduces the number of errors found in the application, and increases user interface consistency.

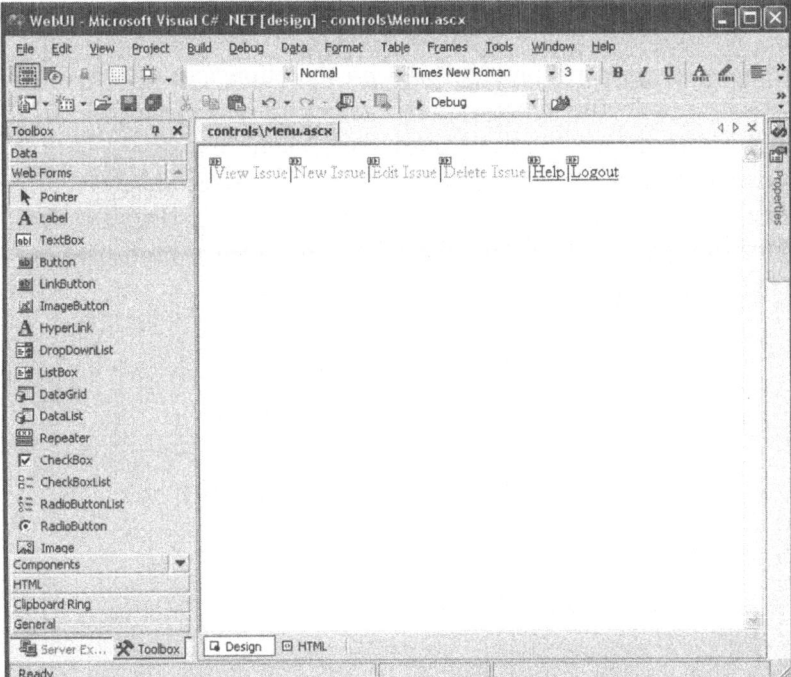

Figure 7-13. The completed IssueSummary.aspx page with the populated form controls

Summary

Building enterprise Web applications with the help of the .NET Framework yields benefits not seen before in traditional ASP, including rapid development, more powerful dynamic data rendering, and greater deployment flexibility. At the center of these benefits are agreed-upon standards, service abstraction, and data binding.

Standards that define how each Web form looks reduce errors and ensure consistency throughout the entire Web application. These standards can be published as HTML templates, which can then be copied and pasted into new Web forms as starting points. Other standards are more or less guidelines that specify whether client scripting is permitted and what amount or type of data can be stored in the session. Services abstraction, with the help of the Business Facade project, allows changes to the underlying data access to not interfere with the application code. Finally, data binding makes the creation of data-enabled Web forms even faster by setting control properties that point to collections. All of these elements come together to build fast, reliable Web applications in a timely manner.

The next chapter implements an enterprise presentation layer as a desktop application. Desktop applications have different strengths and weaknesses when compared to Web applications. One thing both have in common, however, is the need for a structured development framework that minimizes errors and encourages reuse. The next chapter presents a framework for rapid application development that incorporates forms inheritance, user controls, application configuration files, and dynamic access to assemblies.

Developing Desktop Applications

THIS CHAPTER DIVES into the world of building enterprise desktop applications using the .NET Framework. Building desktop applications is quite different from building Web applications, but the implementation of both is nearly identical within the Visual Studio .NET environment. This chapter begins by answering the question "When should I build a desktop application?" The chapter then presents a classical application design pattern that is formulated into a structured application framework to enable you to quickly build a scalable enterprise application. Next, the chapter shows examples that implement data binding and extend application usability. Finally, the chapter presents an approach to application internalization as well as a method for packaging system resources into a shared assembly.

Building a Desktop Application Framework

As the previous chapter demonstrated, a structured application framework can go a long way in accelerating application development, reducing errors, and encouraging reuse. The same concepts hold true for building desktop applications. Before organizing a desktop application framework, you need to answer the question "When is an application implemented as a desktop application rather than a Web application?"

Deciding to Build a Desktop Application

During the dot-com boom, this was a simple question to answer; no matter what your requirements were, you built a Web application. In reality, the answer to this question is in the product requirements. The requirements may not necessarily specify a Web platform vs. a desktop platform, but they should outline specific needs such as global accessibility and access to local system resources. These are often the two most important factors in deciding which platform to target.

Global accessibility is a requirement that needs to be broken into two different parts: connectivity and target platform. If global connectivity is defined as building an application that can be accessed by any user connected to the Internet, then either application type will suffice. Desktop applications can be just as Internet accessible as native Web applications. The real question is target platform. If it is known that the target platform is certainly a Microsoft Windows platform, then a desktop application is ideal. If it is completely unknown or known to be a non-Windows platform, then a native Web application is ideal.

Access to local system resources is the other deciding factor. If the application requirements outline a need to access resources, such as local data files, Registry settings, or Component Object Model (COM) objects, then a desktop application will be required. Desktop applications will also have the advantage of rendering more quickly without the latency that comes with parsing a text-based Hypertext Markup Language (HTML) document. In fact, separate threads of execution might be spawned to perform lengthy business processing without presenting the appearance of "locking up" the user interface.

Understanding the Model-View-Controller Architecture

The roots of the modern three-tier application architecture stem from a classic architecture known as the *Model-View-Controller (MVC) pattern*. This classic design pattern has often been used by applications that require multiple views of the same data. The MVC pattern is based on a clean separation of application elements into three specific categories: models, views, and controllers. The model represents the application data. The views display all or a portion of the model. The controllers handle events that impact the model or views.

Because of this separation, multiple views and controllers can interact with the same underlying model. Furthermore, you can add new types of views and controllers that integrate into the model without requiring changes to the model.

Events cause the controller to change the model, the view, or both. When a controller changes the model's data, all dependent views automatically update. Similarly, when a controller changes a view, the view pulls data from the model to refresh itself. Figure 8-1 illustrates the relationship between the model, the views, and the controller.

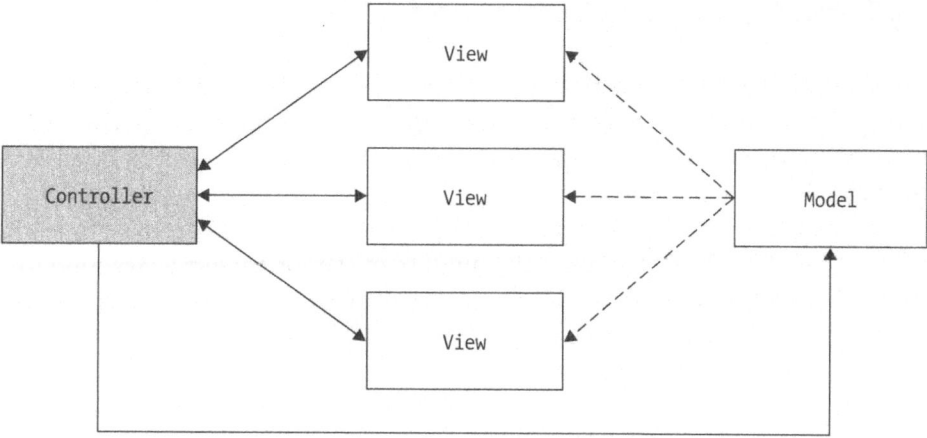

Figure 8-1. The relationships between the model, views, and controller

Defining the Application Model

The model abstracts application data and has the capability to notify views when its values change. It contains only the data and functionality that serves a specific purpose. If you need to model two groups of unrelated data and functionality, then you should create two separate models.

In the context of a desktop application, the Data Access project can represent the model. The data binding capabilities of the views can represent the ability for the model to notify connected views of changes.

Implementing the Application Views

The views display all or part of the model to the user and change in response to changes in the model. There can be multiple views of a model, with each view rendering the model differently. By definition, a view can also aggregate any number of child views.

In the context of a desktop application, you might implement views as windows. The granularity can even vary from a simple textbox control to a complete Windows form. A Multiple Document Interface (MDI) application serves as a nice application model to implement an MVC pattern because multiple child forms can represent application data differently.

Implementing the Application Controller

The controller is the means by which the user interacts with the views and model. The controller is responsible for mapping user action to application response. The model, views, and controller must be tightly bound by references to each other.

In the context of a desktop application, the controller is simply a collection of event handlers. You can create any number of event handlers to respond to user commands that result in either changes displayed within the user interface or changes to the application data.

Applying Multiple Document Interfaces

Although the Single Document Interface (SDI) is the most common approach to application layout, enterprise applications often require more flexibility to display multiple types of data at the same time.

The purpose of MDI applications is to display multiple documents to the user at the same time. Each document is displayed in its own child window, leaving the parent frame with the ability to switch focus between documents. Each document is also capable of displaying a different representation of the same data. One form might display application data in a table format while another document displays the same data in a chart. This application model lends itself well to the MVC pattern, which is founded upon hosting different views of the same model.

Creating the MDI Parent

The most important element of the MDI application is the MDI parent form. The parent form contains and provides space for all child forms. The child forms, in turn, display the various views of the application data.

You create the parent form like any other Windows form in the Visual Studio .NET environment. The difference is that the parent form must have its IsMDIContainer property set to True. The parent form is also the startup form for the application, containing the Main method. It should, therefore, also include the application menu and status bar controls. Figure 8-2 shows the IssueTracker main form implemented as an MDI container form.

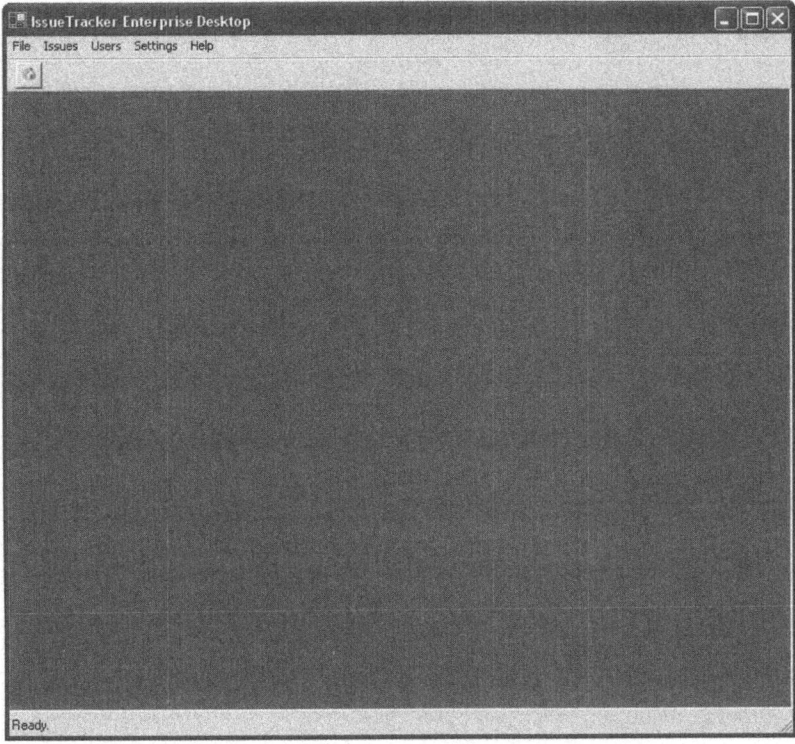

Figure 8-2. The IssueTracker main form and MDI container

Creating MDI Children

The next step in implementing an MDI application is to create one or more child forms. You create the child form like any other Windows form in the Visual Studio .NET environment. You can create any number of child forms to display application data differently and interact with the user.

The first form implements an All Issues view within the IssueTracker database, as shown in Figure 8-3. The simple form includes a single control (a list view control) that will display a variable number of rows in its details mode.

The FormIssueDetails form, shown in Figure 8-4, implements the details view for a specific issue. This form includes a larger number of controls, including labels, textboxes, and combo boxes.

After you create an MDI child form, you can display it within the parent form with only a few lines of code. Listing 8-1 demonstrates the initialization and display of an MDI child form within the FormMain_Load method of the parent container.

Figure 8-3. Displaying a summary collection within a list view control

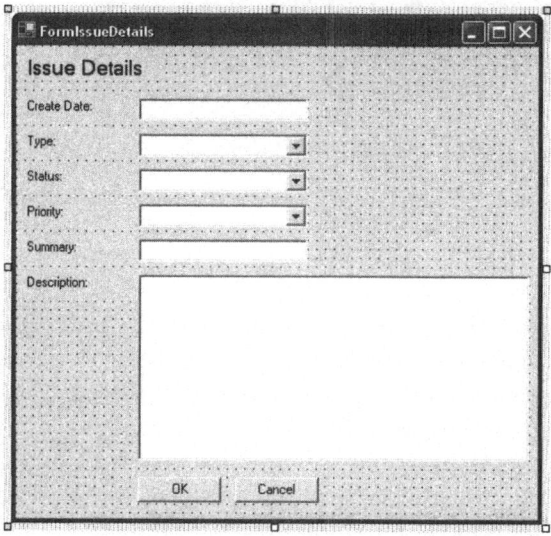

Figure 8-4. Displaying the details of an issue

Listing 8-1. Displaying a Child Form Within the MDI Parent

```
private void FormMain_Load( object sender, System.EventArgs e )
{
    FormIssueSummary dlgSummary = new FormIssueSummary();
    dlgSummary.MdiParent = this;
    dlgSummary.Show();

    return;
}
```

The code first instantiates a new instance of the FormIssueSummary class. After creating the form object, the code sets its MdiParent property to point to the main form and enables the Show method to be called to display the form. Figure 8-5 shows the result of the code as the child form is displayed within the parent.

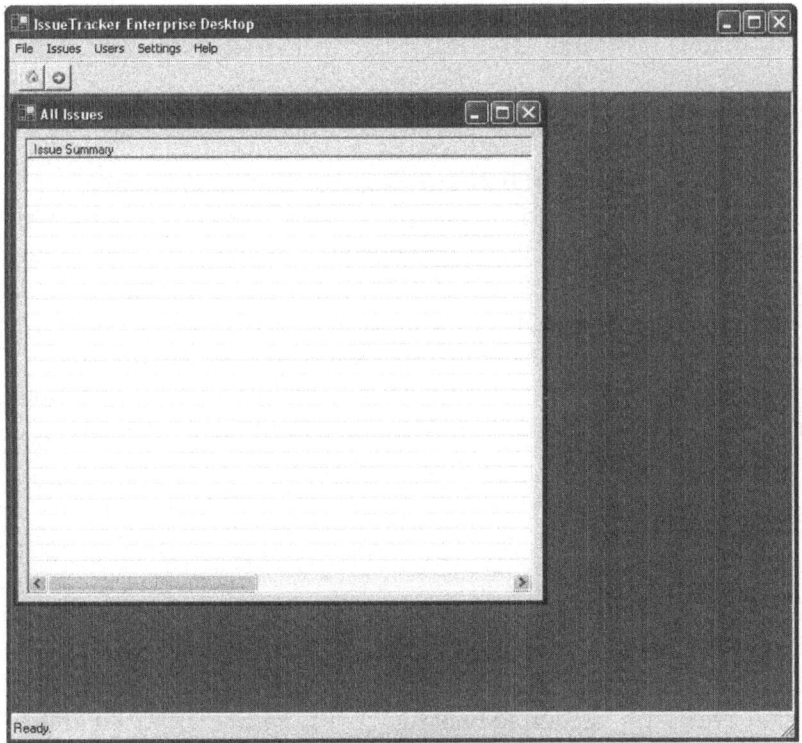

Figure 8-5. The IssueTracker main form and MDI container

NOTE *When an MDI parent form closes, each MDI child form generates a Closing event before the MDI parent is able to generate a Closing event. Clearing an MDI child's Closing event will not prevent the MDI parent's Closing event from being raised.*

Sharing Data Between MDI Children

Sharing data between forms is an eventual necessity with many different approaches. You should exchange data between forms as business objects managed by the Business Rules project.

You can pass business objects by value or by reference; choosing the right method will depend upon the application's needs. Passing business objects by value results is the most common and results in a separate local copy of the business object being created and used. Passing business objects by reference results in the exchange of a pointer to the original object. Changes made to the passed object result in changes to the original object.

Creating a Plug-in Framework

Applications implementing an MDI user interface can display any number of child forms. Therefore, there should not necessarily be a reason to limit the type of forms to only those packaged with the application. Creating a plug-in framework can extend the functionality of an enterprise far beyond its original intent. In many cases, supporting customization within an enterprise application further extends its reach and adoption rate. This is where the MVC architecture pulls everything together. The controller directs the application flow, the model retrieves and updates the data, and the view presents everything to the user.

Creating the Controller

The controller is the most complex element of an MVC architecture. Its responsibilities must include managing multiple viewers and exchanging business objects, all based on user interaction.

As Figure 8-6 illustrates, the implementation of the controller puts it in the middle of the application. Its function is based on configuration information that identifies what business objects and what actions trigger specific views to be displayed. For example, an Issue business object and a View action might display one form while a User object and a New action display a completely different form. This outlines a specific need for mapping the relationships between business objects, actions, and forms.

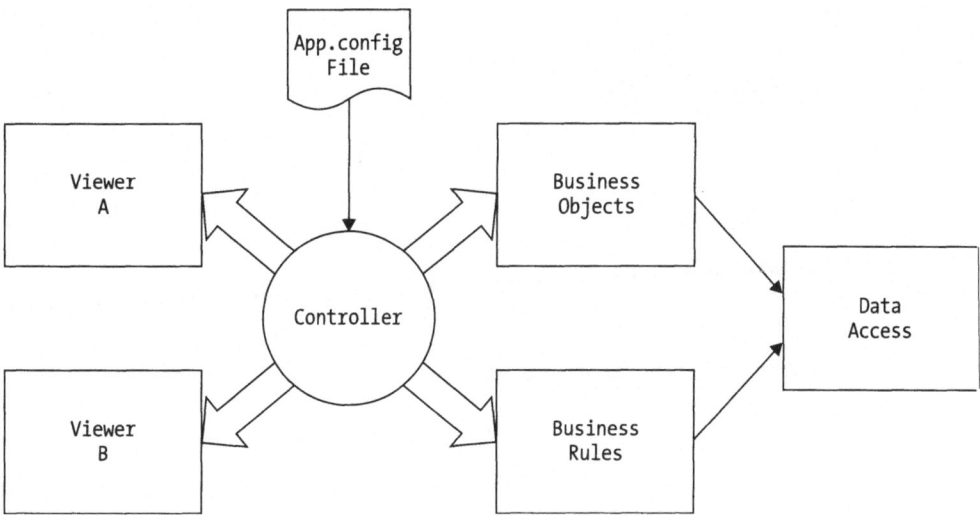

Figure 8-6. The role of the controller in an MVC architecture

Mapping Objects to Actions

The controller is only as strong as its mappings. To keep the controller flexible, it should not know any specifics about what business objects it is working with or which forms should be displayed. It should only know that a combination of business objects and actions results in the display of forms. It is expected that the forms will know what to do with the business objects they receive.

The first step is to add a new Class Library project to the IssueTracker solution, named *ApplicationFramework*. Controller-related code needs to reside in a separate assembly because references can only be made to .dll files, not .exe files. Because the controller will need to manage a mapping of objects and actions to forms, there needs to be a structure for capturing such information. Listing 8-2 outlines the ObjectMappingEntry class, which represents a single action mapping. The controller will manage an array of ObjectMappingEntry objects to select the correct form in response to user action.

Listing 8-2. The ObjectMappingEntry Class

```
public class ObjectMappingEntry
{
    string _Viewer;
    string _BusinessObjectName;
    Controller.ControllerActions _Action;

    public string Viewer
    {
```

```
            set
            {
                _Viewer = value;
            }
            get
            {
                return _Viewer;
            }
        }

        public string BusinessObjectName
        {
            set
            {
                _BusinessObjectName = value;
            }
            get
            {
                return _BusinessObjectName;
            }
        }

        public Controller.ControllerActions Action
        {
            set
            {
                _Action = value;
            }
            get
            {
                return _Action;
            }
        }
    }

}
```

The ObjectMappingEntry class is essentially a simple structure of three data members and supporting get and set accessor methods. Each data member is needed to help the controller take action. The BusinessObjectName property specifies which business object this mapping entry applies to, such as Issue or UserCollection. The Action property is based on the ControllerActions enumeration defined within the Controller object. It specifies which action is being taken. The Viewer property simply labels which MDI child form needs to be displayed in response to a specific business object and action.

NOTE *Because viewers may potentially be loaded from foreign assemblies, the Viewer property must be fully qualified with its namespace, such as WinUI.FormIssueSummary.*

Implementing the Controller

With the ObjectMappingEntry class defined, you can implement the Controller class to take action based on entry values. Listing 8-3 outlines the code that implements the Controller object and directs the application flow based on user actions.

Listing 8-3. The Controller Object

```
public class Controller
{
    //definition of action types
    public enum ControllerActions
    {
        New = 1,
        View = 2,
        Edit = 3,
        Delete = 4
    }


    //reference to the controller MDI parent
    static private Form _ParentForm;

    //container for all of the individual object mappings
    static ArrayList _ObjectMappings = new ArrayList();


    //property accessor to set parent form
    public Form ParentForm
    {
        set
        {
            _ParentForm = value;
        }
    }
```

```
public Controller()
{
    //hard-code new issue mapping
    ObjectMappingEntry entry;

    entry = new ObjectMappingEntry();
    entry.Action = ControllerActions.View;
    entry.BusinessObjectName = "IssueCollection";
    entry.Viewer = "WinUI.FormIssueSummary";
    _ObjectMappings.Add( entry );

    entry = new ObjectMappingEntry();
    entry.Action = ControllerActions.View;
    entry.BusinessObjectName = "Issue";
    entry.Viewer = "WinUI.FormIssueDetails";
    _ObjectMappings.Add( entry );

    entry = new ObjectMappingEntry();
    entry.Action = ControllerActions.New;
    entry.BusinessObjectName = "Issue";
    entry.Viewer = "WinUI.FormIssueDetails";
    _ObjectMappings.Add( entry );

    return;
}


public static void Process( object argObject, ControllerActions argAction )
{
    //based on mapping, display specific form
    foreach( ObjectMappingEntry objMapping in _ObjectMappings )
    {
        //find the right business object
        if( argObject.GetType().Name.CompareTo(
            objMapping.BusinessObjectName ) == 0 )
        {
            //find the right action
            if( objMapping.Action == argAction )
            {
                //start the viewer
                Type typeViewer = Assembly.GetExecutingAssembly().GetType(
                    objMapping.Viewer );
```

```
        Form formViewer = (Form)Activator.CreateInstance(typeViewer);
        formViewer.MdiParent = _ParentForm;
        formViewer.Show();

        break;
      }
    }
  }
  return;
}
}
```

First, the Controller class implements the ControllerActions enumeration. This describes what action is being taken by the user against a specific business object or collection. In most cases, New, View, Edit, and Delete is sufficient, but you can add additional actions as necessary.

Next, the Controller's properties are implemented. The ParentForm property specifies the MDI parent that contains the controller. This is necessary so that the Controller can assign the MDI parent to new child forms that are created and displayed. The _ObjectMappings array is a collection of ObjectMappingEntry items. When the Controller is asked to take action, this ArrayList will be searched for an applicable mapping to use.

Next, the code implements the Controller's class constructor. This is currently where hard-coded object-action mappings are being added. Later, these mappings will migrate into an external configuration file. Table 8-1 describes three object mappings.

Table 8-1. Sample Summary of Object to Action to Forms

BUSINESS OBJECT	CONTROLLER ACTION	CHILD FORM
IssueCollection	View	WinUI.FormIssueSummary
Issue	View	WinUI.FormIssueDetails
Issue	New	WinUI. FormIssueDetails

Finally, the code implements the Process method to take the action. This method accepts two parameters: a business object to process and an action to take. The method begins by iterating through the ArrayList, inspecting object mappings. The business object's data type compares against business object labels stored within the ObjectMappingEntry. If it finds a matching object name,

Chapter 8

it also checks the ControllerActions for a match. If it also finds a matching action, then the Controller object can display the appropriate form.

Again, the Controller object has no awareness of any specific form, and there is no FormIssueSummary variable available to create a new instance. So, the Controller object turns to the assembly. The Assembly.GetExecutingAssembly method points to the assembly running the active code—in this case, WinUI.exe. Because the FormIssueSummary object is defined within the same assembly, you can use the GetType method to return a Type object for the named object. The Activator.CreateInstance method uses the Type object to instantiate the class and present the child form.

Applying the Controller to the MDI Parent

Now that you have implemented the Controller object, you can put it to use. The IssueTracker application begins by displaying the FormIssueSummary child form. A mapping has already been defined that binds an IssueCollection object and a View action to the FormIssueSummary child form. In Listing 8-4, the Form_Load event handler only needs to populate an IssueCollection object and pass it along to the Controller.

Listing 8-4. The MDI Application's Form_Load Event Handler

```
private void FormMain_Load( object sender, System.EventArgs e )
{
    IssueCollection myColl = new IssueCollection();
    Controller.Process( myColl, Controller.ControllerActions.View );
    return;
}
```

In this case, the IssueCollection is empty. Later, you will populate it with actual data. The collection and a ControllerAction will be passed to the static Process method. The Process method will reference its collection of mappings and display the appropriate child form.

Applying the Controller to the MDI Child

Using the Controller object need not be limited to MDI parents. Child forms, or any other object class that needs to direct form actions, can also use the Controller class. In Listing 8-5, the FormIssueSummary class uses the Controller class to display the FormIssueDetails child form in response to double-clicking a row.

Listing 8-5. Using the Controller Class to Process User Actions

```
private void listView1_DoubleClick(object sender, System.EventArgs e)
{
    Issue myIssue = new Issue();
    myIssue.IssueID = 101;

    Controller.Process( myIssue, Controller.ControllerActions.View );
}
```

Essentially, the code functions the same way. When the user double-clicks a row in the list view control, its event handler creates a new Issue object, sets its properties, and passes it to the Controller object's Process method along with a ControllerAction value set to View.

Creating the Model

The model element of the MVC architecture already exists with the abstractions that the Business Facade and Business Rules projects provide. The child forms use these projects and their methods to set and get values from the model. Listing 8-6 demonstrates a child form's use of the model by implementing the Form_Load event handler for the FormIssueSummary form.

Listing 8-6. Filling a List View with Summary Data

```
private void FormIssueSummary_Load(object sender, System.EventArgs e)
{
    IssueManager mgrIssues = new IssueManager();
    IssueCollection collIssues = mgrIssues.GetAllIssues();

    foreach( Issue issueItem in collIssues )
    {
        listView1.Items.Add( issueItem.Summary );
    }

    return;
}
```

The event handler begins by instantiating an IssueManager object provided by the Business Facade project. The IssueManager returns a collection of Issue objects that abstract values stored in the database. This collection is then iterated to add rows to the list view control. Figure 8-7 shows the final outcome.

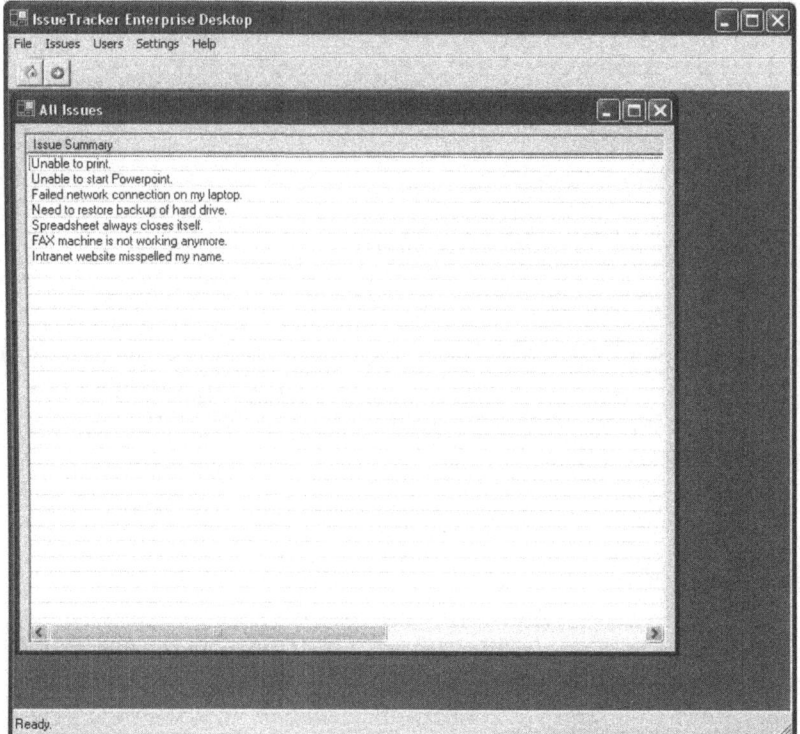

Figure 8-7. The summary view of all issues

The Form_Load event handler is similar for the FormIssueDetails form. You can even apply data binding to child form controls, as shown in Listing 8-7.

Listing 8-7. Data Binding with Form Controls

```
private void FormIssueDetails_Load(object sender, System.EventArgs e)
{
    IssueManager managerIssue = new IssueManager();
    Issue issue = managerIssue.GetIssue( m_intIssueID );

    txtEntryDate.DataBindings.Add( "Text", issue, "EntryDate" );
    cboType.DataBindings.Add( "Text", issue, "TypeID" );
    cboStatus.DataBindings.Add( "Text", issue, "StatusID" );
    cboPriority.DataBindings.Add( "Text", issue, "PriorityID" );
    txtSummary.DataBindings.Add( "Text", issue, "Summary" );
    txtDescription.DataBindings.Add( "Text", issue, "Description" );

    return;
}
```

Again, you have put IssueManager to use. This time, you have invoked the GetIssue method along with a specific Issue ID. You then used .NET's data binding to bind the populated Issue object each relevant form control. Figure 8-8 shows the filled FormIssueDetails form.

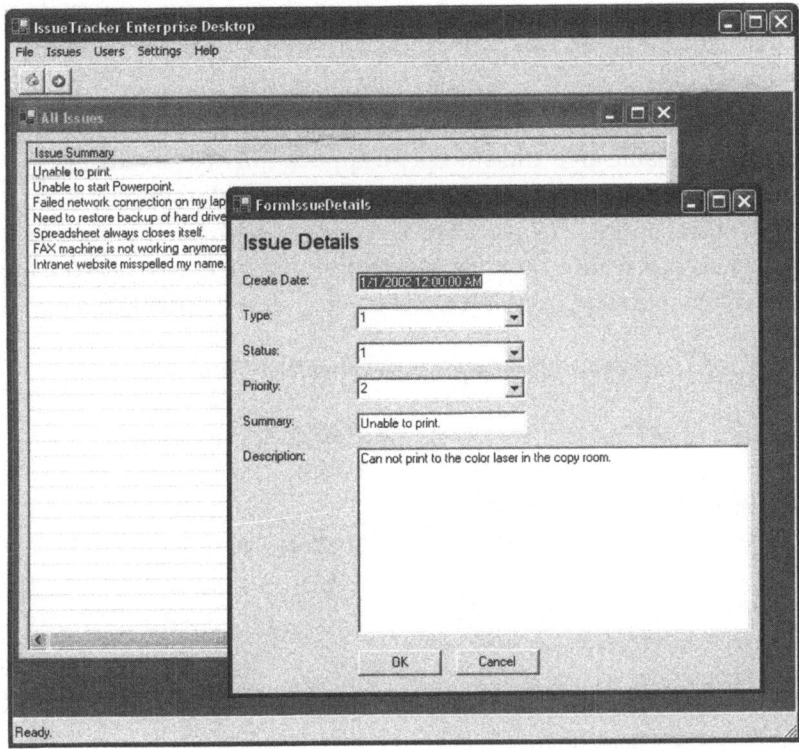

Figure 8-8. Data binding form fields to a data collection

So far, the controller and model elements of the MVC architecture have largely completed the application. The application starts with a Form_Load event handler that uses the Controller class to display a summary form. The DoubleClick event handler in that form uses the Controller class to display a details form.

Simple MDI child forms have worked out well to this point, but to round out a solid application framework, you need to attend to the view area.

Creating Extendable Viewers

So far, the standard MDI user interface methodology has worked out well to implement an MVC architecture. However, to turn MDI into an extendable solution—rather than a flexible solution—you need to put some additional elements into place, including consistent viewer implementation, the ability to load viewers dynamically, and the ability to retrieve controller settings from an external file. You can fulfill these three basic needs with the help of three additional .NET concepts: forms inheritance, external assembly sharing, and application configuration files.

Loading Forms from an External Library

Another characteristic of application extensibility is to load viewers at runtime that might become available after the enterprise application has already been deployed. The .NET Framework's reflection capabilities radically simplify this. Listing 8-8 revisits the Controller object's Process method with an approach to instantiating form objects from a separate assembly. In this implementation, the Controller class can load a form even if it exists in a separate assembly file.

Listing 8-8. An Improved Process Method for the Controller Class

```
public static void Process( object argObject, ControllerActions argAction )
{
    //based on mapping, display specific form
    foreach( ObjectMappingEntry objMapping in _ObjectMappings )
    {
        //find the right business object
        if( argObject.GetType().Name.CompareTo(
            objMapping.BusinessObjectName ) == 0 )
        {
            //find the right action
            if( objMapping.Action == argAction )
            {
                Assembly asm = Assembly.Load( objMapping.Viewer.Substring( 0,
                    objMapping.Viewer.IndexOf( '.' ) ) );

                Type typeViewer = asm.GetType( objMapping.Viewer );

                FrameworkViewer formViewer =
                    (FrameworkViewer)Activator.CreateInstance( typeViewer );

                formViewer.MdiParent = _ParentForm;
                formViewer.Show();
            }
        }
    }

    return;
}
```

The most significant difference is that the form object's Type is not obtained from the application via the GetExecutingAssembly method but rather from a foreign assembly via the Assembly.Load method. The Assembly.Load method loads a named assembly into the application's domain by name. In this case, a substring operation pulls the namespace from the fully qualified name. Otherwise, there is little or no difference from the original implementation.

NOTE *This version of the Process method will no longer display forms defined within the same executable file. In general, a separate assembly should manage all forms, including those deployed with the application. Product upgrades may be as simple as replacing the assembly.*

Extending Windows Forms Through Inheritance

Just like Web forms, Windows forms should also adhere to standards set by an application framework. If there is to be any sort of plug-in framework, it will only be possible through implementation consistency. One effective way to enforce that consistency is through published interfaces. Another way to enforce consistency is through forms inheritance.

Forms inheritance enables a new Windows form to be created by inheriting from an existing form class. This is helpful in building a plug-in framework because you can create a base form that implements basic operational tasks, such as registering forms, returning menu information, and returning a toolbar icon. Rather than implementing this functionality over and over, the inherited form can benefit from the functionality defined in the base class.

Add a new Windows form to the ApplicationFramework project by selecting it in the Solution Explorer and choosing Add ➤ Add Windows Form. Next, enter *FrameworkViewer.cs* for the new filename. This will become the base class from which future application viewers will inherit. All that remains is to add the necessary viewer functionality to this form.

To demonstrate possible functionality that might appear in the base class, consider the following: The Controller class has identified four different states that viewers might operate in: New, View, Edit, and Delete. The application framework guidelines might decide that the only difference between a viewer in a New state and a viewer in an Edit state is that data fields are read-only when in the View state. If all viewers in the View state are read-only, then it makes sense to disable all fields in one central location. Listing 8-9 outlines the FrameworkViewer base class, which includes the functionality that evaluates the View mode of the viewer and disables all data entry fields as needed.

Listing 8-9. Implementing the FrameworkViewer Base Class

```csharp
public class FrameworkViewer : System.Windows.Forms.Form
{
    private Controller.ControllerActions _ViewMode;

    public Controller.ControllerActions ViewMode
    {
        set
        {
            _ViewMode = value;
        }
    }

    public FrameworkViewer()
    {
        InitializeComponent();
    }

    private void InitializeComponent()
    {
        this.Load += new System.EventHandler(this.FrameworkViewer_Load);
    }

    private void FrameworkViewer_Load(object sender, System.EventArgs e)
    {
        if( ViewMode == Controller.ControllerActions.View )
        {
            //set all edit and list controls to read only
            foreach( Control controlItem in Controls )
            {
                if( controlItem.GetType().Name.CompareTo( "TextBox" ) == 0 ||
                    controlItem.GetType().Name.CompareTo( "ComboBox" ) == 0 ||
                    controlItem.GetType().Name.CompareTo( "ListBox" ) == 0 )
                {
                    controlItem.Enabled = false;
                }
            }
        }

        return;
    }
}
```

The code behind the FrameworkViewer class appears like many other form classes. The first element added is a ControllerActions member that identifies the state of the form as New, View, Edit, or Delete. Next, a property accessor allows the controller to set that value. The default constructor that follows is essentially the one provided by Visual Studio. The InitializeComponent method, however, includes only a single statement that designates a Form_Load event handler. This event handler is implemented in the method that follows. The event handler iterates through the form's collection of controls and evaluates their Type values. If a control has a Type value that matches a textbox, combo box, or list box, then the control is disabled. This has the effect of rendering any viewer that is initialized in the View state as read-only.

To take advantage of this functionality, the Controller class needs to set the View mode when the view is initially created. Make the following changes to Listing 8-8 to support this new framework feature:

```
Type typeViewer = asm.GetType( objMapping.Viewer );
FrameworkViewer formViewer =
    (FrameworkViewer)Activator.CreateInstance( typeViewer );
formViewer.ViewMode = argAction;
formViewer.MdiParent = _ParentForm;
formViewer.Show();
```

Turning a Child Form into a Viewer

Turning any MDI child form into a FrameworkViewer is an easy step. The only change necessary is in the class declaration of the form's code-behind page. The class declaration for the FormIssueDetails class now looks like the following:

```
public class FormIssueDetails : FrameworkViewer //System.Windows.Forms.Form
```

The code compiles normally, and you can still edit the form within the Visual Studio form designer. Once converted, the viewer has access to all the benefits that the application framework provides. Figure 8-9 shows the FormIssueDetails viewer as it appears in its View state.

In the case of third-party integrators who do not have code or project access, add a new project reference to the framework assembly by clicking Add Reference, selecting the Projects tab, clicking the Browse button, and pointing to the ApplicationFramework file. Next, add a Windows form to the project and change its base class to FrameworkViewer as specified earlier.

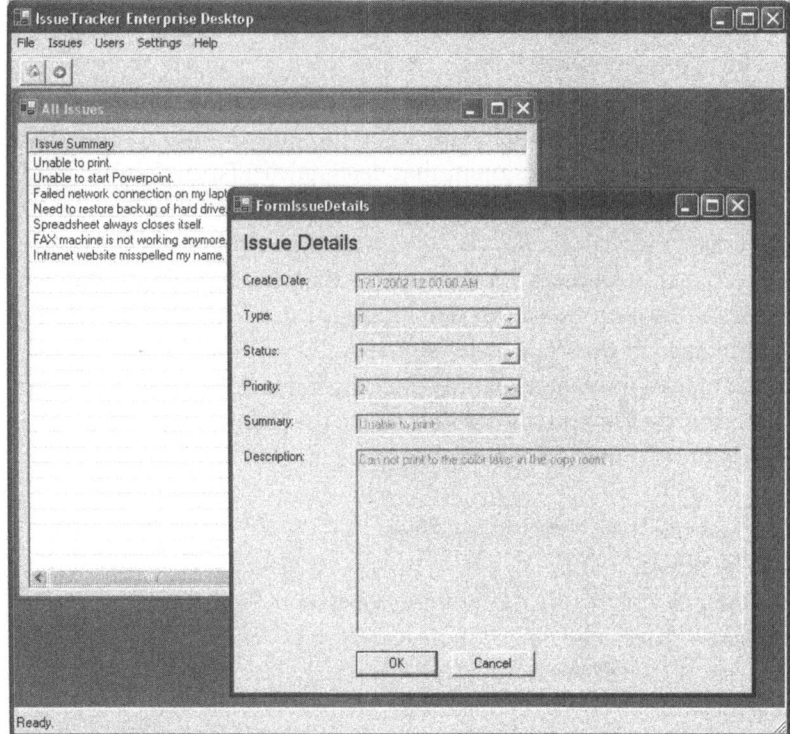

Figure 8-9. The completed FormIssueDetails in its View state

After saving the changes to the source file, preview the form in the form designer. All form code including properties, placed controls, and events are inherited. Like all other objects, the rules of object-oriented inheritance apply when it comes to private, public, and protected methods and attributes.

Retrieving Settings from the Application Configuration File

Earlier, Table 8-1 outlined the application's object-action-form mappings, which defined how the Controller object should respond to a specific user action. Listing 8-3 hard-coded this information directly into the Controller object's constructor. This is far from flexible, and you should certainly externalize it into a configuration file. Coincidentally, the .NET Framework provides services for storing application information into an Extensible Markup Language (XML) file. Create a text file named after the application executable file, app.config, and enter the information outlined in Listing 8-10. Next, save the app.config file to the WinUI project folder and add it as an existing item to the WinUI project. Finally, update the following statement within the AssemblyInfo.cs file:

```
[assembly: AssemblyConfiguration("app.config")]
```

Listing 8-10. Storing Application Configuration Settings in the app.config File

```xml
<?xml version="1.0" encoding="utf-8" ?>
<configuration>
    <configSections>
        <sectionGroup name="Viewers">
            <section name="Include" />
        </sectionGroup>
    </configSections>

    <Viewers>
        <Include BusinessObjectName="IssueCollection" Action="2"
            Viewer="ApplicationFramework.FormIssueSummary" />
        <Include BusinessObjectName="Issue" Action="2"
            Viewer="ApplicationFramework.FormIssueDetails" />
        <Include BusinessObjectName="Issue" Action="1"
            Viewer="ApplicationFramework.FormIssueDetails" />
        <Include BusinessObjectName="Object" Action="3"
            Viewer="ApplicationFramework.FormDataManager" />
    </Viewers>

</configuration>
```

The app.config file contains the same information that was hard-coded into the constructor of the Controller class. With the migration to an external file, you can update the constructor to look more like Listing 8-11.

Listing 8-11. Accessing the app.config File for Controller Settings

```csharp
public Controller()
{
    ObjectMappingEntry entry;

    XmlDocument xmldoc = new XmlDocument();
    xmldoc.Load( "WinUI.exe.config" );
    XmlNode root = xmldoc.DocumentElement;

    try
    {
        XmlNodeList xnodelist =
            root.SelectNodes( "/configuration/Viewers/Include" );

        foreach( XmlNode xnode in xnodelist )
        {
```

```
                    //create a new entry object
                    entry = new ObjectMappingEntry();

                    //translate the integer into a ControllerAction
                    switch( int.Parse(xnode.Attributes["Action"].Value) )
                    {
                        case 1:
                            entry.Action = ControllerActions.New;
                            break;
                        case 2:
                            entry.Action = ControllerActions.View;
                            break;
                        case 3:
                            entry.Action = ControllerActions.Edit;
                            break;
                        case 4:
                            entry.Action = ControllerActions.Delete;
                            break;
                    }

                    //set the BusinessObjectName
                    entry.BusinessObjectName =
                        xnode.Attributes["BusinessObjectName"].Value;

                    //set the viewer name
                    entry.Viewer = xnode.Attributes["Viewer"].Value;

                    //add this mapping to the collection
                    _ObjectMappings.Add( entry );

                }

            }
            catch( Exception x )
            {
                EventLog systemLog = new EventLog();
                systemLog.Source = "IssueTracker";
                systemLog.WriteEntry( x.Message, EventLogEntryType.Error, 0 );
            }

            return;

    }
```

The AppSettingsReader object is a useful tool for pulling custom application attributes from an app.config file. Its only downside is that it expects all values to be represented by a key name-value pair. For representing collections of related values, you can use XPath to navigate to specific nodes and extract specific values. First, XPath navigates to the node containing all the viewer entries. Next, a new ObjectMappingEntry object is created and each child node is iterated to retrieve the necessary viewer attributes. Values are pulled that indicate the action, business object name, and viewer name for each mapping that is stored into the ArrayList.

Adding Dynamic Data to Windows Forms

Chapter 7, "Building Web Applications," described data binding as a powerful mechanism used to create a connection between form controls and the underlying application data. This connection enables a form control to read and write values stored in databases and in other structures, such as arrays and collections. Data binding is just as effective at setting form control properties at runtime for Windows forms as it is for Web forms.

A valid data source for data binding is any data collection that supports indexed access to the elements of the collection—specifically, any collection implementing the IList interface, such as DataSets, arrays, and ArrayLists.

Applying Data Binding

Simple data binding connects a single value within a data source to a single property of a form control. In Listing 8-7, the Form_Load event handler for the FormIssueDetails form binds edtEmailAddress.Text to Dat_Issue.EmailAddress. In this case, the Bindings collection of the edtEmailAddress textbox control manages simple data binding.

Complex data binding binds a list control to a collection of data elements. You implement complex data binding to bind each list control to its respective data source. In Listing 8-12, the new data entry form displays three combo box controls that retrieve their list options from validation tables.

NOTE *For each combo box control, be sure to set the DropDownStyle property to DropDownList. Otherwise, a user will be able to enter their own text values rather than choose ones from a list.*

Listing 8-12. Filling Combo Box Controls with Complex Data Binding

```
private void FormIssueDetails_Load(object sender, System.EventArgs e)
{
    //reference the application's DataSet object
    ReferenceDataManager mgrReference = new ReferenceDataManager();

    //bind the validation data
    cboPriority.DataSource = mgrReference.GetPriorities();
    cboPriority.DisplayMember = "PriorityLabel";
    cboPriority.ValueMember = "PriorityID";

    cboType.DataSource = mgrReference.GetIssueTypes();
    cboType.DisplayMember = "TypeLabel";
    cboType.ValueMember = "TypeID";

    cboStatus.DataSource = mgrReference.GetStatuses();
    cboStatus.DisplayMember = "StatusLabel";
    cboStatus.ValueMember = "StatusID";

    txtEntryDate.Text = DateTime.Now.ToString();


    if( ViewMode == Controller.ControllerActions.View ||
        ViewMode == Controller.ControllerActions.Edit )
    {
        IssueManager managerIssue = new IssueManager();
        Issue issue = managerIssue.GetIssue( m_intIssueID );

        txtEntryDate.DataBindings.Add( "Text", issue, "EntryDate" );
        cboType.DataBindings.Add( "Text", issue, "TypeID" );
        cboStatus.DataBindings.Add( "Text", issue, "StatusID" );
        cboPriority.DataBindings.Add( "Text", issue, "PriorityID" );
        txtSummary.DataBindings.Add( "Text", issue, "Summary" );
        txtDescription.DataBindings.Add( "Text", issue, "Description" );
    }

    return;
}
```

This updated version of the Form_Load event handler for the FormIssueDetails form has a couple of advancements over its predecessor in Listing 8-7. First, an instance of the ReferenceDataManager is created from the Business Facade project. This object accesses the underlying reference tables that are bound to the combo box controls. Three properties complete each data binding. The DataSource property identifies the data collection to which to bind. The DisplayMember property identifies the data column to appear as in the Text field. The ValueMember property identifies the numeric value stored in the database.

The other advancement is that the original data binding of field values only occurs when the form is displayed in a View or Edit state. The resulting form appears in Figure 8-10 as a new issue is entered.

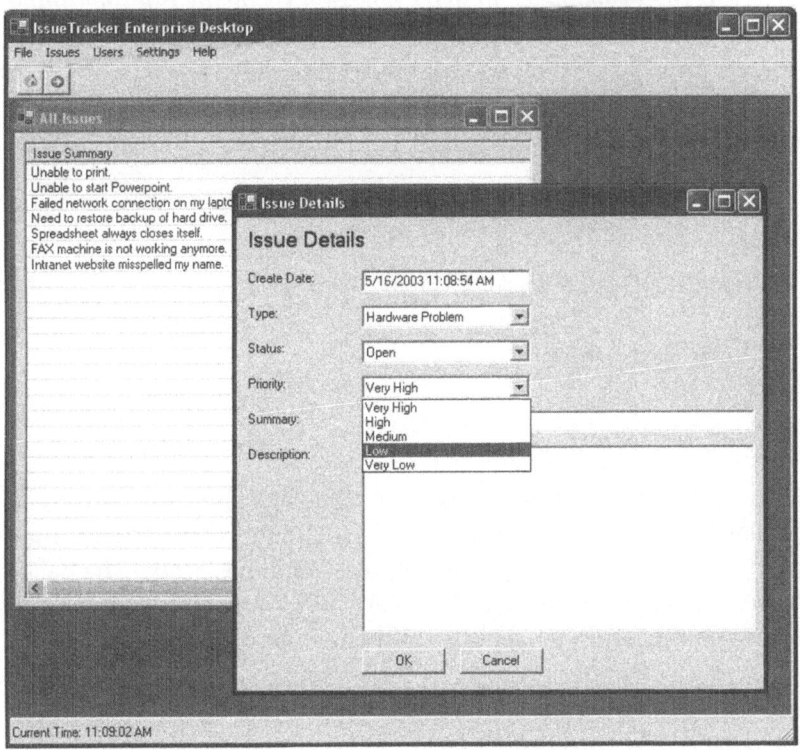

Figure 8-10. Filling combo box controls with complex data binding

Setting the Data Binding Context

Windows forms also support a binding context between a data source and a set of form controls. The BindingContext property points to a data collection to which one or more form controls are bound. This property also maintains the current position within the data collection. This enables a form to track its position within a collection and inform controls about the object in the data collection to which they should bind. As the current position changes, controls update to reflect the change in data.

To use a binding context, implement the simple data binding outlined in Listing 8-6. You bind each Label.Text property to a column value in the current record of the Dat_Issue table using the control's DataBindings property. Because the BindingContext maintains the tableIssues object, changing the current object requires incrementing or decrementing the Position property of the data collection. In Listing 8-13, the currently viewed object is identified by the form's BindingContext property.

Listing 8-13. Selecting the Viewable Data in a Collection Using the BindingContext

```
private void btnBack_Click(object sender, System.EventArgs e)
{
    BindingContext[managerIssue].Position—;
    return;
}

private void btnNext_Click(object sender, System.EventArgs e)
{
    BindingContext[managerIssue].Position++;
    return;
}
```

Listing 8-13 implements the event handler for the Back and Next buttons in the FormIssueView form. The Next button's Click event handler increments the Position property of the data source managed by the BindingContext. The Back button's Click event handler decrements the Position property. This enables the form to cycle through the issues in response to the Next and Back buttons.

Displaying Data in a DataGrid

The DataGrid control is probably one of the most important controls available to the enterprise developer. It displays information stored in an array, collection, or DataTable as a series of columns and rows. You can optionally edit each row in place, allowing changes to be reflected in the source data as the user moves from one row to another. When the DataGrid displays a DataSet, the user can also move across related DataTable objects by navigating their relationships.

To see the capabilities of the DataGrid control, you can create another Windows form, named FormDataManager, and add it to the ApplicationFramework project. You can use this form to view and set rows of reference data, allowing the application administrator to customize the application. Table 8-2 outlines this form's five form controls.

Table 8-2. Windows Form Controls Appearing Within the FormDataManager Viewer

CONTROL ID	CONTROL TYPE
datagridTypes	DataGrid
datagridPriorities	DataGrid
datagridStatuses	DataGrid
btnOK	Button
btnCancel	Button

Listing 8-14 displays a collection of records in each DataGrid control by setting the DataSource property to the collection of objects that will be displayed. Set the DataSource property of the DataGrid control to the application's reference DataSet object. Then, set each DataMember to a reference table appropriate for each control.

Listing 8-14. Data Binding DataGrid Controls to DataTables

```
private void FormDataManager_Load(object sender, System.EventArgs e)
{
    datagridTypes.DataSource = mgrReference.GetEntireDataSet();
    datagridTypes.DataMember = "Val_IssueType";

    datagridStatuses.DataSource = mgrReference.GetEntireDataSet();
    datagridStatuses.DataMember = "Val_IssueStatus";

    datagridPriorities.DataSource = mgrReference.GetEntireDataSet();
    datagridPriorities.DataMember = "Val_Priority";

    return;
}
```

The problem with only setting a DataSource property to an entire DataTable is that all of the columns that make up the DataTable will be displayed. Because you might only want to show a couple of columns, you will need to apply a table style.

To apply a table style, select a DataGrid control, such as datagridTypes, and view its list of properties. Select the TableStyles property and click the ... button to display the DataGridTableStyles Collection dialog box. This dialog box lets you create table styles for one or more tables that belong to any data collection, such as a DataSet. If a DataSet has five separate tables, then you can create and stylize five separate table styles. Each table style defines how a DataGrid control should appear for the specified table. Properties include read-only state, specific row and column sizes, colors, grid lines, visibility of headers, and so on. Click the Add button to create a new table style named tablestyleTypes then set the MappingName property to the name of the DataTable to display. Figure 8-11 shows the DataGridTableStyle Collection Editor dialog box settings for the Val_IssueTypes table.

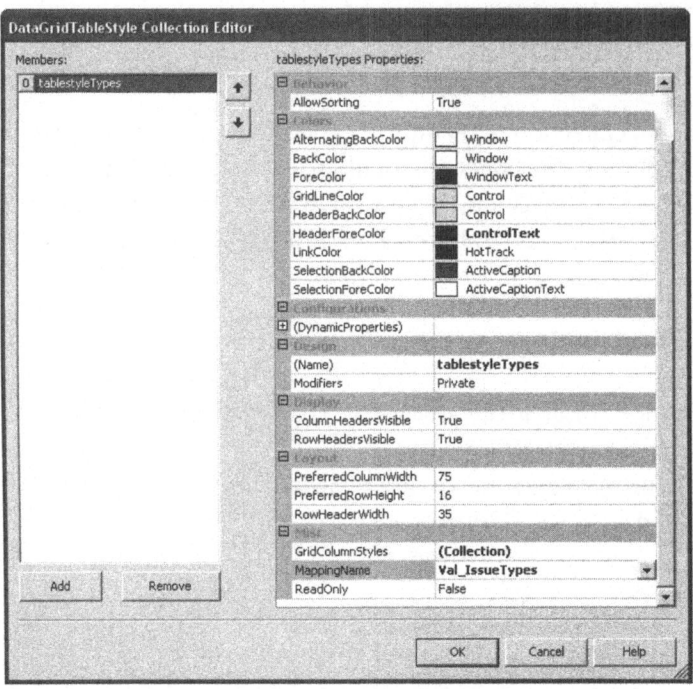

Figure 8-11. The DataGridTableStyle Collection Editor dialog box

Just as you can create multiple table styles for a data structure, you can create multiple column styles for each table. By default, if you do not specify any column styles, then every column in a DataTable object will display. By adding column styles, you can specify which columns to include and how they should be appear. You can also customize the format of string values, such as dates, using string formatting specifiers. Appendix C, "Using String Format Specifiers," contains a list of the most common format specifiers.

NOTE   *You can create a hidden column containing reference IDs by setting the column width to zero.*

To add column styles to a table style, select the GridColumnStyles property in the DataGridTableStyle Collection Editor dialog box and click the ... button. The DataGridColumnStyle Collection Editor dialog box appears. You can add individual column styles by clicking the Add button and filling in the appropriate column properties. Figure 8-12 shows some of the settings used by the Val_IssueTypes dialog box.

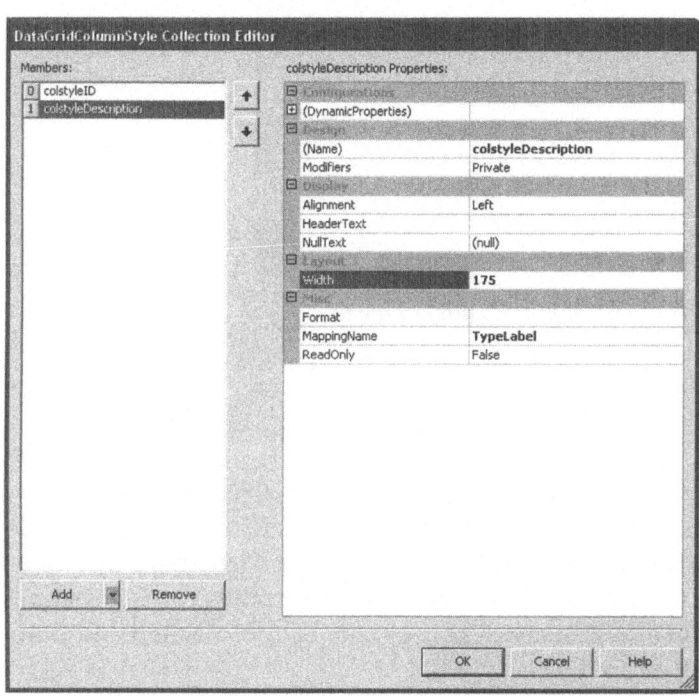

Figure 8-12. Setting column styles with the DataGridColumnStyle Collection Editor dialog box

Filling in the table and column styles within the Visual Studio .NET environment definitely saves a lot of time. The properties set within the table and column style editors translates to pages of code that create and customize a series of DataGridTableStyle and DataGridTextBoxColumn objects. Figure 8-13 shows the completed child form that displays the three DataGrid controls containing reference information.

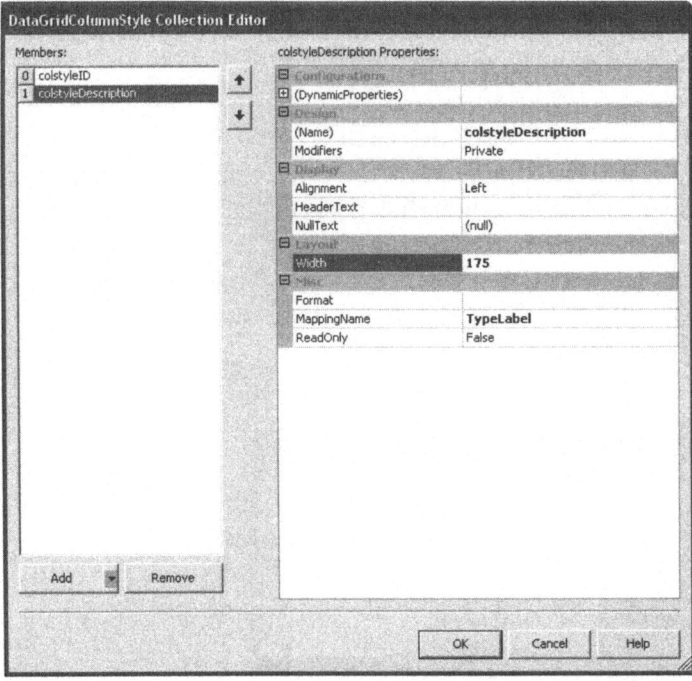

Figure 8-13. The completed FormDataManager viewer

Displaying Current Time with the Timer Control

Often it is necessary for an application to perform an activity at specific intervals. The Timer control enables this functionality by generating an event at specified intervals. You define the actual length of the interval with the Interval property, measured in milliseconds. When the control is enabled, a Tick event is raised at every interval. The key methods of the Timer control are Start and Stop, which turn the timer on and off, respectively.

To add a timed response to a form, select the Timer component from the Toolbox and drag into the specified form. Next, set the Interval property for the timer in terms of milliseconds to determine how much time will pass before the next Tick event is generated. In Listing 8-15, the IssueTracker application uses a timer to periodically check the time and display it to the user as a local clock.

NOTE *The more often a timer event occurs, the more processor time is used in responding to the event. This can slow down the overall application performance. Avoid setting a time interval smaller than needed.*

Listing 8-15. Implementing a Timer Control to Display the Time

```
private void InitializeTimer()
{
    Timer1.Interval = 1000;
    Timer1.Enabled = true;
}

private void Timer1_Tick( object Sender, EventArgs e )
{
    statusbar.Text = "Current Time: " + DateTime.Now.ToLongTimeString();
}
```

Set the Enabled property to true to start the timer. The Tick event will begin to occur, executing the target procedure at the set time interval. Set the Enabled property to false to stop the timer because setting the interval to 0 does not cause the timer to stop.

Extending Application Usability

When it comes to enterprise application development, building an application that is scalable and reliable comes first. You should always implement extended usability features last, when basic functionality is near completion. That being said, completed applications or first release applications can always benefit from usability improvements. These improvements can include improving responsiveness from the application, making data management more convenient, remembering user preferences, or localizing the user interface for a target culture.

Keeping the Application Responsive with Threads

Improving application responsiveness is always a big win with customers. In the information age, nobody wants to wait any longer than absolutely necessary, especially when it comes to data entry or data analysis. Applications that demonstrate any sort of lag can be perceived as slow and undesirable. When time permits, you should profile and review code to find room for improvement.

One common problem that desktop applications experience is the feeling of a "locked-up" application when a lengthy function is in progress. This is often attributed to a process that does not yield any processor cycles back to the user interface to refresh. When a user switches to another application and then switches back, a hole in the application remains.

Lengthy functions should execute on separate threads of execution. Listing 8-16 presents the same code as Listing 8-5 with one exception: A new call is made to a method named StallForTime.

Listing 8-16. Adding a Long Delay Method in Response to User Action

```
private void listView1_DoubleClick(object sender, System.EventArgs e)
{
    //call a really long process...
    StallForTime();

    Issue myIssue = new Issue();
    myIssue.IssueID = 101;

    Controller.Process( myIssue, Controller.ControllerActions.View );
}
```

As Listing 8-17 reveals, the StallForTime method is true to its name and eats up processor cycles while the user waits for the Controller object to present the next view. If the user performs a context switch to another application and back, the IssueTracker application will only show an application frame and no user interface. Assuming that the next view does not depend on the results of the lengthy process, the StallForTime method can execute within its own thread of execution.

Listing 8-17. Implementing a Simple Delay Method

```
public void StallForTime()
{
    for( int i = 0; i < 100000; i++ )
    {
        for( int j = 0; j < 100000; j++ )
            ;
    }
    System.Diagnostics.Debug.WriteLine( "Finished!" );
}
```

Listing 8-18 creates a separate line of execution for the StallForTime method. Two lines of code and no changes to the lengthy method result in a clean and quick user interface. This time, as the application is running, the form is able to repaint itself as it becomes invalidated.

Listing 8-18. Shifting the Delay Method to Another Thread for Better Application Response

```
private void listView1_DoubleClick(object sender, System.EventArgs e)
{
    //call a really long process...
    Thread threadProcess = new Thread( new ThreadStart( StallForTime ));
    threadProcess.Start();

    Issue myIssue = new Issue();
    myIssue.IssueID = 101;

    Controller.Process( myIssue, Controller.ControllerActions.View );
}
```

Adding Drag and Drop Functionality

Drag and drop functionality can be effective at streamlining user steps within an enterprise application. You can accomplish this implementation by handling a series of events, such as DragEnter, DragLeave, and DragDrop. These events store all of the necessary information to carry out a drag and drop process within their event arguments.

Dragging Data from a Control

Dragging operations typically begin with a MouseDown event generated by a control containing an object to be dragged. In the case of FormMain, you select the lstIssues list view control and implement a new event handler to respond to the MouseDown event (see Listing 8-19).

Listing 8-19. Beginning the Drag Process

```
private void lstIssues_MouseDown( object sender,
    System.Windows.Forms.MouseEventArgs e )
{
    ListViewItem itemSelected = lstIssues.SelectedItems[0];

    lstIssues.DoDragDrop( itemSelected.SubItems[0].Text,
        System.Windows.Forms.DragDropEffects.Copy );

    return;
}
```

The MouseDown event handler responds to the event by invoking the DoDragDrop method belonging to the originating control. This method takes two parameters. The first parameter represents the object being dragged. You can use any data, from a simple string to a complex object, as a parameter. In this case, the data object is a string that represents the numeric value of the selected Issue object. The second parameter describes how the data is to be dragged. Table 8-3 summarizes the drag methods supported by the DragDropEffects structure.

Table 8-3. The DragDropEffects Elements Identifying How Data Should Be Dragged

PROPERTY	DESCRIPTION
All	The data is copied, removed from the drag source, and scrolled in the drop target.
Copy	The data is copied to the drop target.
Link	The data from the drag source is linked to the drop target.
Move	The data from the drag source is moved to the drop target.
None	The drop target does not accept the data.
Scroll	Scrolling is about to start or is currently occurring in the drop target.

Because the list view and tree view controls are used most often for initiating drag and drop operations, they both have a specific event handler, ItemDrag, for this purpose. Listing 8-19 would more accurately look like Listing 8-20.

Listing 8-20. Beginning the Process with a Drag

```
private void lstIssues_DragLeave( object sender,
    System.Windows.Forms.MouseEventArgs e )
{
    ListViewItem itemSelected = lstIssues.SelectedItems[0];

    lstIssues.DoDragDrop( itemSelected.SubItems[0].Text,
        System.Windows.Forms.DragDropEffects.Copy );

    return;
}
```

Dropping Data into a Control

Once dragging has started, something needs to accept the drop. The cursor changes when it crosses over areas of the form where dropping is supported. Areas can accept dropped data by setting the AllowDrop property and handling the DragEnter and DragDrop events.

In the Properties window, set the AllowDrop property to true. Next, add an event handler to respond to the DragEnter event. Listing 8-21 implements the DragEnter event handler. An If statement performs type-checking to ensure the data being dragged is an acceptable type. Next, the code sets the effect that will happen when the drop occurs in the DragDropEffects property.

Listing 8-21. Determining If a Drop Should Be Allowed

```
private void FormMain_DragEnter( object sender,
    System.Windows.Forms.DragEventArgs e )
{
    if( e.Data.GetDataPresent( DataFormats.Text ) )
        e.Effect = DragDropEffects.Copy;
    else
        e.Effect = DragDropEffects.None;
    return;
}
```

You can define custom DataFormats as long as the custom object is specified as serializable. Next, you need to implement the DragDrop event handler, as outlined in Listing 8-22. The GetData method retrieves the data being dragged.

Listing 8-22. Ending the Process with a Drop

```
private void FormMain_DragDrop( object sender,
    System.Windows.Forms.DragEventArgs e )
{
    //close the active MDI child
    if( this.ActiveMdiChild != null )
        this.ActiveMdiChild.Close();

    //initialize the new MDI child
    this.dlgViewIssue = new FormIssueView();
    dlgViewIssue.MdiParent = this;
    dlgViewIssue.Dock = System.Windows.Forms.DockStyle.Fill;
```

```
//supply the IssueID carried through the Drag process
dlgViewIssue.SetIssueID( int.Parse( e.Data.GetData(
        DataFormats.Text ).ToString() ) );


//display the new MDI child
dlgViewIssue.Show();


return;
}
```

Saving User Preferences with the System Registry

Enterprise applications will often need to store user preferences within the Windows system Registry. The Registry hosts information from the operating system as well as information from applications hosted on the machine. Working with the Registry may compromise security if it stores plain-text passwords and other sensitive information. You should give careful attention to what is stored in the Registry to ensure that it poses no threat to system or user security.

Reading and Writing Registry Keys

Each Registry entry comprises two primary elements: name and value. Each entry is also stored in a collection of keys and subkeys. Any parent key may have one or more child keys, each with one or more names and values. Figure 8-14 shows a snapshot of the Registry Editor highlighting the IssueTracker application settings node.

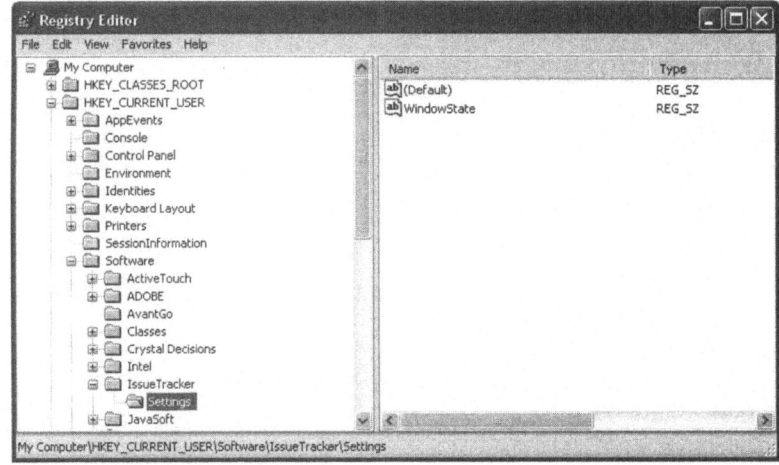

Figure 8-14. Viewing the system Registry with the Registry Editor

The Registry and RegistryKey classes, provided by the .NET Framework, offer services to read and write Registry settings. To include support for system Registry access, include the necessary namespace:

```
using Microsoft.Win32;
```

The Registry class implements the base Registry keys that can access Registry subkeys and their values. Listing 8-23 shows the application's FormLoad event handler and how it accesses application settings from the Registry.

Listing 8-23. Reading from the System Registry at the Start of the Application

```
private void FormMain_Load(object sender, System.EventArgs e)
{
    RegistryKey  regkeyAppRoot =
        Registry.CurrentUser.CreateSubKey("Software\\IssueTracker\\Settings");

    String strWindowState = (String)regkeyAppRoot.GetValue("WindowState");

    if( strWindowState != null && strWindowState.CompareTo("Maximized") == 0 )
        WindowState = System.Windows.Forms.FormWindowState.Maximized;

    else if(strWindowState != null && strWindowState.CompareTo("Minimized") == 0)
        WindowState = FormWindowState.Minimized;

    else
        WindowState = FormWindowState.Normal;

    return;
}
```

The RegistryKey object holds a reference to the specified subkey. Its GetValue method retrieves the Registry value and assigns it to a string variable. Because the return value is a string, it is evaluated to set the window state as maximized or minimized. Listing 8-24 writes the window state value to the Registry upon application closing.

Listing 8-24. Writing to the System Registry upon Application Close

```
private void FormMain_Closing( object sender,
    System.ComponentModel.CancelEventArgs e )
{
    //save the window state
    String strPath = "Software\\IssueTracker\\Settings";
```

```
        String strWindowState = "";

        RegistryKey  regkeyAppRoot = Registry.CurrentUser.CreateSubKey( strPath );

        if( WindowState == FormWindowState.Maximized )
            strWindowState = "Maximized";

        else if( WindowState == FormWindowState.Minimized )
            strWindowState = "Minimized";

        else
            strWindowState = "Normal";

        regkeyAppRoot.SetValue( "WindowState", strWindowState );

        return;
    }
```

Evaluating Registry Access Permissions

The RegistryPermission class, which is in the System.Security.Permission namespace, controls the ability to access Registry variables. Registry variables should not be stored in memory locations where code without RegistryPermission can access them. Similarly, when granting permissions, grant the least privilege necessary to get the job done. For more information, see RegistryPermission and System.Security.Permissions.

Registry permission access values are defined by the RegistryPermissionAccess enumeration. Table 8-4 details the members of the RegistryPermissionAccess enumeration.

Table 8-4. The Registry Access Permissions

VALUE	DESCRIPTION
AllAccess	Create, read, and write access to Registry variables
Create	Create access to Registry variables
NoAccess	No access to Registry variables
Read	Read access to Registry variables
Write	Write access to Registry variables

You can create combinations of permissions, such as permitting read and write access while denying create access, with a bitwise OR operation. Also, when working with deployment projects, you can also use the Registry Editor to specify Registry keys and values that should be added to the Registry of the target computer.

Building Internationalization into the Application

When developing world-ready applications, you must focus attention on a variety of issues throughout the application design and development process. Addressing internationalization requirements early in the design phase will minimize the amount of time and money required to produce quality localized applications for the languages that are intended to be supported.

Targeting a Culture with CultureInfo

The CultureInfo object manages culture-specific information, such as the associated language, sublanguage, country/region, calendar, and cultural conventions. Additional attributes of the CultureInfo object manage the default formats for dates, times, currency, and numbers:

```
using System.Globalization;
```

Although the CultureInfo object is not a language setting, it does contain information related to settings for a geographical region. Table 8-5 presents a sample of the available culture codes available to the enterprise developer.

The CultureInfo object provides a number of useful properties. Among them, CurrentCulture is most often referenced to programmatically set the cultural preference. To set an application's cultural setting to German in Germany, set the CurrentCulture to de-DE:

```
Thread.CurrentThread.CurrentCulture = new CultureInfo("de-DE");
```

You represent a culture by both a language and a region because a language is often spoken in more than one country or region. In the case of German, the language is also popularly spoken within Austria and Switzerland.

By default, the Windows operating system sets the CurrentCulture property. The user sets this property by changing the User Locale through the Regional Options dialog box in the Control Panel or by changing settings related to user locale, such as currency, number, date, and time formats.

Table 8-5. Abridged List of the Cultural Identifiers Supported by the CultureInfo Object

CULTURE CODE	LANGUAGE, COUNTRY
	Invariant culture
ar-SA	Arabic, Saudi Arabia
ar-AE	Arabic, United Arab Emirates
zh-HK	Chinese, Hong Kong SAR
zh-CN	Chinese, China
da-DK	Danish, Denmark
nl-BE	Dutch, Belgium
nl-NL	Dutch, The Netherlands
en-AU	English, Australia
en-CA	English, Canada
en-GB	English, United Kingdom
en-US	English, United States
fr-BE	French, Belgium
fr-CA	French, Canada
fr-FR	French, France
de-AT	German, Austria
de-DE	German, Germany
el-GR	Greek, Greece
it-IT	Italian, Italy
it-CH	Italian, Switzerland
ru-RU	Russian, Russia
es-MX	Spanish, Mexico
es-ES	Spanish, Spain

To ensure that an application uses the default formats provided by the .NET Framework for currency, numbers, date, and time for a specified culture, override the User Locale defaults in your application's code. To do this, create a CultureInfo object with the useUserOverride parameter set to false. The default settings on the user's system will be overridden by the .NET Framework's default settings.

Formatting Foreign Dates and Times

The DateTime structure provides methods such as ToString and Parse that perform culture-sensitive operations on a DateTime object. The DateTimeFormatInfo object typically formats and displays the value of a DateTime object based on a specific culture. The DateTimeFormatInfo object defines how DateTime values are formatted and displayed, depending on the culture.

In the IssueTracker application, you can modify the timer event handler to display the current date in the status bar, formatted to either the English or German culture (see Listing 8-25). Using ShortDatePattern, the date February 7, 2001 is formatted as 2/7/2001 for the English (en-US) culture and 07.02.2001 for the German (de-DE) culture.

Listing 8-25. An Updated Timer Event Handler Displaying the Date in a Different Culture

```
private void timerMain_Tick(object sender, System.EventArgs e)
{
    String strDateOutput = "";
    DateTime dateNow = DateTime.Now;

    // Sets the CurrentCulture property to U.S. English.
    Thread.CurrentThread.CurrentCulture = new CultureInfo( "en-US" );

    // Displays dt, formatted using the ShortDatePattern
    // and the CurrentThread.CurrentCulture.
    strDateOutput = dateNow.ToString( "d" );

    // Creates a CultureInfo for German in Germany.
    CultureInfo cultureinfo = new CultureInfo( "de-DE" );

    // Displays dt, formatted using the ShortDatePattern
    // and the CultureInfo.
    strDateOutput += " [";
    strDateOutput += dateNow.ToString( "d", cultureinfo );
    strDateOutput += "]";

    statusbarMain.Panels[0].Text = strDateOutput;

    return;
}
```

When working with methods provided by the DateTime structure, be aware that the members such as DateTime.Day, DateTime.Month, and DateTime.Year are based on the Gregorian calendar. Even if the current calendar changes, the Gregorian calendar still performs the calculations. This prevents the mathematics performed by the methods from being corrupted by a user's settings. Listing 8-26 shows how to display a message to the user that displays a date 30 days from the current date.

Listing 8-26. Performing Date Mathematics with the DateTime Object

```
public void DisplayReminderMessage()
{
    Thread.CurrentThread.CurrentCulture = new CultureInfo("en-US");

    DateTime dateNow = DateTime.Now;
    dateNow = dateNow.AddDays(30);

    MessageBox.Show( "A 30 Day reminder will be sent on: " +
        dateNow.ToString("d") );

    return;
}
```

Formatting Foreign Numbers

Another property of the CultureInfo object is NumberFormat, which interacts with the NumberFormatInfo object to define how currency, decimal separators, and other numeric symbols are formatted and displayed based on culture (see Listing 8-27). The decimal number 10000.50 is formatted as 10,000.50 for the English (en-US) culture and 10.000,50 for the German (de-DE) culture.

Listing 8-27. Formatting a Currency Value According to a Culture

```
public String GetFormattedCurrency( int intAmount, String strCulture )
{
    CultureInfo culture = new CultureInfo( strCulture );

    return intAmount.ToString( "c", culture );
}
```

In this method, you format an integer using the NumberFormatInfo standard currency format ("c") for the specified CurrentCulture. The culture argument can be any of the identifiers listed in Table 8-5. The formatted amount is not actually converted from one currency value to another. Only its currency representation is modified.

NOTE *The .NET Framework and Microsoft Windows XP set the default currency symbol to the Euro for the 12 unified European nations. Older versions of Windows will still set the default currency symbol to the local currency for these nations.*

Applications running on all versions of Windows operating systems set the default currency symbol from the settings on the user's computer. As mentioned, this setting might be incorrect. To ensure that an application uses the .NET Framework's default settings, create a CultureInfo object and set the useUserOverride parameter to false.

Packaging Application Resources

Nearly every production-quality application needs to use resources. A resource is any nonexecutable data that is logically deployed with an application. A resource might be displayed in an application as error messages or as part of the user interface. Resources can contain data in a number of forms, including strings, images, and persisted objects. Storing your data in a resource file allows you to change the data without recompiling your entire application. Note that in order to write persisted objects to a resource file, the objects must be serializable.

The .NET Framework supports the creation and localization of application resources as well as a model for packaging and deploying localized resources. Application resources are localized for specific cultures to build translated versions of applications. An application loads the appropriate localized resources based on the value of the CultureInfo.CurrentUICulture property. This value is set either in the application code or by the common language runtime for the current user on the local computer.

You can deploy application resources in satellite assemblies because satellite assemblies only contain resource files and not any application code. In the satellite assembly deployment model, an application is created with one default assembly, the main assembly, and several satellite assemblies. One satellite assembly should be created for each culture that the application supports. Because the satellite assemblies are not part of the main assembly, certain resources can easily be replaced or updated without replacing the application's main assembly.

To localize a Windows form, set the Localizable form property to true and save the project. A language translator can use the Windows Resource Localization Editor application to load the form and create the localized version by changing the text and control sizes. Figure 8-15 illustrates using the resource editor while the View Issue page is translated into German. Having a translator change the control text makes perfect sense. However, allowing a translator to be able to change the control's dimensions or locations is also important because the translated labels may require larger control dimensions. The editor does not permit a translator to access or modify the functional source code bound to the form.

 NOTE *You can launch the Windows Resource Localization Editor from C:\Program Files\Microsoft Visual Studio .NET 2003\ SDK\v1.1\Bin\WinRes.exe.*

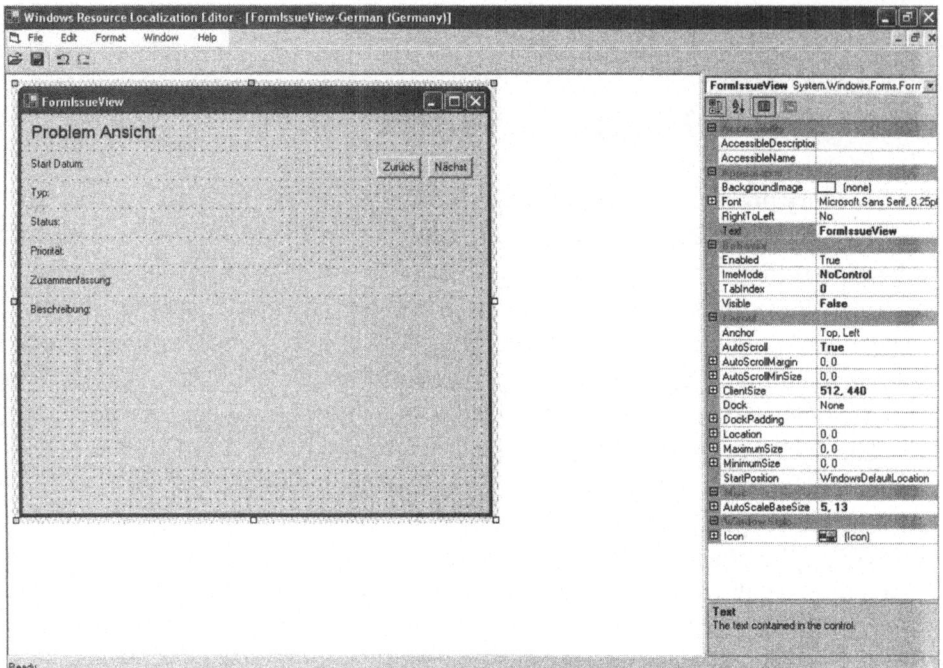

Figure 8-15. Editing a form resource in the Windows Resource Localization Editor

After the translator edits the resource, you can save the form with an associated culture code—in this case, de-DE, for Germany. The resource is deployed along with the rest of the application. Upon execution, the application checks the local culture settings. If they are set to de-DE, as would be expected in Germany, then the application displays the localized form. If a culture is specified that is not localized, then the default form is displayed—in this case, English.

Summary

Windows form clients provide an alternative presentation layer for an enterprise application. Although Web form clients offer a great deal of flexibility, they lack a lot of the rich client-side functionality that Windows forms can provide. An enterprise application has many requirements that typical desktop applications do not face, such as reliability, scalability, and usability.

Implementing an enterprise application as a desktop solution requires much of the same detailed planning that a Web application demands. Having an application framework in place can help minimize errors and encourage reuse. More important, a flexible application framework that can support plug-in views can support adding new views to the application after it has already been deployed. This level of flexibility supports application customization and third-party integration, which are key factors in encouraging application adoption. Before defining an application framework, you need to plan a solid architecture. This chapter presented the classic MVC architecture supported by the MDI user interface methodology to help define that underlying framework.

Business productivity counts on the reliability of an enterprise application and often cannot afford downtime attributed to bugs. Enterprise applications need to support a wide variety of users, from the nontechnical to the Information Technology (IT) professional. Windows forms can effectively address the needs of enterprise application development with an open and flexible framework.

In the next chapter, you will see more details relating to XML and Web services. First, the chapter reviews what XML is and how it works. Next, the chapter broadens these concepts and shows how to create Web services that expose enterprise application functionality.

CHAPTER 9

Using XML and Web Services

VARIOUS CHAPTERS OF THIS BOOK have mentioned Extensible Markup Language (XML) documents and their ability to represent structured data in a flat file. This chapter looks closer at XML and explains why the technology is important to the extended enterprise. Then, building from your understanding of XML, this chapter introduces the concept of Web services and the components that make up Web services. This chapter continues to expand the IssueTracker application by building out the Web service layer of the IssueTracker application to produce a Web service integration platform for any Web-enabled application to use.

Understanding the Extensible Markup Language

As described in Chapter 6, "Automating Business Processes," XML is a flexible language used to create documents that share formatting and data for document exchange over the Web. A business document written in XML can be viewed and edited with any text editor and is usually easy to read. XML usage is most prominent with businesses that exchange documents in an environment where neither side wants to depend on the technology the other side is using.

Reviewing the Evolution of XML

The primary purpose of XML is to deliver structured data. Sources of structured data can include spreadsheets, business functions, and databases. Overall, XML is a set of rules for designing textual representations of structured data. XML is not a programming language, and it does not require a programmer to interact with it. It is extensible and platform independent, and it supports internationalization and localization.

XML looks much like Hypertext Markup Language (HTML) in that it is organized into tags (words bracketed by < and >) and attributes. Although HTML specifies what each tag and attribute means and how the text between the tags is formatted in a browser, XML uses the tags to identify blocks of data and their relationships, leaving the interpretation of the data to the application that reads it.

Although XML is text, it is not intended to be read by people. Data sources, such as spreadsheets, business functions, and databases, often store that data on disk, usually using a binary format. One advantage of a text format is that it allows people, if necessary, to look at the data without the program that produced it. Text formats also allow developers to more easily debug applications. Like HTML, XML files are text files that people should not have to read but could if necessary.

Before the emergence of XML, there was Standard Generalized Markup Language (SGML), which was developed in the early 1980s. SGML has been a standard since 1986, and it is widely used for large documentation projects. The development of HTML started in 1990. The development of XML started in 1996 and has been a World Wide Web Consortium (W3C) recommendation since February 1998. The designers of XML took the best parts of SGML, guided by the experience with HTML, and produced something that is as powerful as SGML but much easier to use. Whereas SGML is mostly used for technical documentation rather than other kinds of data, XML is the opposite.

XML is license free, platform independent and widely supported. Choosing XML as the basis for a project gives you access to a large and growing number of tools, applications, and developers.

Resolving Conflicts with XML Namespaces

XML namespaces clearly identify elements within an XML document that would otherwise lead to ambiguity. For example, if an XML document containing Issue information merges with another document containing User information, certain elements within the resulting document may experience a name collision, as demonstrated in Listing 9-1.

Listing 9-1. issuedata.xml

```
<Dat_Issue>
    <IssueID>1</IssueID>
    <TypeID>1</TypeID>
    <EntryDate>2002-08-15T00:00:00.0000000-07:00</EntryDate>
    <StatusID>1</StatusID>
    <Summary>Unable to print</Summary>
    <Description>I can not print any PowerPoint files on the //MKT-GROUP
        printer in the lobby.</Description>
    <PriorityID>1</PriorityID>
    <User>
        <Firstname>Larry</Firstname>
```

```
        <Lastname>Dalton</Lastname>
        <Description>Marketing Director</Description>
        <EmailAddress>larryd@sample.com</EmailAddress>
        <UserType>1</UserType>
    </User>
</Dat_Issue>
```

The problem appears when an XML document uses a <Description> tag to describe an Issue and later to describe a User. An application has no way of knowing how to process the <Description> tag differently unless it has some additional information outside of the document.

Namespaces address this problem by extending the data model to fully qualify element and attribute names. The purpose of a qualified name is to allow applications to more clearly identify a tag or attribute name. You construct qualified names with a prefix, a colon, and a local name. The prefix identifies a specific Uniform Resource Identifier (URI) as defined in RFC 2396. The local name specifies any identifier used locally within the document:

```
qualified_name = <namespace_identifier : local_name>
```

Namespaces remove ambiguity from XML documents just as class namespaces do in the C# language. Including namespaces in XML documents occur in two separate steps, the namespace reference and the namespace usage. Listing 9-2 replaces all local tag names with qualified tag names.

Listing 9-2. issuedata.qualified.xml

```
<Dat_Issue
    xmlns:issue="http://www.enterprisedotnet/xml/issue"
    xmlns:user="http://www.enterprisedotnet/xml/user">
    <issue:IssueID>1</issue:IssueID>
    <issue:TypeID>1</issue:TypeID>
    <issue:EntryDate>2002-08-15T00:00:00.0000000-07:00</issue:EntryDate>
    <issue:StatusID>1</issue:StatusID>
    <issue:Summary>Unable to print</issue:Summary>
    <issue:Description>I can not print any PowerPoint files on the //MKT-GROUP
        printer in the lobby.</issue:Description>
    <issue:PriorityID>1</issue:PriorityID>
    <user:User>
        <user:Firstname>Larry</user:Firstname>
        <user:Lastname>Dalton</user:Lastname>
        <user:Description>Marketing Director</user:Description>
        <user:EmailAddress>larryd@sample.com</user:EmailAddress>
        <user:UserType>1</user:UserType>
```

```
        </user:User>
</issue:Dat_Issue>
```

In this case, the elements prefixed with *issue:* are associated with a namespace that has a URI of `http://www.enterprisedotnet/xml/issue`, and those prefixed with *user:* are associated with a namespace that has a URI of `http://www.enterprisedotnet/xml/user`.

The namespace prefixes map to the complete namespace URI as attributes of the first element. Because XML namespaces significantly increase the size of the document and make the text more difficult to read, documents may define a single default namespace. Listing 9-3 demonstrates using a default namespace.

Listing 9-3. issuedata.default.xml

```
<Dat_Issue
    xmlns="http://www.enterprisedotnet/xml/issue"
    xmlns:user="http://www.enterprisedotnet/xml/user">
    <IssueID>1</IssueID>
    <TypeID>1</TypeID>
    <EntryDate>2002-08-15T00:00:00.0000000-07:00</EntryDate>
    <StatusID>1</StatusID>
    <Summary>Unable to print</Summary>
    <Description>I can not print any PowerPoint files on the //MKT-GROUP
        printer in the lobby.</Description>
    <PriorityID>1</PriorityID>
    <user:User>
        <user:Firstname>Larry</user:Firstname>
        <user:Lastname>Dalton</user:Lastname>
        <user:Description>Marketing Director</user:Description>
        <user:EmailAddress>larryd@sample.com</user:EmailAddress>
        <user:UserType>1</user:UserType>
    </user:User>
</Dat_Issue>
```

In this case, a prefix maps to the User namespace but not the Issue namespace. Therefore, all of the local element and attribute names will use the Issue namespace by default and not require the issue: prefix. The result is a much smaller and easier-to-read XML document.

Enforcing Structure with XML Schemas

An XML *schema*, also referred to as an *XML Schema Definition (XSD)*, describes the structure and rules for processing XML documents. Its purpose is to define the working elements of an XML document and to define the elements and attributes that can appear within a document. This enables the XML parser to determine if the document is valid or invalid, as illustrated in Figure 9-1.

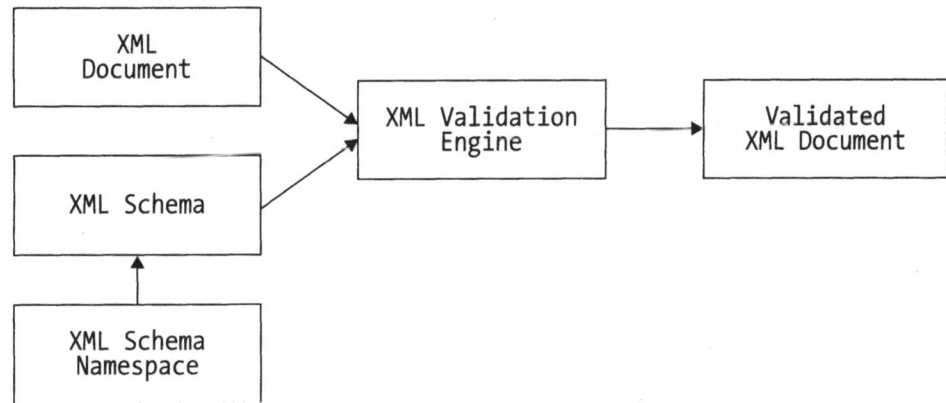

Figure 9-1. The XML document validation process

The schema also defines how many child elements exist, which elements are child elements, and in which order the child elements must appear. Finally, a schema defines whether an element is empty or can include text, which data types are expected for each element, and their default values. Listing 9-4 summarizes the IssueTracker DataSet schema.

Listing 9-4. DataSetIssueTracker.xsd (Partial Listing)

```xml
<?xml version="1.0" encoding="UTF-8" ?>
<xs:schema id="DataSetIssueTracker"
    xmlns="http://www.tempuri.org/DataSetIssueTracker.xsd"
    xmlns:xs="http://www.w3.org/2001/XMLSchema"
    targetNamespace="http://www.tempuri.org/DataSetIssueTracker.xsd"
    attributeFormDefault="qualified"
    elementFormDefault="qualified">

<xs:element name="DataSetIssueTracker">
<xs:complexType>
<xs:choice maxOccurs="unbounded">
<xs:element name="Dat_Issue">
    <xs:complexType>
        <xs:sequence>
            <xs:element name="IssueID" type="xs:long" />
            <xs:element name="TypeID" type="xs:int" minOccurs="0" />
            <xs:element name="UserID" type="xs:long" minOccurs="0" />
```

```
                    <xs:element name="EntryDate" type="xs:dateTime" minOccurs="0" />
                    <xs:element name="StatusID" type="xs:int" minOccurs="0" />
                    <xs:element name="Summary" type="xs:string" minOccurs="0" />
                    <xs:element name="Description" type="xs:string" minOccurs="0" />
                    <xs:element name="PriorityID" type="xs:int" minOccurs="0" />
                </xs:sequence>
            </xs:complexType>
        </xs:element>
        <xs:element name="Dat_User">
            <xs:complexType>
                <xs:sequence>
                    <xs:element name="UserID" type="xs:long" />
                    <xs:element name="Password" type="xs:string" minOccurs="0" />
                    <xs:element name="Firstname" type="xs:string" minOccurs="0" />
                    <xs:element name="Lastname" type="xs:string" minOccurs="0" />
                    <xs:element name="EmailAddress" type="xs:string" minOccurs="0" />
                    <xs:element name="UserType" type="xs:int" minOccurs="0" />
                    <xs:element name="CreateDate" type="xs:dateTime" minOccurs="0" />
                </xs:sequence>
            </xs:complexType>
        </xs:element>
        </xs:choice>
        </xs:complexType>
        <xs:unique name="Dat_Issue_Constraint" msdata:ConstraintName="Constraint1"
            msdata:PrimaryKey="true">
            <xs:selector xpath=".//mstns:Dat_Issue" />
            <xs:field xpath="mstns:IssueID" />
        </xs:unique>
        <xs:unique name="Dat_User_Constraint" msdata:ConstraintName="Constraint"
            msdata:PrimaryKey="true">
            <xs:selector xpath=".//mstns:Dat_User" />
            <xs:field xpath="mstns:UserID" />
        </xs:unique>
        </xs:element>
    </xs:schema>
```

NOTE *By default, new XML documents have a default namespace set to* http://www.tempuri.org/. *See the "Changing the Default Namespace" section later within this chapter to learn how to modify this setting.*

The most noticeable characteristic of the XSD in Listing 9-4 is that all tags have an xs: prefix. This prefix maps to the XML schema namespace at http://www.w3.org/2001/XMLSchema. This listing outlines the valid data values, field types, constraints, and relationships for the Dat_Issue and Dat_User data tables contained within the application's DataSet object.

Expressing DataSets in XML

As described in Chapter 2, "Accessing Data in ADO.NET," the DataSet class is useful for managing large amounts of data pulled from the database. This in-memory representation of the database includes representations of tables, table relationships, and field constraints. The DataSet is also capable of reading and writing its data and schema to XML. You fill DataSets from XML using the ReadXml method, and they output XML with the WriteXml method. Listing 9-5 implements a possible data export method for the Business Facade project that writes the contents of a filled DataSet to a specified file or a returned string.

Listing 9-5. Exporting XML Data from the ReferenceDataSet Object

```
public string ExportDataToXml( string strFilename )
{
    string strXmlData = "";

    try
    {
        //check to see if filename is valid
        if( strFilename != null && strFilename.Length > 0 )
        {
            System.IO.StreamWriter streamWrite =
                new System.IO.StreamWriter( strFilename );

            _AppDataComponent.ReferenceDataSet.WriteXml( streamWrite,
                XmlWriteMode.WriteSchema );

            streamWrite.Close();
        }
        else
        {
            //return xml output as a string
            strXmlData = _AppDataComponent.ReferenceDataSet.GetXml();
        }
    }
```

```
catch( Exception x )
{
    EventLog systemLog = new EventLog();
    systemLog.Source = "IssueTracker";
    systemLog.WriteEntry( x.Message, EventLogEntryType.Error, 0 );
}


    return strXmlData;
}
```

In this method, a string parameter provides the export method a value that represents an export filename. If the filename is valid, then the code creates and initializes a new StreamWriter object with the export filename. Next, the WriteXml method attached to the ReferenceDataSet object generates an XML representation of itself and writes it to the specified stream writer. If the filename is not valid, then the code creates and returns only a string representation of the ReferenceDataSet object. You might use the string representation of the DataSet's XML data for exchanging information between Web services.

In addition to producing XML, a DataSet object is also capable of reading XML as a data source. It can read XML content from a string parameter, an input stream, or a path to an XML file. Listing 9-6 presents an import method that takes XML data and populates the ReferenceDataSet object.

Listing 9-6. Importing XML Data into the ReferenceDataSet Object

```
public void ImportDataFromXml( string strXmlData, string strFilename )
{
    try
    {
        if( strFilename != null && strFilename.Length > 0 )
        {
            //pull xml from file
            System.IO.StringReader streamRead = new System.IO.StringReader(
                strFilename );

            _AppDataComponent.ReferenceDataSet.ReadXml( streamRead,
                XmlReadMode.ReadSchema );
        }
        else
        {
            //pull xml from string argument
```

```
    System.IO.StringReader readerXml = new System.IO.StringReader(
        strXmlData );

    _AppDataComponent.ReferenceDataSet.ReadXml( readerXml,
        XmlReadMode.IgnoreSchema );
    }
}
catch( Exception x )
{
    EventLog systemLog = new EventLog();
    systemLog.Source = "IssueTracker";
    systemLog.WriteEntry( x.Message, EventLogEntryType.Error, 0 );
}

return;
}
```

This method passes two arguments to point the way to XML data. The first parameter is a string object containing the actual XML data. The second parameter is a string that represents a filename where the XML data is stored. If the filename is valid, it extracts the XML data from the file. The code creates and initializes a new StringReader object with the supplied filename. Next, the ReadXml method attached to the ReferenceDataSet object pulls the XML data from the file with the help of the string reader. If the filename is not valid, then the ReadXml method uses the string reader to pull the XML data from the string argument. This approach supports interaction with desktop applications that can access the local file system and Web services capable of only exchanging data represented by string objects.

 NOTE *If a DataSet object already contains data, the new XML data is added to the existing DataSet. The ReadXml method does not merge XML data that has matching primary keys. To overwrite an existing row, you must use the ReadXml method to create a new DataSet. Then, the new DataSet merges with the existing DataSet.*

Listings 9-5 and 9-6 use two important methods that the DataSet class provides for reading and writing data to and from XML. Table 9-1 outlines all the methods that the DataSet object provides for interacting with XML as well as schema data.

Table 9-1. XML-Related Methods Provided by the DataSet Object

METHOD	DESCRIPTION
GetXml	Returns a string containing an XML representation of the data in the DataSet object.
GetXmlSchema	Returns a string containing the XSD for the XML returned by the GetXml method.
WriteXml	Writes the XML representation of the data in the DataSet object to a Stream object, a file, a TextWriter object, or an XmlWriter object. This XML can either include or omit the corresponding XSD.
WriteXmlSchema	Writes the XSD for the DataSet to a Stream object, a file, a TextWriter object, or an XmlWriter object.
ReadXml	Reads the XML written by the WriteXml method.
ReadXmlSchema	Reads the XSD written by the WriteXmlSchema method.

Understanding the Web Service Framework

Web services represent a significant part of the .NET application architecture. In the .NET vision, developers can construct an application using multiple Web services that work together to provide data and services for the application. The Web service model is a general model for building applications for any operating system that supports communication over the Internet, as illustrated in Figure 9-2. This model is also referred to as a *Service Oriented Architecture (SOA)*.

A *Web service* is a piece of application logic that is accessible using standard Web protocols. The Web service framework combines the best aspects of component-based development and Web development. As components, Web services represent packaged functionality that can be reused without concern about how the service is implemented. As a Web solution, Web services are not accessed by distributed protocols, such as the Component Object Model (COM), Remote Method Invocation (RMI), or Internet Inter-ORB Protocol (IIOP). Web services are accessed by open Web protocols, such as HTTP(S) and XML.

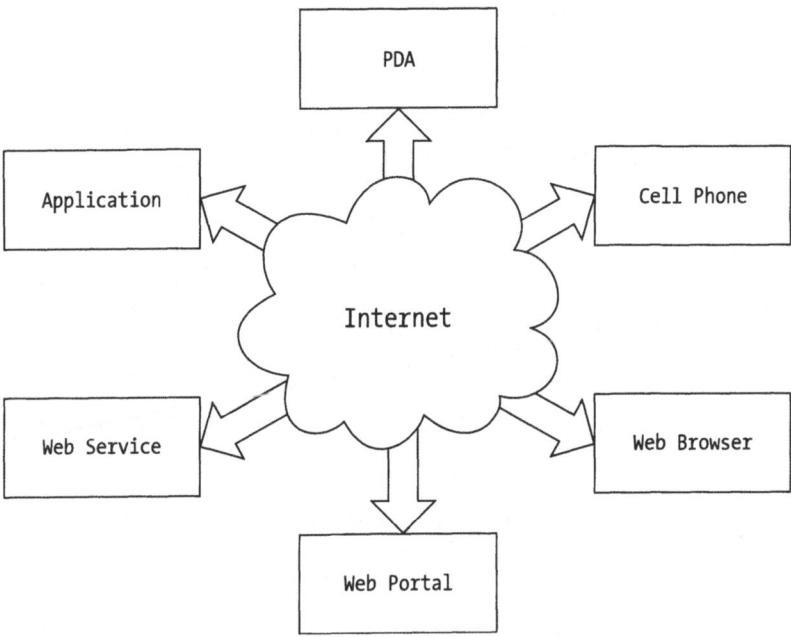

Figure 9-2. A connected environment where Web services reach a variety of clients

You define a Web service interface in terms of the messages it sends and receives. You can implement Web service clients on any platform and in any programming language as long as they can send and receive the specified messages.

As mentioned, Web services depend upon a collection of open specifications to interoperate with clients on multiple platforms. These specifications define a standard way to represent data, format messages, describe services, and discover services and their providers.

Exploring the Web Service Specifications

The power behind Web services is in their interoperability with clients and other services existing on different platforms. Web services can achieve this interoperability only through published open standards, as illustrated in Figure 9-3. These standards describe Web services at all functional levels, including communication protocol, service description, and service discovery. (The following sections explain the protocols in Figure 9-3.)

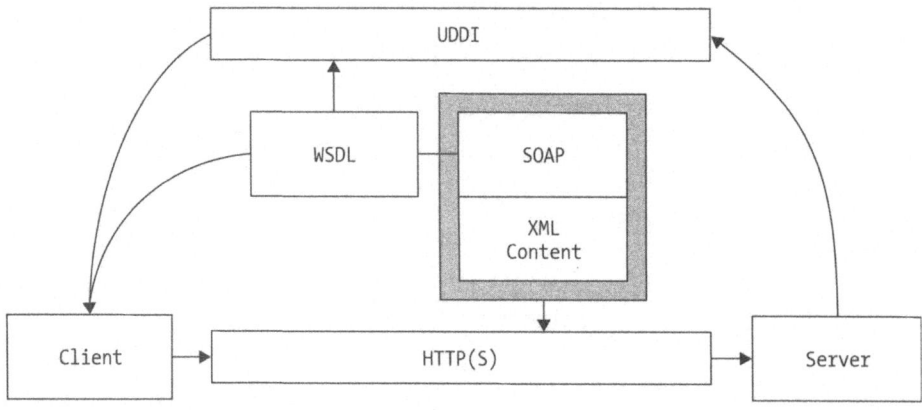

Figure 9-3. Relationships between the Web service protocols

Specifying a Communication Protocol

The Hypertext Transmission Protocol (HTTP) is the fundamental transport technology that carries messages between a Web service and a client. HTTP has been adopted as the default transport protocol largely because of its popularity and flexibility. Because HTTP requests usually channel through socket port 80 for Web browser support, it is an ideal candidate for channeling services. You can also use HTTPS, the securely encrypted variation of HTTP, for Web service communication, but the encryption/decryption process significantly slows down the communication.

NOTE *For additional information about the HTTP specification, see* http://www.w3c.org/Protocols.

The Simple Object Access Protocol (SOAP) is an XML-based document that contains the messages that exchange data between a Web service provider and client. SOAP specifies the message header for request and response messages as well as the structure for the embedded data. Although SOAP is typically carried by the HTTP(S) protocol, there is no specific requirement for it. That is, any carrier protocol that the Web service client and server both understand can transport a SOAP message. The greatest benefit SOAP offers is that it has already been implemented on many different hardware and software platforms. You can use SOAP to link different systems within and outside of the enterprise. Many attempts to create a common communication protocol that could be used for systems integration have been attempted, but none of them have had the wide-spread adoption that SOAP has. This is because SOAP uses existing XML parsers and HTTP libraries to do most of the hard work.

NOTE *You can find additional information on the SOAP specification on the W3C Web site at* http://www.w3c.org/2000/xp/Group.

Describing Available Web Services

The Web Services Description Language (WSDL) is an XML-based document that describes the basic format of Web service requests and responses. WSDL describes what a Web service can do, where it resides, and how to invoke it. WSDL is to SOAP as the Interface Definition Language (IDL) is to the Common Object Request Broker Architecture (CORBA) or COM. However, because WSDL is represented in XML, it is readable and editable. Also, it is language independent and standards based. This makes it ideal for describing XML Web service interfaces that are also accessible from a wide variety of platforms and programming languages. In addition to describing message contents, WSDL defines where the service is available and what communication protocol talks to the service. This means that the WSDL file defines everything required to write a program to work with an XML Web service.

NOTE *Additional information on the WSDL specification is available on the W3C Web site at* http://www.w3.org/TR/wsdl.

Discovering Other Web Services

Universal Description, Discovery, and Integration (UDDI) is a platform-independent open framework for describing services, discovering businesses, and integrating business services using the Web. It is also referred to as *the Yellow Pages of Web services*. UDDI is driven by all major platform and software providers, as well as marketplace operators and e-business leaders. These technology and business pioneers are acting as the initial catalysts to quickly develop UDDI and related technologies. The UDDI protocol is the building block that will enable businesses to quickly, easily, and dynamically find and transact with one another using their preferred applications. A directory of Web services based on UDDI also includes several ways to search for the services you need to build your applications. For example, you can search for providers of a service in a specified geographic location or for businesses of a specified type. The UDDI directory will then supply information, contacts, links, and technical data to allow you to evaluate which services meet your requirements.

> **NOTE** *Additional information on the UDDI specification is available on the UDDI Web site at* http://www.uddi.org/about.html.

Architecting Web Services in .NET

Web service clients are only concerned with the external interfaces of a Web service. As long as a client application can send and receive specified messages, it does not need to know anything about the internal workings of the Web service. From the enterprise developer perspective, a well-planned Web service architecture is critical to offering highly available and reliable Web services. Figure 9-4 shows an abbreviated version of the Web service architecture for the IssueTracker application.

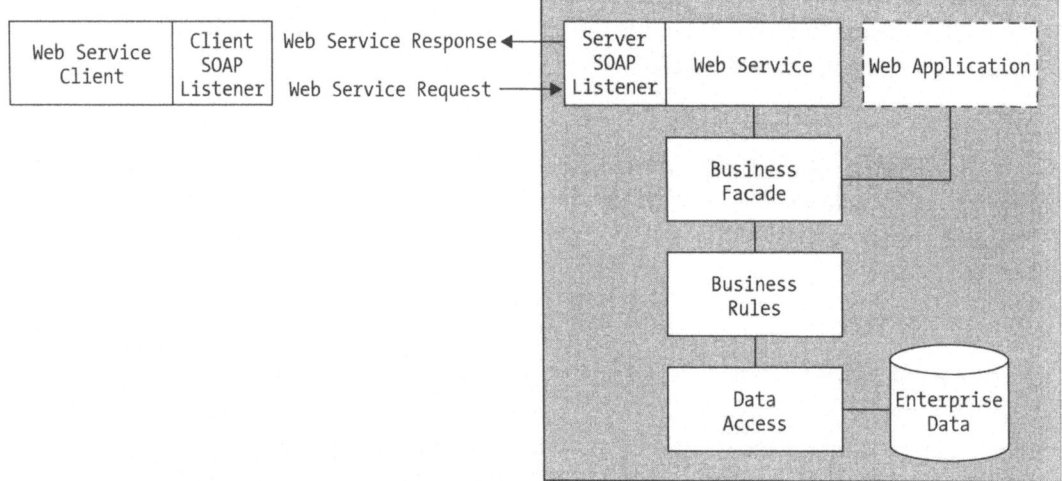

Figure 9-4. The IssueTracker Web service architecture

This view of the IssueTracker application focuses on the five most relevant architectural layers. At the bottom of the architecture is the application database, which persistently manages all enterprise data. Sitting beside the database is the Data Access layer, which manages the data retrieval and storage functions.

The Business Rules layer manages internal business objects and processes. The Business Facade layer provides a simple interface that maps Web service methods to internal business objects and processes. The Web Service layer is essentially a wrapper for the Business Facade layer that exposes functionality to Web service clients. The Business Facade layer interacts directly with the Business Rules and Data Access layers to deliver high-level functionality. Web service clients interact with the Web services through the Web service listener. The listener is responsible for receiving incoming messages containing requests for service, parsing the messages, and invoking the appropriate Web service method. If the Web service method returns a response, the listener is also responsible for packaging the response into a message and sending that back to the client. The listener also handles requests for contracts and other details about the Web service.

NOTE   *An emerging revenue stream for growing enterprises is to wrap existing data and services with a Web service layer and charge subscription access. However, supporting Web services requires a highly available and reliable environment. An enterprise application needs to be architected for sustaining the overwhelming load that Web services will bring.*

Building Enterprise Web Services

Creating a new Web service in Visual Studio .NET is easy because the New Project Wizard does just about everything for you. In general, the steps to creating a new Web service involve creating a new project, implementing the Web service methods, testing the service, and building a service client.

In Visual Studio .NET, building Web services is similar to building Web forms. Rather than having an .aspx file extension, Web services have an .asmx extension. Both file types also have a code-behind page with an additional .cs file extension. The biggest difference is that Web services have no user interface elements. They are essentially used for machine-to-machine data exchange only.

Expanding the Web Service Project

The IssueTracker enterprise application will leverage the power of Web services to expose existing data and services to third-party integrators. Any client application interested in accessing Issues or Users managed by IssueTracker only needs to send and receive SOAP messages.

As part of the Visual C# Distributed Application project, Visual Studio .NET has already created a Web service project containing a single default Web service identified as *WebService1.asmx*. The existing Web service project resides under the C:\Inetpub\wwwroot\IssueTracker_WebService directory. From the Solution Explorer, select WebService as the startup project type.

Because the Web service project will expose functionality provided by the Business Facade project, you need to create a reference to the Business Facade project. Open the Solution Explorer and select the References node under the Web service project. Next, open the pop-up menu and select Add Reference. In the Add Reference dialog box, select the Business Facade project, click Select, and then click OK to close the box.

Adding a New Web Service

Currently, Web services have little to offer in the area of security. They are based upon a technology stack of openly published specifications, their messages and content are transmitted in plain-text XML, and their request and response messages are typically transmitted over the open HTTP. A new specification, WS-Security, is in the works to resolve security concerns. For now, however, it is up to the individual developer to implement security functionality.

One of the most common, and minimal, approaches to Web service security is to implement an access key approach. In this approach, a user makes an initial Web service call, providing login credentials encrypted over a secure HTTPS connection. The program validates the login and returns an access key. All subsequent Web service method invocations then require the same valid key to perform its service.

The IssueTracker application will implement a new Web service that receives the login credentials, validates them with the help of the existing LoginManager, generates a new access key, and returns that key to the Web service caller. Begin by returning to the Solution Explorer and setting the Web service project as the startup project. Next, open the project's pop-up menu and select Add ➤ Add Web Service. The familiar Add New Item dialog box appears with the Web Service icon already highlighted. Enter *LoginServices.asmx* for the new Web service filename, as shown in Figure 9-5.

Visual Studio .NET creates a new LoginServices.asmx file and displays it in the design view. Because you can do little in the design view, switch to the code view by clicking the Switch to Code View link. The Web service source code is minimal. The necessary namespace references are in place, along with a class definition, a default constructor, and a couple of methods that initialize and dispose of the object. However, the file compiles cleanly into a Web service with no methods. To implement the ValidateLogin method within the LoginServices Web service, add the source code shown in Listing 9-7.

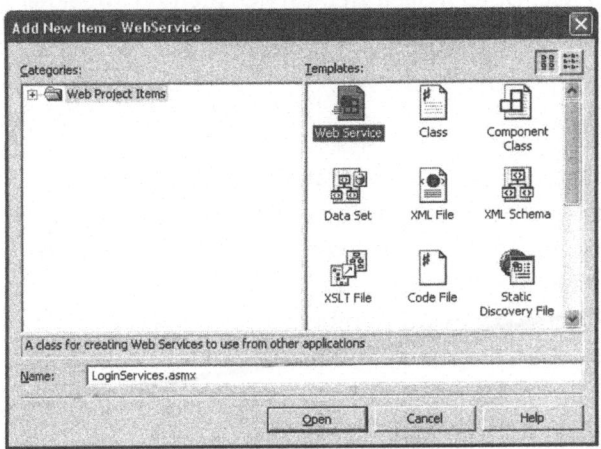

Figure 9-5. Creating a new Web service with the Add New Item dialog box

Listing 9-7. LoginServices.cs in the Web Service Project

```
[WebMethod(EnableSession=true)]
public string ValidateLogin( string strEmailAddress, string strPassword )
{
    //instantiate the LoginManager object
    UserManager mgrLogin = new UserManager();

    //validate login by getting the user data
    User objUser = mgrLogin.GetUser( strEmailAddress, strPassword );

    if( objUser != null )
    {
        //if successful, return the key
        if( Session[strEmailAddress] == null )
            Session[strEmailAddress] = 1;

        return Session.SessionID;
    }

    //if not successful, return error message
    return "ERR: Unable to validate login.";
}
```

This method begins with a WebMethod attribute. Attaching the WebMethod attribute to a public method indicates that the method is to be exposed as part of an XML Web service. The EnableSession parameter indicates whether session state is enabled for the Web service. Otherwise, a Web service method appears just like any other method within the framework:

```
[WebMethod(EnableSession=true)]
```

First, the code creates an instance of the LoginManager object. Next, the Web service parameters pass to the ValidateLogin method to authenticate the supplied credentials. If the program approves the login credentials, then it generates an access key and returns to the Web service caller.

You can generate a unique access key in any number of ways. The IssueTracker application creates an HttpSessionState variable to store the e-mail address of the user logging in:

```
Session[strEmailAddress] = 1;
```

The SessionID property serves as a nice key because it is unique, it can be tied back to a specific login, and it has a built-in expiration. You can easily complement the ValidateLogin method with another that checks to determine if the access key is valid. Add the method shown in Listing 9-8 to the same source file.

Listing 9-8. Adding Capability to Validate a Login Key

```
[WebMethod(EnableSession=true)]
public string CheckKey( string strKey )
{
    //determine if key is still valid
    if( Session.SessionID.CompareTo( strKey ) == 0 )
        return "OK: The Key is still valid.";

    else
        return "ERR: The Key is not valid.";
}
```

This method takes the access key generated by the ValidateLogin Web service method and determines if it is valid. Because the access key is essentially the SessionID value for the caller of this method, this method only needs to perform a quick comparison. With the two most important Web service methods complete, it is time to test them.

Testing a New Web Service

Visual Studio .NET makes testing Web services just as easy as writing them. With the Web service project selected as the startup project, run the debugger by pressing F5. The LoginServices test page displays, listing the two public Web service methods, as shown in Figure 9-6. Each method displays a link to a page that tests that specific method. Begin by clicking the ValidateLogin link.

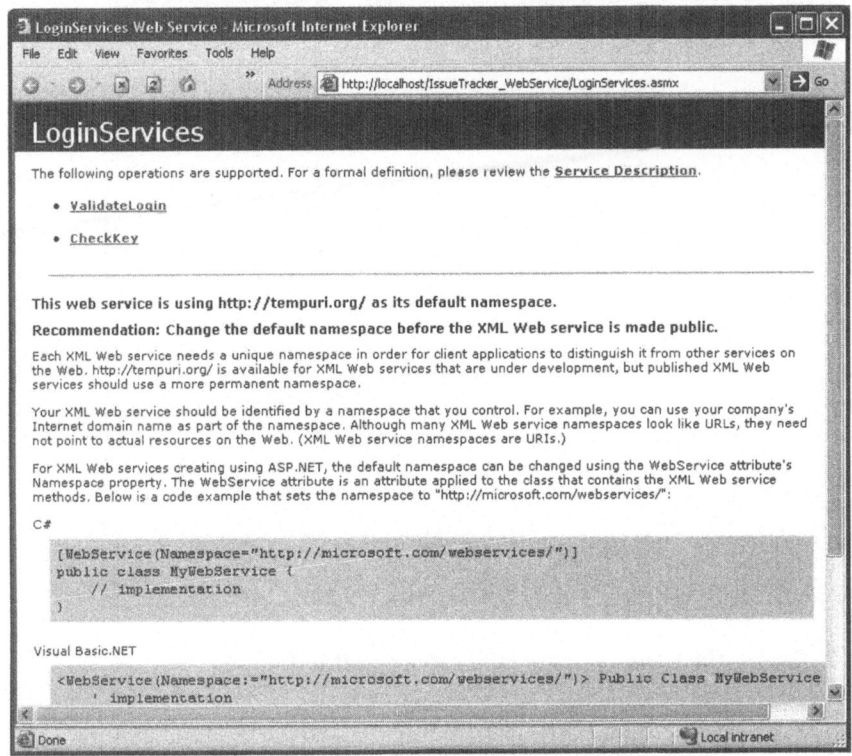

Figure 9-6. The LoginServices Web service test page

 NOTE *A number of developers have experienced problems debugging Web services, receiving the following error: "Unable to generate a temporary class (result=1)." To resolve the problem, try modifying the security permissions on the specified directory by adding a new user, named machine_name\aspnet, and assigning it full directory privileges. See MSDN Article #Q322886 at* http://support.microsoft.com/ default.aspx?scid=kb%3ben-us%3b322886 *for more information.*

Clicking the method name displays another test page, as shown in Figure 9-7. This page lists the method parameters along with fields to enter test parameters. Next, enter a valid IssueTracker login or the word *test* for the e-mail address and password and then click the Invoke button.

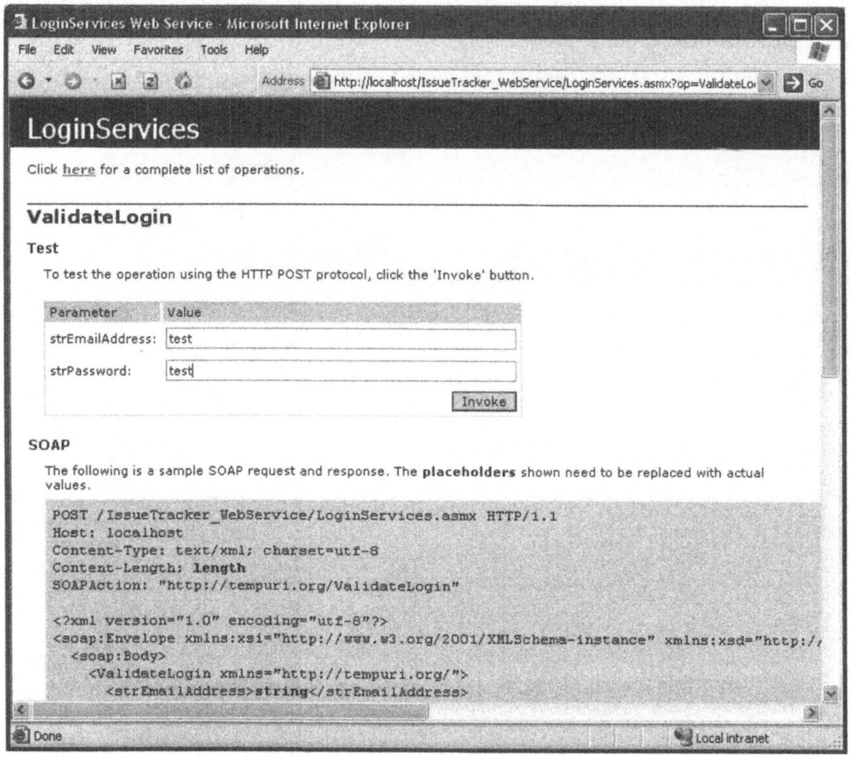

Figure 9-7. Testing the ValidateLogin Web service method

The results of the Web service display in an XML document. In this case, the test returns a cryptic string that represents the access key for unlocking the remaining Web services:

```
<?xml version="1.0" encoding="utf-8" ?>
<string xmlns="http://tempuri.org/">qd1ai155wf5tpn45wgjfx223</string>
```

As an additional test, return to the initial test page and click the CheckKey link. In the CheckKey method test page, enter the same access key and click the Invoke button. If all goes well, the result should be the following confirmation message:

```
<?xml version="1.0" encoding="utf-8" ?>
<string xmlns="http://tempuri.org/">OK: The Key is still valid.</string>
```

The Web service method test page also provides additional debugging information. Specifically, it displays the actual SOAP request and response messages coming to and from the Web service.

Examining the SOAP Request

A SOAP request comprises two elements, the HTTP request and the XML content that supplies the method parameters. Even without an explanation of the SOAP specification, it is not difficult to understand what most of it means. This is radically different from the CORBA and Distributed Component Object Model (DCOM) protocols, which are binary, not self-describing, and difficult to trace.

Although HTTP is used to deliver SOAP messages, SOAP can be carried over any other transport protocol, including Simple Mail Transfer Protocol (SMTP), the Internet e-mail protocol. The header differs between transport layers, but the XML content remains the same:

```
POST /IssueTracker_WebService/LoginServices.asmx HTTP/1.1
Host: localhost
Content-Type: text/xml; charset=utf-8
Content-Length: length
SOAPAction: "http://tempuri.org/ValidateLogin"


<?xml version="1.0" encoding="utf-8"?>
<soap:Envelope xmlns:xsi="http://www.w3.org/2001/XMLSchema-instance"
xmlns:xsd="http://www.w3.org/2001/XMLSchema"
xmlns:soap="http://schemas.xmlsoap.org/soap/envelope/">
  <soap:Body>
    <ValidateLogin xmlns="http://tempuri.org/">
      <strEmailAddress>string</strEmailAddress>
      <strPassword>string</strPassword>
    </ValidateLogin>
  </soap:Body>
</soap:Envelope>
```

A SOAP request is typically sent as an HTTP POST request with the content type set to text/xml and a SOAPAction field set to either an empty string or the name of the SOAP method. The SOAPAction field informs a Web server that an incoming SOAP message is on the way so that it can process, route, or filter the request. When the Web server receives the request, it first checks that the request has a SOAPAction field. If it does, it forwards it to the destination .asmx file; otherwise, it redirects to the default Web service test page.

The XML content of the SOAP request comes in three sections: the Envelope, Header, and Body. The Envelope defines the namespaces used by the rest of the SOAP message. Table 9-2 describes these namespaces.

Table 9-2. Summary of the SOAP Envelope Namespaces

NAMESPACE	DESCRIPTION
xmlns:SOAP-ENV	SOAP Envelope namespace
xmlns:xsi	XML schema for instances
xmlns:xsd	XML schema for data types

The Header is optional; it carries extended information relating to authentication, transactions, and payments. Any element in a SOAP processing chain can add or delete items from the Header. If a Header is present, it must be the first child node of the Envelope. Because the ValidateLogin method is simple and contains extended information, the Header is absent.

The Body represents the main content of the message. When SOAP performs a Web service method invocation, the Body contains a single element that includes the method name, arguments, and Web service target address. The Body element must be the first child element of the Header element. If the Header element is not present, then the Body element must be the first child of the Envelope element. The first child node of the Body element identifies the Web service method to be invoked. That element's children represent the parameters passed to the method.

The SOAP parameters can either be typed or untyped. The default SOAP encoding scheme uses the xsi:type attribute to indicate an XSD type. XSD defines several basic types, including int, byte, short, boolean, string, float, double, date, time, and URL. It also specifies a format for sending arrays and blocks of opaque data. Because SOAP is intended to be platform and language neutral, XSD does not define formats for encoding objects or structures unique to a single language.

Examining the SOAP Response

A SOAP/HTTP response is also returned as an XML document within a standard HTTP reply whose content type is set to text/xml. The XML document structure is just like the request except that the Body contains the encoded method result. The namespace of the result is the original target object URI, and the base name is the name of the method that was invoked. The XSI/XSD tagging scheme is optionally used to denote the type of the result. The SOAP standard does not specify what should be returned from a void method, but most implementations simply omit the <return> tag of the Body:

```
HTTP/1.1 200 OK
Content-Type: text/xml; charset=utf-8
Content-Length: length
```

```
<?xml version="1.0" encoding="utf-8"?>
<soap:Envelope xmlns:xsi="http://www.w3.org/2001/XMLSchema-instance"
xmlns:xsd="http://www.w3.org/2001/XMLSchema"
xmlns:soap="http://schemas.xmlsoap.org/soap/envelope/">
  <soap:Body>
    <ValidateLoginResponse xmlns="http://tempuri.org/">
      <ValidateLoginResult>string</ValidateLoginResult>
    </ValidateLoginResponse>
  </soap:Body>
</soap:Envelope>
```

Exposing Existing Services As Web Services

As with most enterprise applications, the purpose of the Web service project is to expose the IssueTracker application functionality for integration into other applications or processes. Therefore, the remainder of the IssueTracker Web service should be dedicated to wrapping the functionality already implemented within the Business Facade project. Because the Business Facade project contains the functionality already packaged within objects, such as IssueManager and UserManager, it makes sense to implement Web services similarly packaged, such as IssueServices and UserServices. An example of wrapping an existing method appears in Listing 9-9 as the GetSpecificIssue Web service method wraps the GetSpecificIssue Business Facade method.

Listing 9-9. IssueServices.cs in the Web Service Project

```
[WebMethod(EnableSession=true)]
public string GetSpecificIssue( string strKey, int argIssueID )
{
    //check key
    LoginServices svcLogin = new LoginServices();

    if( svcLogin.CheckKey( strKey ).StartsWith( "OK" ) )
    {
        BusinessFacade.IssueManager mgrIssues = new
            BusinessFacade.IssueManager();

        return mgrIssues.GetSpecificIssueXml( argIssueID );
    }

    return null;
}
```

Similar to a new Web service method, the implementation begins with the WebMethod property. However, rather than returning a simple string value as in the previous example, this method returns a longer string that represents a DataSet in XML. The method accepts two input parameters: the access key and an identifier indicating which Issue data to return. After validating the access key, the method creates a new IssueManager object and invokes the GetSpecificIssueXml method outlined in Listing 9-10.

Listing 9-10. Implementing the GetSpecificIssueXml Business Facade Method

```
public string GetSpecificIssueXml( int argLongIssueID )
{
    string strOutput;
    Issue objIssue = new Issue();

    strOutput = _ObjectManager.SelectOneAsXML( objIssue, argLongIssueID );
    return strOutput;
}
```

The GetSpecificIssueXml method appears in the Business Facade project and is similar to the GetSpecificIssue method. The difference between the two methods is probably obvious: In one case, an Issue object is returned, and in the other, a string is returned that formats the Issue as XML. Otherwise, this method works just like its GetSpecificIssue counterpart. It creates a new Issue object and passes it along with an ID to the business object manager.

The business object manager implemented within the DataAccess project adds a new public method that selects a specific Issue and returns it as XML rather than an Issue business object. Listing 9-11 implements the new SelectOneAsXml method.

Listing 9-11. Retrieving an Issue Record As XML

```
public string SelectOneAsXML( BusinessObject objSource, int intObjectID )
{
    bool boolStatus = false;
    string strObject;
    string strStoredProc;
    string strOutput = "";
    SqlParameter parameter;
    SqlCommand command;

    try
    {
        //get the object name
```

```
        Type objType = objSource.GetType();
        strObject = objType.FullName.Substring( objType.FullName.IndexOf(".")+1);

        //get the stored procedure name
        strStoredProc = "app_";
        strStoredProc += strObject;
        strStoredProc += "SelectAsXml";

        //initialize the command
        command = new SqlCommand( strStoredProc, dataComponent.sqlConnection );
        command.CommandType = CommandType.StoredProcedure;

        //add the ID parameter
        parameter = new SqlParameter( "@" + strObject + "ID", SqlDbType.Int );
        parameter.Direction = ParameterDirection.Input;
        parameter.Value = intObjectID;
        command.Parameters.Add( parameter );

        //open the connection and execute query
        dataComponent.sqlConnection.Open();
        XmlReader reader = command.ExecuteXmlReader();

        reader.MoveToContent();
        strOutput = reader.ReadOuterXml();
        reader.Close();

    }
    catch( Exception exception )
    {
        EventLog systemLog = new EventLog();
        systemLog.Source = "IssueTracker";
        systemLog.WriteEntry( exception.Message, EventLogEntryType.Error, 0 );
    }
    finally
    {
        dataComponent.sqlConnection.Close();
    }

    return strOutput;
}
```

The SelectOneAsXml method is a variation of the existing SelectOne method. The only minor differences include a new stored procedure, a different data reader, and a different return type. The new stored procedure appears in

Listing 9-12 and differs by adding the FOR XML AUTO statement described in Chapter 2, "Accessing Data in ADO.NET." Instead of processing records with a SqlDataReader, records are processed with an XmlReader object. The XmlReader produces a string value containing an XML representation of the selected Issue.

Listing 9-12. The app_IssueSelectAsXml Database Stored Procedure

```
CREATE PROCEDURE dbo.app_IssueSelectAsXml
(
    @IssueID int
)
AS

SET NOCOUNT ON;

SELECT IssueID, TypeID, UserID, EntryDate, StatusID, Summary, Description,
PriorityID, ModifiedDate FROM Dat_Issue WHERE (IssueID = @IssueID) FOR XML AUTO;
GO
```

The modified stored procedure returns a string that represents the Issue in XML format. Otherwise, it appears almost identical to its app_IssueSelect counterpart. Listing 9-13 presents an example of the XML code produced as a result of the new query.

Listing 9-13. XML Output from the GetSpecificIssue Web Service Method

```
<?xml version="1.0" encoding="utf-8" ?>
<string xmlns="http://tempuri.org/"><Dat_Issue IssueID="1" TypeID="1"
    UserID="1" EntryDate="2002-01-01T00:00:00" StatusID="1"
    Summary="Unable to print. " Description="Can not print to the color laser
    in the copy room." PriorityID="2" ModifiedDate="2002-01-01T00:00:00" />
</string>
```

Changing the Default Namespace

As Web services emerge, there may be cases where Web service names and method names will collide. As mentioned earlier, namespaces uniquely identify a Web service method. By default, Visual Studio .NET assigns the default namespace of http://tempuri.org/. To change from this default, edit the namespace accordingly:

```
[ WebMethod( EnableSession=true,
Namespace="http://www.mynamespace.net/webservices/" ) ]
```

Addressing Web Service Security

Initially, developers saw SOAP as an HTTP-based protocol and assumed that HTTP security would be adequate for SOAP. This was largely driven by the fact that thousands of Web applications are running daily using HTTP security. Therefore, the current SOAP standard assumes that security is a transport issue, relying upon technologies such as HTTPS and digitally signed certificates.

As SOAP extended its reach to become a more general-purpose protocol running on top of a number of transports and on a number of devices, security became a bigger issue. HTTP provides several ways to authenticate which user is making a SOAP call, but there are no means to propagate this identity when the message is routed from HTTP to an SMTP transport.

Specifications are already in the works to build upon SOAP to provide additional security features for Web services. The WS-Security specification defines a complete encryption framework, and the WS-License specification defines techniques for guaranteeing the identity of the client and ensuring that only authorized clients can use a Web service. In the meantime, it is up to the enterprise developer to implement a sufficient level of security. The access key approach to Web service access is a common practice.

Building a Web Service Client

As mentioned, a Web service client can take many shapes including other Web services, Web applications, desktop applications, console applications, cellular phones, Personal Digital Assistants (PDAs), and any other device capable of sending and receiving SOAP messages. To demonstrate, let's implement the application login functionality of the IssueTracker Windows form application using LoginServices.

Begin by opening the Solution Explorer in Visual Studio .NET and selecting the WinUI project as the startup project. Next, open the pop-up menu for the WinUI project and select Add Web Reference. When the Add Web Reference dialog box appears, enter the Uniform Resource Locator (URL) that points to the LoginServices Web service file in the Address field of the Add Web Reference dialog box:

```
http://127.0.0.1/IssueTracker_WebService/LoginServices.asmx
```

After entering the Web service URL and clicking the Go button, you will see the Web service test page. Enter the namespace associated with the Web service. Generally, Web service namespaces are the reverse designations of domain names, such as net.mynamespace.www, as shown in Figure 9-8.

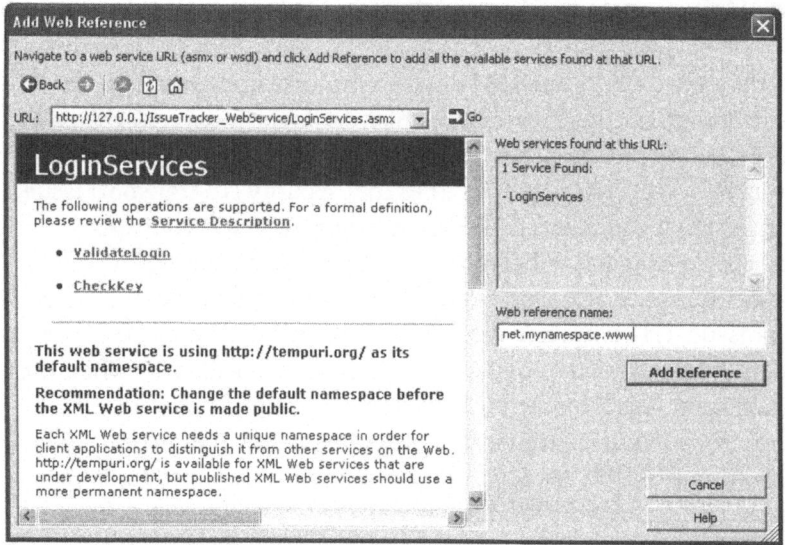

Figure 9-8. Importing a service with the Add Web Reference dialog box

The Web service test page displays the two Web service methods created earlier. Alternatively, you can browse the Microsoft UDDI registry for available Web services by clicking the Add Web Reference button in Visual Studio. The Solution Explorer updates with a new Web References node. This node displays a reference to the locally hosted LoginServices Web service, as shown in Figure 9-9.

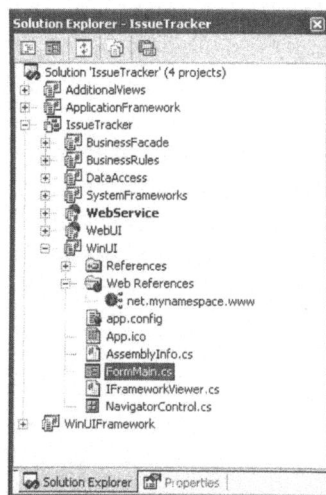

Figure 9-9. The Web references associated with the IssueTracker WinUI project

When Visual Studio .NET creates a Web reference to a Web service, it also implicitly creates a new proxy class. This proxy class abstracts the Web service and provides an object that can be instantiated and interacted with in code. The enterprise developer is not concerned with structuring SOAP messages and using HTTP methods to invoke a remote Web service. Rather, you create and invoke a Web service object just as any other C# object. Listing 9-14 interacts with a LoginServices proxy object to validate an IssueTracker login.

Listing 9-14. FormLogin.cs in the WinUI Project

```csharp
private void btnOK_Click(object sender, System.EventArgs e)
{
    string strWebServiceResponse = "";

    net.mynamespace.www.LoginServices wsLogin =
        new net.mynamespace.www.LoginServices();

    strWebServiceResponse = wsLogin.ValidateLogin( edtEmail.Text,
        edtPassword.Text );

    if( strWebServiceResponse.StartsWith( "ERR" ) == false )
    {
        m_strAccessKey = strWebServiceResponse;
        m_boolLoggedIn = true;
        Close();
    }
    else
        System.Windows.Forms.MessageBox.Show( "Login Failed." );

    return;
}
```

This event handler begins by instantiating the Web service proxy object. The Web reference listed in the Solution Explorer indicates that the namespace for this object would be net.mynamespaces.www.LoginServices. The object is initialized and the login credentials are supplied as parameters to the ValidateLogin method. The results of the Web service method are returned in a string variable for the event handler to interpret. Depending upon the results of the Web service, the event handler either accepts the login or rejects it.

Interpreting the Web Service Description

As mentioned, a WSDL document describes the interfaces and bindings of a Web service. Web services are collections of network endpoints, known as *ports*. These ports are identified with network bindings that enable description reuse. The protocol and data format for a specific port represents a binding. Therefore, you define a port by associating a network address with a reusable binding. Table 9-3 summarizes the key elements found in the WSDL document.

Table 9-3. Tag Elements That Define the WSDL Specification

ELEMENT	DESCRIPTION
Types	A container for data type definitions using a type system, such as XSD
Message	An abstract definition of the data being communicated
Operation	An abstract description of an action supported by the service
Port Type	An abstract set of operations supported by one or more endpoints
Binding	A concrete protocol and data format specification for a particular port type
Port	A single endpoint defined as a combination of a binding and a network address
Service	A collection of related endpoints

A completely filled WSDL document can span several pages depending on the number of different data type and methods defined for the Web service. The following code listings present the WSDL document for the LoginServices Web service. The listing has five major blocks.

As you can see in Listing 9-15, the WSDL document begins with a basic page declaration and identifies the document encoding format. Next, the XML namespaces are defined in the definitions block of the WSDL document.

Listing 9-15. The Definitions Element of a Sample WSDL File

```
<?xml version="1.0" encoding="utf-8" ?>
<definitions xmlns:http="http://schemas.xmlsoap.org/wsdl/http/"
    xmlns:soap="http://schemas.xmlsoap.org/wsdl/soap/"
    xmlns:s="http://www.w3.org/2001/XMLSchema" xmlns:s0="http://tempuri.org/"
    xmlns:soapenc="http://schemas.xmlsoap.org/soap/encoding/"
    xmlns:tm="http://microsoft.com/wsdl/mime/textMatching/"
    xmlns:mime="http://schemas.xmlsoap.org/wsdl/mime/"
```

```
targetNamespace="http://tempuri.org/"
xmlns="http://schemas.xmlsoap.org/wsdl/">
```

With the page declaration and namespace definition out of the way, the WSDL defines the data types referenced by the Web service methods (see Listing 9-16). This block comprises four principal entries that represent the SOAP messages transmitted to and from each Web service method. Each message identifies the piece of data it is carrying. For example, the message that invokes the ValidateLogin method carries two string data elements, named strEmailAddress and strPassword. The message generated in response to this method is ValidateLoginResponse and carries a single string data element, named ValidateLoginResult.

Listing 9-16. The Types Element of a Sample WSDL File

```
<types>
<s:schema elementFormDefault="qualified"
    targetNamespace="http://tempuri.org/">

    <s:element name="ValidateLogin">
        <s:complexType>
            <s:sequence>
                <s:element minOccurs="0" maxOccurs="1" name="strEmailAddress"
                    type="s:string"/>
                <s:element minOccurs="0" maxOccurs="1" name="strPassword"
                    type="s:string" />
            </s:sequence>
        </s:complexType>
    </s:element>

    <s:element name="ValidateLoginResponse">
        <s:complexType>
            <s:sequence>
                <s:element minOccurs="0" maxOccurs="1"
                    name="ValidateLoginResult" type="s:string" />
            </s:sequence>
        </s:complexType>
    </s:element>

    <s:element name="CheckKey">
        <s:complexType>
            <s:sequence>
                <s:element minOccurs="0" maxOccurs="1" name="strKey"
```

```
                        type="s:string" />
            </s:sequence>
        </s:complexType>
    </s:element>

    <s:element name="CheckKeyResponse">
        <s:complexType>
            <s:sequence>
                <s:element minOccurs="0" maxOccurs="1" name="CheckKeyResult"
                    type="s:string" />
            </s:sequence>
        </s:complexType>
    </s:element>

    <s:element name="string" nillable="true" type="s:string" />
</s:schema>
</types>
```

The message element describes the data being exchanged between the Web service providers and consumers (see Listing 9-17). Each Web method has two messages: input and output. The input describes the parameters for the Web method; the output describes the return data from the Web method. Each message contains zero or more <part> parameters, one for each parameter of the Web method. Each parameter associates with a concrete type defined in the <types> container element.

Listing 9-17. The Message Element of a Sample WSDL File

```
<message name="ValidateLoginSoapIn">
    <part name="parameters" element="s0:ValidateLogin" />
</message>
<message name="ValidateLoginSoapOut">
    <part name="parameters" element="s0:ValidateLoginResponse" />
</message>
<message name="CheckKeySoapIn">
    <part name="parameters" element="s0:CheckKey" />
</message>
<message name="CheckKeySoapOut">
    <part name="parameters" element="s0:CheckKeyResponse" />
</message>

<message name="ValidateLoginHttpGetIn">
    <part name="strEmailAddress" type="s:string" />
```

```
        <part name="strPassword" type="s:string" />
    </message>
    <message name="ValidateLoginHttpGetOut">
        <part name="Body" element="s0:string" />
    </message>
    <message name="CheckKeyHttpGetIn">
        <part name="strKey" type="s:string" />
    </message>
    <message name="CheckKeyHttpGetOut">
        <part name="Body" element="s0:string" />
    </message>

    <message name="ValidateLoginHttpPostIn">
        <part name="strEmailAddress" type="s:string" />
        <part name="strPassword" type="s:string" />
    </message>
    <message name="ValidateLoginHttpPostOut">
        <part name="Body" element="s0:string" />
    </message>
    <message name="CheckKeyHttpPostIn">
        <part name="strKey" type="s:string" />
    </message>
    <message name="CheckKeyHttpPostOut">
        <part name="Body" element="s0:string" />
    </message>
```

Ports are channels through which Web service request and response messages
are communicated. Ports types might include SOAP, HTTP-GET, HTTP-POST, and
SMTP. You need to map each port type to specific Web service methods, which in
turn map to the specific messages that carry data to and from the Web service. To
map a method to a request-response pair of messages, they must appear in the
<operation> element (see Listing 9-18).

Listing 9-18. The Ports and Channels Element of a Sample WSDL File

```
<portType name="LoginServicesSoap">
    <operation name="ValidateLogin">
        <input message="s0:ValidateLoginSoapIn" />
        <output message="s0:ValidateLoginSoapOut" />
    </operation>
    <operation name="CheckKey">
        <input message="s0:CheckKeySoapIn" />
        <output message="s0:CheckKeySoapOut" />
```

```
        </operation>
    </portType>

    <portType name="LoginServicesHttpGet">
        <operation name="ValidateLogin">
            <input message="s0:ValidateLoginHttpGetIn" />
            <output message="s0:ValidateLoginHttpGetOut" />
        </operation>
        <operation name="CheckKey">
            <input message="s0:CheckKeyHttpGetIn" />
            <output message="s0:CheckKeyHttpGetOut" />
        </operation>
    </portType>

    <portType name="LoginServicesHttpPost">
        <operation name="ValidateLogin">
            <input message="s0:ValidateLoginHttpPostIn" />
            <output message="s0:ValidateLoginHttpPostOut" />
        </operation>
        <operation name="CheckKey">
            <input message="s0:CheckKeyHttpPostIn" />
            <output message="s0:CheckKeyHttpPostOut" />
        </operation>
    </portType>
```

Bindings specify how Web service methods expect the data to be encoded. The SOAP specification contains predefined rules for doing this. This involves a transition from abstract data types, messages, and operations to concrete physical representations of the messages transmitted. The concrete aspects of operations are defined in the <binding> element (see Listing 9-19).

The name of the binding can be anything, but you must use the same name for the binding attribute of the <port> element. Inside the <binding> element, there is an extension element called <soap:binding>. It specifies the transport protocol used, whether it is HTTP or SMTP, and the style of request.

Listing 9-19. The Types Operations of a Sample WSDL File

```
<binding name="LoginServicesSoap" type="s0:LoginServicesSoap">
    <soap:binding transport="http://schemas.xmlsoap.org/soap/http"
        style="document" />

    <operation name="ValidateLogin">
        <soap:operation soapAction="http://tempuri.org/ValidateLogin"
            style="document" />
```

```
        <input>
            <soap:body use="literal" />
        </input>
        <output>
            <soap:body use="literal" />
        </output>
    </operation>

    <operation name="CheckKey">
        <soap:operation soapAction="http://tempuri.org/CheckKey"
            style="document" />
        <input>
            <soap:body use="literal" />
        </input>
        <output>
            <soap:body use="literal" />
        </output>
    </operation>

</binding>

<binding name="LoginServicesHttpGet" type="s0:LoginServicesHttpGet">
    <http:binding verb="GET" />

    <operation name="ValidateLogin">
        <http:operation location="/ValidateLogin" />
        <input>
            <http:urlEncoded />
        </input>
        <output>
            <mime:mimeXml part="Body" />
        </output>
    </operation>

    <operation name="CheckKey">
        <http:operation location="/CheckKey" />
        <input>
            <http:urlEncoded />
        </input>
        <output>
            <mime:mimeXml part="Body" />
        </output>
    </operation>
```

```
        </binding>
        <binding name="LoginServicesHttpPost" type="so:LoginServicesHttpPost">
            <http:binding verb="POST" />

            <operation name="ValidateLogin">
                <http:operation location="/ValidateLogin" />
                <input>
                    <mime:content type="application/x-www-form-urlencoded" />
                </input>
                <output>
                    <mime:mimeXml part="Body" />
                </output>
            </operation>

            <operation name="CheckKey">
                <http:operation location="/CheckKey" />
                <input>
                    <mime:content type="application/x-www-form-urlencoded" />
                </input>
                <output>
                    <mime:mimeXml part="Body" />
                </output>
            </operation>

        </binding>
```

Finally, the <service> element defines the interface for the entire Web service with the exposed Web service name defined as an element attribute (see Listing 9-20). This element also identifies endpoints publicly available and maps them to the ports defined earlier in the WSDL. In all three cases, the SOAP endpoints map to a single .asmx Web service implementation file.

Listing 9-20. The Service Element of a Sample WSDL File

```
<service name="LoginServices">

    <port name="LoginServicesSoap" binding="so:LoginServicesSoap">
        <soap:address  location="http://localhost/Issue.../LoginServices.asmx"
/>
    </port>

    <port name="LoginServicesHttpGet" binding="so:LoginServicesHttpGet">
```

```
        <http:address location="http://localhost/Issue.../LoginServices.asmx" />
    </port>

    <port name="LoginServicesHttpPost" binding="so:LoginServicesHttpPost">
        <http:address location="http://localhost/Issue.../LoginServices.asmx" />
    </port>

</service>
</definitions>
```

It quickly becomes clear how a WSDL specification for a Web service can be self-describing. The <service> element represents the entry point for the entire Web service. This element describes the service in terms of entry points, referred to as *ports*. The <binding> element maps these ports to a specific communication protocol. The <portType> element maps defined ports to Web service methods, referred to as *operations*. Each <operation> element comprises an input and output message. Each <message> element defines parts of its message and, in some cases, references a parameter data structure. These data structures are defined in the <Types> element. Finally, all blocks come together to comprehensively describe a single Web service for publishing.

Publishing Web Service Availability

As mentioned, UDDI is a technology that lets Web service clients dynamically find Web service providers. You can browse a UDDI registry by service descriptions or by businesses descriptions. The results of a UDDI search provide information about the business or service. Most important, UDDI entries provide WSDL descriptions of Web services, allowing a client to dynamically bind to the listed Web service without requiring any other integration information. The typical process for using UDDI is in a publish-find-bind process, as illustrated in Figure 9-10.

A provider of Web services registers itself and publishes its available services. This information appears in the UDDI White Pages. Business information such as the name, address, telephone number, and other contact information becomes available for others to find. This business information is stored in a BusinessEntity object, which in turn contains information about services, categories, contacts, URLs, and other documents relating to that business.

Web service clients use UDDI to find a specific Web service. Organized information about Web services appear in the UDDI Yellow Pages. This information groups Web services by common functionality and stores them in a BusinessService object.

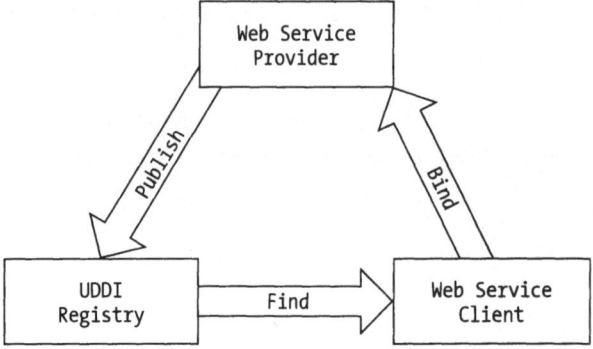

Figure 9-10. The relationship between Web service provider, registrar, and client

Web service clients connect to and interact with Web services after they have found them. Technical information about Web services, including the details necessary to invoke a Web service, appear in the UDDI Green Pages. This includes URLs, information about method names, argument types, and related documents, which are stored in the BindingTemplate object. Web service specifications are defined in a UDDI document called a *type model* or *tModel*. Usually, the tModel contains a WSDL file that describes a SOAP interface to a Web service.

Developers and organizations can publish the availability of Web services with any available UDDI registry. You can find information about registering as an organization and publishing an available Web service at `http://uddi.microsoft.com`.

Discovering Web Services with UDDI

You browse a UDDI registry through a Web service. Web service clients can connect to the Microsoft UDDI registry by pointing to the UDDI Inquiry interface:

`http://uddi.microsoft.com/inquire`

Just as your own Web services have a test page, the Microsoft UDDI Inquiry Web service also provides a Web browser–supported test page. All public Web service methods display, including those that return business, service, binding, and tModel details. An easier method of searching the UDDI registry is through the Add Web Reference dialog box, as shown in Figure 9-11.

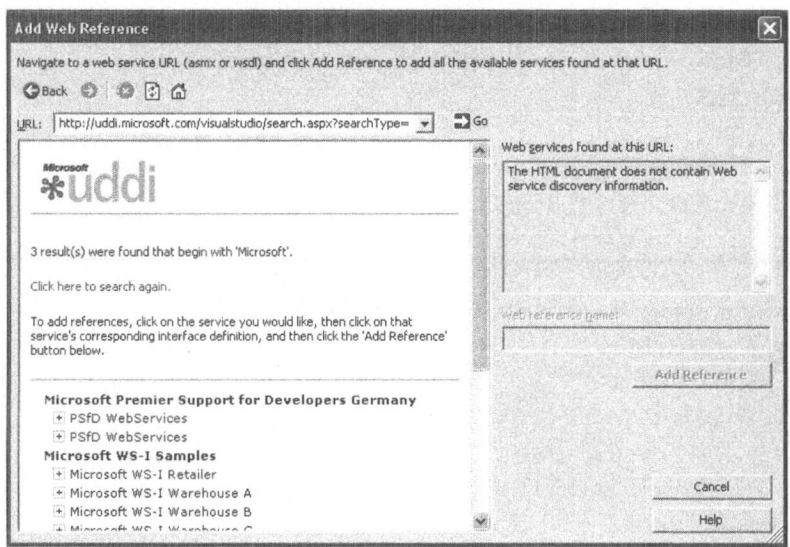

Figure 9-11. Searching for external Web services in the UDDI registry

To find information about a business or service, enter the name into the displayed edit field. In Figure 9-11, the user has entered *Microsoft* as the provider name. This has the same effect as invoking the FindBusiness method of the UDDI Inquiry Web service with the following request:

```
<find_business generic="1.0" xmlns="urn:uddi-org:api">
        <name>Microsoft</name>
</find_business>
```

The result of the FindBusiness method is another XML document that contains detailed business information about Microsoft:

```
<businessList generic="1.0"
    operator="Microsoft Corporation"
    truncated="false"
    xmlns="urn:uddi-org:api">

    <businessInfos>
        <businessInfo businessKey="0076B468-EB27-42E5-AC09-9955CFF462A3">
            <name>Microsoft Corporation</name>
            <description xml:lang="en">
                Empowering people through great software -
                any time, any place and on any device is Microsoft's
                vision. As the worldwide leader in software for personal
```

```
                            and business computing, we strive to produce innovative
                            products and services that meet our customer's
                    </description>

                    <serviceInfos>
                        <serviceInfo
                            businessKey="0076B468-EB27-42E5-AC09-9955CFF462A3"
                            serviceKey="1FFE1F71-2AF3-45FB-B788-09AF7FF151A4">
                            <name>Web services for smart searching</name>
                        </serviceInfo>
                        <serviceInfo
                            businessKey="0076B468-EB27-42E5-AC09-9955CFF462A3"
                            serviceKey="8BF2F51F-8ED4-43FE-B665-38D8205D1333">
                            <name>Electronic Business Integration Services</name>
                        </serviceInfo>
                        <serviceInfo
                            businessKey="0076B468-EB27-42E5-AC09-9955CFF462A3"
                            serviceKey="611C5867-384E-4FFD-B49C-28F93A7B4F9B">
                            <name>Volume Licensing Select Program</name>
                        </serviceInfo>
                        <serviceInfo
                            businessKey="0076B468-EB27-42E5-AC09-9955CFF462A3"
                            serviceKey="A8E4999A-21A3-47FA-802E-EE50A88B266F">
                            <name>UDDI Web Sites</name>
                        </serviceInfo>

                    </serviceInfos>
                </businessInfo>
            </businessInfos>
</businessList>
```

The returned XML message provides useful information, such as a unique UDDI identifier for retrieving additional information, a business description, and a list of offered services. Any SOAP-enabled software or device can browse the UDDI registry for a specific service and then dynamically bind to the service to access the desired information or services.

Validating Web Service Accessibility

As mentioned, Web services are intended for interoperability with applications and devices existing on multiple operating platforms. To ensure a successful Web service deployment and to minimize customer frustration, it is important to test newly developed services with validation tools that check the structure of a Web service's related documents, such as WSDL and SOAP messages. Many tools are emerging that validate Web service documents:

```
http://www.gotdotnet.com/services/wsdl/wsdlverify.asmx?op=ValidateWSDL
```

The WsdlVerify Web service validates WSDL documents to ensure that they are well formed and contain all the necessary information to bind to a Web service. The previous URL points to the test page shown in Figure 9-12. Simply enter the URL of your hosted Web service to determine if it is valid. In most cases, WSDL documents generated by Visual Studio .NET do not need customization and in turn do not need validation. However, it is always useful to check.

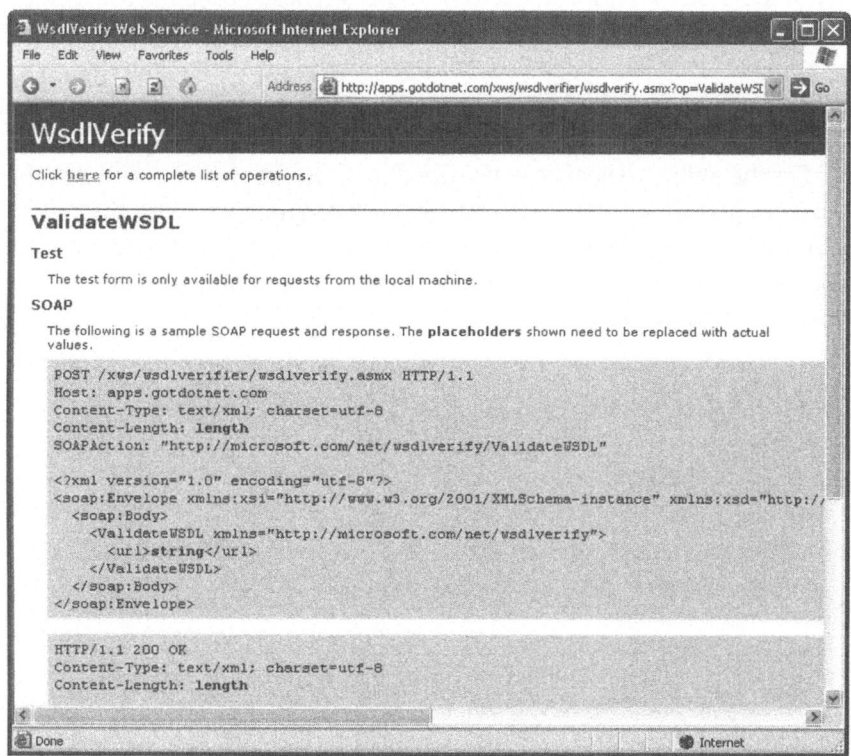

Figure 9-12. The WsdlVerify utility Web service

Summary

XML remains a powerful technology for exchanging self-describing data between applications. Initially grasping XML is a challenge, but once you put it to use, you will see its simplicity. Its self-describing characteristic makes it an ideal method of exchanging information between Web services. As you have seen, Web services depend heavily upon XML for describing nearly every aspect of the Web service, especially in the data passed between the client and service.

The DataSet object includes powerful functionality to generate XML documents and to initialize its own data structure from an XML source document. In addition, Visual Studio .NET makes it easy to quickly create new Web services capable of exposing existing functionality to potential customers looking to license legacy data and services. New Web services can announce their availability as they are published to public directories, such as UDDI. Similarly, Visual Studio .NET includes sophisticated functionality for easily importing and using discovered services.

Bear in mind that a Web service strategy should be planned and well thought out. Simply adding a service layer over existing code can lead to complications, specifically in the areas of performance and security. These problems will lead to more customer frustration than customer satisfaction. You need to build an enterprise application to support Web services from the beginning and design it for scalability accordingly. You should not consider Web services to be products or solutions in themselves. They are an additional feature to your enterprise application; they offer the ability to license your core data or functionality over the Web.

The next chapter describes the reporting services integrated with the Visual Studio .NET environment. The chapter begins with an overview of reporting and then breaks down the report-building steps. It covers everything necessary to build a typical enterprise report.

Integrating Reporting Services

THIS CHAPTER EXPLORES the reporting services available to .NET enterprise developers for producing high-quality, interactive reports. This chapter begins with a description of Crystal Reports and its tight integration with the Visual Studio .NET environment. Next, it reviews the report-building process, covering all the steps from designing the report to integrating it in an application. Finally, this chapter puts everything together by creating a new report and integrating it into the IssueTracker application.

Delivering Enterprise Reporting

Enterprise data must be printed at some point, so reporting services are a vital part of any enterprise application. Printed reports need to appear professional with accurate data and clear formatting. Developers can always write code to enable a Windows or Web application to loop through database records and print the results. However, anything beyond basic formatting—such as data consolidation, multiple-level totals, charting, and conditional formatting—can become complicated.

The Visual Studio .NET environment comes with Crystal Reports, a sophisticated reporting tool developed by Crystal Decisions. You can use it to quickly create complex and professional-looking reports such as the one shown in Figure 10-1. Crystal Reports is tightly integrated with Visual Studio .NET and provides a visual designer to quickly create and format reports.

Benefiting from an Enterprise Reporting Toolkit

An enterprise reporting toolkit such as Crystal Reports offers enterprise developers a number of advantages for quickly building a reporting service. Applications benefit from the option of using a thin Web client or a rich Windows form client to display reports. In addition, Crystal Reports provides report viewers that operate within a Web browser or a desktop application. You can also create interactions between the form controls and the report viewer.

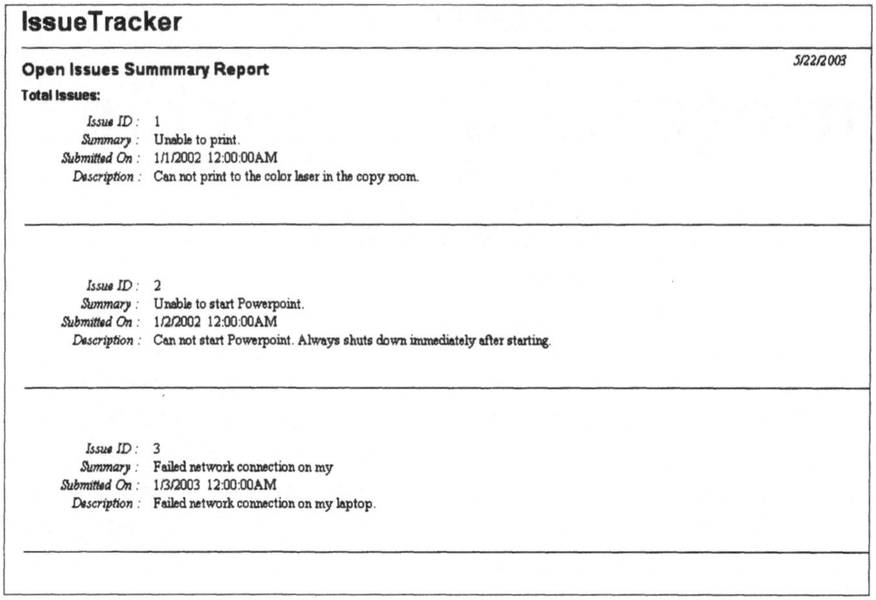

IssueTracker

Open Issues Summmary Report   *5/22/2003*

Total Issues:

    Issue ID : 1
   Summary : Unable to print.
Submitted On : 1/1/2002 12:00:00AM
 Description : Can not print to the color laser in the copy room.

    Issue ID : 2
   Summary : Unable to start Powerpoint.
Submitted On : 1/2/2002 12:00:00AM
 Description : Can not start Powerpoint. Always shuts down immediately after starting.

    Issue ID : 3
   Summary : Failed network connection on my
Submitted On : 1/3/2003 12:00:00AM
 Description : Failed network connection on my laptop.

Figure 10-1. IssueTracker's Open Issues Summary Report

You can specify viewer properties at design time and interact with other controls at runtime. With runtime customization, users can view different reports or change the format, data selection, or export options of an existing report. Finally, developers benefit from the rich object model that Crystal Reports provides. The report object model exposed by the reporting engine allows developers to add code that enables the Windows form viewer control to interact with other user interface controls in the same page. For example, a Windows form viewer can interact with a button or combo box to provide users with export and formatting options.

Summarizing the Report-Building Process

The report-building process happens in four distinct steps: creating the report, layout out the report, implementing the viewer, and distributing the reporting components.

Creating the Report

The entire process starts with the creation of a blank report template. Once you have created the template, you can assign a data source for the report because

Crystal Reports connects directly to databases through ADO.NET database drivers. Each driver handles a specific database type or database access technology. To provide the most flexible data access to developers, two different models of data access pull or push values, as illustrated in Figure 10-2.

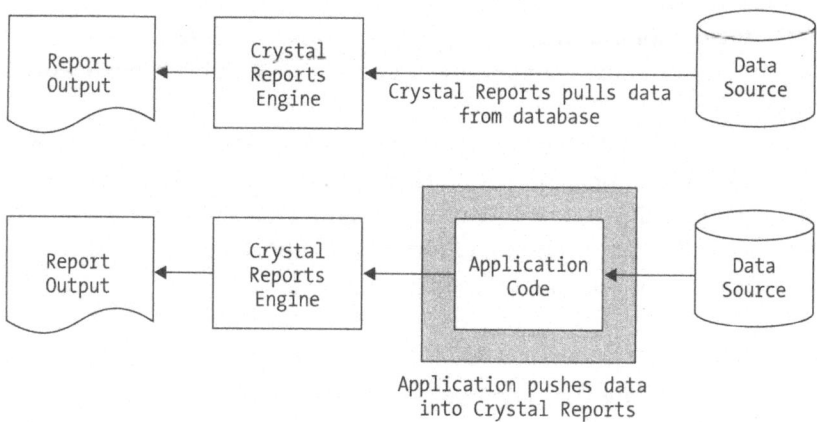

Figure 10-2. Comparing data push and data pull models

In the data pull model, the database driver connects to the database and pulls the data on demand. With this data model, Crystal Reports handles the connection to the database and the SQL extract command that retrieves the data. This is the default data retrieval methodology.

Alternatively, the data push model requires the application to connect to the database, execute a SQL command to create a RecordSet or DataSet object that matches fields in the report, and pass that object to the report. This data model enables the developer to build connection pooling into the application and to filter the data before Crystal Reports receives it.

Laying Out the Report Template

The next step in building a new report is to lay out the report template. Each report includes database connections, different report sections, and report objects. Using the Crystal Reports designer, you lay out reports graphically in Visual Studio. The designer starts when you add a new blank report to a project.

You need to specify one or more report data sources—specifically, database tables from which the report will extract data. In most cases, you need to join individual database tables so that you can associate rows in one table with rows in another. The design environment provides intelligent linking of database tables and presents a user interface to manually set table links.

You also need to define and implement report sections. The report designer is divided into several report sections. You implement reports by dragging objects from the Field Explorer into each report section. The report data associated with a report object will vary depending upon the section into which you place the report objects.

Finally, you need to add individual report objects to a report. Their section placement determines their behavior. First, drag a report object from the Field Explorer and drop it into the body of the report. Second, use either the Properties window or the pop-up menu to format the report object.

Report objects come in the following categories:

- **Database fields**: These are tables and columns that represent the insertion point for extracted data. The tables and columns listed are based on the specified data sources.

- **Formula fields**: These are user-defined data fields that apply data transformation formulas against other fields.

- **Parameter fields**: These are user-defined data fields that are set by parameters passed to the report at runtime.

- **Group name fields**: These are user-defined fields that group all extracted rows together.

- **Running total fields**: These are user-defined fields that conditionally total the number of extracted records independent of grouping.

- **SQL expression fields**: These are user-defined data fields that apply SQL statements for optimized data extraction performance.

- **Special fields**: These are built-in fields that are specific to reports, such as page count, print date, author, and report file path.

- **Unbound fields**: These are strongly typed placeholders that participate in display formulas.

- **Charts**: These are graphical representations of extracted data.

- **Subreports**: These are nested reports that are defined elsewhere.

- **Text objects**: These are formatted text labels that display static information.

- **Line and box objects**: These are objects that draw a simple line or box for adding visual effects to a report.

- **Picture objects**: These are objects that load a picture from a file for display within a report page.

Creating Application Viewers

Both Windows forms and Web forms can contain a report viewer that displays the generated report to the application user. The Windows form viewer supports a number of features, including data export and file format conversion. You can also customize the viewer to add or remove functionality exposed to the user through toolbar buttons. The Web form viewer displays reports in Hypertext Markup Language (HTML) 3.2 and 4.0 one page at a time. You can export a report into different file formats using the Crystal Reports reporting engine.

Application users can set printing properties from a viewer's toolbar or keep the default print settings. Users can also export a report into a number of different file formats. These formats support easy integration into other applications including the following:

- Adobe Acrobat (.pdf)

- Crystal Reports for Visual Studio .NET (.rpt)

- HTML 3.2 and 4.0 (.html)

- Microsoft Excel (.xls)

- Microsoft Rich Text (.rtf)

- Microsoft Word (.doc)

- Plain-text files (.txt)

- Microsoft Exchange public folders

Distributing Reporting Components

The last step of the report-building process is distributing the reporting components. The Crystal Reports engine is distributable as a merge module that can be combined with an application's normal setup program. For Web applications, all reporting elements reside on a single server.

Creating a New Enterprise Report

The report-building process begins by creating a new report template and setting its data source. The reporting engine connects to databases through drivers written for specific data source types. To provide the most flexible data access to applications, database drivers support both a pull and a push model of data access.

You can use the database drivers both at design time and at runtime. At design time, the database driver identifies the schema of the source data and fills the table entries in the Field Explorer. In most cases, this process involves connecting to a database and selecting the tables, views, or stored procedures to specify the schema. During runtime, the report will use the same database driver used to create the report. If data is pushed into the report, the report will select the appropriate driver to handle the supplied RecordSet or DataSet object.

Adding a New Report Template

A report exists independently of its type of viewer. The best way to begin a reporting project is to create the report template. Begin by creating a new Class Library project named *EnterpriseReports*. Once created, select the new project in the Solution Explorer and choose Add ➤ Add New Item from its context menu. Select the Crystal Report template and enter the name *OpenIssuesReport.rpt*, as shown in Figure 10-3.

Adding a new Crystal Report template triggers the Crystal Report Gallery, as shown in Figure 10-4. This dialog box allows you to start creating a new report based on the Report Expert, a blank report, or an existing report.

A Report Expert is a wizard that walks you through the report creation process. Each Report Expert begins with a data source definition. There are seven different Report Experts that assist in the creation of the following report types: Standard, Form Letter, Form, Cross-Tab, Subreport, Mail Label, and Drill Down.

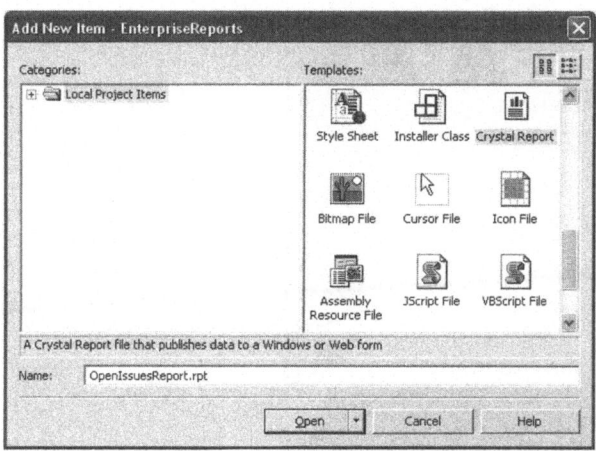

Figure 10-3. Creating a new report with the Add New Item dialog box

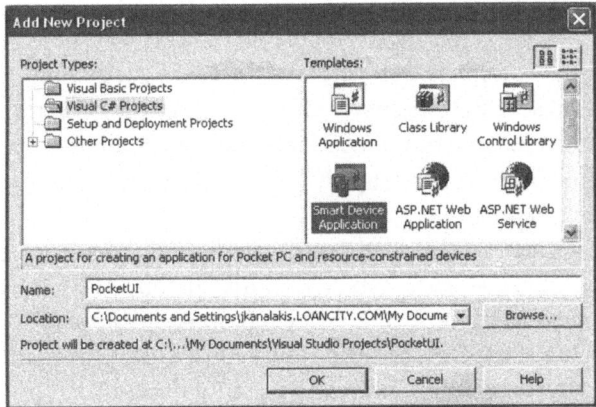

Figure 10-4. Selecting the Report Expert in the Crystal Report Gallery

The Standard Report Expert is the most generic of the experts. It guides the developer through the process of choosing a data source and linking database tables, as shown in Figure 10-5. It also helps add fields and specify grouping, summarization, and sorting criteria. This expert also displays a Chart tab for creating different types of charts and a Select tab for filtering specific rows of data. The Style tab contains predefined layouts for formatting data to help give the report a professional look.

The Form Letter Report Expert creates form letters that access the database for customer mailing information. It offers much of the functionality found in the Standard Report Expert, but it adds a Form Letter tab to specify the text and database fields that will appear in each section of the letter. The Form Letter tab can also import text that has been created in another application.

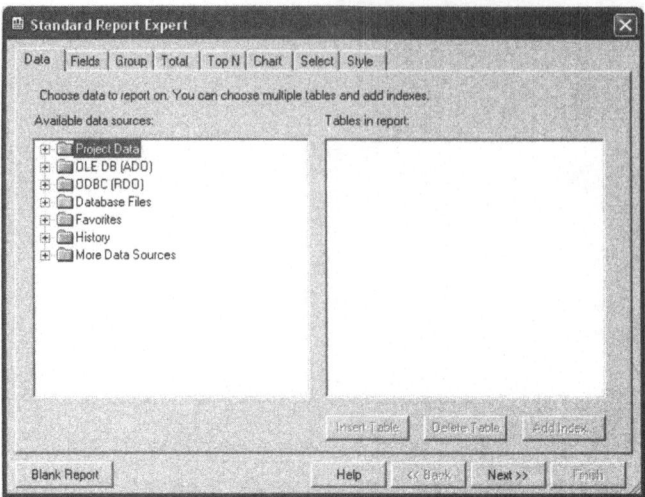

Figure 10-5. The Standard Report Expert

The Form Report Expert creates reports that can be printed on predefined forms, such as company invoices and statements. It offers much of the functionality found in the Standard Report Expert, but it also features a Form tab to specify a company logo image or form. You can apply logos and forms to the header or the Details section of a report.

The Cross-Tab Report Expert creates a report that displays data as a cross-tab object. Three additional tab pages—Cross-Tab, Style, and Customize Style—define the format of the cross-tab report. A cross-tab object is represented as a grid that returns values based on criteria supplied to it. Data appears as rows and columns that help users compare data and identify trends.

The Subreport Expert creates a main report and a subreport at the same time. It offers much of the functionality found in the Standard Report Expert for creating the main report. An additional Subreport tab page defines a new or existing report as the subreport. You create new subreports by repeating the steps found in the Standard Report Expert.

The Mail Label Report Expert creates a report formatted to print on a mailing label of any size. The Label tab lets you select a commercial label type or define a custom layout of rows and columns for any style of multicolumn report.

The Drill Down Report Expert creates a report that hides sections and makes them available for viewing only through a drill-down process. It offers much of the functionality of the Standard Report Expert. An additional Drill tab displays a list of sections that you can hide. Hidden sections do not appear on the report until you select the appropriate field. Typically, you will use hidden data for summaries and totals.

Specifying a Reporting Data Source

Because data access is at the center of the report-building process, each Report Expert requires a data source to be specified at the beginning. You can bind a report to any number and type of data sources. You can specify additional data sources (after you have completed a Report Expert) by selecting the report and choosing Database ➤ Add/Remove Database from its context menu to display the Database Expert, as shown in Figure 10-6.

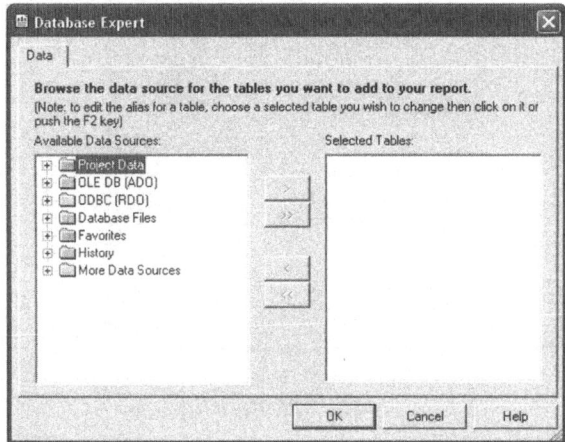

Figure 10-6. The Database Expert designates referenced data sources.

In the Database Expert, expand the OLE DB (ADO) tree node and select Microsoft OLE DB Provider for SQL Server. Click Next and select the source Server to enter the database server login parameters. Enter *IssueTracker* as the source database and click Next. Leave the default settings listed in the Advanced Information dialog box and click Finish.

This creates a new database connection, which can be expanded in the Database Expert's Available Data Sources tree list. Expand the IssueTracker node to see the list of individual tables. Add all the tables in the Selected Tables list and click OK. Next, the Database Expert displays the Links tab, as shown in Figure 10-7.

The Links tab displays the join relationships between all the tables selected. The Dat_Issue table is the master table with joins into Val_IssueType, Dat_User, Val_Status, and Val_Priority. The Data Expert does a great job of automatically linking tables. To add an additional link, click one table field and drag it to another. For example, bind Dat_Issue.AuthorID to Dat_User.UserID and click the OK button to complete the process.

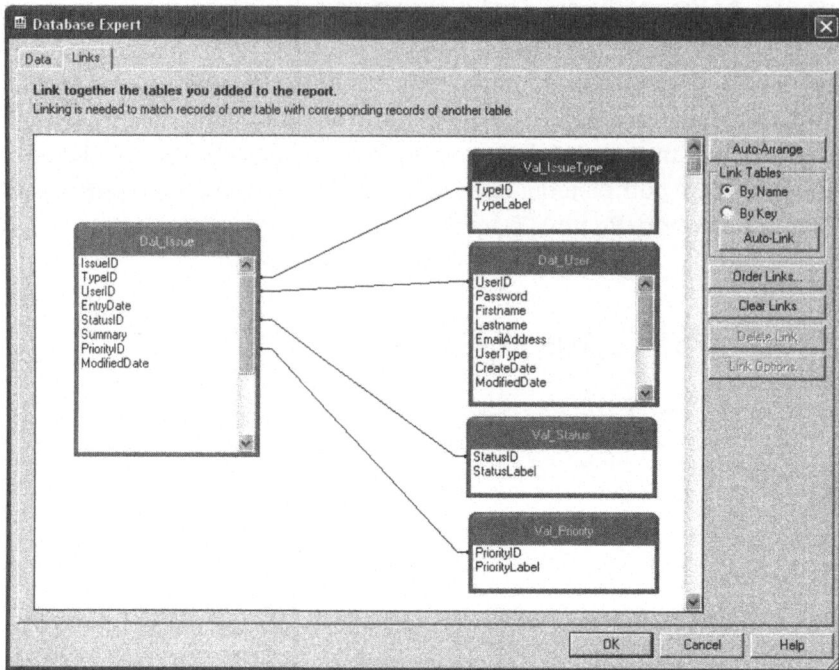

Figure 10-7. The Database Expert maps database table relationships.

Performing the Report Layout

The report layout steps consist of the following: adding report sections, adding report objects, adding data filters, organizing the data, and formatting the data.

Organizing Reports into Sections

First, you need to define and implement report sections. The report designer comes in several report sections, including the Report Header, Page Header, Details, Report Footer, and Page Footer. You can drag report objects from the Field Explorer into a report section. The report data associated with that report object varies depending upon where you place the report objects. If you insert a chart object into the Report Header section, for example, the chart will appear only once at the beginning of the report and will summarize all the data contained in the report. If you insert a chart object into the Group Header section, on the other hand, a separate chart will appear at the beginning of each group that summarizes the data contained within that group.

Adding Report Formatting Objects

Crystal Reports provides a number of report formatting objects that help the developer create truly customized forms and reports. The Field Explorer lists the field objects that add dynamic elements to the report. Drag a field object from the Field Explorer into a report section to mark the placement of extracted data. In the case of the OpenIssuesReport template, expand the Database Fields and Dat_Issue nodes. Drag a few of the listed column references into the Details section of the report, as shown in Figure 10-8.

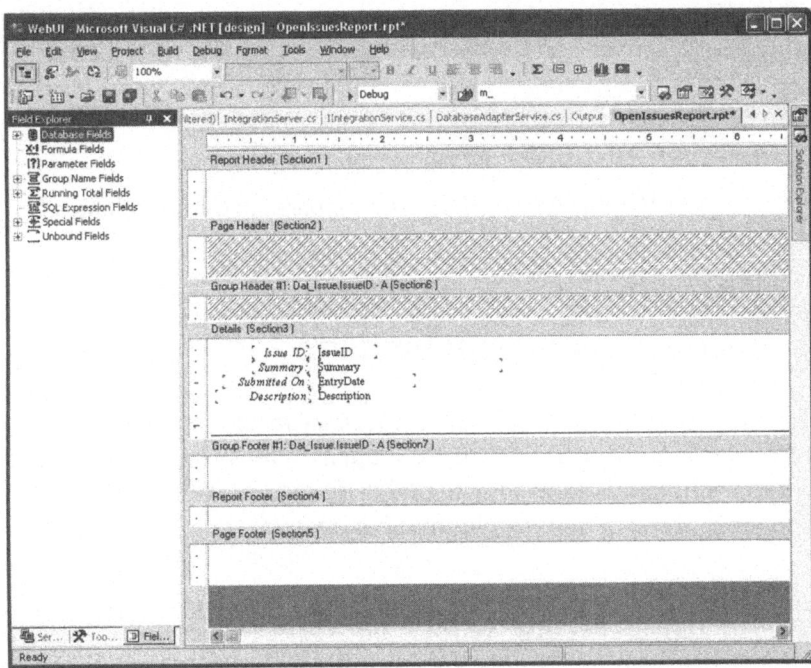

Figure 10-8. You use field objects to lay out data and text within the body of a report.

Text objects display static text and create titles, headings, and label summaries. If necessary, text objects can hold database fields as well as create custom forms and letters.

Properties define how the different reporting objects will appear in the final report. This includes special formatting such as font selection, border definition, paragraph spacing, and hyperlink definitions. You can open the object's Format Editor (shown in Figure 10-9) by selecting a placed report object and choosing Format from the pop-up menu.

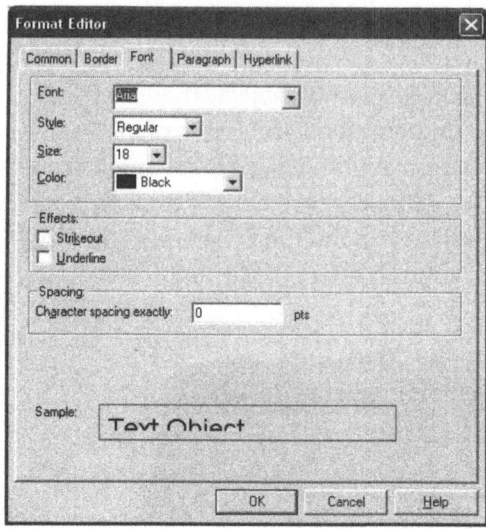

Figure 10-9. The object's Format Editor dialog box defines the format of placed report objects.

Filtering Necessary Application Data

In many cases, such as in OpenIssuesReport, not every record in a database is desired—only those issues that are still marked open. In these cases, you need to apply a filter to select a certain subset of the table data. In Crystal Reports, you filter data using record selection formulas and parameters.

Filtering Data Using Record Selection Formulas

When you select a field to appear on a report, data values from every record in the table display by default. In many cases, you may not want to include all the values and instead display a subset of those values. Crystal Reports provides a formula language that specifies any type of record selection. In most cases, the powerful record selection flexibility that the formula language provides is not necessary. For simpler record selection, use the Select Expert.

Open the Select Expert by selecting Report ➤ Select Expert from the pop-up menu. Choose the table source that needs to be filtered. As Figure 10-10 shows, the source can be an existing report field that has been placed within the report or any field selection from an associated data source.

After you have selected the source field, click the OK button to enter the specific filter criteria. You can add any number of select filters to narrow down the desired record selection. Each select filter comprises a database field, a comparative operator, and a value, as shown in Figure 10-11. You can use any of the dozen comparative operators as well as a custom formula. For OpenIssuesReport, select the data field Dat_Issue.IssueID, choose the Is Equal To operator, and enter 0 for the value.

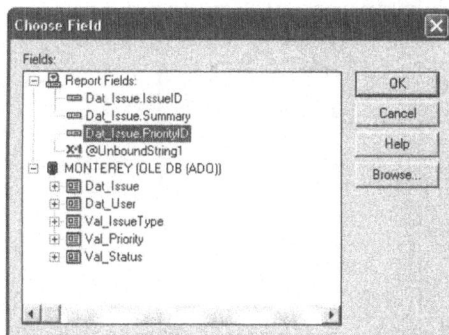

Figure 10-10. Select Expert filtering field selection

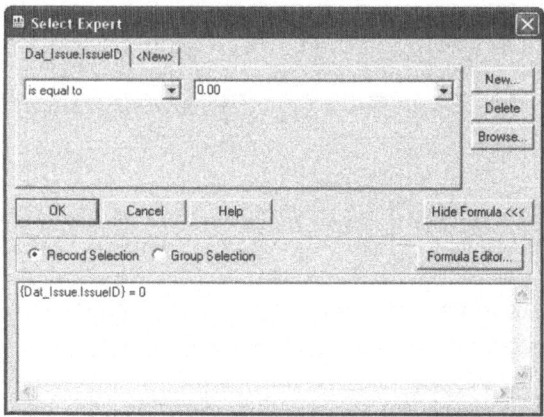

Figure 10-11. Creating a select filter to retrieve specific records

When you select specific records, the report will be based only on the records that meet those conditions. If there is a need to select records based on part of the data within a specific field, then you need to create a record selection formula using the formula language. For example, you could evaluate the area code within a telephone number and then do a record selection based on that. To create a selection formula, open the report's pop-up menu and select Report ➤ Edit Selection Formula ➤ Records. The Record Selection Formula Editor displays, as shown in Figure 10-12.

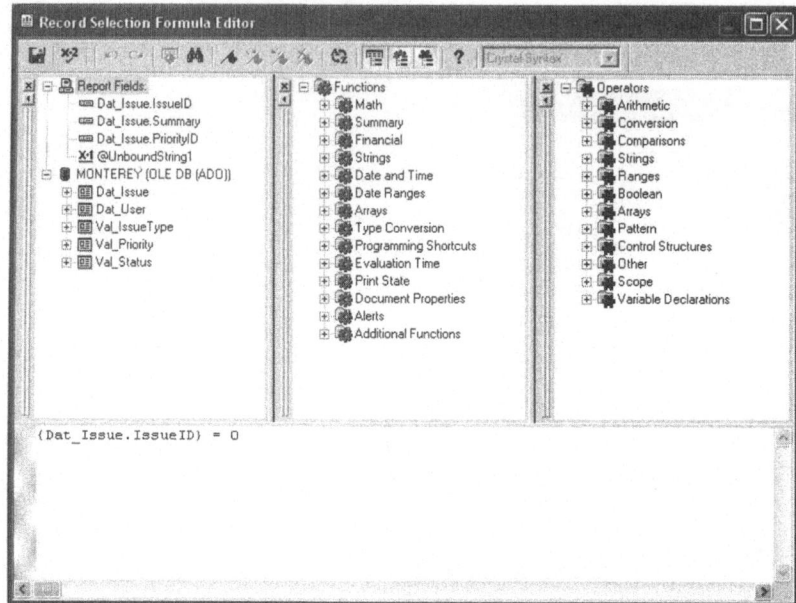

Figure 10-12. Creating presentation formulas with the Record Selection Formula Editor

Filtering Data Using Parameters

Parameter fields prompt the application user to enter additional information before generating the report. The information users enter determines what appears in the report. For example, in a report used by salespeople, a parameter might ask the user to choose a region. The report would return the results for the specific region instead of returning the results for all of the regions. Though it is useful to be aware of this feature, all reporting parameters should be captured by the application user interface and supplied to the report programmatically. Relying upon a Crystal Reports dialog box makes the report appear loosely integrated with the application. Figure 10-13 illustrates the awkward dialog box presented to the user when prompted to enter an issue priority.

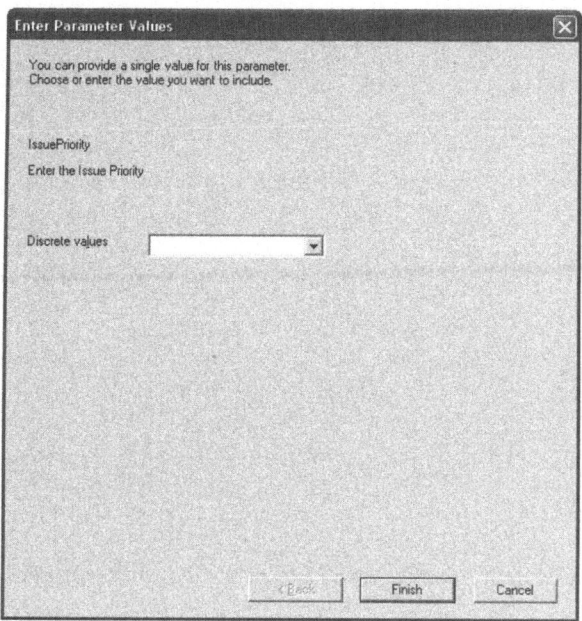

Figure 10-13. The Enter Parameter Values dialog box captures runtime input parameters.

Organizing Related Data Together

When you insert a database field into a report, the data within the field appears in the order in which it appears in the database. Grouping, sorting, and totaling functions turn disorganized data into useful information on a report.

Grouping Values Together

Most reports need to break data into sections so reports are easier to read and analyze. You can usually achieve this by grouping reported data. To create a report group, select the report, open the pop-up menu, and select Insert ➤ Group. In the Insert Group dialog box, select the field to be sorted and grouped by, as shown in Figure 10-14. Select the sort direction from the second drop-down list.

Reports can also specify headers that label each group. By default, this group header displays the value of the field being grouped. Because this report is grouped by Dat_IssueID.PriorityID, the relative priority value displays at the change of each group. In the case of OpenIssuesReport, you can make the header even more readable by adding a text object that labels the group header.

315

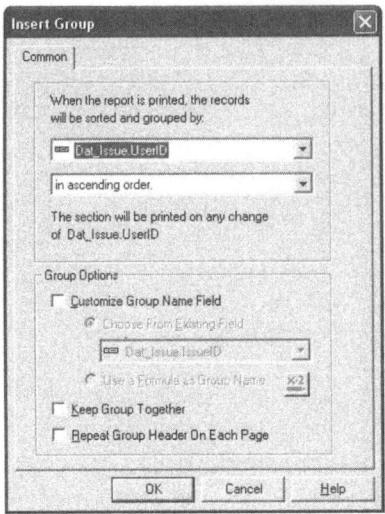

Figure 10-14. The Insert Group dialog box selects a field to be sorted and grouped.

To display a different value, such as the Issue author's name, you can customize the group name field by choosing an alternate data field or by creating a formula. When the Insert Group dialog box closes, two new sections appear in the report: Group Header #1 and Group Footer # 1. This is how Crystal Reports represents the existence of groups within a report and provides the developer with an area to enhance the group header and footer.

Sorting Column Data

When you add a database field to a report, the data values display in the report in the order in which they exist in the database. Sorting records helps organize data within a report so users can find and interpret reported information.

Data sorting is based on two criteria: the field to be sorted and the sort direction. The sort field is the data field that specifies the order in which data will be presented in a report. You can specify any data field as a sort field, including formula fields. The field's data type determines the method by which the data from that field is sorted.

The sort direction is the order in which data values appear in a report. Ascending order presents numeric values from smallest to largest and text values alphabetically. By default, Crystal Reports sorts data records in ascending order based on the values specified in the sort field. Descending order presents numeric values from largest to smallest and text values reverse alphabetically.

To sort data records displayed in a report, open the report's pop-up menu and select Report ➤ Sort Records. This opens the Record Sort Order dialog box, as shown in Figure 10-15. Select the data field to be sorted and click the > button to add it to the Sort Fields list. Next, specify the sort direction as Ascending or Descending. If sorting by more than one field, select the second data field and add it to the Sort Fields list. The order of the fields listed in the Sort Fields list represents the order in which report data will be sorted. Set the Ascending or Descending sort direction to the fields added to the Sort Fields list.

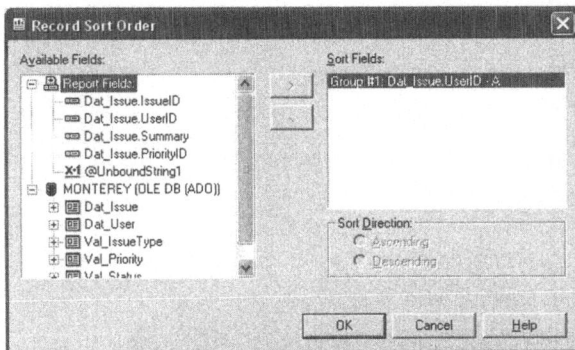

Figure 10-15. The Record Sort Order dialog box

Totaling Numerical Values

Totaling can be as simple as providing the grand total at the bottom of a list of records or as complex as showing a running total based on conditions specified by a formula. In Crystal Reports, you can embed two types of totals within a report that help analyze data: subtotals and running totals.

A subtotal is a simple summary that sums all numeric values within a group. To create a subtotal, open the report's pop-up menu and select Insert ➤ Subtotal. The Insert Subtotal dialog box displays, as shown in Figure 10-16. Select the field to be subtotaled and the field that specifies the record sorting and grouping.

Running totals offer more control over how the total is calculated and are ideal for any of the following: displaying totals record by record, displaying a total value independent of grouping, displaying a total value conditionally, and displaying a total value after a group selection formula has been applied.

To create a running total for a group, open the Field Explorer, select the Running Total Fields entry, and open the pop-up menu, as shown in Figure 10-17. Selecting New opens the Create Running Total Field dialog box, as shown in Figure 10-18.

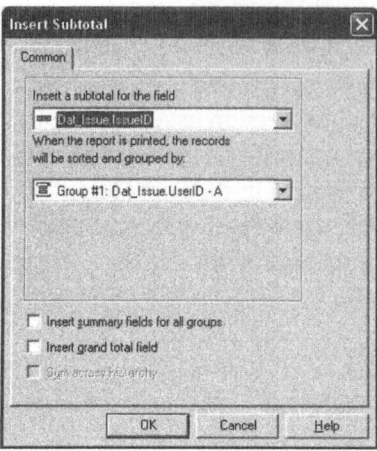

Figure 10-16. The Insert Subtotal dialog box specifies the field that must be summed.

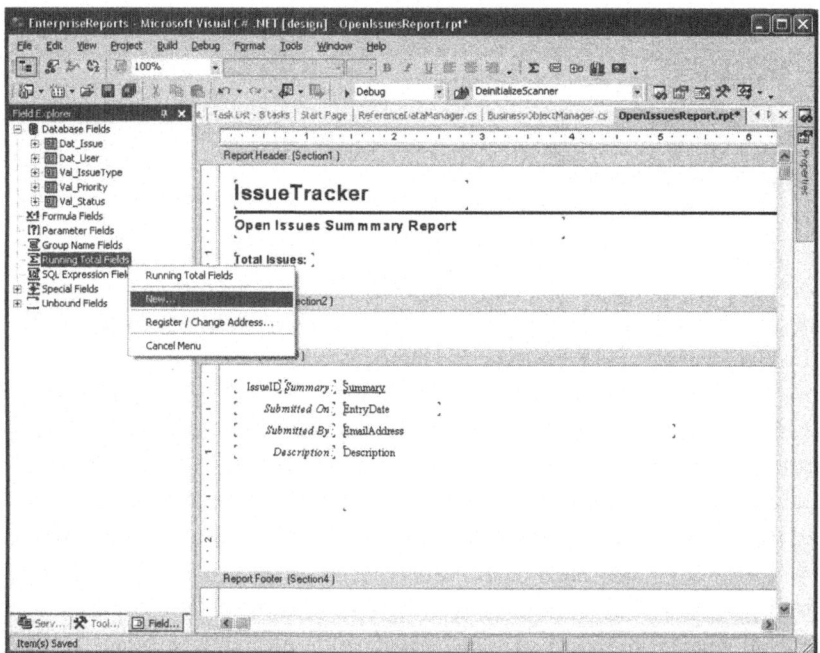

Figure 10-17. The Insert Grand Total dialog box

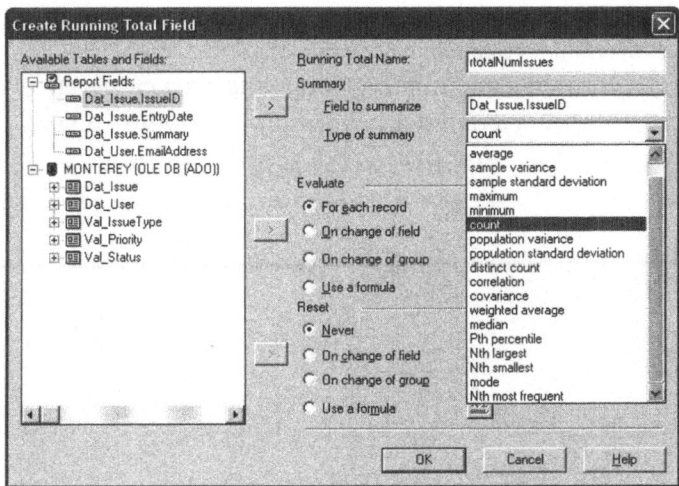

Figure 10-18. The Create Running Total Field dialog box

Next, specify a reference name for the running total and specify the fields to be totaled. In this example, the running total will keep track of the number of records displayed within a group. Select Dat_Issue.IssueID from the available report fields and click the > button pointing to the Summary section. Specify the Type of Summary option as Count. The Evaluate section of this dialog box determines how the field is updated; for this example, choose For Each Record. Finally, keep the Reset value at its default value of Never and click OK. The rtotalNumIssues field becomes immediately available in the Field Explorer; you can now place it into the Group Footer section of the report.

Enhancing Report Presentation

Although simple reports are effective in communicating important data to users, Crystal Reports offers a number of enhancements that make a report stand out. Some of these enhancements include adding charts; changing the presentation of dates, numbers, and other values; hiding unwanted sections; and performing additional formatting touches.

Inserting Graphical Charts

Crystal Reports supports sophisticated and colorful charts to be embedded within any report. Charting is an effective tool for presenting data and is valuable as a data analysis tool. Users can drill down into a chart and reference a chart's legend for detailed information. In most cases, charts represent summary and subtotal information at the group level. Charts can also represent summaries, subtotals, row data, formula data, running totals, and even cross-tab summaries. To embed a chart within a report, open the report's pop-up menu and select Insert ➤ Chart. The Chart Expert dialog box displays, as shown in Figure 10-19.

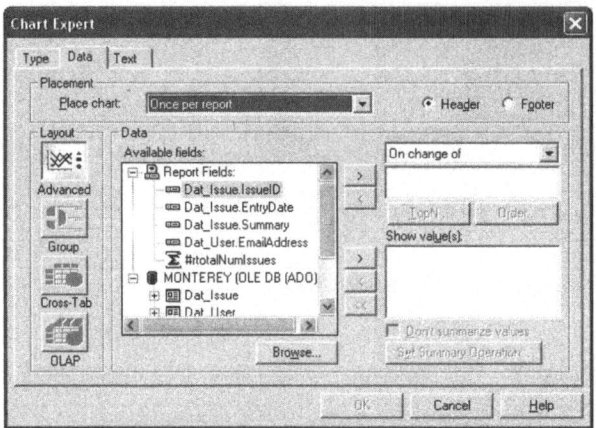

Figure 10-19. The Chart Expert dialog box

The Chart Expert dialog box has three tabs. In the Type tab, select the type of chart to be generated. Available options include Bar, Line, Area, Pie, and a few variations. To accept the default options for the chart and axis formatting options, select the Automatically Set Chart Options box. Otherwise, two additional tabs appear to manually set the chart and axis formatting options. In the Data tab, specify how often the chart should appear within the report with the Place Chart selection. Also, specify whether the chart should be placed in the header or footer of the report. In addition, specify the database fields upon which the charts should be based. Finally, you can use the Text tab to override the default wording of chart-related labels, such as title, subtitle, footnote, group title, and data title.

Inserting Nested Subreports

A *subreport* is simply a report embedded within another report. You can aggregate several unrelated subreports into a composite report that presents multiple views of the same data. In most cases, reports with a large number of records in a section can appear in an on-demand subreport. The subreport appears as a hyperlink within the primary report. When the primary report is opened, the large volume of data to be retrieved for the subreport is not retrieved until the user selects the hyperlink.

To insert a subreport, open the pop-up menu for the report and select Insert ➤ Subreport. Drag the subreport border object into the report section. Select to use a report within the project, use another existing report, or create a new report for the subreport. Selecting the On-Demand Subreport checkbox enables the subreport to retrieve the data as needed. Otherwise, all subreport data will be retrieved with the parent report.

You use the Link tab, shown in Figure 10-20, to create the hyperlinks in the main report that bind to the subreport. Start by selecting the field in the main report from which you want to hyperlink. The Available Fields list box is filled with report fields that already have been added to the main report. Next, use the Field Link options to specify which main report field supplies a parameter to the subreport and the data upon which the subreport is based.

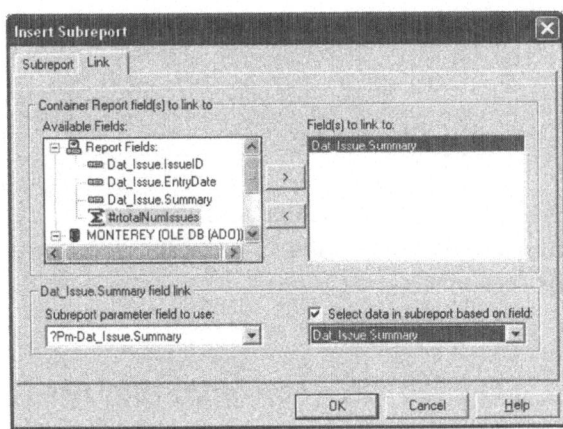

Figure 10-20. The Insert Subreport dialog box

Inserting Cross-Tab Results

A cross-tab report is any report that displays a spreadsheet-like view of data organized into rows and columns. You can use cross-tab reports to compare data and identify trends. In Crystal Reports, a cross-tab object consists of three elements: rows, columns, and summary fields.

To insert a cross-tab object, select the report's pop-up menu and select Insert ➤ Cross-Tab. Drag the subreport border object into the report section. The Format Cross-Tab dialog box appears, as shown in Figure 10-21. Next, add the desired fields to the Rows, Columns, and Summarized Field areas. Select the Style tab to select a cross-tab design, or click the Customize Style tab to create your own Cross-Tab design. When finished, click OK—a placeholder for the Cross-Tab table will appear.

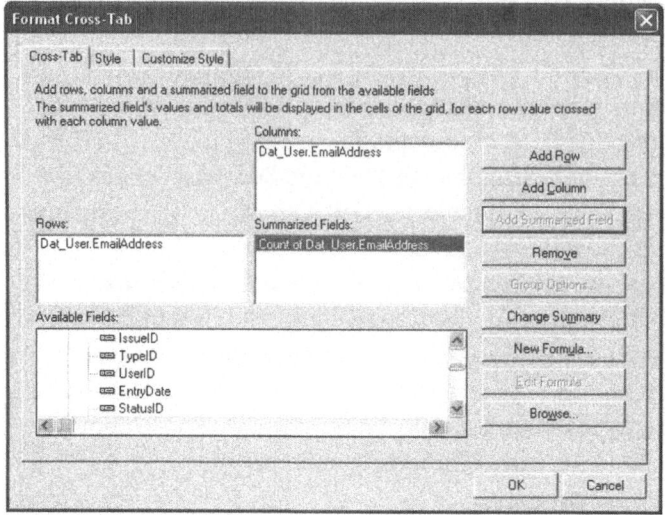

Figure 10-21. The Format Cross-Tab dialog box

Adding Report Viewers to Applications

After you have created a report, you can view it in a client application. Both desktop applications and Web applications can include a Crystal Reports viewer capable of loading and displaying a selected report.

Adding Reporting Capability to Desktop Applications

Any Windows application can display a report within a Windows form using the Crystal Reports Windows form viewer. In addition to displaying reports, the report viewer is also able to interact with other form controls that can dynamically update the report. Displaying a report in a Windows application requires the following steps: adding a report viewer to a form, binding a report to the report viewer, and interacting with other controls within the form.

Adding a Report Viewer to a Windows Form

To display a report in a desktop application, you must add a report viewer to the form. Begin by creating a Windows form named *ReportViewer.cs* as described in

Chapter 8, "Developing Desktop Applications." Next, open the Visual Studio .NET Toolbox and drag the CrystalReportViewer control onto the form.

You can resize or move the report viewer around within the form and ideally anchor it to resize as the form is resized. The properties of the report viewer can initialize at design time or in response to user-driven events at runtime.

Before a report can display in the report viewer, however, you must bind a report object to the viewer. You can do this by assigning the ReportSource property of the report viewer to a path pointing to the .rpt file.

A report can bind at design time to initialize a report viewer or at runtime to display a variety of reports based on the user selection. The report viewer can also bind to a report that is available as a report Web service.

Interacting with Windows Forms Controls

The report viewer can interact with other controls within a Windows form with the help of the report object model exposed by the reporting engine. You can add code to a form's source file that responds to specific events and sets report viewer properties.

In the ReportViewer form, add two buttons: btn_Next and btn_Previous. These buttons will direct the report viewer to move to the next page or the previous page of the report. From the Visual Studio .NET form editor, select the Next button and choose the events view in the Properties window. Create an event handler for the Click event named *btnNext_Click,* as shown in Figure 10-22.

Once you have created an event for a form object, the form's code view opens and points to the newly created event handler. Inside the event handler, the code is free to set the report viewer's properties or invoke its methods:

```
private void ShowNextPage(object sender, System.EventArgs e)
{
    reportViewer.ShowNextPage();
}
private void ShowPrevPage(object sender, System.EventArgs e)
{
    reportViewer.ShowPreviousPage();
}
```

In this example, clicking the Next button advances the displayed report to the next page.

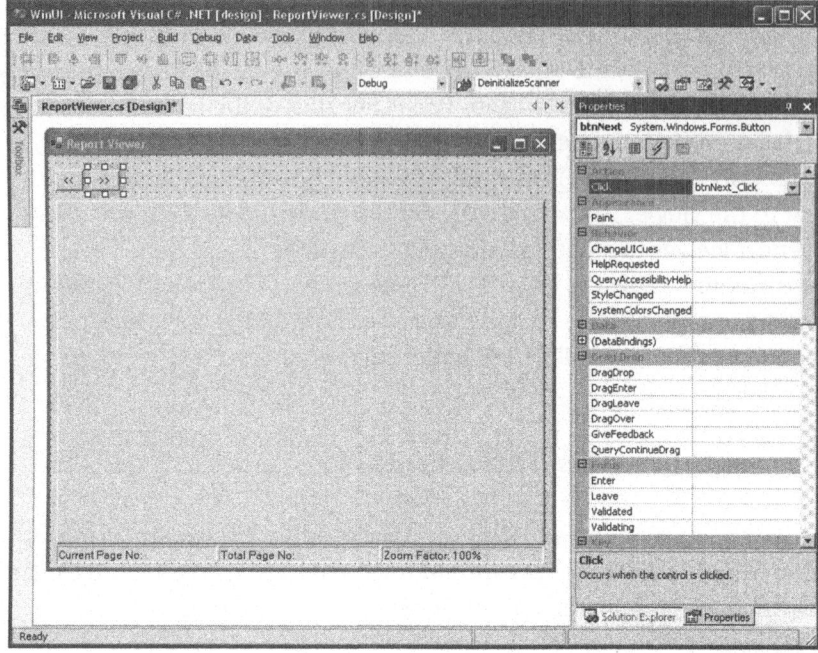

Figure 10-22. Creating an event handler that links a button to the report viewer

Adding Reporting Capability to Web Applications

Web applications can also display reports using the Crystal Reports Web form viewer. The Web form viewer can interact with other Web form controls and can dynamically update the report being displayed. Displaying a report in a Web application requires the following steps: adding a report viewer to a form, binding a report to the report viewer, and interacting with other controls within the form.

If an exception is immediately thrown and the Web form is unable to load the viewer, check to ensure that the ASP.NET system account has read-write access to the viewer files. Open the File Explorer and point to the following directory: \Program Files\Microsoft Visual Studio .NET\Viewers. Open the Folder Properties dialog box, click the Security tab, and click the Add button. Next, enter a new user reference as follows:

```
<machine_name>\ASPNET
```

Next, close the Folder Properties dialog box by clicking OK. Finally, set folder permissions for this user to Read, Write, and Modify. This should eliminate the exception and allow the report to display normally.

Adding a Report Viewer to a Web Form

To display a report in a Web application, you must add a report viewer to the form. Begin by creating a Web form named *ReportViewer.aspx* as described in Chapter 7, "Building Web Applications." Next, open the Visual Studio .NET Toolbox and drag the CrystalReportViewer icon onto the form. Visual Studio .NET adds the following registration code to the HTML view of the ReportViewer.aspx file:

```
<%@ Register TagPrefix = "cr" Namespace="CrystalDecisions.Web"
    Assembly="CrystalDecisions.Web" %>
```

Later in the HTML, the following code designates the insertion point for the Crystal Reports viewer:

```
<cr:CrystalReportViewer id=crystalViewer runat="SERVER"
    Width="350px" Height="50px">
</crystal:CrystalReportViewer>
```

Interacting with Web Forms Controls

The report viewer can interact with other controls within a Web form in the same manner as the Windows form. You can add code to a form's source file that responds to specific events and sets report viewer properties.

In the ReportViewer Web form, add two buttons: btn_Next and btn_Previous. These buttons will also direct the Web report viewer to move to the next page or the previous page of the report. From the Visual Studio .NET form editor, select the Next button and choose the events view in the Properties window to create an event handler for the Click event named *btnPrevious_Click*, as shown in Figure 10-23.

Crystal Reports allows specific data values to be entered as parameters before generating reports. The Web form viewer also supports the hosting of such reports. You can design a Web application to retrieve user input through a Web form control and pass the input as a parameter to the report hosted by the Web form viewer using the ParameterFieldInfo property of the CrystalReportViewer object.

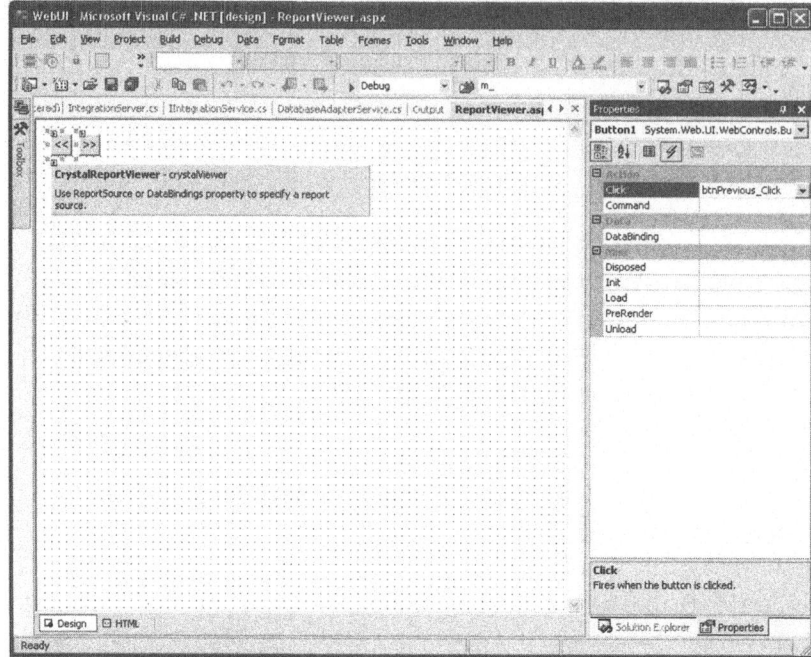

Figure 10-23. Creating an event handler that links a button to the report viewer

Improving Performance with Report Caching

Web form viewers have the added capability of caching reports on the server for more efficient retrieval. Because the caching function leverages the ASP.NET caches, only reports displayed in a Web form viewer can be cached, not reports displayed in a Windows form viewer. The Web form viewer uses caching when different users call the Uniform Resource Locator (URL) for the same dynamic page, such as `http://localhost/MyProject/ReportViewer.aspx`.

Report caching begins when you add a report to any Web project. For example, when you added the OpenIssuesReport.rpt file to the project, you automatically created an OpenIssuesReport.cs file in the project directory. The newly created OpenIssuesReport class is derived from the CrystalDecisions.Engine.ReportClass class. Table 10-1 describes the ReportClass methods and properties.

You can create a cached report instance in code by invoking the object's default constructor. Because the OpenIssuesReport object is derived from ReportDocument, the resulting instance can bind to a Web form viewer to cache it:

```
OpenIssuesReport cachedOpenIssuesReport = new OpenIssuesReport();
```

Then, you can use the cached report object as is or customize it to meet specific needs. Finally, you bind the cached report instance directly to the Web form viewer:

```
reportViewer.ReportSource = cachedOpenIssuesReport;
```

The Web form viewer control initializes the cached report instance with data and the current state of the report. On cache timeout, the cache is flushed and the Web form viewer control reinitializes the cache with the current report state. As with all cached pages interacting with a database, refreshing a cached report will result in additional database access. To limit unnecessary load on the database, the Web form viewer toolbar disables the Refresh icon by default.

Table 10-1. Relevant ReportClass Methods and Properties

NAME	DESCRIPTION
CreateReport	Creates an instance of the strongly typed report
GetCustomizedCacheKey	Returns the default cache key to the ASP.NET cache
CacheTimeOut	Returns a timeout value for the ASP.NET cache, CachedReportConstants.DEFAULT_TIMEOUT, by default
IsCacheable	Returns a value indicating if the report is cacheable and is True by default
ShareDBLogonInfo	Indicates if database login should be shared and is False by default

Adding Reporting Capability to Web Services

You can also publish a report as a Web service. A report Web service can be accessed by any application operating on any platform that uses an appropriate viewer. When you add a report to a Web service project, Visual Studio .NET compiles the Web service into a DLL and generates an Extensible Markup Language (XML) file that describes the public functions, input parameters, data types, and return data types exposed by the Web service. The DLL and the XML files are both published to the Web server as a Web service. Any client can invoke the Web service via Hypertext Transfer Protocol (HTTP) and Simple Object Access Protocol (SOAP) to pass the XML data to the Web service.

Once you have published the report Web service on a Web server, any Web-enabled application can consume it on the client side. Users can drag the report Web service from the Visual Studio .NET Server Explorer into a desktop application or a Web application. A Web Services Description Language (WSDL) file is automatically generated on the client.

Creating a Reporting Web Service

Creating a report Web service begins with a new Web application or Web service project in Visual Studio .NET. First, add a new or existing report template to the project. In the case of the IssueTracker application, the OpenIssuesReport.rpt file will do. Second, select the report template in the Solution Explorer and open its pop-up menu. Select the Publish As Web Service menu item.

This creates a new file and adds it to the project with the same name as the report template, but with an .asmx file extension. This file is the source code for the newly created report Web service. You can easily modify the code to invoke another Web service or to perform additional security functions. Rebuild the solution to compile the Web service and make it available to clients. Once built, the Web service becomes available in the Server Explorer. You can also test it by entering the Web service URL into a Web browser, as shown in Figure 10-24.

Creating a Reporting Web Service Client

When the report Web service is published, its classes, objects, methods, properties, and return values are available in XML and therefore can be transmitted across the Web. Client applications can access this Web service and interact with the report and its data without needing anything other than the ability to read XML.

The report Web service client can be either a Windows application with a Windows form viewer or a Web application with a Web form viewer. In either case, the viewer displays the report by connecting to the report Web service for that report. The first step is to create a proxy class that abstracts the report's Web service. Begin by selecting Project ➤ Add Web Reference from the Visual Studio .NET menu. In the Add Web Reference dialog box, enter the URL that points to the location of the newly created report Web service, as shown in Figure 10-25.

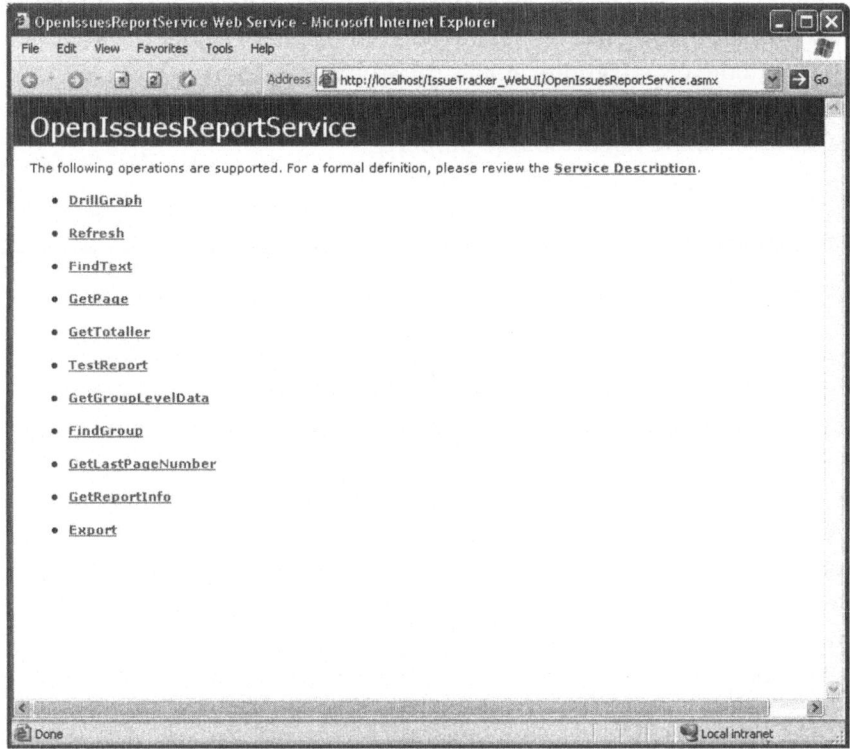

Figure 10-24. Testing the report Web service with Internet Explorer

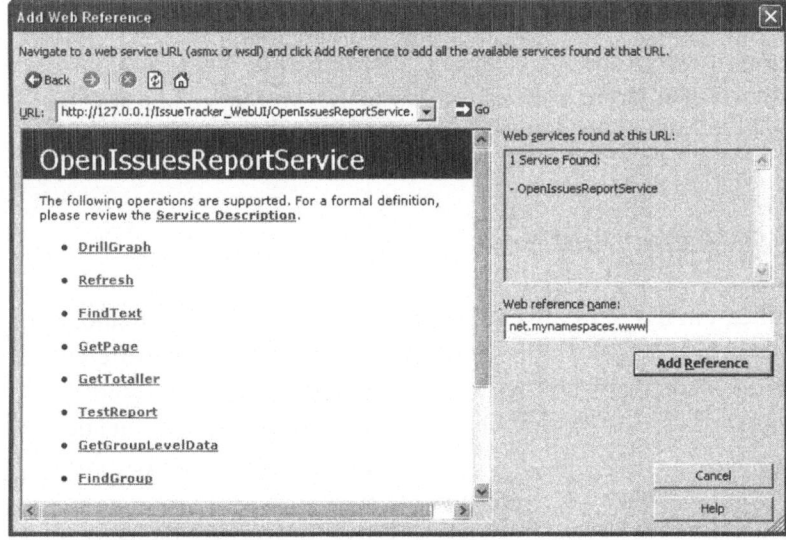

Figure 10-25. Adding a Web referece to a Visual Studio .NET project

After adding a new Web reference to the report Web service, Visual Studio adds a new entry for the Web service in the Solution Explorer under the Web References tree node. Visual Studio creates the Web service proxy object with which the C# code can interact. You can use the proxy object directly to load the report and assign it to the ReportSource property:

```
IssueTracker.OpenIssuesReport reportService = new IssueTracker.OpenIssuesReport();
reportService.Load();
reportViewer.ReportSource = reportService;
```

In this case, the code creates an object, calls a Load method, and sets the ReportSource property. The compiled code establishes an HTTP connection to the OpenIssuesReportService Web service and exchanges SOAP messages that contain XML-based information about the report.

In the Web service example, a single Web service abstracts a single report. However, server file reports represent a Web service gateway that serves as a single entry point for multiple reports. All server file reports share the same report Web service file, such as ServerFileReportService.asmx. You select the specific report to display by setting the ReportPath property of the ServerFileReport object. The ReportPath property specifies the relative path of the report on the server.

Distributing Enterprise-Wide Reports

You can deploy Crystal Reports for Visual Studio .NET as single-tiered or multi-tiered applications. As described in Chapter 1, "Introducing .NET and Enterprise Architecture," tiers are different application layers that specialize in a specific form of processing to maximize scalability.

Distributing Reporting-Enabled Applications

A Windows application that contains all report components locally, including the report file and reporting engine, represents either a one-tiered or two-tiered deployment; the presentation and logic exists on one tier, and the database exists on another. This type of deployment is best suited for applications that rely heavily on client-side processing. If any changes to a report are required, then the application needs to install an update.

A Web application that hosts a local report file for processing typically represents a three-tiered deployment: presentation on one tier, business logic on a second tier, and the database on the third tier. The Web server processes requests sent from the client side. Application users require only a browser to access the application. All report components reside on the server and can be updated centrally.

A report Web service is a report that has been published, or exposed, for consumption by a Web-enabled application. Applications connect over the Web to a report Web service existing on an application server, consume the exposed report, and display the report for users in a report viewer. Typically, users require only a thin client to view report Web services. All other report components reside with the report Web service on a remote application server. Changes made to the report Web service are reflected immediately in the application.

Distributing the Crystal Reports Runtime

You need to package and distribute Crystal Reports runtime files with the enterprise application. Deciding which runtime files to package depends upon the features used, such as charts and formula functions. Another variable is the data source used by the reports and the exporting options available to the application user. The Microsoft Installer (MSI) includes Microsoft Merge (MSM) modules for applications to use to simplify distribution. Chapter 14, "Installing .NET Applications," dives deeper into the details of building installation packages. This section highlights the components and modules relevant to reporting.

The Crystal Reports merge modules reside in the C:\Program Files\Common Files\Merge Modules directory. There are different merge modules, depending on the target components and languages. These modules come three categories: managed components, database access, and KeyCode.

The managed components handle the distribution of all the managed components, including the Windows form viewer, Web form viewer, and all of the Crystal Decisions namespace objects. The database access module handles the distribution of all the other files needed to get the reports to run, including database, export, and charting drivers. The KeyCode module handles the installation of the Crystal Decisions KeyCode so that your users are not asked to register their version of Crystal Reports when viewing reports.

Access to the Crystal Reports reporting engine packed with Visual Studio .NET does not limit the number of user connections. However, it is essentially a performance-limited version intended for development and small group use only. If a report is requested while the server is operating at its internal performance limit, the request will be delayed until the server load drops below this limit. In this case, the server writes a message in the event log. If the delay extends beyond a certain point of time, the server will throw an OutOfLicense exception.

NOTE *You can find Crystal Reports licensing information online at* http://www.crystaldecisions.com/net/licensing.

Summary

This chapter outlined the steps involved in creating a report for an enterprise application using the Crystal Reports solution embedded within the Visual Studio .NET environment. The chapter introduced different elements of report building with the goal of building professional-looking, interactive reports. Creating reports with a template-based solution, such as Crystal Reports, enables reports to be flexible enough to be rendered in different viewers for both Windows and Web applications.

The next chapter takes the .NET Framework on the road and explores mobile application development. It covers developing mobile applications for two types of mobile applications: Compact Framework applications for Personal Digital Assistant (PDA) devices and Microsoft Mobile Internet Toolkit (MMIT) applications for Web-enabled cellular phones. Both frameworks add mobile capabilities to the enterprise application.

Deploying .NET Applications on Wireless Devices

CONNECTIVITY TO ENTERPRISE DATA AND SERVICES is essential to any large corporation. Desktop applications provide a rich and powerful interface that connects users to enterprise resources. Web applications extend the reach of the enterprise by connecting users to the enterprise over greater distances. In the wireless world, users connect to enterprise resources regardless of where they are.

Microsoft offers two powerful development platforms that enable mobile application development for the enterprise: the .NET Compact Framework for Smart Devices and the Microsoft Mobile Internet Toolkit (MMIT). These tools take different approaches to building mobile applications, and each offers specific strengths depending on the purpose of the mobile application. This chapter explores how to build mobile applications that extend the reach of the enterprise. The chapter outlines both mobile development platforms and provides specific examples that reflect the needs of typical mobile enterprise applications.

Exploring the .NET Compact Framework

Mobile applications and wireless applications are not necessarily the same thing. The key difference between the two is where they store data. In many cases, users need to operate outside of the enterprise but still need to interact with or reference critical enterprise data. Typically, a wireless application uses its wireless connection to retrieve real-time enterprise data straight from the source. A mobile application can store critical data locally (on the device itself) and synchronize with the enterprise data at specific intervals. Handheld computers, such as Personal Digital Assistants (PDAs), have grown tremendously powerful and popular. Typical PDAs include a color display, an optimized microprocessor, generous storage space, and, naturally, the Microsoft Windows operating system.

The .NET Compact Framework is a mobile application development platform that targets *smart devices*. Smart devices are largely consumer electronic devices, such as Pocket PC devices, that have embedded microprocessors, memory, and an operating system. The Compact Framework is essentially a scaled-down version (approximately 12 percent) of the .NET Framework. A large number of library classes have been removed, especially those related to ASP.NET. Otherwise, everything else—from multiple language support to managed code and the common language runtime—is still available. Microsoft is also actively engaging PDA manufacturers to integrate the .NET Compact Framework into devices' standard Read-Only Memory (ROM) images.

In Visual Studio .NET, a smart device application's user interface uses the same form designer that is used to build desktop applications. The only difference is that a number of user interface controls have either been removed from the Toolbox or substituted with new device-specific controls.

The Compact Framework also provides a subset implementation of ADO.NET that includes a SQL Server CE .NET data provider. This allows device applications to locally replicate critical enterprise data for users who need to work outside of the enterprise.

Understanding the Platform Architecture

As mentioned, the Compact Framework is essentially a scaled-down version of the .NET Framework that has been ported to the Pocket PC operating system. The Compact Framework enables applications to interact with the native operating system of the device, including accessing native operating system services. Both the Compact Framework and the native applications can run side by side on the same device without the user really knowing which is the native application and which is the Compact Framework application. The Compact Framework's application domain host, also a native application, starts an instance of the common language runtime environment and manages the application's access to all device resources. Figure 11-1 illustrates the .NET Compact Framework platform architecture.

As Figure 11-1 illustrates, all Compact Framework applications run within a runtime environment called an *application domain*. The application domain host is essentially a native application that starts an instance of the common language runtime. The Compact Framework application interacts with the application domain like any other operating system process. Just as in the full .NET Framework, the Compact Framework ensures that all managed resources used by a .NET Framework application are freed and returned to the operating system when the application ends.

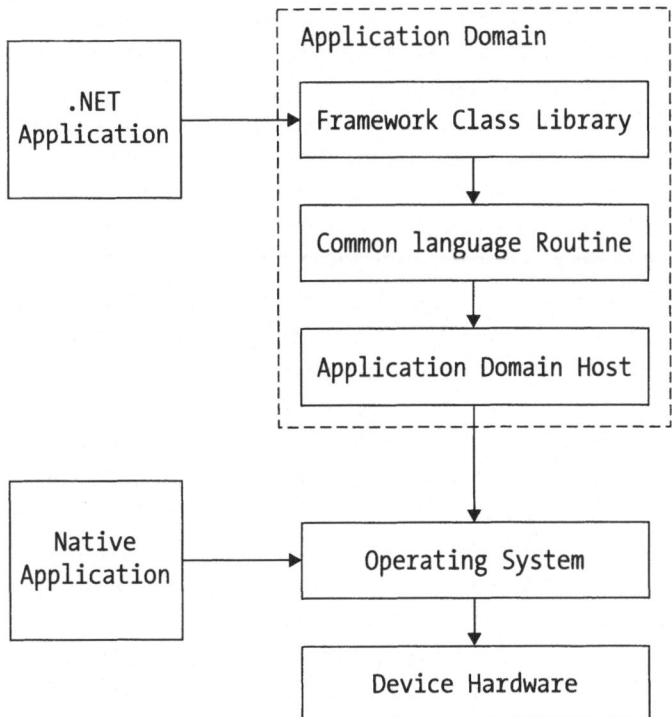

Figure 11-1. The Compact Framework platform architecture

The .NET Compact Framework uses available system memory carefully. No Read-Access Memory (RAM) is accessed until the application starts, and all RAM is immediately released when the application terminates. The operating system is not required to have its own memory protection, and exceptions are always thrown when unowned memory is accessed.

When memory is low, the Compact Framework releases internal data structures that the application does not need. This enables the application to continue running when available memory is low. If the application requires more memory than is available, the Compact Framework cleanly closes the application and releases all underlying resources.

Building Device Applications for the Enterprise

Developing device applications for the enterprise requires significantly more planning than their desktop counterparts. This is largely because of the limitation of resources, such as display area and memory storage. Therefore, device applications require special design emphasis in two critical areas: simplicity and usability.

In a device application, simplicity refers to how easily the application interacts with users. Typically, PDA device users want to perform quick searches and easily enter data without a complicated user interface. In general, device applications should not attempt to mirror their desktop counterparts by supporting an enormous list of features. Rather, they should identify the two or three most important functions of the enterprise application and implement them cleanly.

In the case of the IssueTracker application, viewing a list of issues, viewing an issue's detail, and creating new issues are probably the most important features. It would be nice to include user management or even reporting functions within the device application, but that would increase the application's complexity. The more functions supported by the device application, the more cluttered the user interface becomes. Menus grow longer and forms become flooded with user controls, making the device application harder to use. If a device application displays multiple views, menus, and controls, it can confuse and frustrate someone trying to perform tasks quickly.

The focus of the mobile enterprise application must center on the capability of entering and managing small amounts of data in short sessions as well as synchronizing data and information with the enterprise data.

To simplify an application's interface, it is important to automate as many processes as possible. If a feature is able to function without user interaction, for example, then it should not have a user interface. When you need to add a new feature, try modifying an already existing feature to incorporate the new one. The user interface design goal should always be to minimize the choices that a user needs to make. You should always keep the number of steps needed to complete tasks to a minimum. To validate a device's user interface, examine the most common activities a user is expected to perform and then determine the minimum number of steps necessary to complete them. Try to find ways to decrease the resulting number of steps.

A simple device application only shows the most important user interface controls within a form. You should place important commands either as buttons within the menu bar or as items in menus. You should display only the most relevant data to the user. Because entering data into a device is usually a pain, try to minimize the amount of data entry that users must perform and find ways to reuse data or obtain it from existing sources. Furthermore, minimize the number of characters and fields the user must edit to complete a task or activity and present common data choices or selections in drop-down list boxes. Where text entry is necessary, try to include functionality that remembers recent (or most often entered) text. Figure 11-2 illustrates IssueTracker's summary page. The Issues list shows only the three most important columns.

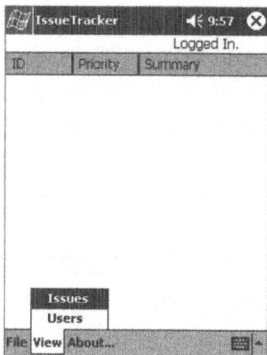

Figure 11-2. Simplicity applied to the IssueTracker's summary page

With a smaller display, device applications require careful planning as to how controls are placed within a form so a user can more quickly and easily accomplish tasks. In most cases, usability often translates into how easily a user can identify and use interface controls. As in desktop and Web application development, device applications should also group similar controls together. Logically grouped controls will be discovered more easily.

Controls should be clearly visible, especially when viewed in dim lighting. Controls should also be large enough to interact with as the user is in motion. Placing user interface controls for frequently used tasks near the top level of the application is always helpful.

Controls should always have enough spacing between each other. Without enough spacing, a user is likely to accidentally select one control while intending to select another. In addition, added spacing helps users who move around while using their device as well as those with limited coordination. At the same time, however, it is important to ensure that controls fit properly within the limited screen space and that they do not overlap. Figure 11-3 illustrates the New Issue form with balanced spacing of user interface controls.

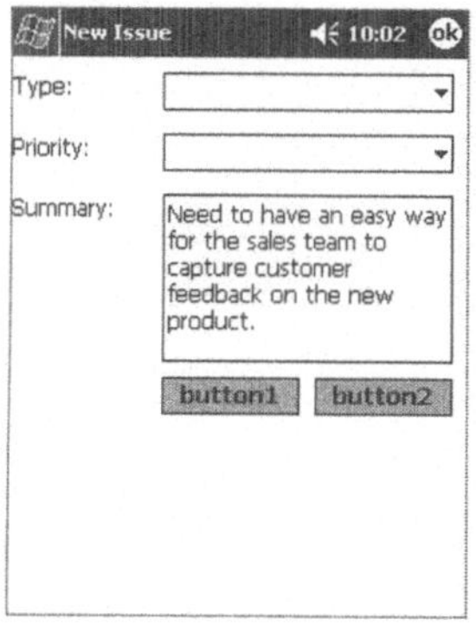

Figure 11-3. Usability applied to the New Issue device application page

Controls should be easy to distinguish from each other with easily recognizable differences. You can make controls easier to identify by using a unique size, position, shape, and contrast. You can simplify device applications by making user interface controls easier to understand through representations such as image icons.

Finally, controls should be predictable and consistent, and they should function the same way in different parts of the application. For example, if clicking a green plus icon adds a new object, such as an Issue, a green plus icon should always be associated with an add function, even when referring to User objects.

Implementing a Smart Device Application

Visual Studio .NET provides a powerful development environment for creating applications for smart devices. With the .NET Compact Framework, developers can create, build, debug, and distribute applications that run on any device configured with the Pocket PC or Windows CE operating system. Implementing a smart device application typically involves creating the project, adding controls to forms, adding event handlers that accomplish specific business tasks, and deploying the application.

Creating the New Project

Creating a new project for a specific device follows the same general process as creating a new project for the desktop. To create a device project, click Add ➤ New Project from the Solution Explorer's context menu. In the Add New Project dialog box, select the Smart Device Application template, enter the project name as shown in Figure 11-4, and then click the OK button.

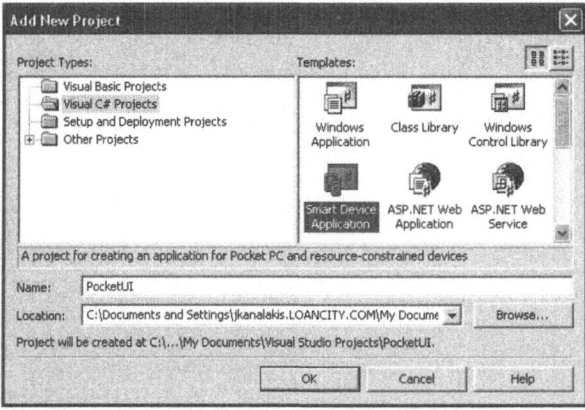

Figure 11-4. Adding a new device application to the IssueTracker solution

Next, the Smart Device Application Wizard starts and prompts you for additional details about the device application. In the case of the IssueTracker application, you will implement a device client that targets the common Pocket PC operating system. Select Pocket PC as the target platform and Windows Application as the project type, as shown in Figure 11-5.

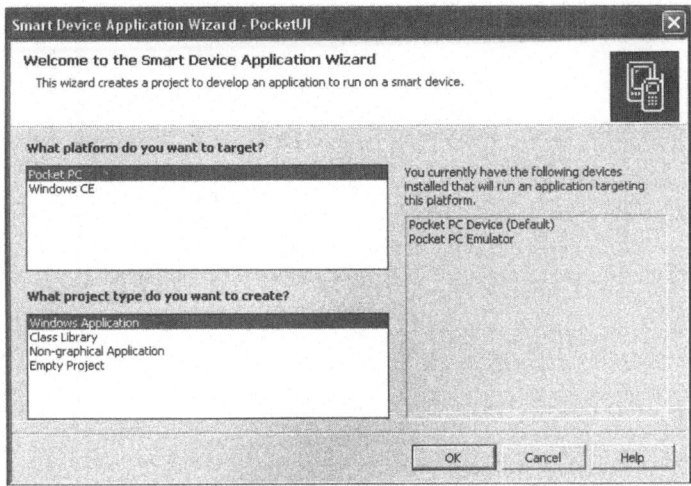

Figure 11-5. Designating the device application's target platform and project type

Adding Forms and Controls

As mentioned, developing a device application's user interface is similar to developing a desktop application's interface. In fact, the form designer shown in Figure 11-6 has only a few differences, such as a different user control list in the Toolbox and a different default form size set to fit within a Pocket PC display area.

You add controls to the form and set properties in the same manner as you do for a desktop application. After placing user interface controls into a form, you can define event handlers to implement the application's business logic.

Building and Deploying the Application

You also build device applications in the same manner as their desktop counterparts. When you select a device project to run from within the design environment, a message box prompts you for the deployment preference, as shown in Figure 11-7. Visual Studio .NET integrates a fully functional device emulator that realistically simulates the Pocket PC environment.

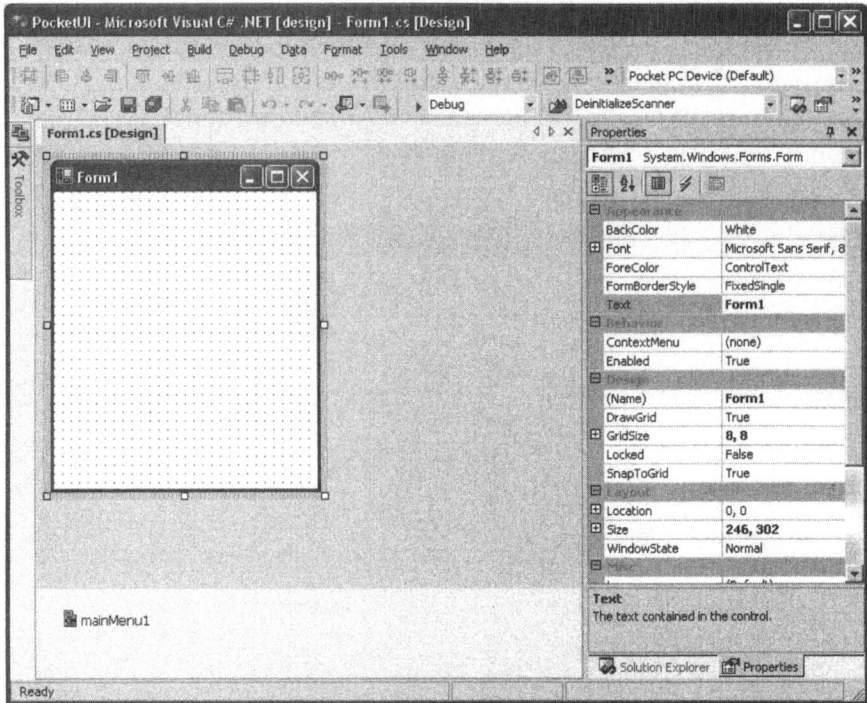

Figure 11-6. Creating device application forms using the form designer

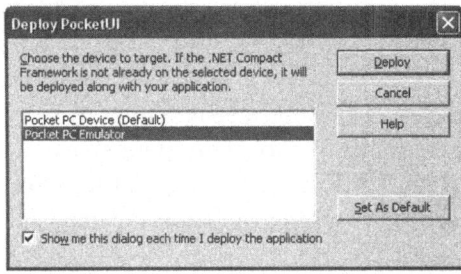

Figure 11-7. Selecting a target deployment platform for the device application

Alternatively, you can package the device application into a cabinet file and deploy it directly to the device. When the mobile application is completed and ready for broad deployment, a cabinet file packaging greatly simplifies the installation process for the user. Individual users may be required to install the mobile client as the device recovers from a completely drained battery or cold boot.

To deploy the device application directly to the device, you must connect with the desktop using ActiveSync or Visual Studio .NET. When deploying from ActiveSync, you must install the cabinet containing the .NET Compact

Framework first. When deploying from Visual Studio .NET, Visual Studio examines the target device to determine if the .NET Compact Framework is already installed. If not, Visual Studio .NET first deploys the Compact Framework, followed by the newly built device application.

Enhancing Smart Device Enterprise Clients

Device applications really differentiate themselves from mobile applications by storing and accessing data locally rather than connecting to a remote server (although devices are also capable of connecting to remote servers via wireless adapters). There are many different approaches to storing data on a device; the two most common approaches are Extensible Markup Language (XML) document exchange and SQL Server CE database storage.

Accessing XML Document Data

Exchanging data using XML documents is a popular form of device data exchange for many reasons. The primary reason for its popularity is simply that many different types of applications are capable of generating XML documents. This enables the device application to access data from a variety of data sources.

Because XML is intended to be a data exchange format and not a data storage format, it is worth mentioning that accessing XML document data is very slow. You should ideally store data in a device database, such as SQL Server CE.

Developers typically configure the data exchange via XML as an automated process. In most cases, applications that generate an XML export document can do so at designated times or intervals and place them into specific directories. At the same time, the ActiveSync application is capable of moving files, along with contacts and appointments, between the desktop and the device. Together, these systems can form the basis of integration between the desktop application and the mobile device. All that remains is the functionality within the device application to read the transferred XML file and display its data. Listing 11-1 implements functionality to read the XML document containing issues generated in Chapter 2, "Accessing Data in ADO.NET," and display them in a list view control, as shown earlier in Figure 11-2.

Listing 11-1. Displaying Form Data from an XML Document

```
private void menuViewIssues_Click(object sender, System.EventArgs e)
{
    string strResponse;
    ListViewItem listItem;
```

```
        //prepare the ListView control, initially hidden from user
        lstViewer.Items.Clear();
        lstViewer.Visible = true;

        try
        {
            //create and populate a new DataSet
            DataSet datasetIssues = new DataSet();
            datasetIssues.ReadXml( "\\Windows\\issues.xml" );

            //iterate through the rows to populate the ListView control
            foreach( DataRow row in datasetIssues.Tables["Dat_Issue"].Rows )
            {
                listItem = new ListViewItem();

                listItem.Text = row["IssueID"].ToString();
                listItem.SubItems.Add( row["PriorityID"].ToString() );
                listItem.SubItems.Add( row["Summary"].ToString() );

                //add the created entry to the ListView control
                lstViewer.Items.Add( listItem );
            }

        }
        catch( Exception x )
        {
            MessageBox.Show( x.Message );
        }

        return;

    }
```

The method begins by declaring working variables, clearing the contents of the list view control, and making the control visible to the user. Next, the method creates an empty DataSet object. Its ReadXml method is invoked to open the local XML file, infer its schema structure, and fill the DataSet with the document's data. Next, each row of the DataSet object is iterated while filling in a ListViewItem object to add to the list view control.

Accessing SQL Server CE Data

Developers with experience building embedded Visual C++ device applications have a number of differences to adapt to when working with the Compact Framework. Most important, native support for data storage in Pocket Access (the Pocket PC version of Microsoft Access) has been dropped in favor of the latest release of SQL Server CE. SQL Server CE has been selected as the preferred device data storage platform largely because of its support for multiple tables, SQL querying, and data replication capabilities. Developing data-driven device applications is essentially divided into four stages: configuring the necessary servers, creating a SQL Server CE database on the device, synchronizing the device's database, and interacting with the device's database.

Configuring SQL Server CE begins on the server side with the installation of an additional setup application, known as Server Tools. This installation configures the Internet Information Services (IIS) server to relay requests between the device and the enterprise SQL Server database. You accomplish this by adding an Internet Server Application Programming Interface (ISAPI) service agent and specifying a virtual directory for the replication service. Incoming Hypertext Transfer Protocol (HTTP) requests from the device are received and managed, as illustrated in Figure 11-8.

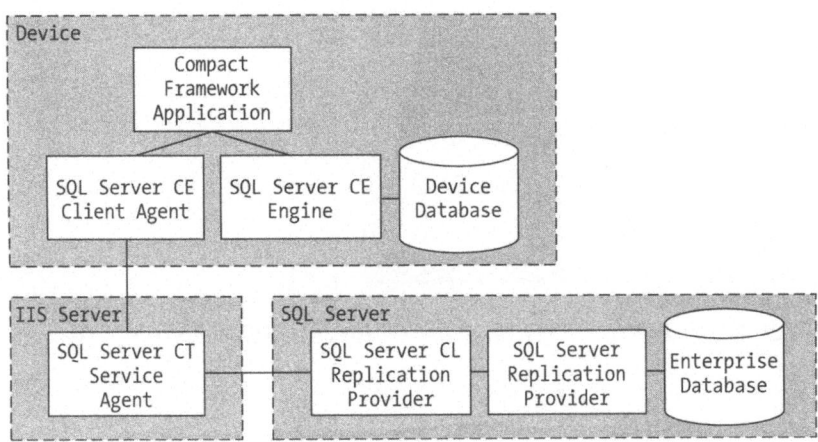

Figure 11-8. The SQL Server CE data replication components

After you have prepared the IIS server, you must configure the enterprise SQL Server database to publish specified data. From the SQL Server Enterprise Manager, choose Tools ➤ Replication ➤ Create and Manage Publications. The Create and Manage Publications dialog box will display. Click the Create Publication button to start the Create Publication Wizard.

During the course of the wizard, you need to select the database to be replicated and choose a publication type. The publication type depends largely on the purpose of the mobile client. In the case of IssueTracker, the purpose of the mobile client is to browse data and enter new data. Therefore, the merge replication type of publication works best. Next, select the publication clients—in this case, select only servers running SQL Server 2000 and devices running SQL Server CE. Finally, the wizard prompts you for the specific data that should be published. Rather than share the entire enterprise schema, specify only the issues, users, and supporting validation tables. When the Create Publication Wizard ends, the enterprise SQL Server database will be capable of replicating useful enterprise data to validated connecting clients. At any time, you can view and modify the publication settings within the Publication Properties dialog box, as shown in Figure 11-9.

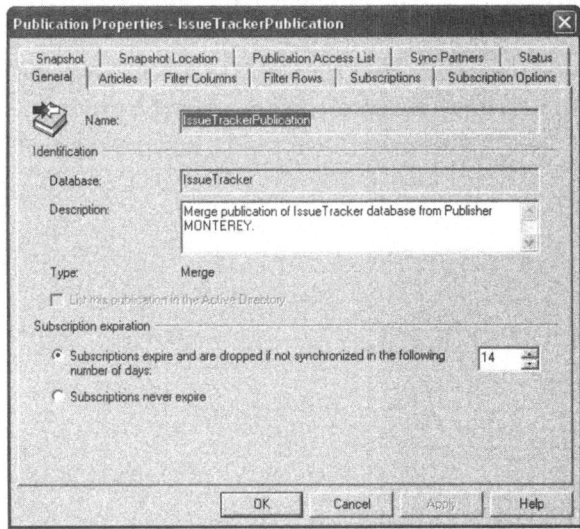

Figure 11-9. SQL Server publication properties define data replication to SQL Server CE.

After you complete the server configuration, you implement the remaining work in the enterprise device application. You must add two administrative functions to the device application: one that creates the device database and another that synchronizes it with the enterprise database.

Begin by adding a project reference to the SQL Server CE namespace. The next time the device application is deployed, the SQL Server CE engine will be deployed to the device along with the Compact Framework binaries. Select Project ➤ Add Reference from the Visual Studio .NET menu. Select the SqlServerCe component, as shown in Figure 11-10.

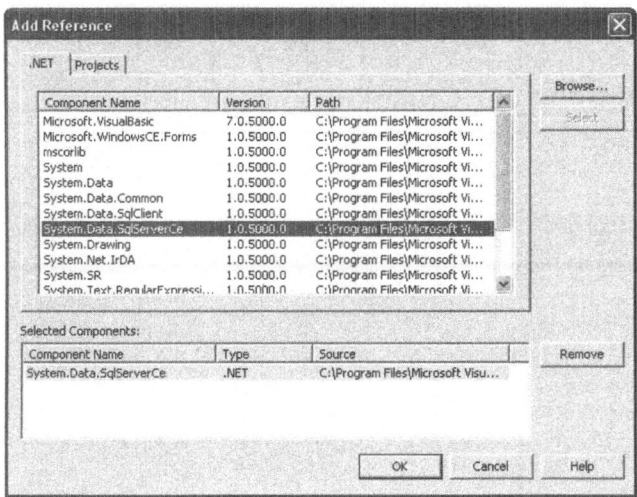

Figure 11-10. Adding the SqlServerCe namespace reference

In the code-behind file, include the necessary namespace using this reference:

```
using System.Data.SqlServerCe;
```

The CreateSqlDatabase method shown in Listing 11-2 creates the device database. The database itself is stored as an .sdf file in the device's My Documents directory.

Listing 11-2. Reading a List of Issues from a Transferred XML Document

```
private void CreateSqlDatabase()
{
    //specify the location of the local device database
    string strDataPath = "\\My Documents\\IssueTracker.sdf";

    try
    {
        //check to determine of local device database already exists
        if( ! System.IO.File.Exists( strDataPath ) )
        {
            //define a connection string and create the device database file
            SqlCeEngine engine = new SqlCeEngine( "Data Source=" + strDataPath );
            engine.CreateDatabase();
        }
    }
```

```
catch( SqlCeException x )
{
    MessageBox.Show( x.Message );
}
catch( Exception x )
{
    MessageBox.Show( x.Message );
}

return;
}
```

The CreateSqlDatabase method begins by identifying the location of the device database file. In this case, the file resides in the device's My Documents folder. Next, the device application determines if the file already exists locally. If not, then it creates the SqlCeEngine with a connection string pointing back to the device database file. The CreateDatabase method actually creates the file. This creates an empty database on the device; you need to add tables and data separately.

After creating the device database, you need to populate it. The device application can create the schema manually through CREATE TABLE statements in SQL, or it can synchronize everything from the enterprise SQL Server. The SynchronizeSqlDatabase method appears in Listing 11-3. Its purpose is to connect to the enterprise database and replicate specific tables, structure, and data.

Listing 11-3. Synchronizing the SQL Server CE Database

```
private void SynchronizeSqlDatabase()
{
    //specify the location of the local device database
    string strDataPath = "\\My Documents\\IssueTracker.sdf";

    //create the data replication object
    SqlCeReplication replication = new SqlCeReplication();

    try
    {
        //define the source of the replication data
        replication.Publisher = "server_name";
        replication.PublisherDatabase = "IssueTracker"; //database name
        replication.Publication = "IssueTrackerPublication";
```

```
            //define the login credentials
            replication.PublisherLogin = "sa";
            replication.PublisherPassword = "";

            //define the subscriber-side connection string
            replication.SubscriberConnectionString =
                "Provider=Microsoft.SQLServer.OLEDB.CE.2.0;"  +
                "Data Source=" + strDataPath;

            replication.Subscriber = "iPAQ Mobile Device";

            //define the location of the IIS replication service agent
            replication.InternetUrl = "http://jkanalakis/sqlce/ssceca20.dll";

            //define the replication mode and begin the process
            replication.ExchangeType = ExchangeType.BiDirectional;
            replication.Synchronize();
        }
        catch( SqlCeException x )
        {
            MessageBox.Show( x.Message );
        }
        catch( Exception x )
        {
            MessageBox.Show( x.Message );
        }

        return;
    }
```

This method begins with the instantiation of the SqlCeReplication object. Next, it sets each replication attribute, including the source database server, source database, and source publication. The publication identifies which source database tables are to be synchronized, how much of the data is accessed, and how the database is synchronized. Connection parameters such as username and password must also be supplied, along with a name that identifies the device and the Uniform Resource Locator (URL) pointing to the ISAPI service agent. The final call to the Synchronize method initiates the data exchange process. When completed, the device's file explorer application can navigate to the My Documents directory and open the .sdf file. The Query Analyzer device application now shows a populated list of tables stored in the device database, as shown in Figure 11-11.

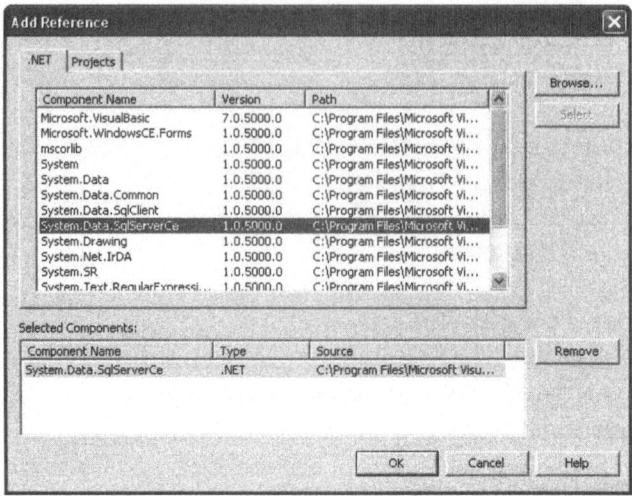

Figure 11-11. The Query Analyzer view of the device database

The final step in developing a data-driven device application is to add the source code that stores and retrieves data records. Data access from a device database works the same way as any of the other ADO.NET data providers. Listing 11-4 outlines the DisplayIssues method, which retrieves a list of issues from the already synchronized device database and displays them in a list view control.

Listing 11-4. Displaying Issues Based on SQL Server CE Data

```
private void DisplayIssues()
{
    string strDataPath = "\\My Documents\\IssueTracker.sdf";
    ListViewItem listItem;

    //create the connection object
    SqlCeConnection conn = new SqlCeConnection( "Data Source=" + strDataPath );

    try
    {
        //open the device database connection
        conn.Open();

        //create and initialize the command
        SqlCeCommand command = conn.CreateCommand();
        command.CommandText = "SELECT IssueID, PriorityID, RTRIM(Summary) " +
            "FROM Dat_Issues ORDER BY IssueID";
```

```
        //execute the query
        SqlCeDataReader reader = command.ExecuteReader();

        //build the display list
        lstViewer.Items.Clear();
        while( reader.Read() )
        {
            //build the display list row entries
            listItem = new ListViewItem();
            listItem.Text = reader.GetInt32(0).ToString();
            listItem.SubItems.Add( reader.GetInt16(1).ToString() );
            listItem.SubItems.Add( reader.GetString(3) );

            lstViewer.Items.Add( listItem );
        }

    }
    catch( SqlCeException x )
    {
        MessageBox.Show( x.Message );
    }
    catch( Exception x )
    {
        MessageBox.Show( x.Message );
    }
    finally
    {
        //close the database connection
        conn.Close();
    }

    return;
}
```

This method begins by initializing a SqlCeConnection object with a connection string that points to the device database file. Next, the connection is opened and a command object is created to perform the database query. After specifying the query, the SqlCeCommand object's ExecuteReader method is invoked. The results of the query are iterated and displayed in a list view control.

The biggest concern related to data-driven device applications is reliability. Ideally, the device database file should be stored or created within Compact Flash (CF) memory. Files stored in CF are immune to critical power loss and cold boots. If not available, however, enterprise applications should attempt to handle data loss as cleanly as possible.

Integrating XML Web Services

XML Web services define a communication framework where messages can be exchanged in a loosely coupled environment using standard protocols. Because Web services are based on standard protocols, just about any client running any operating system can integrate with them, including device applications.

The problem with Web service integration is performance. Retrieving data over a wireless HTTP connection and rendering its resulting data in a form is a lengthy process. Unfortunately, the remoting framework is included in the Compact Framework, so faster binary communication is not available.

Because Web services can pull data straight from the enterprise database, its data is up-to-date. In the IssueTracker device application, two data retrieval systems are in place. First, the high-level issue information is retrieved from a locally synchronized device database. This provides the best possible performance. Next, the user can optionally request to view the issue details in a form that pulls its data from the Web service created in Chapter 9, "Using XML and Web Services." Any additional data entered at the last minute still appears in the details view, as shown in Figure 11-12.

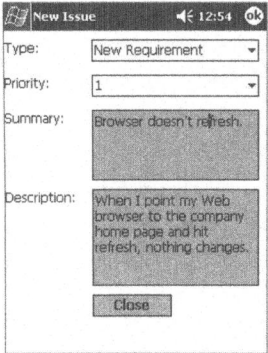

Figure 11-12. The issue details form

Implementing the issue details form begins to look similar to the Web service client created in Chapter 9, "Using XML and Web Services." It begins with a Web reference that needs to be added to the project. Select the new PocketUI project within the IssueTracker Solution Explorer. From the context menu, click References ➤ Add Web Reference. The Add Web Reference dialog box appears, as shown in Figure 11-13. You can use the Add Web Reference dialog box to either enter a URL pointing to a specific Web service or browse a Universal Description, Discovery, and Integration (UDDI) registry for any other available Web services. Enter the URL that points to the issues retrieval Web service developed in Chapter 9 (http://server_name/IssueTracker_WebService/IssueServices.asmx) and click the Go button.

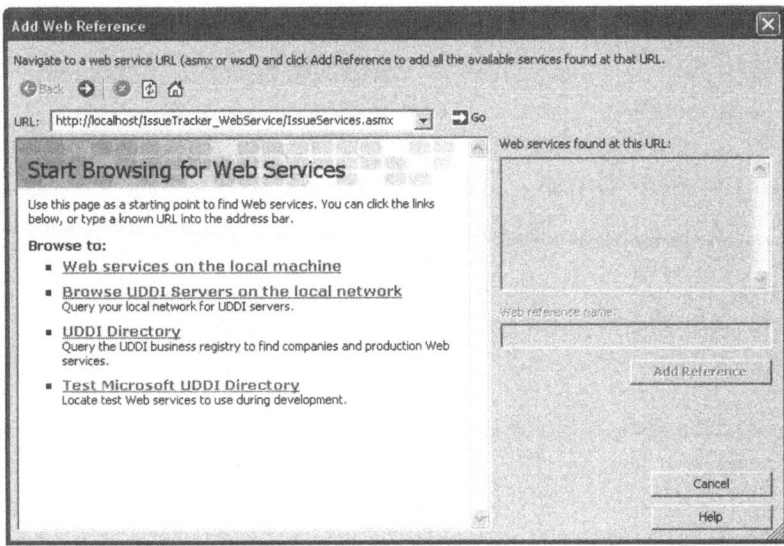

Figure 11-13. Adding a Web reference to an existing Web service

Next, the Add Web Reference dialog box displays a test view of the Web service, listing all exposed methods. Click the Add Reference button to establish the project reference to this Web service. Visual Studio .NET adds the reference to the Web service, which is noticeable within the Solution Explorer. Although the underlying files, such as .wsdl and .disco files, are named to match the Web service, the Web reference's name matches the source server name. Fortunately, you can rename the node within the Solution Explorer to also match the Web service. In this case, the Web reference named *jkanalakis* has been renamed to *IssueService*. This way, the namespace appearing within the source code makes more sense when reading.

The code that interacts with the Web service is fairly small (see Listing 11-5). When you establish a Web reference, Visual Studio .NET creates a proxy class that abstracts access to the Web service. Instead of formatting Simple Object Access Protocol (SOAP) headers and messages, the Web service client can simply interact with the Web service as if it were any other object.

Listing 11-5. Displaying Issue Details Based on Data Retrieved from a Web Service

```
private void FormViewIssue_Load( object sender, System.EventArgs e )
{
    try
    {
        //instantiate the Web service proxy
        IssueService.IssueServices webserviceIssue =
            new IssueService.IssueServices();
```

```
        //invoke the Web service method
        string strResponse = webserviceIssue.GetSpecificIssue( m_strPassword,
            m_longIssueID );

        //initialize a new DataSet
        DataSet dsIssue = new DataSet();

        //initialize an XmlTextReader with the Web service results
        XmlTextReader xreader = new XmlTextReader( strResponse,
            XmlNodeType.Element, null );

        //feed the Web service response to the DataSet
        dsIssue.ReadXml( xreader );

        //Set the display fields based on values within the DataSet
        lblPriority.Text =
            dsIssue.Tables["Dat_Issue"].Rows[0]["PriorityLabel"].ToString();
        lblType.Text =
            dsIssue.Tables["Dat_Issue"].Rows[0]["TypeLabel"].ToString();
        txtSummary.Text =
            dsIssue.Tables["Dat_Issue"].Rows[0]["Summary"].ToString();
        lblAuthor.Text =
            dsIssue.Tables["Dat_Issue"].Rows[0]["Lastname"].ToString().Trim() +
            ", " +
            dsIssue.Tables["Dat_Issue"].Rows[0]["Firstname"].ToString().Trim();
        txtDescription.Text =
            dsIssue.Tables["Dat_Issue"].Rows[0]["Description"].ToString();
    }
    catch( Exception x )
    {
        MessageBox.Show( x.Message );
    }

    return;
}
```

In Listing 11-5, the FormViewIssue form connects to the IssueServices Web service to return specific details about a selected issue. First, the automatically generated Web service proxy object, webserviceIssue, is instantiated. Next, a specific Web service method, GetSpecificIssue, is invoked. This method is supplied with a password and a specific issue ID. The Web service response is captured as a string, and an XmlTextReader is used to map the raw XML in the string into a schema-inferred DataSet object. Finally, the form's user interface elements are set to various fields of the DataSet.

Displaying Graphics Within a Form

It is common for any application to display a splash screen that identifies the software creator at startup. In just about every case, the splash screen is represented by an image containing text about the application and its producer. The picture box control can easily create and render simple images. However, anything more than simply displaying the image, such as drawing a border, is beyond its capabilities. Another approach to rendering an image that supports customization is to use the drawing methods available within the System.Drawing namespace. Figure 11-14 illustrates using the System.Drawing methods to create the splash screen for the IssueTracker device application.

Figure 11-14. Displaying a graphic as an application splash screen

You can use just about any image format to render the splash screen, including .bmp, .jpg, and .gif files. The process begins by creating the source image and adding it to the PocketUI project with its Build Action property set to Content. Listing 11-6 outlines the specific steps involved in manually rendering the image.

Listing 11-6. Displaying the IssueTracker Splash Screen

```
public class FormSplash : System.Windows.Forms.Form
{
    private System.Windows.Forms.Timer timerSplash;
    private Bitmap m_bmpImage;
    private int m_intTimeElapsed = 0;
    private int m_intTimeInterval = 100;
```

```
private int m_intTimerDuration = 2000;


//initializes the source image and timer interval
private void FormSplash_Load(object sender, System.EventArgs e)
{
    try
    {
        //create and initialize the bitmap object
        m_bmpImage = new Bitmap( "\\Windows\\app_splash.jpg" );

        //activate the timer
        timerSplash.Interval = m_intTimeInterval;
        timerSplash.Enabled = true;
    }
    catch( Exception x )
    {
        MessageBox.Show( x.Message );
    }
    return;
}

//handles the Tick event and determines if enough time has elapsed
private void timerSplash_Tick(object sender, System.EventArgs e)
{
    try
    {
        //compare the elapsed time against the expected duration
        if( m_intTimeElapsed >= m_intTimerDuration )
        {
            //time is up, close the splash screen
            timerSplash.Enabled = false;
            Close();
        }
        else
        {
            //still waiting, increment the elapsed time
            m_intTimeElapsed += m_intTimeInterval;
        }
    }
    catch( Exception x )
    {
        MessageBox.Show( x.Message );
    }
```

```
        return;
    }


    //display the bitmap image
    protected override void OnPaint( PaintEventArgs e )
    {
        try
        {
            //initialize a Graphics engine object and draw the image
            Graphics graphics = e.Graphics;
            graphics.DrawImage( m_bmpImage, 1, 1 );
        }
        catch( Exception x )
        {
            MessageBox.Show( x.Message );
        }
        return;
    }
}
```

The client side of the splash screen code exists in a few lines of code within the main form. The parent form only needs to instantiate the FormSplash object and display it. After a determined elapsed time, the splash screen will close itself and allow the application to continue:

```
private void FormMain_Load( object sender, System.EventArgs e )
{
    FormSplash splash = new FormSplash();
    splash.ShowDialog();
    return;
}
```

Integrating Native Device Functionality

The Compact Framework does not support interop services with Component Object Model (COM) objects. However, you can access native operating system services and custom DLL methods with the help of platform invoke services.

An example of the platform invocation services is audio playback. Although a Compact Framework method is not available for audio playback, you can access the native device services packaged within the coredll.dll file. You can abstract the details of the platform invocation into a single object. Listing 11-7 adds a new class, SoundLayer, to the PocketUI project.

Listing 11-7. An Audio Playback Layer Based on Platform Method Invocation

```
using System;
using System.Runtime.InteropServices;

public class SoundLayer
{
    //specify the bitwise control flags
    [Flags]
    public enum AudioBitFlags : int
    {
        FILENAME = 0x00020000,
        ASYNC = 0x0001
    }

    //import a method from an unmanaged dll
    [DllImport("coredll")]
    private static extern bool PlaySound( string szSound, IntPtr hMod,
        AudioBitFlags flags );

    //abstract the external function with an exposed static play method
    public static void Play( string strFilename )
    {
        try
        {
            PlaySound( strFilename, IntPtr.Zero,
                AudioBitFlags.FILENAME | AudioBitFlags.ASYNC );
        }
        catch( Exception x )
        {
            MessageBox.Show( "Unable to playback sound file." );
        }
        return;
    }

}
```

The first step is to add a reference to the Compact Framework's interop services. Next, the class defines a set of bitwise flags that are required by the native method. Flag values are packaged nicely into an enumerator to allow named referencing. Next, the class identifies the PlaySound method as exported from an unmanaged DLL (specifically, coredll.dll). Finally, the exposed static method, Play, is implemented. This method wraps the exported DLL method to minimize impacts on the application client in the event a different implementation is used in the future.

The client code comes down to a few simple lines. In Listing 11-8, the PlayAlertSound method calls the Play method defined in the SoundLayer class. Because the Play method is marked as static, a new instance of the SoundLayer object is not necessary.

Listing 11-8. Accessing the Audio Playback Layer

```
public void PlayAlertSound()
{
    //sound file should be added to project with 'Content' build type
    SoundLayer.Play( "\\Windows\\AlertSound.wav" );
}
```

Given the limited processing power that devices offer, there will most likely be a need to display a "busy" cursor to inform the user that the device has not frozen but rather that it needs time to continue processing. Although these cases should be kept to a minimum, it sometimes cannot be helped. Simple file access and Web service invocation can easily take a few seconds, leaving the user to wonder if everything is still operating normally. Listing 11-9 uses platform invocation to change the cursor state from normal to busy and back.

Listing 11-9. Changing the Device Cursor Based on Platform Method Invocation

```
//import a method from an unmanaged dll
[DllImport("coredll.dll")]
private static extern int LoadCursor(int zeroValue, int cursorID );

//import a method from an unmanaged dll
[DllImport("coredll.dll")]
private static extern int SetCursor( int cursorHandle );

// show or hide the wait cursor
public void ShowWaitCursor( bool boolShowWait )
{
    try
    {
        int cursorHandle = 0;

        if( boolShowWait )
        {
            //load the busy cursor
            cursorHandle = LoadCursor( 0, 32514 );
```

```
        }

        SetCursor( cursorHandle );
    }
    catch( Exception x )
    {
        MessageBox.Show( "Unable to set cursor." );
    }
    return;
}
```

The ShowWaitCursor works similarly to the PlaySound method. A couple of external methods, LoadCursor and SetCursor, are imported from the coredll.dll file. Next, the method accepts a boolean flag that determines if the busy cursor, 32514, should display or the default system cursor, 0, should display.

With support for platform invocation services, the Compact Framework leaves the door open to extensibility, much like its desktop counterpart. It provides enterprise application developers with the tools needed to build extensions to mobile clients capable of presenting a familiar user interface and supporting local data storage. The next section explores an alternative platform for building truly wireless applications with even more limited resources.

Exploring the Microsoft Mobile Internet Toolkit

Wireless devices, such as Web-enabled cellular phones, serve a different function from PDAs. Rather than storing data such as contact information, messages, and schedules locally, cellular phones are used exclusively for communication and information retrieval. The simplest example of information access via cellular phone is an everyday call to 411 for information. Web-enabled cellular phones have taken this concept to the next level by removing the human element on the information provider side and replacing it with Web content. This is the basis for the Microsoft Mobile Internet Toolkit (MMIT).

Essentially, MMIT is an extension to the existing ASP.NET services. Mobile applications are composed of source files that abstract a user interface. When a mobile device connects to the server, its device profile is detected and the abstracted user interface is formatted specifically for the connecting device. The connecting mobile device does not need to install any local software to interact with the enterprise application.

Communication between the mobile client and the server is typically conducted over port 80 using the Wireless Application Protocol (WAP). WAP is similar to the standard HTTP Web protocol but is optimized for mobile devices. WAP leverages a binary transmission for improved compression of data optimized for low bandwidth. WAP sessions are also forgiving to intermittent and unreliable connections.

Content displayed within a mobile device is formatted in the Wireless Markup Language (WML). Like its Hypertext Markup Language (HTML) counterpart, WML is a tag-based format for describing content. WML addresses many of the inefficiencies found in HTML, including the large amounts of text-based data to be sent across a low bandwidth connection. Also, HTML content is unable to be cleanly displayed on the small displays of mobile devices.

In Visual Studio .NET, a mobile application's user interface uses the same form designer used to build ASP.NET Web applications. There are only a few noticeable differences. First, a number of user interface controls have been removed from the Toolbox, and new device-specific controls have been added. Next, you can draw multiple content forms per page. Also, there is no support for absolute positioning of form controls, only relative positioning. Finally, there are a number of limitations related to session management.

Understanding the Platform Architecture

MMIT enables applications to be rendered on mobile devices produced by different manufacturers with different device capabilities. Its underlying platform architecture is based on three elements: device detection, device formatting, and Web communication. Figure 11-15 illustrates the MMIT platform architecture.

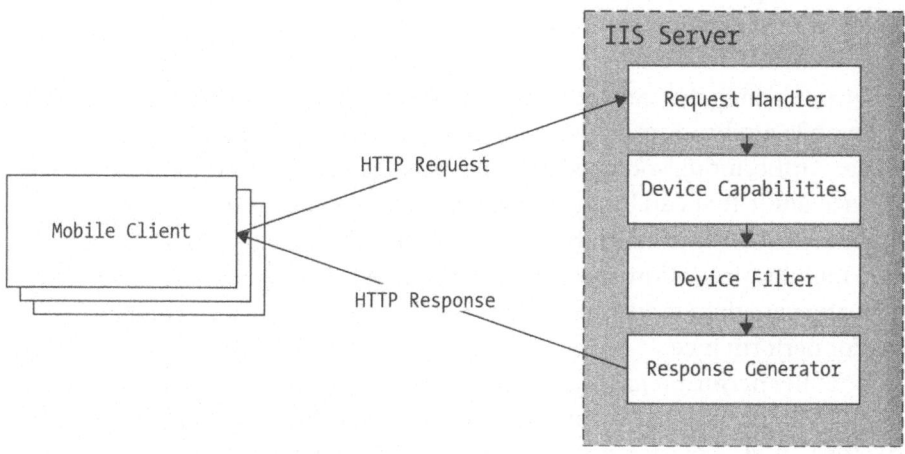

Figure 11-15. The MMIT platform architecture

The only way to render an application on different mobile devices is to apply the appropriate formatting. That begins with device capability detection. Both the HTTP and WAP protocols embed information about Web requests within their request headers. These incoming request headers determine the device capabilities of the connecting device and determine the best method of formatting a response. There are a number of available output formats for a variety of mobile devices, including HTML, Compact HTML (cHTML), and WML.

You compose the user interfaces created for mobile applications generically. In other words, the application developer has little influence over the final positioning of user interface controls when rendered on a specific device. Device filters manage the specific layout mapping between the abstract user interface defined in the form designer and the final output of the mobile application.

The functionality that binds everything together is the existing ASP.NET framework. This includes page processing and life cycle, request and response communication, and session management. Adding capability detection and device formatting to existing ASP.NET services makes MMIT a logical choice for building mobile applications.

Building Mobile Applications for the Enterprise

Developing mobile applications for the enterprise requires even more planning than Compact Framework device applications or their natural Web application counterparts. This is largely because of the tighter restrictions on resources, such as display area, memory capacity, and speed. Therefore, mobile applications require additional design constraints to those imposed by Compact Framework applications. These include the constraints of portability and speed.

Where Compact Framework applications could expect to operate on devices running the WinCE or Pocket PC operating systems, MMIT applications may not know for sure which device platforms they will support. As a result, you need to design mobile applications with broad functionality in mind and a simple user interface. Furthermore, you need to design mobile applications to integrate custom device filters that can bridge the gap to unknown devices.

With a low-bandwidth Internet connection, especially one that charges per minute, mobile application speed is important. Mobile applications must take even greater care than their Web application counterparts when it comes to optimizing for performance.

A lot of the performance impact depends on how the mobile application is laid out. WML specifies the organization of content differently than HTML. In HTML, the contents of each page are completely viewable. In WML, however, a page may be composed of separate viewable forms of related content. When a mobile page is referenced, the page and all of its embedded forms are downloaded into local memory. Switching between the individual display forms appears to be fast because there is not a request to the server.

You need to organize content, therefore, into related blocks. In the case of IssueTracker, searching for an issue, viewing a list of issues, and viewing a specific issue's details are all implemented as different forms within a page. The application requires only a single request to the server to pull down all the necessary forms.

Implementing a Mobile Internet Application

Visual Studio .NET provides a development environment for creating mobile applications. With MMIT, developers can create and distribute applications that run on just about any mobile device capable of Web browsing. Implementing a mobile application typically involves creating the project, adding forms and controls to pages, adding event handlers that accomplish specific business tasks, and deploying the application.

Creating the New Project

Creating a new project for a mobile application follows the same general process as creating a new Web application project. To create a mobile project, click Add ➤ New Project from the Solution Explorer's context menu. In the Add New Project dialog box, select the ASP.NET Mobile Web Application template, enter the project name as shown in Figure 11-16, and then click the OK button.

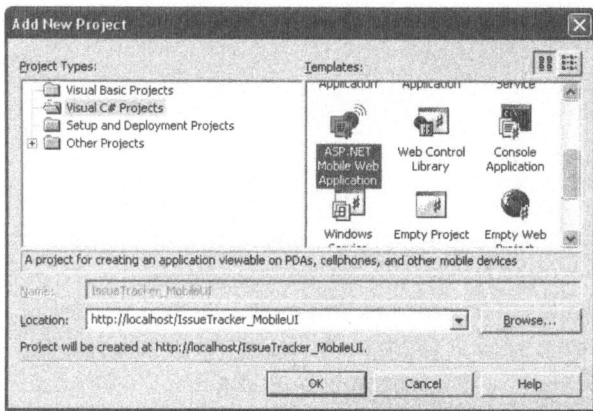

Figure 11-16. Adding a new mobile Web application project

This creates the mobile application project along with a handful of supporting files. The MobileWebForm1.aspx.cs file contains the source code for handling events and user interface formatting. The assemblyInfo.cs file contains attributes that describe the assembly built by the project. The global.asax file responds to application-level events sent by ASP.NET or by HttpModules. The web.config file contains settings specific to the mobile application.

Adding Pages and Forms

The foundation element of a mobile application is a page. Like any other Web application, a mobile application page is referenced by a specific URL. As mentioned, a page is composed of one or more display forms, each containing the user interface controls that implement the user experience. An important difference between mobile applications and standard Web applications is that only one form displays on a mobile device at a time. In a mobile application, the first form within a page is considered to be the default form displayed.

The reason for supporting multiple display forms per page is based largely on state management and performance reasons. There is little support for saving state between mobile application pages. By implementing multiple display forms per page, applications can more easily pass state information from one form to another.

Another reason for supporting multiple display forms within a page is to optimize for performance. Rather than slowly downloading one page after another, it requires a single performance hit to download one larger page and then quickly navigate among locally cached forms. Also, mobile applications are able to pass state data between forms within a page, rather than slowly pass state data back to the server. All forms within a page share a single code-behind source file, supporting sharing and reuse of methods as well as minimizing the mobile application's overhead.

Adding Forms and Controls

Unlike the design of Web applications, mobile applications have limited influence over how user interface controls appear with the mobile application. Forms do not support the absolute placement of controls. You must place controls into a form in their logical order of use from left to right and from top to bottom. You cannot set controls to specific dimensions. As a result, building display forms in the form designer does not provide an accurate representation of how they will be rendered on a mobile device. Figure 11-17 illustrates the minimal control that application developers have over mobile form layout. User interface controls fall vertically down a form with the expectation that there is little display width.

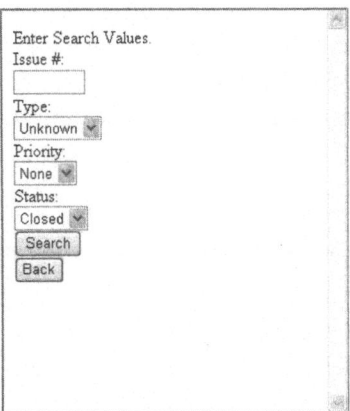

Figure 11-17. Setting the BreakAfter property to true renders one control per line.

The only exception to the limited placement of controls within a form relates to line breaks. Some devices are capable of displaying multiple controls on a single line, and other devices display only a single control per line. If devices are capable, the BreakAfter property enables side-by-side placement of form controls. Devices supporting line breaks automatically adapt the rendering for side-by-side layout. Setting the BreakAfter property to false places controls side by side on all capable devices. Figure 11-18 sets the BreakAfter property to false to produce a user interface that is a bit easier to use.

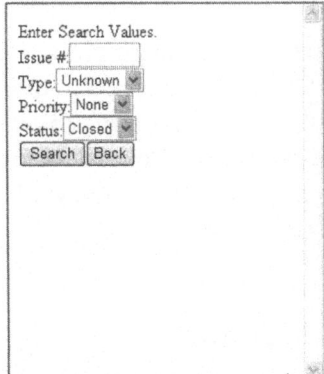

Figure 11-18. Setting the BreakAfter property to false renders multiple controls per line.

Panels are another tool that help organize user interface controls within a form. Panels work well for applying specific styles across multiple controls. Typically, forms will try to render as many user interface controls as possible on a device display. Panels, however, can define pagination and grouping of related controls. You add them from the Toolbox to the form and later fill them with additional user interface controls. All embedded controls inherit the properties defined for the panel. This creates a clean method of showing or hiding multiple controls all at once.

Adding Event Handling

User interface controls within a mobile form define events in the same manner as their Web application counterparts. The only difference is that all event handling is processed on the server rather than the client. When a button control is clicked, the containing page is posted back to the server where the event parameters are examined. Event handlers that correspond to events execute on the server. When the event handler completes, the server sends the page back to the mobile device with the applied changes.

Applying Style Sheets to Mobile Forms

A *style sheet* defines one or more styles that specify the appearance of controls when they are rendered. When placed into a display form, the style sheet control enables specific style information to be defined and applied to a specific user interface control, a collection of controls within a container, or all controls within the same page. You can attach only one style sheet control to a page or control, but not within a form or panel.

After adding a style sheet control to a page, the Styles Editor defines its specific properties. The dialog box displays the styles that have been defined in the Defined Styles dialog box. All defined styles must be based on a style type shown in the Style Types list. When you select and add a style type to the Defined Styles list, you add the defined style as an instance of that style type. In addition, you can create multiple defined styles based on the same style type.

Testing Mobile Applications with Device Emulators

Mobile device emulators are valuable tools for testing mobile applications. Most manufacturers of mobile devices encourage application developers to build and test solutions for their mobile devices. Companies, such as Ericsson and Nokia, provide toolkits freely downloadable to registered users. These toolkits include mobile device emulators that simulate the look and feel of a specific device. As Figure 11-19 illustrates, you can use these emulators to test mobile applications, saving you the cost of purchasing the physical devices.

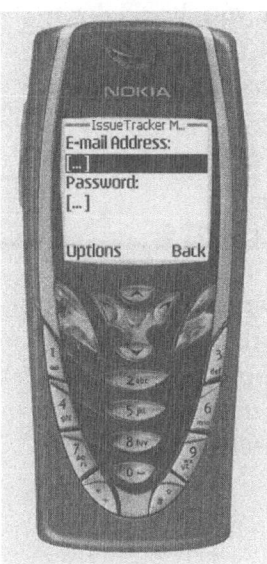

Figure 11-19. The IssueTracker mobile login form displayed in the Nokia 7210 emulator

By default, when a mobile device application starts within Visual Studio .NET, the application interface is rendered in plain HTML and displayed within the default Web browser. You can quickly modify Visual Studio to start a third-party device emulator instead. After downloading and installing the emulator, open Visual Studio. Select File ➤ Browse With from the menu. In the Browse With dialog box, click the Add button and enter the executable file path and label for the device emulator.

 NOTE *Most emulators can accept a parameter representing the URL to a starting page. Specify a %URL variable where Visual Studio should insert the starting page's location.*

From the Solution Explorer, select the starting .aspx mobile form and choose Browse With from its context menu. In the Browse With dialog box, select the newly added device emulator. The next time the mobile application launches, it should appear within the selected device emulator.

You can download the Ericsson WML toolkit and emulator from the Ericsson Mobility World Web site (http://www.ericsson.com/mobilityworld).

The mobile emulator used for the examples in this chapter is the Nokia 7210, bundled with the Nokia Mobile Internet Toolkit 4.0. You can download the toolkit and emulator from Nokia's developer forum (http://www.forum.nokia.com).

In addition to downloading and installing an emulator, you should download and install the Device Update 2 for .NET Framework 1.1. This update includes updated browser capabilities for new mobile devices. You can download it from http://www.asp.net/mobile/deviceupdate.aspx.

Enhancing Mobile Internet Enterprise Clients

There is much more to building a mobile client for the enterprise than creating forms, adding controls, and processing events. Features such as enabling a secure login, pulling data from Web services, dynamically binding form controls, and displaying graphics are necessary to round out the functionality. These features help shift the enterprise mobile client from being a useless showpiece to being a valuable extension of the enterprise application.

Implementing a Secure Mobile Login

Security in mobile applications is just as important as within the other application platforms. MMIT provides services that help validate user access. The IssueTracker mobile client uses the FormsAuthentication object to ensure user identity. To implement the login functionality, add a new mobile Web form to the project and name the page *app_login.aspx*. Add the user interface controls as shown in Figure 11-20.

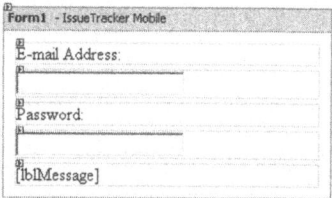

Figure 11-20. The mobile application login page, app_login.aspx

The System.Web.Security namespace provides many security-related objects described later in Chapter 13, "Understanding .NET Security and Cryptography." In the app_login.aspx.cs code-behind file, begin with an additional namespace reference to the Security services:

```
using System.Web.Security;
```

Add an event handler that responds to the Login button's Click event. Rather than process the user login with a Web service, as with the Compact Framework version of the application, the mobile login can be performed with the FormsAuthentication object. Listing 11-10 outlines the login authentication process.

Listing 11-10. Implementing Forms Authentication for Mobile Clients

```
private void btnLogin_Click(object sender, System.EventArgs e)
{
    try
    {
        if( FormsAuthentication.Authenticate( txtUsername.Text, txtPwd.Text ) )
        {
            FormsAuthentication.SetAuthCookie( txtLogin.Text, false );
            MobileFormsAuthentication.RedirectFromLoginPage(txtLogin.Text, true);
        }
        else
        {
            lblMessage.Text = "Login Failed.";
        }
    }
    catch( Exception x )
    {
        EventLog systemLog = new EventLog();
        systemLog.Source = "IssueTracker";
        systemLog.WriteEntry( x.Message, EventLogEntryType.Error, 0 );
    }
    retrun;
}
```

The event handler performs the user authentication. When a user requests any page belonging to the mobile application without having been authenticated, they will be redirected to this login page. The FormAuthentication object performs the user authentication based on the supplied username and password. If the authentication fails, the page displays a message and the user is not permitted to continue. Otherwise, if the authentication succeeds, the user is redirected to the originally requested page.

The application logout uses the same security object. The logout event handler invokes the FormsAuthentication's SignOut method to close the user session. The user is then redirected to the login page where the process can start again:

```
private void btnLogout_Click(object sender, System.EventArgs e)
{
    MobileFormsAuthentication.SignOut();
    RedirectToMobilePage( "app_login.aspx", true );

    return;
}
```

To support Forms Authentication, you need to modify the web.config file to identify the valid credentials. The settings shown in Listing 11-11 should replace (not append to) the existing authentication settings. Specifically, you need to specify the authentication mode to Forms. If two separate <authentication> blocks exist within the web.config file, it will generate a configuration error.

Listing 11-11. Form Security Changes to the web.config File

```
<authentication mode="Forms" >
    <forms loginUrl="app_login.aspx" name="issuetracker" timeout="60" path="/" >
        <credentials passwordFormat="SHA1">
            <user name="jkanalakis"
                password="5BAA61E4C9B93F3F0682250B6CF8331B7EE68FD8"/>
            <user name="mwilliams"
                password="5BAA61E4C9B93F3F0682250B6CF8331B7EE68FD8"/>
        </credentials>
    </forms>
</authentication>

<authorization>
    <deny users="?" />
</authorization>

<sessionState cookieless="true"/>
```

The changes to the <authentication> block specify the use of FormsAuthentication as the mode of user authentication. The <credentials> block specifies the encoding format of the included passwords, either the SHA1 or MD5 format. This block also specifies the valid usernames and passwords for application access. The HashPasswordForStoringInConfigFile method within the FormsAuthentication object created the encoded value for the passwords. The following short method demonstrates how a utility application can use the HashPasswordForStoringInConfigFile method:

```
public string GetEncodedPassword( string strPassword )
{
```

```
    return FormsAuthentication.HashPasswordForStoringInConfigFile( strPassword,
        "SHA1" );
}
```

The changes to the <authorization> block specify that anonymous users should be denied access to the application. Also, because of the security risks associated with cookies, the <SessionState> tag specifies that cookies should not be used to manage the session.

Integrating XML Web Services

Web services can be just as useful for mobile applications as they are for Web applications. There should be some special considerations before implementing Web services connectivity, specifically relating to performance. Mobile applications are fairly slow to start with; integrating Web services will only slow the application further. Also, without a busy cursor or progress bar, there is not a clean way to give the user the sense that something is still happening. Listing 11-12 integrates a Web service to retrieve the list of issues from the enterprise database.

Listing 11-12. Integrating Web Service Data into a Mobile Application Form

```
private void FormViewIssue_Load( object sender, System.EventArgs e )
{
    try
    {
        IssueCollection issues = "";

        //instantiate the Web service proxy
        net.mynamespace.www.IssueServices wsIssues =
            new net.mynamespace.www.IssueServices();

        //invoke the Web service method
        issues = wsIssues.GetAllIssues();

        if( strWebServiceResponse.StartsWith( "ERR" ) == false )
        {
            foreach( Issue objIssue in issues )
            {
                lstIssues.Items.Add( "[" + objIssue.IssueID + "]" +
                    objIssue.Summary.Substring(0,10) + "..." );
            }
        }
        else
```

```
        {
            System.Windows.Forms.MessageBox.Show( "Login Failed." );
        }


    }
    catch( Exception x )
    {
        EventLog systemLog = new EventLog();
        systemLog.Source = "IssueTracker";
        systemLog.WriteEntry( x.Message, EventLogEntryType.Error, 0 );
    }
    return;
}
```

This method begins with an instantiation of the Web service proxy object, where all of the SOAP-based connections to the Web service are implicitly made. Next, the GetAllIssues Web service method is invoked and its resulting XML is stored in a local string variable. Next, a new DataSet object is instantiated. An XmlTextReader object is also created and initialized with the string returned from the Web service. The XmlTextReader is passed to the DataSet's ReadXml method. This results in the DataSet interpreting and forming the data structure of the returned XML document as well as populating itself with the XML data. From then on, the DataSet's rows are iterated and the issues list is built for display. The issue summary text is intentionally truncated to shorten the displayed text. Figure 11-21 illustrates the resulting list of issues that displays.

The user is able to scroll through the list of issues and select one to view its details. The load time for the page is based on the size of the underlying data.

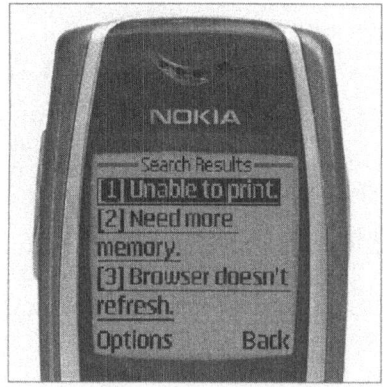

Figure 11-21. Displaying issues extracted from a Web service

Data Binding Mobile Form Controls

You can data bind mobile form controls to a data source in the same manner as you do for the rest of the ASP.NET framework. The only difference between the two is capacity. Because the mobile client will be connecting over low bandwidth and will have a small display area, it is important to minimize the amount of data exchanged. In Figure 11-22, the IssueTracker mobile application has an intermediate step that helps minimize the volume of data accessed when displaying issues.

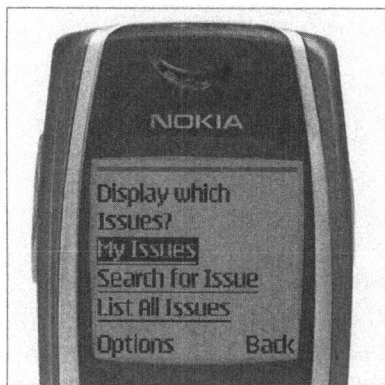

Figure 11-22. Helping the user navigate large DataSets

The intermediate step to data retrieval is data filtering. In the IssueTracker application, data comes into three categories: issues related to the user, issues resulting from a search, and all issues stored in the database. Categorizing the underlying data reduces the user's frustration over waiting for the whole list of issues to be retrieved.

For smaller data collections, such as validation data, it is usually safe to continue with standard data binding to mobile form controls. In the case of FormSearch, you implement the drop-down list entries that contain searchable issue types, priorities, and the status using data binding (see Listing 11-13).

Listing 11-13. Data Binding to Mobile Form Controls

```
private void Page_Load(object sender, System.EventArgs e)
{
    try
    {
        DataAccess.DataAccessComponent data = new
            DataAccess.DataAccessComponent();
```

Chapter 11

```
        lstType.DataSource = data.GetDataSetIssueTracker().Val_IssueType;
        lstType.DataBind();

        lstPriority.DataSource = data.GetDataSetIssueTracker().Val_Priority;
        lstPriority.DataBind();

        lstStatus.DataSource = data.GetDataSetIssueTracker().Val_Status;
        lstStatus.DataBind();
    }
    catch( Exception x )
    {
        EventLog systemLog = new EventLog();
        systemLog.Source = "IssueTracker";
        systemLog.WriteEntry( x.Message, EventLogEntryType.Error, 0 );
    }
    return;
}
```

Listing 11-13 creates an instance of the DataAccessComponent object to retrieve the application's DataSet object. For each mobile form control, the code assigns the DataSource property to the respective DataSet table. The code then sets the DataTextField and DataValueField properties to the Description and ID columns of the table. Finally, the DataBind method is invoked to establish the binding. Figure 11-23 demonstrates the results, where the user can select from a list of options pulled from the DataSet.

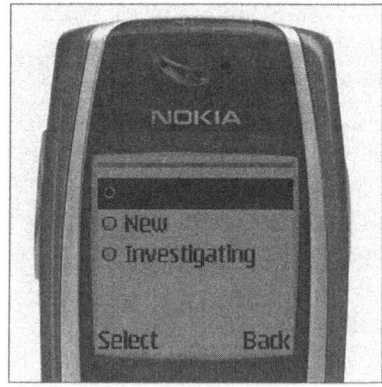

Figure 11-23. Selecting an issue status from a data-bound list control

Displaying Graphics Within a Mobile Form

Some mobile devices are capable of displaying graphics. Graphics are an effective way to communicate information in a quickly recognizable format. As more mobile devices become available with support for graphics, you can develop more usable mobile interfaces. In the meantime, it is important to target specific devices and test their graphical support through emulators. It may take time to determine which graphic format, such as .bmp or .gif, renders best on each targeted device.

A practical use for images within mobile clients is to present a chart to the user. You can place any static image into a mobile form with the help of the MobileControls.Image object. After placing the image control into a mobile form, set its ImageUrl property to the source of the graphic. Presenting a chart based upon dynamic data works similarly. Instead of placing an image control within a mobile form, you can create a new mobile user control.

Mobile user controls function similarly to the Web user controls described in Chapter 7, "Building Web Applications." They also serve a similar function, bringing consistency to an online application. In this case, a mobile user control will implement a simple mobile chart. Begin by selecting the IssueTracker_MobileUI project within the Solution Explorer. Next, select Add ➤ Add New Item from its context menu to create a new mobile Web user control named *MobileChart.ascx*, as shown in Figure 11-24.

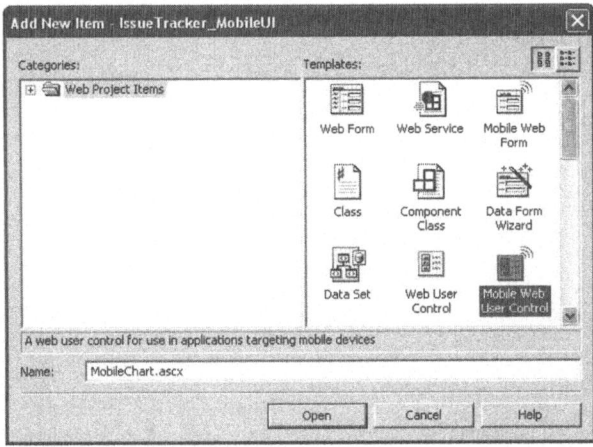

Figure 11-24. Creating a new mobile user control

Place an image control, imgChart, into the new user control. Double-click the control's design surface to create a Page_Load event handler. In the page's event handler, you can add code to dynamically create a chart, save it as a .gif, and return it to the mobile client. Listing 11-14 lists the completed event handler.

Listing 11-14. Creating a Dynamic Chart in a Mobile User Control

```
private void Page_Load(object sender, System.EventArgs e)
{
    Point pointStart;
    Point pointEnd;

    try
    {
        SolidBrush brush = new SolidBrush( Color.Blue );
        Bitmap bmpChart = new Bitmap( 80, 80 );

        Graphics g = Graphics.FromImage( bmpChart );
        g.Clear( Color.White );

        pointStart = new Point( 1, 1 );
        pointEnd = new Point( 10, 40 );
        g.DrawLine( new Pen( brush, 2 ), pointStart, pointEnd );

        pointStart = pointEnd;
        pointEnd = new Point( 20, 20 );
        g.DrawLine( new Pen( brush, 2 ), pointStart, pointEnd );

        pointStart = pointEnd;
        pointEnd = new Point( 30, 50 );
        g.DrawLine( new Pen( brush, 2 ), pointStart, pointEnd );

        pointStart = pointEnd;
        pointEnd = new Point( 40, 45 );
        g.DrawLine( new Pen( brush, 2 ), pointStart, pointEnd );

        pointStart = pointEnd;
        pointEnd = new Point( 60, 45 );
        g.DrawLine( new Pen( brush, 2 ), pointStart, pointEnd );

        Font fontLabel = new Font( "Arial", 8 );
        g.DrawString("1  2  3  4  5  6", fontLabel, brush, 1,50 );

        bmpChart.Save( @"c:\inetpub\wwwroot\issuetracker_mobileui\chart.gif",
            ImageFormat.Gif );

        imgChart.ImageUrl = "http://127.0.0.1/issuetracker_mobileui/chart.gif";

    }
```

```
catch(Exception x)
{
    EventLog systemLog = new EventLog();
    systemLog.Source = "IssueTracker";
    systemLog.WriteEntry( x.Message, EventLogEntryType.Error, 0 );
}

    return;
}
```

The Page_Load event handler begins by creating SolidBrush, Bitmap, and Graphic objects. The brush specifies that the color of the chart should appear in blue. The bitmap specifies the dimensions of the drawing surface as being 80 pixels wide by 80 pixels high. The code then creates the graphics engine based on the bitmap specifications and immediately sets it to a white background. The next few lines of code arbitrarily draw lines from point to point to simulate a line chart. Ideally, they should reflect useful values such as sales or losses over time. Finally, the chart is written to the image file chart.gif.

After you have implemented the MobileChart.ascx control, you can place it into a mobile form to render it like any other static image. Figure 11-25 illustrates the use of the MobileChart mobile user control. If a mobile user control does not appear as expected or at all, check the AppliedDeviceFilter settings and apply available device filters as needed to display the control within your emulator.

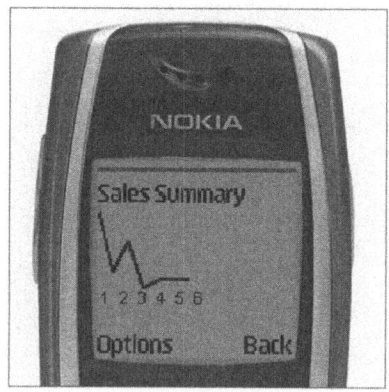

Figure 11-25. Using the MobileChart mobile user control

Although accessibility to enterprise data is the primary function of an enterprise mobile application, it must also be easy to use. Using graphics in mobile forms works best when they serve a functional purpose. When creating the images, be sure to keep the file size and display size as small as possible. Always test different image formats with different emulators for the best results.

Summary

The .NET Framework provides useful tools for developing mobile enterprise applications in the form of two different platforms, the Compact Framework and the MMIT. Both platforms are seamlessly integrated into the Visual Studio .NET environment. Building applications for Pocket PC devices closely resembles building desktop applications. Building Web-enabled cellular applications closely resembles building ASP.NET Web applications.

It is becoming increasingly difficult to determine which of the two frameworks to adopt when implementing a mobile solution for the enterprise. This is largely because of a convergence of the two technologies. PDAs are now available with built-in wireless capabilities, and cellular phones are now available with rich user interfaces. At this point, determining which solution to use still depends largely on where the data is being stored. The Compact Framework targets devices with local data storage capabilities, and the MMIT targets devices that access data from a remote server.

Regardless of which platform you select, the key to a successful mobile enterprise application is simplicity. You cannot expect mobile applications to support the full set of features that their desktop-based or Web-based counterparts implement. Enterprise application developers must look closely at the core services their products offer and extend only those services to the mobile client.

The next chapter introduces application integration, .NET style. An introduction to application integration describes the value in interfacing existing applications with new .NET applications. Then, the chapter assembles a new integration platform that puts XML, XSLT, and remoting to work.

CHAPTER 12

Integrating .NET Applications

ENTERPRISES OFTEN WANT pieces of their data and services to be accessible over the Web to partners, suppliers, customers, and remote employees. Enterprises can realize this by building a Web application that can access and manage data stored within existing information systems. With the .NET Framework, enterprises have the ability to build applications that can extend the reach of their existing information systems across the Internet. This chapter explores the delicate field of application integration and applies some of the technologies described earlier to build integration solutions.

Defining an Application Integration Strategy

Integrating new applications with existing legacy applications has always been a challenge. Legacy applications often include traditional enterprise applications, such as Enterprise Resource Planner (ERP) systems, transaction processing systems, database management systems, and various business-specific applications developed within the enterprise. The goal of application integration is to seamlessly bind existing application data and functionality to other business applications.

An integration project needs to be implemented without requiring changes to the legacy application or its data. An integration project must also assure that none of its newly added components cause any data inconsistencies or compromise the integrity of the existing data. The selected application integration strategy needs to be clearly defined. The strategy should list and address the predicted integration challenges, identify the type of integration necessary, and address security concerns.

Exposing the Integration Challenges

Generally, enterprises have built up their legacy information systems incrementally over time. As a business grows, it often finds it necessary to combine existing applications, even if they operate on different hardware platforms or were written in different programming languages. Enterprises usually end up with clusters of disparate business functions and data across their networks. A lack of integration between applications leads to information and process inconsistencies throughout the enterprise. Enterprise-wide integrations are always an expensive and risky undertaking. Some of the integration challenges include the following:

- **Merging different application architectures**: Legacy applications are often written in different programming languages and target different operating platforms without any mechanism for sharing information.

- **Combining different client models**: Legacy applications present technology and administrative restrictions, such as new user account creation, that are difficult to overcome.

- **Addressing different transaction mechanisms and security**: Legacy applications may apply transactions and security that are difficult to integrate. Some applications may control access to their resources through transactions, and others offer limited or no support for transactions.

- **Resolving data inconsistencies**: Legacy applications may use different data storage mediums in different formats for storing data requiring significant data mapping and/or transformations.

When developing a .NET application that integrates with a legacy application, keep the legacy application's functional limitations in mind. Design the integration solution to consider such limitations. It may be necessary to support transactions with rollback capabilities that span across multiple applications.

Understanding the Types of Integration

There are three different types of integration: inbound, outbound, and bidirectional. From the perspective of the new application, an *inbound* integration is passive and only exposes data and services to other applications. An *outbound* integration is active and interacts with the data and services provided by other applications. A *bidirectional* integration is both inbound and outbound. There is equal use of services between the new and legacy applications. You can also differentiate these three types of integration by the types of communication they use.

Synchronous communication involves a synchronous interface, which provides request-reply communication between a new application and a legacy application. When a new application wants to interact with the legacy application, it invokes an exposed function within the legacy application and then waits until the function completes before returning with a reply. The reply contains the results of the function's legacy execution.

Asynchronous integration involves an asynchronous interface, which enables a new application to call a remote function within the legacy application and then continue its own processing. The remote function within the legacy application processes that request and then returns an appropriate response to the application. The new application does not suspend its own processing while the remote function executes. Rather, the new application continues its work and receives a notification with the results of its request.

Message-based integration requires a connection to a queue-based or publish-subscribe messaging system. With queue-based messaging, a queue, independent from both the sender and receiver, serves as a message buffer between two communicating applications. One application sends a message to this queue, and another receives messages from it. With publish-subscribe messaging, publishers produce messages and subscribers listen to messages in which they are interested.

Building Awareness of Integration Security

An enterprise depends on its existing information systems to serve its business activities. Information loss or unauthorized access can be extremely costly. Enterprises require that the security of their legacy applications must never be compromised. Integrating applications must provide access to legacy applications without creating new security threats.

Enterprises must clearly establish the requirements for a secured environment. They must also weigh the cost of implementing, administering, and running a secure system against the security needs of individual applications. It is best for new applications to require only the minimum level of access allowed by the legacy applications. New applications should also reduce the level of access for less sensitive information or where the system is less vulnerable to threats. Enterprises need to establish their security requirements before mapping the architecture for legacy application integration. The integration project should do the following:

- Support a consistent end-to-end security architecture across all legacy application tiers.

- Fit into the existing security environment and infrastructure supported by the legacy application.

- Support authentication and authorization of users who are accessing the legacy application.

- Be transparent to new application components. This includes support for enabling end users to log on only once to the enterprise environment and access multiple enterprise information systems.

- Enable new applications to be portable across security environments that enforce different security policies.

Achieving these goals depends on the cost vs. benefit tradeoffs for the security requirements. The more that the integration project takes care of security requirements for the application, the easier the new application development effort will be.

A new application should clearly specify security requirements. This includes security roles, method permissions, and the authentication approach for the legacy application login.

When in doubt, a separate security component can manage security. A programmatic interface can be exposed through which new applications can manage security. The security component interface allows the new application to make access control decisions based on the role associated with the login.

Architecting an Integration Platform

Application integration is often, but not always, a one-to-one effort. A new application might need to access functionality or data contained within an older legacy application. As you develop the new application, you can make direct mappings into the legacy application to access the needed data or functionality.

Although one-to-one integrations are common, one-to-many integrations produce the greatest benefits. With one-to-many integrations, an existing application's data or functionality is exposed and documented. Any new application will be able to integrate with the existing application.

Figure 12-1 shows the key elements that make up the integration platform. These elements include application adapters, the integration server, the data mapping and transformation engine, environment configuration, and the underlying communication mechanism.

You can package these elements into three new projects and add them to the IssueTracker solution. The IntegrationServer project is a Windows service that runs on a central server. The integration server processes incoming messages, maps fields from one application format into another, and sends on the message to the destination application.

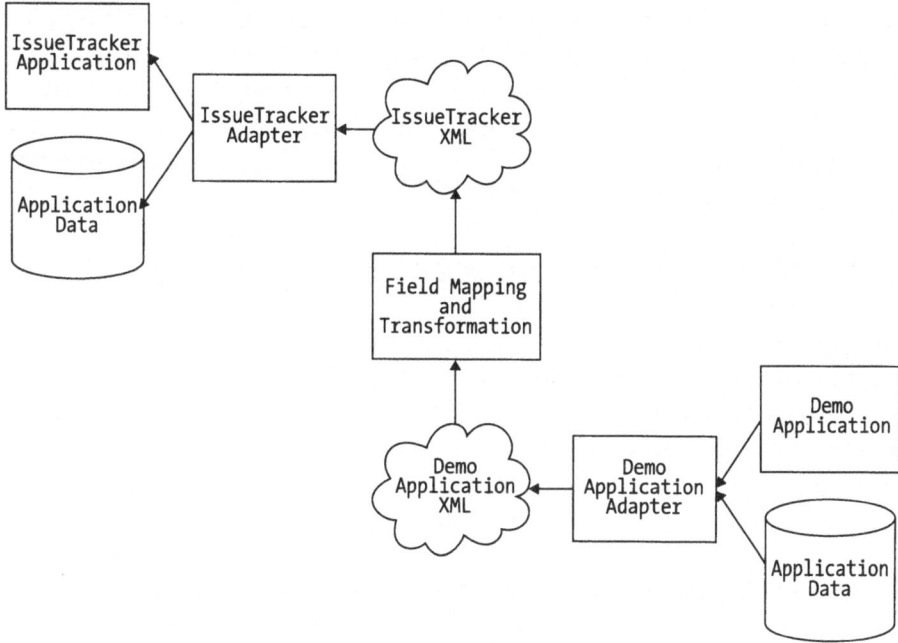

Figure 12-1. Key components of the application integration platform

The IntegrationCommon project is a Class Library project. This produces a shared assembly that defines common data types used between the integration server and the application adapters.

The IntegrationAdapter project is a Windows service that runs on the computer hosting an integrated application. The role of the integration adapter is to natively interact with the integrated application and exchange data with the integration server.

Creating Integration Adapters

There are many different methods of integrating applications. Selecting a method of integration is based upon which integration interfaces, if any, are exposed. Implementing an adapter framework will keep an application integration platform flexible. You can create different adapters that natively interact with an application. The adapter can turn around and format that data into a normalized representation with which the rest of the integration platform can work.

An integration adapter needs to perform four specific tasks: read a configuration file, access data from an application, format that data into a normalized structure, and communicate data back to the integration server. Adapters also need to be implemented consistently within the integration platform, which is an ideal use of an interface.

Defining the Adapter Interface

The integration adapter interface defines the methods necessary to implement an adapter that plugs into the integration platform. Creating an adapter interface will also be required later for remoting communication between the adapter and the integration server. Begin by creating a new Class Library project named *IntegrationCommon*. Next, add a new class, named *IIntegrationAdapter.cs*, to the new project and implement the interface that appears in Listing 12-1.

Listing 12-1. Adding the IIntegrationAdapter Interface to the IntegrationCommon Project

```
namespace IntegrationCommon
{
    public interface IIntegrationAdapter
    {
        void LoadConfigurationData();
        string ReadRecord( int intRecordID );
        string ReadAllRecords();
        bool WriteRecords( string strData );
        string SendToServer( string strData );
    }
}
```

The interface comprises five basic methods: LoadConfigurationData, ReadRecord, ReadAllRecords, WriteRecords, and SendToServer. The LoadConfigurationData method loads the adapter-specific settings, such as a connection string to the target database. The ReadRecord method takes an identifier as a parameter, reads that record of data, formats the data as Extensible Markup Language (XML), and sends that XML to the integration service. The ReadAllRecords method performs essentially the same tasks but returns all data records instead of one specific record. The WriteRecords method takes a parameter that contains XML data to be written into the application database. The SendToServer method handles the details of packaging and sending the application-specific XML to the integration server.

Creating a Direct Database Access Adapter

The simplest method of application integration is direct database access. In this case, the adapter can use ADO.NET functionality to retrieve data directly from an application's database. Assume the integrated application, DemoApp, has data stored in SQL Server with the table structure shown in Table 12-1.

Table 12-1. The DemoDat Database Table Example

COLUMN NAME	DATA TYPE
ID	int
SubmittedOn	datetime
Priority	char(16)
Severity	char(16)
Condition	char(16)
ShortDescription	char(256)
LongDescription	text
ComposedBy	char(256)

The direct database integration adapter implements the IIntegrationAdapter interface and runs locally on the computer hosting the application to be integrated. Begin by creating a new Windows service, named *IntegrationDatabaseAdapter*. After you have created the project in Visual Studio, rename the Service1 file to *DatabaseAdapterService* and change all code references from Service1 to *DatabaseAdapterService*. Next, add a project reference to the IntegrationCommon assembly. After adding the code reference, modify the class declaration and add the necessary interface methods. Listing 12-2 presents the DatabaseAdapterService class definition with the added interface methods and new class variables. The Windows service code generated by Visual Studio .NET has also been wrapped within #region tags so that it may be conveniently collapsed and hidden from view.

Listing 12-2. Creating the DatabaseAdapterService Class

```
public class DatabaseAdapterService  : System.ServiceProcess.ServiceBase,
IntegrationCommon.IIntegrationAdapter
{

    private void LoadConfigurationData()
```

```
    {
        return;
    }

    public string ReadRecord( int intRecordID )
    {
        return null;
    }

    public string ReadAllRecords()
    {
        return null;
    }

    public bool WriteRecords( string strData )
    {
        return false;
    }

    private string SendToServer( string strData )
    {
        return null;
    }

    #region Visual Studio .NET generated Windows service code
    //...
    #endregion
}
```

Specifying that this class implements the IIntegrationAdapter interface requires the implementation of the LoadConfigurationData, ReadRecord, ReadAllRecords, WriteRecords, and SendToServer methods. For now, temporary stub methods are inserted into the code to continue testing the Windows service.

Before a Windows service can be started, it will need to include a service installer. To add an installer, open the Windows service source file in the empty form designer. Next, right-click the form and select Add Installer from the context menu. Visual Studio will create a new file (ProjectInstaller.cs) and add two new components (serviceProcessInstaller1 and serviceInstaller2). Next, select the serviceProcessInstaller1 component and open its properties as shown in Figure 12-2. Set the account to *LocalSystem* to enable the service to be started and logged in under the local system account.

Next, display the properties for the serviceInstaller1 component. Set the display name, such as DatabaseAdapterService, that should be associated with this service when added to the list of services. Then, save and rebuild the service.

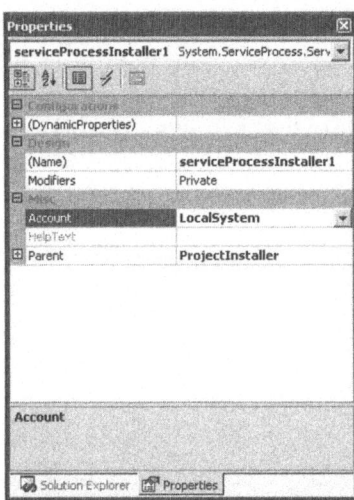

Figure 12-2. Setting the login mechanism for the new Windows service

You cannot start a Windows service in the Visual Studio .NET debugger. You must first install the service from the .NET command prompt. Click the Windows Start button and select Programs ➤ Microsoft Visual Studio .NET 2003 ➤ Visual Studio .NET Tools ➤ Visual Studio .NET Command Prompt. Next, browse to the output directory where you can find the DatabaseAdapterService.exe file. Enter the following command to install the service:

```
installutil DatabaseAdapterService.exe
```

This command installs the new DatabaseAdapterService into the Windows environment. Next, you can start the service either from the Services section of the Control Panel or by entering the following statement at the command prompt:

```
net start DatabaseAdapterService
```

Remember to stop the service before changing and rebuilding it within the Visual Studio .NET environment. Uninstalling the service is not necessary when making code changes and rebuilding, but you should uninstall when you finish development to test the setup project. To completely uninstall the service, enter the following:

```
installutil /u DatabaseAdapterService.exe
```

The normalized representation of exchanged application data will be XML. One approach to formatting the data is to load the records into a DataSet object, set a filter for the desired records, and create an XML representation of that data as described earlier in Chapter 9, "Using XML and Web Services." A faster approach, however, is to format the data in a SQL SELECT statement using the FOR XML AUTO specifier. Listing 12-3 presents a new stored procedure that extracts a record as XML data.

Listing 12-3. The XML Extraction Stored Procedure

```
CREATE PROCEDURE [dbo].[adapter_ReadRecord]
(
    @ID int
)
AS
SET NOCOUNT ON;

SELECT ID, SubmittedOn, Priority, Severity, Condition, ShortDescription,
LongDescription, ComposedBy FROM DemoDat WHERE ID = @ID FOR XML AUTO;
GO
```

This stored procedure is similar to the one created in Chapter 9, "Using XML and Web Services," in that it uses the FOR XML AUTO statement to produce XML as the result of the query. You can implement the ReadRecord adapter method using this stored procedure and return XML from the DemoApp database. Be sure to add references to the System.XML and System.Data.SqlClient namespaces. Listing 12-4 shows the complete listing for the ReadRecord method.

Listing 12-4. Retrieving a Database Record As XML

```
public string ReadRecord( int intRecordID )
{
    string stroutput = null;
    XmlReader reader = null;
    SqlConnection connection = null;
    SqlParameter parameter = null;
    SqlCommand command = null;

    try
    {
        //later, connection string is retrieved from a configuration file
        connection = new SqlConnection(
            "workstation id=MONTEREY;packet size=4096;user id=sa;data " +
            "source=MONTEREY;persist security info=False;" +
            "initial catalog=DemoApp" );
```

```
        connection.Open();

        command = new SqlCommand( "adapter_ReadRecord", connection );
        command.CommandType = CommandType.StoredProcedure;

        //add the ID parameter
        parameter = new SqlParameter( "@ID", SqlDbType.Int );
        parameter.Direction = ParameterDirection.Input;
        parameter.Value = intRecordID;
        command.Parameters.Add( parameter );

        reader = command.ExecuteXmlReader();
        reader.MoveToContent();

        stroutput = reader.ReadOuterXml();
    }
    catch( Exception x )
    {
        EventLog systemLog = new EventLog();
        systemLog.Source = "Integration Adapter";
        systemLog.WriteEntry( x.Message, EventLogEntryType.Error, 0 );
        systemLog.Dispose();
    }
    finally
    {
        reader.Close();
        connection.Close();
        connection.Dispose();
        command.Dispose();
    }

    return SendToServer( stroutput );
}
```

This implementation of the ReadRecord method begins by opening a connection to the database. In a later section, the LoadConfiguration method will be implemented to retrieve this connection string from an external configuration file. After opening the connection, this method fills the stored procedure parameters, creates an XmlReader object, and invokes the query. After processing the stored procedure, the reader reads the produced XML content and passes it to the SendToServer method. The produced XML content appears in Listing 12-5.

Listing 12-5. The Resulting XML Produced by the ReadRecord Method

```
<DemoDat ID="2053" SubmittedOn="2004-11-15T00:00:00" Priority="High "
    Severity="2 " Condition="Open " ShortDescription="Having trouble
    accessing my voicemail. " LongDescription="Everytime I try to listen to
    my voicemail, a recording says my password needs to be changed. Even
    after changing my password, I still can't listen to the messages."
    ComposedBy="Connie Teed" />
```

Creating a Document Exchange Adapter

Another type of adapter may not get data from a database but rather from an export file. The original intention might have been to package and export large amounts of data from one computer, send to another location, and then import the data files into another computer.

Although document exchange integration is often considered the least reliable form of integration, it still persists today. Integration through document exchange has also evolved down to dependency upon two prominent document formats: Comma-Separated Values (CSV) and XML.

CSV is one of the oldest and most popular document formats for application integration. The CSV file format is supported by a large number of applications that can read and write data in the CSV file format, including Microsoft Excel. Its popularity lies within its simplicity. Essentially, an application identifies what data it intends to export. Then, the application creates a plain-text file containing multiple lines of data. Each line contains a row of data delimited by the comma character and terminated by a new line character. There is no underlying data structure and no concept of data types in the CSV file format.

Suppose that the DemoApp application exports rows of data into the CSV file AppDemoData.csv. The data structure might look the same with columns that output an ID, a submit date, a priority, a severity, a description, and an author:

```
ID,SubmittedOn,Priority,Severity,Condition,ShortDescription,ComposedBy
2053,2004-11-15,High,2,Open,Having trouble accessing my voicemail,JP Batson
2054,2004-11-15,Medium,1,Open,Printer always prints,Anke
```

ADO objects can access this CSV file convert it into XML with the help of a DataSet object. Listing 12-6 implements the ReadAllRecords method for a different Windows service adapter, FileAdapterService, which also implements the IIntegrationAdapter interface. You need to add references to the System.Xml and System.Data.OleDb namespaces.

Listing 12-6. Retrieving Data Records from a CSV File As XML

```
public string ReadAllRecords()
{
    string strOutput = "";
    OleDbConnection connection = null;
    OleDbDataAdapter adapter = null;
    DataSet datasetFileData = null;

    try
    {
        connection = new OleDbConnection(
            "Provider=Microsoft.Jet.OLEDB.4.0;" +
            "Data Source=" + "c:\\" + ";" +
            "Extended Properties=\"text;HDR=YES;FMT=Delimited\"" );

        adapter = new OleDbDataAdapter( "select ID, SubmittedOn, Priority, " +
            "Severity, Condition, ShortDescription, ComposedBy from " +
            "appdemo.csv", connection );

        datasetFileData = new DataSet( "DemoDat" );

        adapter.Fill( datasetFileData );
        strOutput = datasetFileData.GetXml();
    }
    catch( Exception x )
    {
        EventLog systemLog = new EventLog();
        systemLog.Source = "Integration Adapter";
        systemLog.WriteEntry( x.Message, EventLogEntryType.Error, 0 );
        systemLog.Dispose();
    }
    finally
    {
        connection.Close();
        connection.Dispose();
        adapter.Dispose();
        datasetFileData.Dispose();
    }

    return SendToServer( strOutput );
}
```

The ReadAllRecords method opens a connection to the source file using the OleDbConnection object. Next, an OleDbAdapter object is initialized with a query expression and a reference to the connection object. Again, the connection string should come from an external configuration file. The OleDbDataAdapter is used to fill a new DataSet object with the contents of the data file. Finally, the DataSet object's GetXml method produces the structured XML text that is passed to the SendToServer method. Listing 12-7 presents the XML that the ReadAllRecords method creates.

Listing 12-7. The XML Retrieved from an Export Document

```
<DemoDat>
    <Table>
      <ID>2053</ID>
      <SubmittedOn>2004-11-15T00:00:00.0000000-08:00</SubmittedOn>
      <Priority>High</Priority>
      <Severity>2</Severity>
      <Condition>Open</Condition>
      <ShortDescription>Having trouble accessing my voicemail</ShortDescription>
      <ComposedBy>JP Batson</ComposedBy>
    </Table>
    <Table>
      <ID>2054</ID>
      <SubmittedOn>2004-11-15T00:00:00.0000000-08:00</SubmittedOn>
      <Priority>Medium</Priority>
      <Severity>1</Severity>
      <Condition>Open</Condition>
      <ShortDescription>Printer always prints</ShortDescription>
      <ComposedBy>Anke</ComposedBy>
    </Table>
</DemoDat>
```

Both adapter services presented should retrieve their settings from an external configuration file to keep the adapters flexible.

Retrieving Adapter Configuration Settings

The integration adapters access settings are stored in an external configuration file. In Chapter 8, "Developing Desktop Applications," application settings were stored in the App.config XML file and retrieved using the XPath objects. The adapters store configuration settings, such as a database connection string or properties related to the export file from which to read.

You can process incoming files with the FileSystemWatcher control. Open FileAdapterService in its design mode. Next, drag the FileSystemWatcher control from the Components tab of the Toolbox into the design space and name the control _DirectoryWatch. Next, add an event handler for this control named *DirectoryWatch_Changed* that handles the Changed event. Listing 12-8 implements the Changed event handler. When changes are detected to directories or files matching the criteria specified by the FileSystemWatcher control, this event handler is notified and supplied with information about the changed file or directory. In this case, the ReadAllRecords method is invoked to perform the specific file processing.

Listing 12-8. Implementing the Changed Event Handler for the FileSystemWatcher Control

```
private void DirectoryWatch_Changed(object sender,
System.IO.FileSystemEventArgs e)
{
    //read the file and send to the server
    ReadAllRecords();
    return;
}
```

Next, you need to set the FileSystemWatcher properties from the configuration file. Create a new text file named *App.config* in the same directory as the Windows service source code. Next, enter the XML definition that appears in Listing 12-9 and add the file to the FileAdapterService project.

Listing 12-9. The Document Integration Adapter Configuration File

```
<?xml version="1.0" encoding="utf-8" ?>
<configuration>
    <appSettings>
        <add key="ConnectionString" value="workstation id=MONTEREY;
            packet size=4096;user id=sa;
            data source=MONTEREY;persist security info=False;
            initial catalog=DemoApp" />
        <add key="Directory" value="c:\\" />
        <add key="FileType" value="*.csv" />
    </appSettings>
</configuration>
```

This application configuration file looks different from the one created in Chapter 8, "Developing Desktop Applications." Rather than defining custom configuration tags using the <configSections> element and then accessing values with the help of XPath, these values are stored as simple name-value pairs within the normal <appSettings> region and accessed with the AppSettingsReader object. Add a reference to the System.Configuration namespace to access the AppSettingsReader object. Listing 12-10 implements the LoadConfigurationData method that retrieves the adapter settings.

Listing 12-10. Retrieving Configuration Settings for the Integration Adapter

```
public void LoadConfigurationData()
{
    AppSettingsReader settings = new AppSettingsReader();

    _DirectoryWatch.Filter = (string)settings.GetValue( "FileType",
        typeof(string) );

    _DirectoryWatch.Path = (string)settings.GetValue( "Directory",
        typeof(string));

    return;
}
```

This method reads the adapter's configuration settings and sets the values for the adapter service. The AppSettingsReader object retrieves the values of various adapter settings based on key name. In this case, the code specifies the type of file to look for and the directory to search.

Creating the Integration Server

The integration server is at the center of the integration platform. While running, it processes incoming messages from source adapters, applies transformations, and forwards the results to the destination adapter. Building the integration server requires a common interface definition, the Windows service application code, and access to an external configuration file.

Defining the Integration Server Interface

You need to add the integration server's interface definition to a new class file named IIntegrationServer.cs within the IntegrationCommon assembly. Listing 12-11 presents the interface code.

Listing 12-11. Defining a Common Integration Server Interface

```
namespace IntegrationCommon
{
    public interface IIntegrationServer
    {
        void ProcessRequest( string strData );
        void SendToAdapter( string strDestination, string strData );
        void LoadConfigurationData();
    }
}
```

The interface outlines three methods. The ProcessRequest method reads the incoming normalized data and performs the necessary data transformations. The SendToAdapter method takes the transformed data and forwards it to the target application adapter. The LoadConfigurationData method loads the externalized application-to-application mappings. All methods need to be packaged into a separate assembly that can be imported into the adapter project.

Creating the Integration Server Engine

To create the integration server itself, create a new Windows service project named *IntegrationServer*. The administrator does not really need to directly interact with the integration server, so there is little need for a user interface. The Windows service simply starts, processes data mapping requests, and shuts down when instructed. Listing 12-12 presents a skeletal version of the integration server. Add project and code references to the IntegrationCommon namespace.

Listing 12-12. Creating the Integration Server Windows Service

```
using System;
using System.Collections;
using System.ComponentModel;
using System.Data;
using System.Diagnostics;
using System.ServiceProcess;


namespace LiquidServer
{
    //changed class declaration - other inherited interfaces
    public class System.ServiceProcess.ServiceBase
```

```
{
    private System.ComponentModel.Container components = null;

    public IntegrationServer()
    {
        InitializeComponent();
    }

    static void Main()
    {
        System.ServiceProcess.ServiceBase[] ServicesToRun;
        ServicesToRun = new System.ServiceProcess.ServiceBase[]
            { new IntegrationServer() };
        System.ServiceProcess.ServiceBase.Run(ServicesToRun);
    }

    private void InitializeComponent()
    {
        components = new System.ComponentModel.Container();
        this.ServiceName = "IntegrationServer";
    }

    protected override void Dispose( bool disposing )
    {
        if( disposing )
        {
            if (components != null)
            {
                components.Dispose();
            }
        }
        base.Dispose( disposing );
    }

    protected override void OnStart(string[] args)
    {
    }

    protected override void OnStop()
    {
    }
}
```

Managing Interapplication Data Mappings

The integration server requires access to the collection of application-to-application mappings. As requests come into the integration server, an ArrayList containing ApplicationMapping objects is searched for matches. When a match is found, the details of the mapping are forwarded to the transformation engine. Listing 12-13 presents the MappingEntry class added to the IntegrationServer project. It is used to store the application-to-application mappings in memory.

Listing 12-13. Managing Application-to-Application Data Mappings with the MappingEntry Object

```
class MappingEntry
{
    string _SourceSchema;
    string _DestinationSchema;
    string _DestinationAddress;
    string _TransformationFile;

    public string SourceSchema
    {
        get
        {
            return _SourceSchema;
        }
        set
        {
            _SourceSchema = value;
        }
    }

    public string DestinationSchema
    {
        get
        {
            return _DestinationSchema;
        }
        set
        {
            _DestinationSchema = value;
        }
    }
```

```csharp
public string DestinationAddress
{
    get
    {
        return _DestinationAddress;
    }
    set
    {
        _DestinationAddress = value;
    }
}

public string TransformationFile
{
    get
    {
        return _TransformationFile;
    }
    set
    {
        _TransformationFile = value;
    }
}
```

```
}
```

The application mappings are loaded from the external configuration file when the integration server is started. The _SourceSchema identifies the application data coming into the integration platform. The _TargetSchema identifies the how the data should appear after its transformation. The _TransformationFile points to the XSL Transformations (XSLT) document responsible for performing the data transformation. The _DestinationAddress identifies the target adapter to receive the transformed data.

Retrieving Server Configuration Settings

The integration server needs to store configuration settings externally to keep itself flexible. Some of these settings include application-to-application mappings that are supported. Because XSLT will be the technology performing the transformations, then each application-to-application mapping will need to match a source XML document with a destination XML document and an XSLT style sheet. Add a new text file named *App.config* to the IntegrationServer project and add the values presented in Listing 12-14.

Listing 12-14. The Integration Service Configuration File

```xml
<?xml version="1.0" encoding="utf-8" ?>
<configuration>
    <configSections>
        <sectionGroup name="AppMappings">
            <section name="Integration" />
        </sectionGroup>
    </configSections>

    <AppMappings>
        <Integration
            SourceSchema="appdemo.xml"
            DestinationSchema="issuetracker.xml"
            DestinationAddress="http://127.0.0.1:3202"
            Transformation="AppDemoToIssueTracker.xslt"
        />
    </AppMappings>
</configuration>
```

The integration adapter configuration file can contain any number of <Integration> elements. Each element represents a single mapping from one application to another. Each mapping is identified by a source XML schema name, a destination schema name, a destination address, and the XSLT style sheet used to perform the transformation. Listing 12-15 implements the LoadConfiguraionData method for the integration server. You also need to add code references to the System.Xml and System.Diagnostics namespaces.

Listing 12-15. Retrieving Configuration Settings for the Integration Server

```csharp
private void LoadConfigurationData()
{
    //object representing a single application-to-application mapping
    MappingEntry entry;

    //using XPath to retrieve the configuration data
    XmlDocument xmldoc = new XmlDocument();
    xmldoc.Load( "IntegrationServer.exe.config" );
    XmlNode root = xmldoc.DocumentElement;

    try
    {
        XmlNodeList xnodelist =
            root.SelectNodes( "/configuration/AppMappings/Integration" );
```

```
        foreach( XmlNode xnode in xnodelist )
        {
            //create a new entry object
            entry = new MappingEntry();

            entry.SourceSchema = xnode.Attributes["SourceSchema"].Value;

            entry.DestinationSchema =
                xnode.Attributes["DestinationSchema"].Value;

            entry.DestinationAddress =
                xnode.Attributes["DestinationAddress"].Value;

            entry.TransformationFile = xnode.Attributes["Transformation"].Value;

            //add this mapping to the collection
            _ApplicationMappings.Add( entry );

        }

    }
    catch( Exception x )
    {
        EventLog systemLog = new EventLog();
        systemLog.Source = "IssueTracker";
        systemLog.WriteEntry( x.Message, EventLogEntryType.Error, 0 );
        systemLog.Dispose();
    }

    return;
}
```

Unlike the adapter configuration settings, the integration server requires a more structured configuration file. XPath is used to navigate the configuration file and initialize a new MappingEntry object before adding it to the ArrayList. Each time a request arrives, the ArrayList is searched for a valid mapping to continue processing.

Performing Data Mapping and Transformation with XSLT

A common issue surrounding all application integration projects is data mapping and transformation. *Data mapping* refers to the process of lining up values in one data source against values in another data source. *Transformation* refers to the process of changing the source data to be capable of being stored in the target data field.

Understanding the Role of Mapping Tables

Data mapping can be as minimal as a field-to-field mapping. An issue priority within the DemoApp table might map directly to a priority field within the IssueTracker table. In more complicated cases, you may need to merge two or more fields in a source table and map them to a single field in another table. The source table may contain first and last name in separate fields, whereas the table stores a single value for name. It quickly becomes clear that you need a structured mechanism to map the source data to the target data. This is traditionally referred to as a *mapping table*. The mapping table typically describes the following:

- The source database, table, and column

- The target database, table, and column

- The transformation function used to convert the data

Because application integration is a constantly changing activity, data field mapping tables are usually external from the application. Along with the mapping table is the transformation library. Transformation libraries contain several custom algorithms for converting source data into target data. Often, Enterprise Application Integrators (EAI) will refer to such a library as *Business Rules*.

Understanding the Role of Transformations

Data transformation can also be as minimal as changing field types. A character array of 32 bytes might need to be trimmed to fit into a character array of 24 bytes. An integer might need to become a long. In more complicated cases, the data itself might need to be intelligently modified. A source data table might store the first name and then last name in a single name column, and the target stores the last name, a comma, and then the first name. A transformation is needed to parse the source data and modify it to be correctly stored in the target database.

Implementing Field Mapping and Transformation with XSLT

The benefit of building an XML-based integration is that it can leverage XSLT style sheets to offer a powerful way to dynamically transform and present data. Just as Cascading Style Sheets (CSS) offer richness to static Hypertext Markup Language (HTML) pages, XSLT style sheets extend the value of XML data. XSLT not only offers the ability to present XML data but also to transform it into completely new data. It provides a mechanism for packaging, exchanging, and presenting XML data.

Like traditional data mapping tables, XSLT can transform data so it can be exchanged between different business systems. XSLT supports the mapping of one XML document into another. One application may represent issue data based on one schema, and another application may represent it with another schema. With XSLT, you can transform the data into an XML representation that matches the target application's schema.

XSLT can also dynamically transform XML documents into HTML documents for Web browser access. Transformations are useful not only for backward compatibility for older browsers but also for transforming data so it can be rendered on new Web browser–enabled devices. Transformations can also convert XML data into many other document formats as needed.

XSLT serves as an ideal solution for mapping source XML documents to target XML documents in a flexible way. However, it is essentially an entirely different language to master. This chapter introduces some of the basics of XSLT. For a deeper understanding of XSLT and how to use it, I recommend *XML Programming: Web Applications and Web Services with JSP and ASP* by Tom Myers and Alexander Nakhimovsky (Apress, 2002).

XSLT is composed of multiple instructions that control the formatting of an output document. Appendix D, "Using XSLT Functions," summarizes the most common XSLT instructions. Applying an XSLT style sheet to one of the source XML documents appearing earlier will produce a new XML document in a format that the target application's adapter can more easily understand. The most common XSLT instructions relate to copying values, evaluating values, looping through groups of elements, and organizing instructions into templates.

Copying Data with XSLT

Because the primary function of XSLT is to transform one XML document into another, it is not surprising that the most common instruction is to perform a straight copy of values from the source document to the target document. The <xsl:copy-of> instruction does just that:

```
<?xml version="1.0"?>
<DemoDat
    xmlns:xsl='http://www.w3.org/1999/XSL/Transform'
    xsl:version='1.0' >

    <Issues>
        <xsl:copy-of select='/DemoDat/Table/ID' />
    </Issues>
</DemoDat>
```

In this case, the <xsl:copy-of> instruction makes a literal copy of the specified source elements into the target document. The only element referenced in
the select statement is <ID>, so only that node is produced in the target document. Applying the previous XSLT statements to the source document presented
in Listing 12-7 produces the following output:

```
<?xml version="1.0" encoding="utf-16"?>
<DemoDat>
    <Issues>
        <ID>2053</ID>
        <ID>2054</ID>
    </Issues>
</DemoDat>
```

Evaluating Data with XSLT

XSLT also provides instructions for performing evaluations against source values
(see Listing 12-16). You can use the <xsl:if> instruction to check a specified value
in the source document and output different values to the target document as
long as there are no else conditions. Inside the <xsl:choose> instruction, the
<xsl:when> instruction uses the same syntax to evaluate source values. If no val-
ues match, then the <xsl:otherwise> instruction is capable of displaying a default
value.

*Listing 12-16. Using the <xsl:if> and <xsl:choose> Instructions to Evaluate Source
Data*

```
<?xml version="1.0"?>
<DemoDat
    xmlns:xsl='http://www.w3.org/1999/XSL/Transform'
    xsl:version='1.0' >
```

```
<Issues>
    <xsl:if test='/DemoDat/Table/ID &lt; 1'>
        <xsl:text>INVALID ID</xsl:text>
    </xsl:if>

    <Severity>
        <xsl:choose>
            <xsl:when test='(/DemoDat/Table/Severity) = 1'>
                <xsl:text>Important</xsl:text>
            </xsl:when>
            <xsl:when test='(/DemoDat/Table/Severity) = 2'>
                <xsl:text>Mild</xsl:text>
            </xsl:when>
            <xsl:when test='(/DemoDat/Table/Severity) = 3'>
                <xsl:text>Unimportant</xsl:text>
            </xsl:when>
            <xsl:otherwise>
                <xsl:text>Unknown</xsl:text>
            </xsl:otherwise>
        </xsl:choose>
    </Severity>
</Issues>
</DemoDat>
```

In this case, the <xsl:if> instruction is used to evaluate the ID value in the source document. If the value is less than 1 (represented by < 1), then an error message is displayed. Because the severity field reacts differently depending upon a value, the <xsl:choose> instruction is used. In each case, the test attribute evaluates an element value against a fixed value. Applying the previous XSLT statements to the source document presented in Listing 12-7 produces the following output:

```
<?xml version="1.0" encoding="utf-16"?>
<DemoDat>
    <Issues>
        <Severity>Important</Severity>
    </Issues>
</DemoDat>
```

Looping Through Data with XSLT

Another significant XSLT instruction relates to iterating through a collection of elements. The <xsl:for-each> instruction cycles through specified elements for processing. This instruction lets the XSLT style sheet process multiple export records during batch processing:

```xml
<?xml version="1.0"?>
<DemoDat
    xmlns:xsl='http://www.w3.org/1999/XSL/Transform'
    xsl:version='1.0' >

    <Issues>
        <xsl:for-each select='/DemoDat/Table'>
            <EnteredBy>
                <xsl:value-of select='ComposedBy' />
            </EnteredBy>
        </xsl:for-each>
    </Issues>
</DemoDat>
```

The <xsl:for-each> instruction begins with a select attribute that points to the starting node of the loop. Each <xsl:value-of> instruction will be relative to the current iteration in the loop. Therefore, its select attribute should only point to the actual element identifier. Applying the previous XSLT statements to the source document presented in Listing 12-7 produces the following output:

```xml
<?xml version="1.0" encoding="utf-16"?>
<DemoDat>
    <Issues>
        <EnteredBy>JP Batson</EnteredBy>
        <EnteredBy>Anke</EnteredBy>
    </Issues>
</DemoDat>
```

The XML resulting from the processing spans all rows of the export file. Additional processing may occur within the for-each operation, including additional for-each instructions.

Organizing XSLT Instructions into Templates

XSLT also provides a mechanism for creating reusable instruction sets, known as *templates*. These templates allow XSLT to be organized into modular and reusable blocks. The <xsl:template> element defines the starting point for a template block. All statements within this block are processed like a normal style sheet:

```
<xsl:template name='GetIssueID' >
    <IssueID>
        <xsl:copy-of select='/DemoDat/Table/ID' />
    </IssueID>
</xsl:template>
```

The GetIssueID template can be called from another template or style sheet using the <xsl:call-template> instruction:

```
<xsl:template name='AppDemoImport' >
<DemoDat>
    <Table>
        <xsl:call-template name='GetIssueID' />
    </Table>
</DemoDat>
</xsl:template>
```

Applying the previous XSLT statements to the source document presented in Listing 12-7 produces the following output:

```
<?xml version="1.0" encoding="utf-16"?>
<DemoDat>
    <IssueID>
        <ID>2053</ID>
        <ID>2054</ID>
    </IssueID>
</DemoDat>
```

Templates can also process parameters just like methods. You define parameters within the template using the <xsl:param> instruction. The instruction specifies the parameter name and default value. In the content region of the template, you reference the parameter by prefixing the variable with a $, such as $id:

```
<xsl:template name='GetSpecificDescription' >
    <xsl:param name='id' select='/DemoDat/Table/ID' />
    <Table>
        <Description><xsl:value-of select='$id' /></Description>
    </Table>
</xsl:template>
```

Other templates or style sheets can supply parameters using the <xsl:with-param> instruction:

```
<xsl:call-template name='GetSpecificDescription'>
    <xsl:with-param name='id' >1</xsl:with-param>
</xsl:call-template>
```

Using a combination of XSLT instructions, you can create different style sheets for each application-to-application mapping. Depending upon the incoming source data, the integration server's ProcessRequest method is called upon to load the appropriate style sheet and perform the data transformation. Listing 12-17 presents the ProcessRequest method responsible for loading and applying style sheets to perform transformations.

Listing 12-17. Invoking XSLT Processing Within the Integration Server

```
public void ProcessRequest( string strData )
{
    string strOutput = "";
    System.IO.StringWriter sWriter = null;

    try
    {
        strData.Replace( "\r", "" );
        strData.Replace( "\n", "" );

        //initialize the source document
        XmlDataDocument xmlDoc = new XmlDataDocument();
        xmlDoc.LoadXml( strData );

        //initialize the transformation engine
        XslTransform xslTransformer = new XslTransform();
        xslTransformer.Load( "c:\\transformation.xsl" );

        //initialize the output string writer
        sWriter = new System.IO.StringWriter();

        //transform the document
        xslTransformer.Transform( xmlDoc, null, sWriter );

        //forward the response to the destination adapter
        strOutput = sWriter.GetStringBuilder().ToString();
        SendToAdapter( "http://127.0.0.1:3202", strOutput );
    }
```

```
        catch( Exception x )
        {
            EventLog systemLog = new EventLog();
            systemLog.Source = "IssueTracker";
            systemLog.WriteEntry( x.Message, EventLogEntryType.Error, 0 );
            systemLog.Dispose();
        }
        finally
        {
            sWriter.Close();
        }

        return;
    }
```

The ProcessRequest method takes the adapter-formatted XML data, removes any line breaks found, and creates an XmlDataDocument object. Next, the XSLT style sheet is loaded into an XslTransform object. An XmlTextWriter is also created to write the generated XML output to a local file. The Transform method performs all of the work by reading the source document, applying the XSLT style sheet, and writing the output to the location specified by the XmlTextWriter.

The XML generated from the transformation should be specific to another adapter capable of inserting the data into the integrated application. The results of this method either can be posted back to a message queue or can be delivered to an adapter method via remoting.

The direct database adapter and the file exchange adapter may be different in their implementations, but they both produce XML that represents application-specific data. The next step is to send this application-specific data to the integration server where it can be mapped and transformed into data that is specific to the new application. Before the adapter and integration server can communicate, you need to define a communication mechanism.

Exchanging Data Between Adapters and the Integration Server

You have two different approaches for managing communication between the adapters and the integration server: messaging and remoting. Messaging communication is typically more reliable and fault tolerant, and remoting typically executes faster.

Exchanging Data with Messaging

Chapter 4, "Applying Reliable Messaging," introduced the concept of real-time messaging and the Microsoft Message Queue (MSMQ) solution. You can use real-time messaging components to communicate messages between the integration adapters and the integration service with a series of messages. Because messages can contain any data that is understood by both sender and receiver, it serves as a reliable solution for exchanging the normalized XML data between applications. You also learned earlier that messages that are exchanged are kept in queues that protect messages from being lost. In general, messaging technologies offer tremendous benefits, including the following:

- Integration adapters can use MSMQ to send messages and then continue processing regardless of whether the integration service is running or reachable over the network.

- When networks become available or the integration services come back online, the messaging server will deliver any waiting messages.

- MSMQ ensures that messages are not lost in transit, delivered out of order, or delivered more than once.

- MSMQ can also route messages efficiently around failed machines and network bottlenecks, leaving administrators to configure redundant communications paths to ensure availability.

- Communicating via messages does not require that components be aware of each other's implementation details. MSMQ services are used to only bridge components, not implement them.

Enabling Messaging Communication in the Integration Adapter

To implement messaging as the communication mechanism for binding the adapter to the integration server, you will need to add a project reference to the messaging services to the adapter project. From Visual Studio .NET, select the adapter project within the Solution Explorer and choose Add ➤ Reference from its context menu. In the Add Reference dialog box, select the System.Messaging.dll component and add a code reference to the System.Messaging namespace. Next, add the SendToServer code to open a connection to a message queue and send the XML contents to the integration server (see Listing 12-18).

Listing 12-18. Implementing Adapter to Server Communication with MSMQ

```
public string SendToServer( string strData )
{
    try
    {
        MessageQueue queue = new MessageQueue( "server\\integrationQueue" );
        queue.Send( "AppDemo", strData );
    }
    catch( Exception x )
    {
        EventLog systemLog = new EventLog();
        systemLog.Source = "Integration Adapter";
        systemLog.WriteEntry( x.Message, EventLogEntryType.Error, 0 );
        systemLog.Dispose();
    }
    finally
    {
        queue.Dispose();
    }

    return strData;
}
```

The SendToServer method connects to a message queue located on the server and sends a message that identifies the application within the message subject heading. The message body contains the application-specific XML created by the adapter.

Enabling Messaging Communication in the Integration Server

Within the integration server, the message queue is checked for new incoming messages sent by the adapters. Listing 12-19 implements a method belonging to the integration server that monitors the message queue and processes incoming messages.

Listing 12-19. Processing Incoming Data Messages in the Integration Server

```
public void ProcessIncomingMessages()
{
    do
    {
        try
```

```
    {
        MessageQueue queue = new MessageQueue( "server\\integrationQueue" );
        Message message = queue.Receive( new TimeSpan(0,0,3) );

        message.Formatter = new XmlMessageFormatter(
            new string[] {"System.String,mscorlib"} );

        ProcessRequest( message.Body );
    }
    catch( Exception x )
    {
        EventLog systemLog = new EventLog();
        systemLog.Source = "Integration Adapter";
        systemLog.WriteEntry( x.Message, EventLogEntryType.Error, 0 );
        systemLog.Dispose();
    }
    finally
    {
        message.Dispose();
        queue.Dispose();
    }

}while ( true );

return;
}
```

As they arrive, the integration server passes the XML contained within the message body to the ProcessRequest method. The ProcessRequest method handles the application-to-application field mapping defined within a specified XSLT template.

Exchanging Data with Remoting

Messaging services provide an excellent means of communication between adapters and the integration service. Another form of communication between these components is *remoting*. The .NET remoting services abstract client-server communication between .NET applications. Specific implementations support a fast binary protocol for real-time communication between client and server as well support for the Simple Object Access Protocol (SOAP) protocol over Hypertext Transfer Protocol (HTTP) for firewall-friendly communication across networks.

Applying a remoting communication framework requires only a few steps: creating a common access assembly, implementing the server, and implementing the client.

Enabling Remoting Communication in the Integration Adapter

The adapter code appears similar on the surface. Add a project reference to the System.Remoting namespace (see Listing 12-20).

Listing 12-20. Implementing Remoting Services Within the Integration Adapter

```
public class DocumentAdapterService : System.ServiceProcess.ServiceBase,
IIntegrationAdapter
{
    private static HttpChannel _Channel = new HttpChannel();
    private static string _IntegrationServerPath = "http://127.0.0.1:3200";
    private static IIntegrationServer _IntegrationService;

    //... other collapsed service and IIntegrationAdapter code

    protected override void OnStart(string[] args)
    {
        try
        {
            LoadConfigurationData();

            ChannelServices.RegisterChannel( _Channel );

            _IntegrationService = (IIntegrationServer)Activator.GetObject(
                typeof( IIntegrationServer ),
                _IntegrationServerPath + "/IntegrationServer.soap" );
        }
        catch( Exception x )
        {
            EventLog systemLog = new EventLog();
            systemLog.Source = "IssueTracker";
            systemLog.WriteEntry( x.Message, EventLogEntryType.Error, 0 );
            systemLog.Dispose();
        }

        return;
    }
}
```

Each integration adapter is a remoting client and a remoting server. Although the adapter needs to invoke methods belonging to the integration server, namely ProcessRequest, the server will also need to forward results by invoking adapter methods. Each adapter will need to be assigned a port address through which to communicate. If one computer is running multiple adapters, then each adapter will need to execute against a separate port number as set within the adapter configuration file.

Enabling Remoting Communication in the Integration Server

When it comes to communication between the adapter and the integration server, only two methods are created: ProcessRequest and SendToAdapter. The ProcessRequest method is exposed to the integration adapters to receive incoming application-specific data. The SendToAdapter method exists to send outgoing data that has been mapped to a specific application format. The application constructor starts the remoting service and then waits to process requests. Listing 12-21 presents the modified IntegrationServer class definition.

Listing 12-21. Implementing Remoting Services Within the Integration Server

```
public class IntegrationServer : System.ServiceProcess.ServiceBase,
IIntegrationServer
{
    private System.ComponentModel.Container components = null;

    static HttpChannel _Channel;
    static int _PortNumber = 3200;
    ArrayList _ApplicationMappings = new ArrayList();

    protected override void OnStart(string[] args)
    {
        try
        {
            _Channel = new HttpChannel( _PortNumber );

            ChannelServices.RegisterChannel( _Channel );

            RemotingConfiguration.RegisterWellKnownServiceType(
                typeof( IntegrationServer ),
                "IntegrationServer.soap",
                WellKnownObjectMode.Singleton );
        }
        catch( Exception x )
```

411

```
        {
            EventLog systemLog = new EventLog();
            systemLog.Source = "Integration Adapter";
            systemLog.WriteEntry( x.Message, EventLogEntryType.Error, 0 );
            systemLog.Dispose();
        }
    }

    protected override void OnStop()
    {
    }
}
```

The IntegrationServer class is where the main integration work happens, when everything is implemented. The class begins with references to remoting framework and the existing IntegrationCommon assembly. The class declaration implements the MarshalByRefObject interface needed for remoting and the IIntegrationService interface needed by the adapters. Static class variables maintain the remoting-related values, and the Main method performs the work of registering a remoting service. First, a new HttpChannel object is created and initialized with a port number to which to listen. Next, that channel is registered and associated with the name *IntegrationServer.soap*. Finally, a ReadLine method keeps the application alive until the user presses the Enter key to shut down the application. The ProcessRequest, SendToAdapter, and LoadConfiguration methods appear in their skeletal forms.

Summary

This chapter looked at challenges and approaches concerning the integration of new .NET applications with existing legacy applications. You saw that there are different types of communication involved, including synchronous, asynchronous, and message-based. This chapter also outlined the impacts of security and the role it plays in enterprise integration. Furthermore, you took a close look at specific integration methods, including direct database access, application programming interfaces, document exchange, and messaging adapters. You looked at how data is transformed from a source data field to a destination data field using XSLT. Finally, you took all of this information and applied it by building an integration platform capable of reading data from a CSV file, from an XML file, or from a database table.

Every integration project has its own set of challenges. You will find that different integration methods will work best with different applications. What is most important is to fully understand the integration requirements, exactly what data is moved to where, what the access permissions are, how frequently should the data be moved, how the data should be transformed, and how to handle errors that might appear. With a clear understanding of the requirements, picking the appropriate integration approach will be much easier.

In the next chapter, you will learn about to the security and cryptography services provided by the .NET Framework. You will use these services to implement user-level and code-level security within an application. A detailed look at encryption reveals methods for scrambling data into an unreadable format that is secure for transmission over the Internet.

Understanding .NET Security and Cryptography

SECURITY IS A CRITICAL PART of every enterprise application. It was not too long ago that a simple login page that validated an entered password against a value stored in a database was enough to protect application data and services. Today, there are many approaches to system infiltration at multiple tiers of an application. Also, there are many more people trying to steal valuable corporate data or maliciously attack online services.

The .NET Framework provides a variety of solutions for adding layers upon layers of security over an enterprise application. These solutions collect user credentials, validate them against an authority, evaluate role membership, and encrypt sensitive data. This chapter describes some of the known techniques of application infiltration, outlines some approaches to protecting applications against security violations, and helps define a policy for enterprise-wide security.

Defining Layers of Application Security

Application security is a broad subject that means different things to different people. Even worse, developers typically take application security lightly during application development or even put it off to the end. However, developers must design effective security into the application and clearly spell it out from the beginning of development. They must decide early what data or functionality to guard and to what extent. Furthermore, they need to weigh data security against application performance.

Ideally, you should implement application security in a layered fashion, applying a variety of solutions that protect the application in different ways. These layers represent fundamental concepts such as authentication, authorization, environment configuration, and data encryption. As Figure 13-1 illustrates, these security layers wrap around application data to significantly increase the complexity of outside infiltration. Individually, each layer may be only a moderate deterrence. Working together, however, the layers pose an effective defense that slows aggressors.

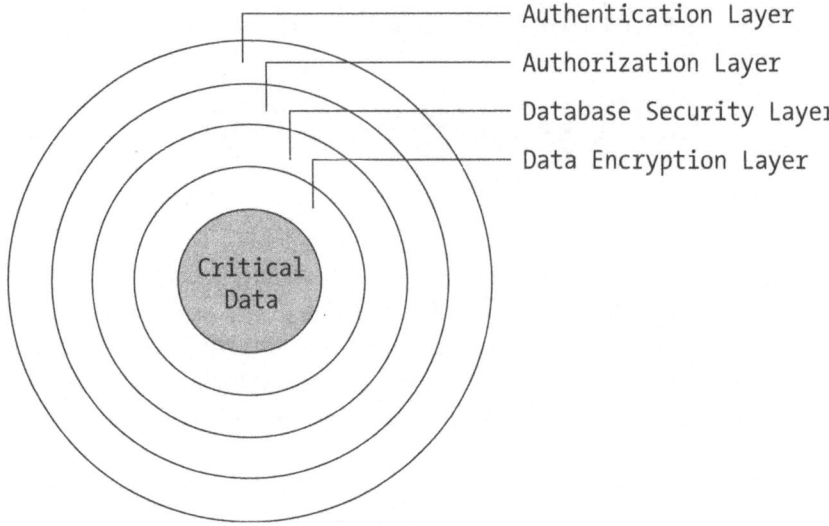

Figure 13-1. Layers of application security

The outermost layer represents basic application security implemented through an authentication service that validates who the user is. The next layer represents an authorization service that identifies what the user can see and do. The next layer represents the environment security such as the database, file server, Web server, or Active Directory that further obstructs access to the underlying data. And, if the application is sensitive enough, the innermost layer represents data encryption that renders the underlying data unreadable.

Understanding the .NET Security Framework

The .NET Framework security services tackle these layers directly. At the center of this framework are objects that abstract a security policy, permissions, principals, and evidence.

Establishing a Security Policy

The security policy is the configurable set of rules that the Common Language Runtime (CLR) references as it determines what, if any, resources can interact with executing code. Network administrators specify the security policy, and the CLR enforces it. You can define a security policy at the enterprise, machine, user, and application levels. When the CLR loads an assembly, it takes the policies and assigns the code groups. During this assignment process, the CLR checks that no permission was denied at a higher level. If it was, the CLR does not assign the permissions. This guarantees that an application configuration cannot overwrite security settings of the enterprise.

Each security policy contains a set of identity permissions that the assembly needs for a code group. The CLR ensures that code can access only the resources and can only invoke code that the security policy allows it to invoke. When an assembly is loaded, the CLR also references the security policy to determine which permissions to grant to the loaded assembly. After reviewing information about specific code, known as *evidence*, the CLR references the security policy to decide how much the code is trusted, which in turn determines what permissions to grant to that assembly.

Identifying the Security Permissions

There are three kinds of permissions: code access, identity, and role based. The System.Security.Permissions object is responsible for abstracting permissions and provides support to implement custom permission objects. Code can request the permissions it needs to access resources or perform operations. The hosting environment can grant permissions to code based on characteristics of the code's identity, what permissions were requested, and how much the code is trusted. Code can also demand that its callers have specific permissions before executing.

Using Principal Objects

A principal object essentially abstracts a user. The .NET Framework security services support three types of principal objects: generic, Windows, and custom. A *generic principal object* represents an unauthenticated user and the roles assigned to him or her. A *Windows principal object* represents a user existing on a Windows server and the server-defined groups to which he or she belongs. An application can define a *custom principal object* in any way that is needed for that particular application. This can extend the basic notion of the principal's identity and roles. An application defining a custom principal must also provide an authentication module with types that implement the principal.

Supplying Identity Evidence

When an assembly is requested, the CLR searches for evidence of its origin. Evidence includes information about the code's publisher, its site, and its zone. Evidence works in conjunction with the security policy to determine which permissions are granted to application domains. Evidence answers the following questions being asked by the CLR:

- From which site does the assembly come?

- From which Uniform Resource Locator (URL) does the assembly come?

- From which zone does the assembly come?

- Who has signed the assembly?

- What is the strong (public or private key) name of the assembly?

Identity permissions and Code Access permissions are only granted if an assembly can show the proper identity evidence. Both are closely related and share the same underlying concept, being derived from the CodeAccessSecurity base class. Applications have no influence over the Identity permissions of an assembly. The CLR simply takes an assembly, examines its evidence, and assigns the identity permissions. To associate a set of identity permissions to a code group, the network administrator must specify them within the security policies.

Implementing Security Concepts

The security services provided by the .NET Framework work together to fulfill three important functions: user authentication, user authorization, and data encryption. *User authentication* validates the credentials supplied by the user. *User authorization* determines the data and services, if any, with which the user is permitted to interact. *Data encryption* encodes sensitive data into an unreadable format for storage or transport.

Validating Specific Users

The first step every security implementation must undertake is user authentication. This process validates user credentials against a specified authority, such as a directory service, a database table, or a configuration file. The three most common implementations of user authentication include Windows Authentication, Forms Authentication, and Passport Authentication.

Applying Basic Windows Authentication

The simplest form of user authentication to implement is Windows Authentication. It is the simplest implementation because the file server does all of the validation work. When a user requests a resource, such as a specific Web page, the Web server determines if the user has been authenticated. If not, they are prompted as shown in Figure 13-2.

Figure 13-2. The Windows Authentication login prompt

The user credentials are validated against the server account for authentication as defined by the Internet Information Services (IIS) directory security options. As Figure 13-3 illustrates, you can configure IIS to perform a variety of security functions, such as basic authentication, digest authentication, or Kerberos/NTLM Windows authentication.

Although this is simplest method of authentication to implement, it is also the least flexible. To validate user accounts, the network administrator must first add them to the server. This might work out within a small-sized or medium-sized enterprise, but it is virtually impossible to open up to any Web accessible user.

Because Windows Authentication is the default user authentication implementation for applications built within Visual Studio .NET, it is already specified in the Web.config file created for new projects. Listing 13-1 displays an excerpt from the default Web.config file generated for a Web application.

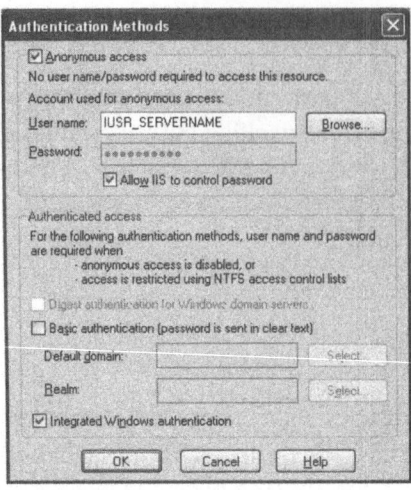

Figure 13-3. Configuring Windows authentication options in IIS

Listing 13-1. Web.config File Set to Windows Authentication Mode

```
<configuration>
    <system.web>
        <authentication mode="Windows" />
    </system.web>
</configuration>
```

When a new Web application starts, however, it does not prompt a connected user automatically for login credentials. This is because the Web.config file does not explicitly demand authentication. To add this functionality, add the additional Extensible Markup Language (XML) tags as outlined in Listing 13-2.

Listing 13-2. Web.config File Set to Refuse Anonymous Connections

```
<configuration>
    <system.web>
        <authentication mode="Windows" />
        <authorization>
            <deny users="?" />
        </authorization>
    </system.web>
</configuration>
```

No additional coding is necessary. The updated Web.config file specifies that any user requesting a page must have a login account on the hosting Web server. Users who are authenticated by the server are permitted to access the resource. Otherwise, all other users must be denied access. The ? value in the <deny> tag specifies that anonymous users are not permitted.

The permissions defined within the Web.config file apply to all files within the same directory. You can set permissions in multiple Web.config files located in different subdirectories or within the same Web.config file using the <location> tag, as outlined in Listing 13-3.

Listing 13-3. Spanning the Web.config Directory Permissions Across Multiple Directories

```
<location path="Pages">
<!- Apply security settings to all files located in the 'Pages' directory ->
    <system.web>
        <authorization>
            <deny users="?" />
        </authorization>
        </system.web>
    </location>
```

Behind the scenes, after the server validates the login credentials, a WindowsAuthenticationModule provider object creates and populates a WindowsPrincipal object and a WindowsIdentity object. Both objects manage the identity of the connected user as well as his or her assigned roles. They are assigned to the local HttpContext (see Listing 13-4).

Listing 13-4. Viewing a User's Login Identity

```
private void Page_Load(object sender, System.EventArgs e)
{
    string strMessage = "";

    if( Request.IsAuthenticated )
    {
        string strUsername = HttpContext.Current.User.Identity.Name;
        strMessage = "<h2>User: " + HttpContext.Current.User.Identity.Name;
        strMessage += "<p>Administrator: ";

        if( HttpContext.Current.User.IsInRole( "Administrators" ) )
            strMessage += "Yes";
        else
```

```
                strMessage +="No";

        strMessage += "</h2>";
        Response.Write( strMessage );
    }
    else
        Response.Write( "<h1>Not authenticated.<h1>" );

    return;
}
```

This listing creates a simple test page to check the status of a login and report if the user has been authenticated. First, it calls the Request object's IsAuthenticated method. If it returns true, the code constructs a string that displays the username as captured by the WindowsIdentity object. Next, the string construction continues as the IsInRole method evaluates whether this user is a member of the Administrators role. (Determining a user membership within a role is another critical security concept covered later in the "Authorizing User Capabilities" section.) Finally, the listing returns the constructed string to the browser for display.

Again, this is a simple method for user validation that might work within the enterprise, but not for applications exposed to the Web. Also, this approach places all the trust into the hands of the file server. If the file server security is breached, the enterprise application is not insulated from that breach.

Applying Web Forms Authentication

An even better approach to user authentication is through Forms Authentication. With this approach, applications manage their own set of credentials rather than referencing the file server or Active Directory. Forms Authentication captures user credentials from a user interface form and validates them against an application-defined authority such as a database table or configuration file. Any user attempting to request access to part of the application is redirected to a central login page, as shown in Figure 13-4.

The application tracks an authenticated user with the help of a client-side cookie. This enables the user to explore the Web application without being constantly prompted to log in. To enable Forms Authentication, edit the Web.config file as shown in Listing 13-5.

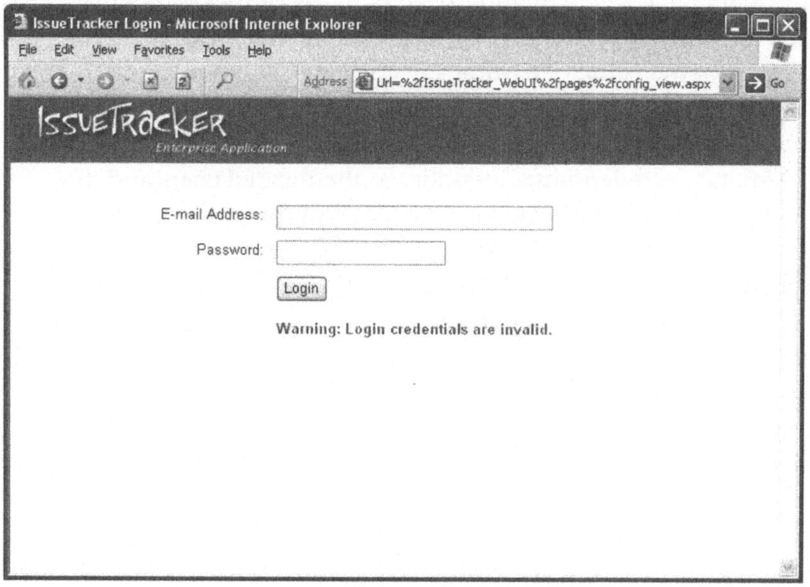

Figure 13-4. The default login form specified for Forms Authentication

Listing 13-5. Enabling Forms Authentication in the Web.config File

```
<authentication mode="Forms">
    <forms name=".ASPXAUTH" loginUrl="pages/app_login.aspx"
        protection="Encryption" timeout="30">
        <credentials passwordFormat="Clear">
            <user name="John" password="openup" />
        </credentials>
    </forms>
</authentication>
<location path="Pages">
    <system.web>
        <authorization>
            <deny users="*" />
        </authorization>
    </system.web>
</location>
```

The changes to the Web.config file include setting the authentication mode to Forms Authentication. The listing also adds an XML tag, <forms>, along with a few custom attributes. The optional name attribute specifies the name of the cookie file created on the client computer. The loginUrl attribute specifies the location of the login page where unauthorized requests should be redirected. The protection attribute specifies how the authentication cookie should be protected. Protection methods include None, Encryption, Validation, and All. Finally, a timeout attribute specifies the number of minutes of inactivity that must elapse before the user is automatically logged out.

Another XML tag, <credentials>, identifies authenticated users and their passwords. Also included is the format used to encrypt the password. In this case, the user *John* has been added with a clear text password of *openup*. Two additional encoding formats are available to hash the password into an unreadable string: SHA1 and MD5. You could represent the same credentials in the following unreadable format:

```
<credentials passwordFormat="SHA1">
    <user name="John" password="3F36690145A773B6B6968827D5A6F19AE819205B" />
</credentials>
```

To obtain an SHA1 hashed representation of a string, the .NET Framework provides a helpful method. The following method generates a hashed string from a clear text string and might be helpful if creating hashed values:

```
private string HashPassword( string strPassword )
{
    return FormsAuthentication.HashPasswordForStoringInConfigFile( strPassword,
        "SHA1" );
}
```

In addition to the changes in the Web.config file, you must also implement the login form to interact with the FormsAuthentication object. Listing 13-6 implements the login button event handler for the login page.

Listing 13-6. Processing the FormsAuthentication Object

```
private void btnLogin_Click(object sender, System.EventArgs e)
{
    if( FormsAuthentication.Authenticate( edtEmail.Text, edtPassword.Text ) )
        FormsAuthentication.RedirectFromLoginPage( edtEmail.Text, false );
    else
        lblWarning.Visible = true;

    return;
}
```

The event handler invokes the static Authenticate method belonging to the FormsAuthentication object, passing the username and password retrieved from the user. If the method returns true, the user is redirected to their originally requested page. If Forms Authentication fails, a label indicates a failed login attempt.

> **NOTE** *It's useful to record the number of consecutive failed login attempts. If three or so consecutive attempts fail, the event should be logged and the account should be inactivated.*

After Forms Authentication validate the user credentials, the code creates a new FormsIdentity object assigns it to a GenericPrincipal object within the local HttpContext. You can extract additional information, such as role membership, from the principal object via the HttpContext.User object.

Although Forms Authentication does not require validation against a server, it appears that validating against a Web.config file is even worse. An even better approach to Forms Authentication is to write a custom authentication method that validates user credentials against an application database (see Listing 13-7).

Listing 13-7. Validating Forms Authentication Against a Database

```
public bool DatabaseAuthenticate( string strUsername, string strPassword )
{
    SqlCommand command;
    SqlParameter parameter;
    bool boolAuthenticated = false;

    //open connection
    SqlConnection conn = new SqlConnection( "server=jkanalakis;" +
        "database=IssueTracker;uid=sa;pwd=" );

    try
    {
        conn.Open( );

        //initialize the command
        command = new SqlCommand( "app_ValidateLogin", conn );
        command.CommandType = CommandType.StoredProcedure;

        //add the email address parameter
        parameter = new SqlParameter( "@EmailAddress", SqlDbType.Char );
        parameter.Direction = ParameterDirection.Input;
        parameter.Value = strUsername;
        command.Parameters.Add( parameter );
```

```
            //add the password parameter
            parameter = new SqlParameter( "@Password", SqlDbType.Char );
            parameter.Direction = ParameterDirection.Input;
            parameter.Value = strPassword;
            command.Parameters.Add( parameter );

            //execute query
            if( (int)command.ExecuteScalar() > 0 )
                boolAuthenticated = true;

        }
        catch( Exception x )
        {
            EventLog systemLog = new EventLog();
            systemLog.Source = "IssueTracker";
            systemLog.WriteEntry( x.Message, EventLogEntryType.Error, 0 );
        }
        finally
        {
            conn.Close();
            conn.Dispose();
        }

        return boolAuthenticated;
    }
```

This method receives a username and a password from the login page. Next, a stored procedure executes to validate the supplied credentials. The stored procedure uses an odd-looking query that performs a case-sensitive comparison by casting the password into a VARBINARY data type. If any records match the query, the login credentials are presumed valid and the method returns true:

```
CREATE PROCEDURE [dbo].[app_ValidateLogin]
(
    @EmailAddress char(256),
    @Password char(16)
)
AS
SET NOCOUNT ON;

SELECT COUNT(*) FROM Dat_User WHERE EmailAddress = @EmailAddress AND
CAST ( RTRIM ( Password ) AS VARBINARY ) = CAST (@Password AS VARBINARY );
GO
```

After validating the user credentials, all that needs to change is the login button's event handler. In Listing 13-8, the updated handler invokes the custom database authentication method instead of the stock Authenticate method.

Listing 13-8. Changes to the Login Event Handler to Support Database Validation

```
private void btnLogin_Click(object sender, System.EventArgs e)
{
    if( DatabaseAuthenticate( edtEmail.Text, edtPassword.Text ) )
        FormsAuthentication.RedirectFromLoginPage( edtEmail.Text, false );
    else
        lblWarning.Visible = true;

    return;
}
```

The last step in the process is to handle the user logout. Because user logout should occur from just about any location within the application, it makes sense that it should be implemented as part of the application framework. A useful way to implement this is with another Web user control. In the IssueTracker solution, add a new Web user control with a single link button control. Set the link button's Label attribute to Logout and its Name attribute to lnkLogout. Finally, implement the link button's event handler as outlined in Listing 13-9.

Listing 13-9. Implementing a Logout Web User Control

```
private void lnkLogout_Click(object sender, System.EventArgs e)
{
    FormsAuthentication.SignOut();
    Session.Clear();
    Response.Redirect( "Pages/app_login.aspx" );

    return;
}
```

This short method simply invokes the SignOut method belonging to the FormsAuthentication object. Next, the Session object is cleaned up, and the user is redirected to the application's login page. You can add this user control to each application page header for consistent logout functionality.

Applying Passport Authentication

Web applications can benefit from the rich credential validation provided by Passport's single sign-on service. This enables users to maintain a single login account valid for a variety of Web services and applications. Because the Passport service also captures user profiles, it reduces unnecessary complexity behind new account creation. Rather than creating new account entry forms to capture user contact information, Passport-enabled Web sites and applications can subscribe to the Passport service to retrieve user profiles based on their login credentials. Figure 13-5 shows the Passport version of the application start page.

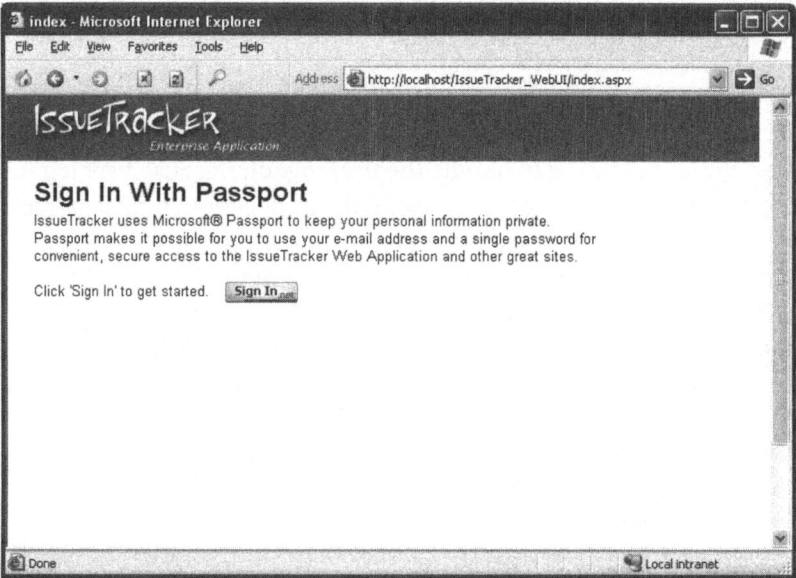

Figure 13-5. Default Passport sign-in page for IssueTracker

In this form, two functional elements are visible to the user: a status label that currently reads *Click 'Sign In' to get started* and a Passport Sign In button. On the Web form, both elements are implemented as simple label controls with Text attributes based upon the Passport login. To enable Passport Authentication, modify the Web.config file to specify Passport as the authentication mode, as outlined in Listing 13-10.

Listing 13-10. Enabling Passport Authentication in the Web.config File

```
<configuration>
    <system.web>
        <authentication mode="Passport"/>
```

```
        </system.web>
    </configuration>
    <authorization>
        <allow users="passport_account@msn.com" />
        <deny users="*" />
    </authorization>
```

In this case, the only user allowed access to the application is passport_account@msn.com. When an unauthorized user requests a Web page, a prompt for Passport Authentication appears, as illustrated in Figure 13-6.

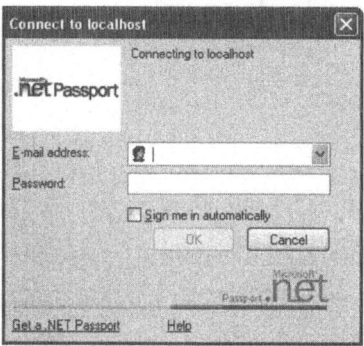

Figure 13-6. The Passport Authentication login prompt

The user credentials are submitted securely to the Passport authority site where they are authenticated. The only other changes necessary are to the application start page, which must display the Sign In button. Listing 13-11 outlines the new application start page, protected by Passport Authentication.

Listing 13-11. Rendering the Passport Sign In/Sign Out Buttons and Status

```
private void Page_Load(object sender, System.EventArgs e)
{
    int intDefault = -1;
    int intTimeWindow = 7200;
    bool boolForceLogin = false;
    string strSrvPath = "http://" + Request.Url.Host + Request.Url.AbsolutePath;

    PassportIdentity passport = new PassportIdentity();

    if( passport.GetFromNetworkServer )
        Response.Redirect( strSrvPath );
```

```
        if( passport.GetIsAuthenticated( intTimeWindow, boolForceLogin, false ) )
            lblStatus.Text = "Click 'Sign Out' to logout.";

        else if( passport.HasTicket )
            passport.LoginUser( HttpUtility.UrlEncode( strSrvPath ),
            intTimeWindow, boolForceLogin, null, intDefault, null, intDefault,
            false, null );
        else
            lblStatus.Text = "Click 'Sign In' to get started.";

        lblPassportBtn.Text = passport.LogoTag2( HttpUtility.UrlEncode( strSrvPath ),
            intTimeWindow, boolForceLogin, null, intDefault, false, null,
intDefault,
            false );

    return;
}
```

This method begins by setting default values required by Passport. Next, it instantiates the PassportIdentity object. Then, the GetFromNetworkServer property indicates true if the Passport server returns the active page. If so, you can clear extra cookie data appended to the URL by redirecting to the active page. The LoginUser method requires an encoded URL that indicates which page the Passport server should redirect to after authenticating the user. Next, a time window indicates how many minutes have elapsed since the last known login. Another parameter indicates if the Passport server should apply the time window of the last manual login or the refresh of the passport ticket. The LoginUser method forces a redirect to the Passport server. If the browser contains a passport ticket, it refreshes. Otherwise, a login on the Passport server is required. In either case, the browser redirects to the active page:

```
passport.LoginUser( HttpUtility.UrlEncode( strSrvPath ),
    intTimeWindow, boolForceLogin, null, intDefault, null, intDefault,
    false, null );
```

This method returns a string pointing to a Sign In button image on the Passport server. When the user clicks the image button, the same steps take place. Users are redirected to the Passport server, returning them to the active page. If the user is already signed in and has an authentication ticket, the image changes to a Sign Out button.

On the server side, Passport is deployed in binary form and must be first downloaded and installed. Also, enabling Passport requires registration and an expensive subscription to the Passport network.

NOTE *You can download the Passport Software Developer Kit (SDK) from Microsoft at* http://www.microsoft.com/netservices/ passport.

Authorizing the User Capabilities

After determining if a user can access an application, the next step is to determine *what* data and services the user is able to access. User authorization determines what system resources an authenticated user may access based upon their defined roles.

Creating Role-Based Security

Role-based security expands upon basic authorization services. As mentioned, basic authorization determines whether a user has sufficient permissions to access an application. Role-based security, however, determines what level of data can be accessed by a user. The process begins with the definition of discrete roles that categorize user profiles. Next, it determines what data each role is permitted to view and whether the role is able to add, edit, or delete data.

The Web.config file specifies which roles are allowed and denied access to server resources within the <authorization> tag. When Windows Authentication mode is applied, the FileAuthorizationModule object performs user and role validation against the Windows NT File System (NTFS) security manager. Similarly, when Forms or Passport Authentication is applied, the UrlAuthorizationModule object performs role validation. You can define any number of roles within the Web.config file:

```
<authorization>
    <allow roles="Administrators" />
    <allow roles="Managers" />
    <allow roles="All" />
    <deny users="*" />
</authorization>
```

The Application_AuthenticateRequest method evaluates role settings in the Web.config file. You can assign roles to a User object by adding them to a string array and passing the object to the GenericPrincipal object. Next, replace the current principal assigned to the HttpContext.User property. Any page within the application can invoke the IsInRole method to match a specified role against one within the passed array, as outlined in Listing 13-12. The role-based permissions provided by the .NET Framework rely largely on the identity and principal objects. Identities represent users within the software or operating system. Principals, however, represent the security context or Windows group of a user. A PrincipalPermission demands a role from a user. If the user has the necessary principal assigned, the request will succeed. PrincipalPermission is therefore an easy way to check role assignments.

Listing 13-12. Assigning a User to a Specific Set of Roles

```
protected void Application_AuthenticateRequest(Object sender, EventArgs e)
{
    HttpApplication application = ( HttpApplication )sender;

    if( application.Request.IsAuthenticated &&
        application.User.Identity is FormsIdentity )
    {
        FormsIdentity identity = (FormsIdentity)application.User.Identity;

        if( identity.Name == "demo" )
        {
            application.Context.User = new GenericPrincipal( identity,
                new string[]
                { "Managers", "All" } );
        }
    }

    return;
}
```

In the Web application code, user authorization is determined by referencing the HttpContext.User object and evaluating the user's role by checking the IsInRole property. Once the specific role is determined, a user interface element can decide to display data. In the case of IssueTracker, the DynamicMenu Web user control comprises three other user Web controls: MenuAdmin, MenuAll, and MenuManager. Each submenu displays commands that apply to a specific role. When the DynamicMenu control loads, it determines the login role of the user and displays the appropriate collection of menus (see Listing 13-13).

Listing 13-13. Dynamically Rendering Application Menus Based on User Role

```
private void Page_Load(object sender, System.EventArgs e)
{
    if( HttpContext.Current.User.IsInRole( "Administrator" ) )
        menuAdministrator.Visible = true;

    if( HttpContext.Current.User.IsInRole( "Manager" ) )
        menuManager.Visible = true;

    if( HttpContext.Current.User.IsInRole( "All" ) )
        menuAll.Visible = true;

    return;
}
```

When the form loads, the current user is evaluated for membership within the Administrator, Manager, and All roles. If so, then the respective menu Web user control becomes visible. This lets a form contain all necessary menus and only display the appropriate menu to the user with sufficient role-based permissions. Figure 13-7 illustrates the use of role-based menus within the IssueTracker application. Two different Web user controls display side by side, one for the Manager role and one for the All users role.

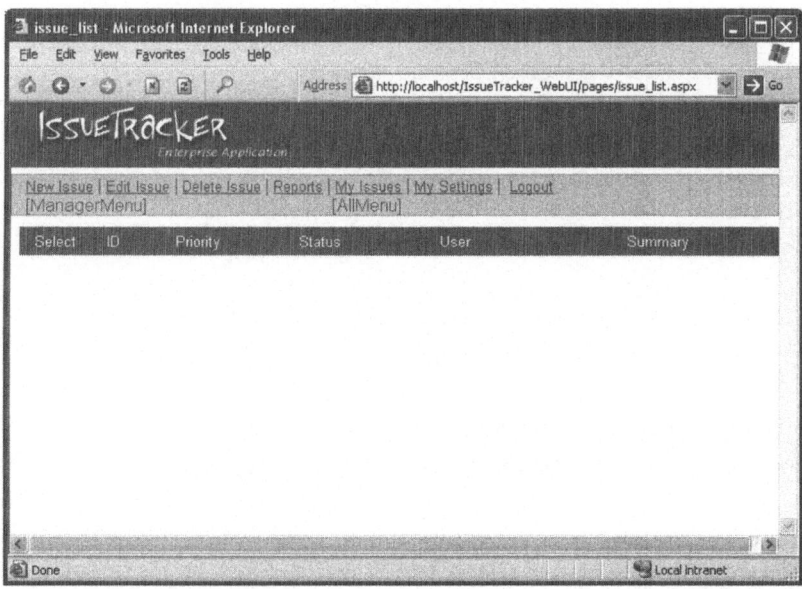

Figure 13-7. Displaying role-based menus in the IssueTracker issues summary view

Using Code Access Security

Code access security protects access to system resources by granting or denying access at the code level. Code access security is applied as an attribute to a class, method, or property. As an object is instantiated or executed, permissions are checked against the current client's principal before being allowed to continue. The PrincipalPermission attribute specifies code access permissions for role-based security. Setting the attribute on an object, method, or attribute can prohibit access to that code (see Listing 13-14).

Listing 13-14. Enabling Code Access Security for Specific Methods and Roles

```
using System;
using System.Security.Permissions;

public class IssueManager
{
    [PrincipalPermission(SecurityAction.Demand, Role="All")]
    [PrincipalPermission(SecurityAction.Demand, Role="Manager")]
    public IssueManager() {}

    [PrincipalPermission(SecurityAction.Demand, Role="All")]
    [PrincipalPermission(SecurityAction.Demand, Role="Manager")]
    public BusinessRules.IssueCollection GetAllIssues(){}

    [PrincipalPermission(SecurityAction.Demand, Role="All")]
    [PrincipalPermission(SecurityAction.Demand, Role="Manager")]
    public BusinessRules.Issue GetSpecificIssue( int argIntIssueID ){}

    [PrincipalPermission(SecurityAction.Demand, Role="All")]
    [PrincipalPermission(SecurityAction.Demand, Role="Manager")]
    public bool InsertIssue( BusinessRules.Issue argIssue ){}

    [PrincipalPermission(SecurityAction.Demand, Role="Manager")]
    public bool UpdateIssue( BusinessRules.Issue argIssue ){}

    [PrincipalPermission(SecurityAction.Demand, Role="Manager")]
    public bool DeleteIssue( BusinessRules.Issue argIssue ){}

}
```

This listing illustrates how you can modify the IssueManager object defined within the Business Facade project to include code access security. In this case, it has been determined that all users are able to view and insert issues. However, only managers are permitted to update or delete issues. The PrincipalPermission attribute specifies the code-level permissions. The SecurityAction.Demand action must verify the user's role before allowing the method to be invoked.

Protecting Data with Encryption

Cryptography secures data that is kept persistent within a file or database by scrambling a readable string into an unreadable string. The .NET Framework provides services either to hash a string or to encrypt a string into an unreadable format using single key or public/private key cryptographic algorithms. The most common use for hashing and encryption is to scramble a password or credit card number for persistence within a file or database.

Applying Data Hashing

Hashing is the process of converting a binary string of variable length into a fixed-length value through an algorithm. The string is manipulated by using its binary representation. A hash is often smaller than the original string and is generally unreadable.

An ideal hash algorithm cannot be reversed to "unhash" a value. Also, any string passed through the same hash algorithm must always produce the same hashed output. If two input strings vary by only one character, they should each produce different hashed output. The only way to decipher a hashed value is to run countless combinations of characters through the hash algorithm until finding a match.

Again, the .NET Framework provides a helpful method for producing an SHA1 or MD5 hash representation of a string. The following method generates a hashed string from a clear text string:

```
private string HashPassword( string strPassword )
{
    return FormsAuthentication.HashPasswordForStoringInConfigFile( strPassword,
        "SHA1" );
}
```

Hashing compares two strings for equality without knowing the actual value of either string, only that they are equal or not. Passwords are perfect examples. Applications that require authentication manage each user's password in a database. When a user logs into the application, his or her password is entered and compared to an entry in the database. If the values match, the user is authenticated. Ideally, a password should be stored as a hashed value in the database.

When the user enters his or her login, that value is also hashed before it is transmitted for verification. Instead of clear text passwords being intercepted by packet-sniffing tools, only unreadable strings are intercepted. The user will only be authenticated if the two hashed values match. Also, anyone who manages to obtain query permissions to the database is still unable to view the data.

Applying Symmetrical Encryption

Unlike hashing algorithms, encryption algorithms encode data in a method that enables them to be decrypted later. Encryption algorithms use keys to encrypt and decrypt data. Encryption keys are usually numeric values that are 32 to 256 bits long and that essentially randomize the encryption algorithm. Data encrypted with same encryption algorithm using two different keys should produce two different results. However, data encrypted with the same key and same algorithm should always produce the same results.

There are two different methods of data encryption: symmetric and asymmetric. *Symmetric encryption* uses a single key for data encryption and decryption. The encryption key exists for the time it takes to encrypt and exchange data and is then destroyed. It is important to keep these session keys secure. Once a session key has been compromised, information can no longer be securely exchanged because anyone with the key can decrypt it.

.NET implements a number of well-known symmetrical encryption algorithms. The .NET Framework provides services for generating random session keys or obtaining pass phrases. Pass phrases are useful when storing information such as a credit card number that might not be retrieved for some time. .NET creates a pass phrase, stores it in a secure location, and then uses it to regenerate the session key when needed to encrypt or decrypt data. Like pass phrases, randomly generated keys can also be saved for later use.

You can use the following methods to take an ordinary string and encrypt it into an unreadable format for storage or transport and later decrypt it for subsequent reading. The CreateKey method, shown in Listing 13-15, creates the private key used to encode and decode the data. The EncryptData method encodes the data and returns an unreadable string. The DecryptData method takes that same string and the private key, and it returns the data into a human-readable string.

Listing 13-15. Public Key Generation Method

```
public void CreateKey( string strPassword, int intSize, ref byte[] byteKey,
    ref byte[] byteIV )
{
    int intIndex;
    byte[] byteData;
```

```
    byte[] byteHash;

    byteData = Encoding.ASCII.GetBytes( strPassword );

    SHA1CryptoServiceProvider providerCrypto = new SHA1CryptoServiceProvider();

    int intLength = intSize / 8;

    byteHash = providerCrypto.ComputeHash( byteData );

    for( intIndex = 0; intIndex < intLength; intIndex++ )
        byteKey[intIndex] = byteHash[intIndex];

    for( intIndex = intLength; intIndex < (2 * intLength); intIndex++ )
        byteIV[intIndex - intLength] = byteHash[intIndex];

    return;
}
```

This method creates a private key for use by the data encryption and decryption methods and leverages the .NET Framework's SHA1 hash creation functionality. The method initially accepts a password that is converted into a byte array. Next, this byte array runs through the SHA1CryptoServiceProvider to create a hashed value. The resulting value is properly sized and used to construct the Initialization Vector (IV). Both the hashed private key and initialization vector are required to perform the encryption and decryption.

The .NET Framework includes symmetric algorithms, such as the Data Encryption Standard (DES), to encrypt data with a single private key. Listing 13-16 presents the EncryptData method that takes a private key generated by the CreateKey method and writes an encrypted value to a memory stream.

Listing 13-16. Data Encryption Method

```
public string EncryptData( string strSource, string strPassword )
{
    byte[] byteIV;
    byte[] byteKey;
    byte[] byteData = Encoding.ASCII.GetBytes( strSource );

    DESCryptoServiceProvider providerCrypto = new DESCryptoServiceProvider();
    byteIV = new byte[providerCrypto.BlockSize/8];
    byteKey = new byte[providerCrypto.BlockSize/8];

    CreateKey( strPassword, providerCrypto.BlockSize, ref byteKey, ref byteIV );
```

```
providerCrypto.Key = byteKey;
providerCrypto.IV = byteIV;

MemoryStream streamMemory = new MemoryStream();
CryptoStream streamCrypto = new CryptoStream( streamMemory,
    providerCrypto.CreateEncryptor(), CryptoStreamMode.Write );

for( int intIndex = 0; intIndex < byteData.Length; intIndex += 4096 )
{
    streamCrypto.Write( byteData, (intIndex*4096),
        byteData.Length - (intIndex*4096) );
}

streamCrypto.FlushFinalBlock();

byte[] byteResult = new byte[streamMemory.Length];

streamMemory.Seek( 0, SeekOrigin.Begin );

streamMemory.Read( byteResult, 0, byteResult.Length );

streamMemory.Close();
streamCrypto.Close();

return Convert.ToBase64String( byteResult );
}
```

This method begins by converting the string data into a byte array with the help of the Encoding object. Next, it creates the hashed value for the key and initialization vector. The key is 8 bytes long and determines how the encrypted output is generated. The initialization vector is appended to the encrypted output to add to the strength of the encryption. Next, a MemoryStream object is created to provide a protected buffer with which to work. The code also instantiates the CryptoStream object to perform the actual encryption. The MemoryStream object maintains the results of the encryption until read into a byte array. Finally, the ToBase64String method converts the byte array into a string.

The DecryptData method appearing in Listing 13-17 functions almost identically except that the CreateDecryptor method creates a DES decryptor. The encrypted data is converted from Base64 into a byte array before passing through the decryptor and finally converting into a normal string with the help of the Encoding object.

Listing 13-17. Data Decryption Method

```
public string DecryptData( string strSource, string strPassword )
{
    byte[] byteIV;
    byte[] byteKey;
    byte[] byteData = Convert.FromBase64String( strSource );

    DESCryptoServiceProvider providerCrypto = new DESCryptoServiceProvider();
    byteIV = new byte[providerCrypto.BlockSize/8];
    byteKey = new byte[providerCrypto.BlockSize/8];

    CreateKey( strPassword, providerCrypto.BlockSize, ref byteKey, ref byteIV );
    providerCrypto.Key = byteKey;
    providerCrypto.IV = byteIV;

    MemoryStream streamMemory = new MemoryStream();
    CryptoStream streamCrypto = new CryptoStream( streamMemory,
        providerCrypto.CreateDecryptor(), CryptoStreamMode.Write );

    for( int intIndex = 0; intIndex < byteData.Length; intIndex += 4096 )
    {
        streamCrypto.Write( byteData, (intIndex*4096),
            byteData.Length - (intIndex*4096) );
    }

    streamCrypto.FlushFinalBlock();

    byte[] byteResult = new byte[streamMemory.Length];

    streamMemory.Seek( 0, SeekOrigin.Begin );

    streamMemory.Read( byteResult, 0, byteResult.Length );

    streamMemory.Close();
    streamCrypto.Close();

    return Encoding.ASCII.GetString( byteResult );
}
```

Encrypting data into a file stream is not very different from encrypting into
a memory stream. With some small effort, you could modify these methods to

write data straight to a data file. This can be a great advantage for applications that must write sensitive data to a persistent file for physical data exchange. This way, if you lose a floppy disk carrying sensitive data at the airport, you can still protect critical enterprise data.

Applying Asymmetrical Encryption

Although symmetric data encryption is effective in keeping sensitive data secure, everything can be easily compromised if the encryption key is exposed. Given that two entities must exchange an encryption key to exchange encrypted data, there exists a real possibility of the key being intercepted. Asymmetric data encryption addresses this situation directly. Unlike symmetric encryption, which uses the same key for encryption and decryption, asymmetric encryption uses two keys: a private key and a public key.

Information encrypted with the private key can only be decrypted with the public key, and information encrypted with the public key can only be decrypted with the private key. The public key is made available to anyone who asks for it, and the private key remains secret. Because the private key is never shared, asymmetric encryption is more secure than symmetric encryption.

The .NET Framework provides implementations of several well-known asymmetric encryption algorithms, such as those offered by RSA Security. The .NET Framework also simplifies the key exchange process. Public keys are exported as a Binary Large Object (BLOB) that can be saved to a file and sent to the client application. Once received, the client application uses the BLOB to reconstruct the public key and encrypt information. A single method call can generate an XML representation of a public key. The XML document can be transferred over a network to another application, and the client application can reconstruct the key with a single method call.

Symmetric and asymmetric encryption algorithms each have their advantages. Symmetric encryption is much faster than asymmetric encryption and is useful for quick encryption and decryption. Furthermore, there is little chance that someone might intercept the key. Asymmetric encryption is more secure because only one of the keys is shared and is ideal for communication over insecure environments, such as the Internet. Because of its relatively slow performance, asymmetric encryption should be reserved for small amounts of data, such as a password, a credit card number, or a symmetric key used for later symmetric encryption.

Summary

Adequate security is important to the success of any enterprise application. With the ever-increasing threat of corporate espionage and Web site hacking, more corporations and government agencies are looking closely at the security services that enterprise solutions offer. The .NET Framework provides security services that have been virtually nonexistent on many platforms such as Windows 98. Such security services make it fairly painless to implement the important authentication, authorization, and encryption services long needed by enterprise applications.

Authentication is the bare minimum form of security that an enterprise application can afford. Windows, Forms, and Passport Authentication all provide an easy method of determining whether a particular user should have access to an application and its data.

Authorization in the form of role-based and code access security work well together to limit how users interact with enterprise data and services. Rather than a simple approved or disapproved login, applications can take control of what interacts with the user. Furthermore, network administrators are now able to decide the resources that applications should be able to access.

Finally, when building applications that store or exchange sensitive data, maintaining privacy must be a primary concern. Hashing and encryption help ensure that information such as passwords and credit card numbers remain private. The .NET Framework provides several classes that simplify the hashing and encryption of data.

The next chapter wraps up the development of an enterprise application by presenting the deployment project. Deploying Web, desktop, and mobile applications is significantly easier with the help of the Visual Studio .NET environment. A functional and user-friendly application setup adds a polished and professional look to an application and helps to ensure that user configurations are consistent.

CHAPTER 14

Installing .NET Applications

THE LAST STAGE of application development is implementing a deployment solution. A deployment solution installs the completed application on a user's computer or networked environment. The installation must be complete with supporting files and Registry values. Successful deployment solutions accomplish this with the least amount of user interaction necessary.

How to deploy an application varies significantly whether you are deploying to a server, to a desktop, or to a device. Although the purpose of a setup program is to create files and folders on a target computer, there are additional issues you need to address. You might need to make Registry updates, create file associations, and render the installation user interface differently from one country to another. This chapter covers all of these topics and explains how Visual Studio .NET helps to simplify them.

Defining the Elements of Application Deployment

A setup program can perform many functions—from basic file copy using the operating system's XCOPY service to a fully scripted setup program loaded with features. In all cases, the setup program must create folders, move files, update the Registry, create file associations, and possibly support localization.

Creating Folders and Moving Files

The primary purpose of a setup program is to install the enterprise application files on a target computer. Because the target file system organization can differ from one computer to another, the deployment project references directories as abstract folders. This ensures that files are installed in their intended locations. Abstract folders can represent nearly every system-related folder, including Program Files, the user's Desktop, Windows, and System. You can copy files to any of these existing folders or to new folders created under them.

Updating the System Registry

Alongside creating folders and moving files is the need to create system Registry keys with default values. Many desktop applications insert user-specific values, environment settings, and even product expiration information into the Registry. The deployment project includes a hierarchical view of a typical Registry structure where you can modify existing Registry keys or add new Registry keys. During installation, the created Registry structure will be applied to the target computer.

Creating File Associations

Document-centric applications also find it useful to create an association between themselves and files that have a specific file extension. Just as a .doc file is normally associated with the Microsoft Word application, an .issue file might be associated with the IssueTracker application. This way, double-clicking the file within the file explorer will automatically start the IssueTracker desktop client. Additionally, you can associate one or more actions with a document, such as Open, Edit, or Copy. You can associate these actions with different installed applications when selected from a document's context menu within the file explorer.

Supporting Localization

Multinational applications need to support localization, not only within the application but also during deployment. The deployment project supports the inclusion of multiple merge files, each containing files related to a specific locale. Merge files are simply packages of individual files that you can use for grouping files in many ways, including by locale. The deployment project also supports localization itself. When running, instructions for each wizard step can appear in the locale's native language.

Examining the Windows Installer Engine

The Windows Installer is an application setup service that is tightly integrated with Windows XP and Windows Server 2003. It functions by referencing packages that contain the distributable application files along with its distribution rules. If any step of the application installation fails, the Windows Installer will roll back the installation, returning the environment to its original state. The Windows Installer also maintains a list of all applications it has previously installed, including their files and Registry values. Figure 14-1 illustrates the different elements of the Windows Installer.

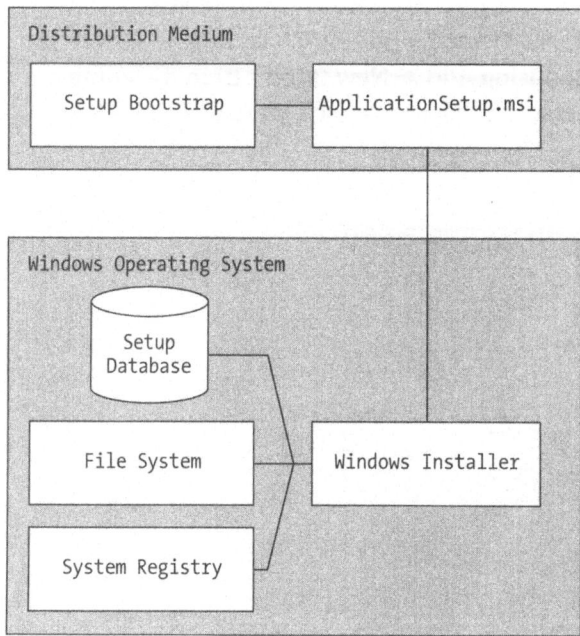

Figure 14-1. The internal elements of the Windows Installer

Maintaining an internal list of installed applications has a number of benefits. If a user accidentally removes an application's file, the Windows Installer is capable of repairing the installation by copying only the missing files from the original distribution package. Also, when the Windows Installer uninstalls an application, it checks to ensure that other installed applications will not be impacted by the removed files or Registry values.

Implementing a Deployment Solution

Visual Studio .NET includes the tools necessary to build deployment projects for desktop applications, Web applications, and device applications. For each target application type, the necessary steps and tools are similar. In all cases, the steps include creating a deployment project, adding necessary files, adding necessary Registry keys, polishing the user interface, and adding any special conditions.

Creating the Deployment Project

You create an installation project just like any other project. Begin by selecting the IssueTracker solution and choosing Add ➤ New Project from the context menu. The Add New Project dialog box displays, as shown in Figure 14-2.

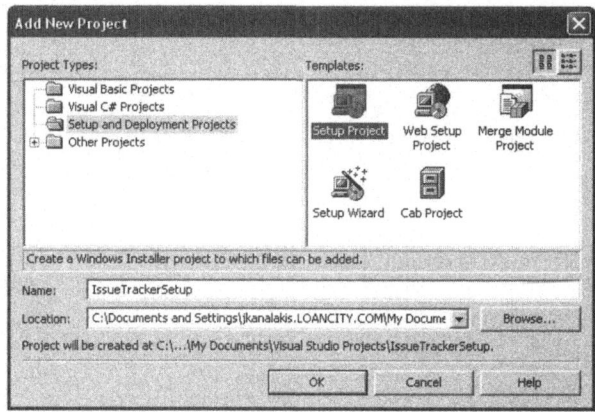

Figure 14-2. Creating a new deployment project in the Add New Project dialog box

Select the Setup and Deployment Projects folder and a template that matches the type of installation project necessary. There are four setup projects to choose from and a wizard that helps determine which of the four templates best matches a particular application.

Specifying the Deployment Project Type

The four standard setup project types target desktop applications, Web applications, merge modules, and cabinet files. The first step in implementing the deployment project is selecting the application type. It is normal for an enterprise application to contain multiple setup projects within one solution. The IssueTracker solution will contain a deployment project for the enterprise Web application, another for the desktop client application, and another for a device application.

Deploying Desktop Applications

The Setup Project template creates a distribution medium for deploying desktop applications. You can configure the project to create folders, move files, set Registry values, and create shortcuts. The output from a setup project is an .msi installer file that contains the application to be deployed, its dependent files, and related application settings.

The Setup Project template is highly configurable. You can customize the user experience to add or remove user steps driving the installation. You can specify the targeted deployment directory and tie it directly back to another project's generated output. Multiple deployment projects might exist within a solution to support different application configurations.

Deploying Web Applications

The Web Setup Project template creates a distribution medium for deploying Web applications. The Web Setup Project template is similar to the standard Setup Project template. Both configure files, folders, Registry keys, actions, and launch conditions that affect deployment to the target computer. However, the Web Setup Project template includes the ability to create virtual directories within the Internet Information Services (IIS) environment.

Distributing Merge Modules

Merge modules package files, resources, and Registry values that multiple applications might share. The output from a merge module project is an .msm file that can be later included by any other deployment project in the same manner that .dll files enable multiple applications to share the same code. And like a .dll, an .msm file cannot be launched independently—only as a part of a completed .msi deployment application.

Distributing Cabinet Files

Cabinets package multiple files into a single file for download. They simply package files or project output into a single compressed file, much like a .zip file. Cabinet project properties specify the level of compression and whether Authenticode signing should be applied. Cabinet files are most widely used in deploying device applications.

Using the Deployment Editors

Visual Studio .NET provides different editors to interact with the deployment project. These editors customize the files to be deployed, the Registry values to be set, the file types to be associated, the user interface forms to be displayed, the custom actions to take, and the launch conditions to evaluate.

Selecting Files with the File Editor

The Deployment File Editor displays folders that abstract the true destination of files installed on the target computer (see Figure 14-3). Several built-in folder abstractions exist, including the Program Files folder, the Windows folder, the System folder, and the Fonts folder. Application files and shortcuts reside in these different abstract folders, relying upon the Windows Installer to resolve the actual directories on the target computer during installation.

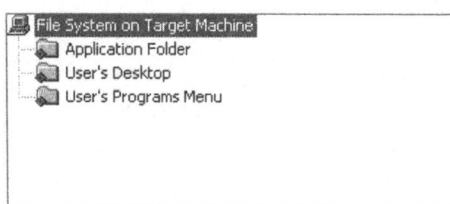

Figure 14-3. Adding distribution files with the Deployment File Editor

Open the Deployment File Editor by selecting the deployment project within the Solution Explorer and choosing View ➤ File System from its context menu. You can add files, assemblies, and project outputs to each abstract folder by selecting the folder name and choosing Add from its context menu. Also, you can create any number of child folders beneath an abstract folder to create any necessary folder structure.

Adding Registry Values with the Registry Editor

The Deployment Registry Editor displays a hierarchy of Registry values that are standard to most versions of the Windows operating system (see Figure 14-4). Additions to the hierarchy of values represent Registry changes that the Windows Installer will need to make during application installation.

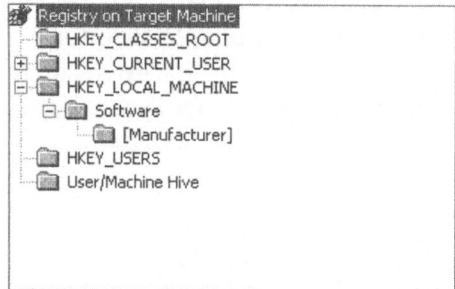

Figure 14-4. Adding new Registry keys using the Deployment Registry Editor

Open the Deployment Registry Editor by selecting the deployment project and choosing View ➤ Registry. You can create any number of Registry keys within the hierarchy by choosing from the nodes' context menus. Registry keys can reference installation variable values, such as [Manufacturer] and [ProductName]. For every new key, you can create a new string, binary, or DWORD value. You can also create Registry keys and values conditionally during install time.

Configuring File Types with the File Types Editor

The Deployment File Types Editor configures the target computer to associate a particular file type with an application based on the file's extension (see Figure 14-5). You accomplish this by adding the document type, associating a file extension with the document type, and then associating an application with the file extension.

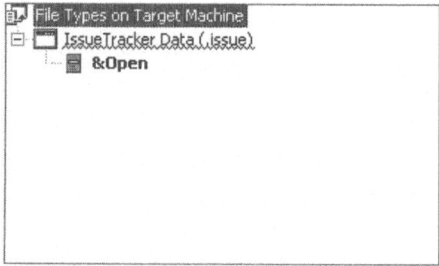

Figure 14-5. Adding document associations using the Deployment File Types Editor

To associate a file type with an application, select the root node within the Deployment File Types Editor. Choose Add File Types from its context menu to add a new document type node beneath the root node. Type a short description for the new file type, such as *IssueTracker Data*. Next, open the Properties view and set the Extensions property to the file extension to be associated. Be sure to not precede the extension with a period. You can associate multiple file extensions by delimiting them with a semicolon. Finally, associate the file extension to an application by selecting the Command property and pointing it to the executable application within the distribution, such as Application Folder ➤ Primary Output from WinUI.

You can also associate multiple actions with a file extension. If a deployment project packages separate applications to open, edit, and copy a specific file, then you can add each separate action to associate the same file extension with different application executables.

> **NOTE** *When taking ownership of a file extension, be sure to check for existing conflicts. You can find a detailed list of known file extensions online at* http://www.filext.com.

Displaying Wizard Steps with the User Interface Editor

You can use the deployment User Interface Editor to add or remove user interface steps displayed within the Setup Wizard during the application deployment (see Figure 14-6). Several predefined dialog boxes exist to collect different information and to present different types of status to the user.

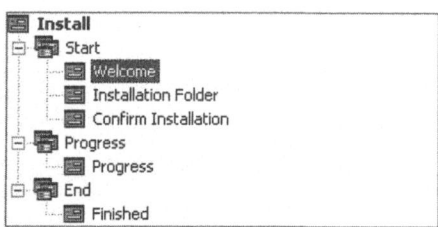

Figure 14-6. Setting wizard steps using the deployment User Interface Editor

Open the deployment User Interface Editor by selecting the deployment project and choosing View ➤ User Interface from its context menu. Although you can display standard setup wizard dialog boxes, such as Welcome, License Agreement, and Destination Folder, Visual Studio .NET also includes several custom dialog boxes to collect custom user choices. These choices are then associated with custom actions that allow the Windows Installer to perform special deployment-related tasks. You can configure each dialog box to display a default Windows Installer message or a custom message.

The editor also separates the general user's view of the setup program from the administrator's view. This function provides the administrator with all steps of the Setup Wizard, including the target folder. Administrators can then create an image of the installation that has optional fields, such as target folder, set to a new default value. Internal company employees could download the image from the local intranet and interact with a limited subset of the Setup Wizard.

Adding Functional Steps with the Custom Actions Editor

The deployment Custom Actions Editor invokes custom actions implemented in external binary files (see Figure 14-7). The Windows Installer supports custom actions that are implemented in .dll, .exe, script, or assembly files to be invoked during the install, uninstall, rollback, or commit stages of the deployment. You can use custom actions for a variety of tasks, including creating or configuring the application data sources.

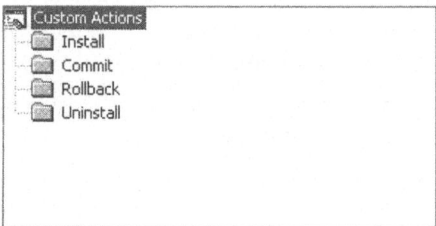

Figure 14-7. Adding custom actions using the deployment Custom Actions Editor

You can invoke custom actions after the actual installation completes; you do not have access to properties set during the installation. To pass information from the install program to a custom action, set the CustomActionData property. Custom actions that fail will result in the entire installation failing, causing a complete setup rollback. You can place conditions on any custom action using the Condition property.

Setting Conditions with the Launch Conditions Editor

The deployment Launch Conditions Editor sets conditions for the installation (see Figure 14-8). Launch conditions allow the setup program to install specific files depending upon tested conditions, such as operating system version or the installed presence of the .NET Framework. To test conditions, the editor also enables searches for files, Registry settings, or registered components.

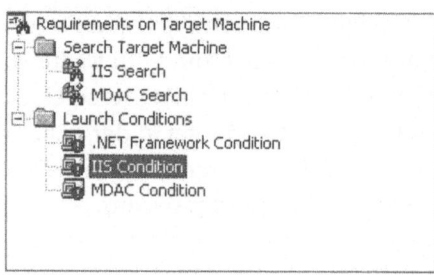

Figure 14-8. Adding launch conditions usng the deployment Launch Conditions Editor

Visual Studio automatically adds a launch condition that checks for the existence of the .NET Framework runtime environment. To add a launch condition to a deployment project, first add search criteria. Select the Search Target Machine node and choose Add File Search. You add new search criteria to the tree, and file search properties appear in the Properties window. Set the file properties necessary to locate the file on the target computer, such as FileName, Folder, MinDate, and MaxDate. Next, create a new launch condition by selecting the Launch Conditions node and choosing Add Launch Condition from its context menu. For the launch condition's properties, select the search criteria to link to, a Uniform Resource Locator (URL) pointing to the download location of the missing files, and an error message to present to the user.

NOTE *You can find a complete reference of the installation properties at* http://msdn.microsoft.com/library/default.asp?url=/library/en-us/msi/setup/properties.asp.

Creating a Windows Application Setup

After selecting a project type and adding a new project to the solution, the next step is to add the distributable application files. Open the deployment File Editor by selecting the setup project in the Solution Explorer, opening its context menu, and choosing View ➤ File System. The Add Project Output Group dialog box will display. Select WinUI as the source project and choose Primary Output, Localized Resources, and Content Files for the distributable files, as shown in Figure 14-9.

This instructs Visual Studio to pull the built .dll or .exe output from the selected project directly into the distribution package. After the output group is selected, Visual Studio attempts to resolve the project's dependencies and inserts additional nodes into the Solution Explorer, as shown in Figure 14-10.

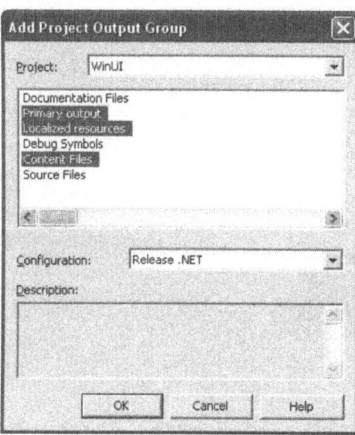

Figure 14-9. Adding project output files to the distribution

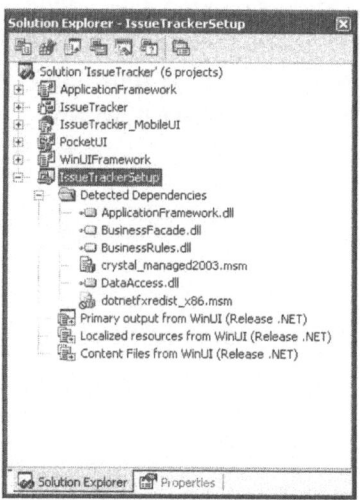

Figure 14-10. The Solution Explorer view of deployment dependencies checked

After specifying the distribution files and validating the dependencies, add the application shortcuts. You can create a shortcut just about anywhere, but it typically appears in the user's Programs menu and Desktop. To add a shortcut to the Desktop, select the User's Desktop entry in the deployment File Editor, open its context menu, and select Create Shortcut to User's Desktop. In the right pane, open the context menu and select Create New Shortcut. In the Select Item in Project dialog box, select Primary Output from WinUI, as shown in Figure 14-11. This creates a shortcut pointing to the application's .exe file. To add a shortcut to any other distributed file, click the Add File button and browse to its location.

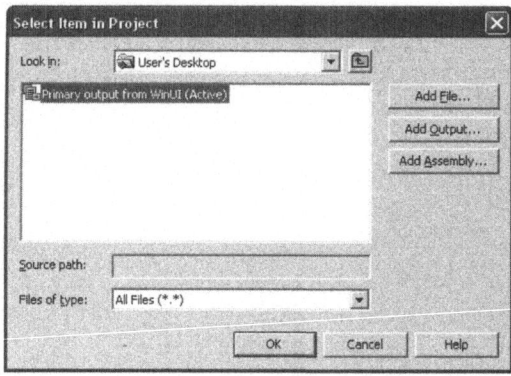

Figure 14-11. Creating application shortcuts linked to project output

After you have created the shortcut, edit the properties to specify a path to an icon or to enter command-line arguments. With folders created, files added, and shortcuts created, a minimal deployment project is complete. After building the setup project, start the .msi file and step through the wizard, as shown in Figure 14-12. Determine if you should add or remove any of the setup wizard steps.

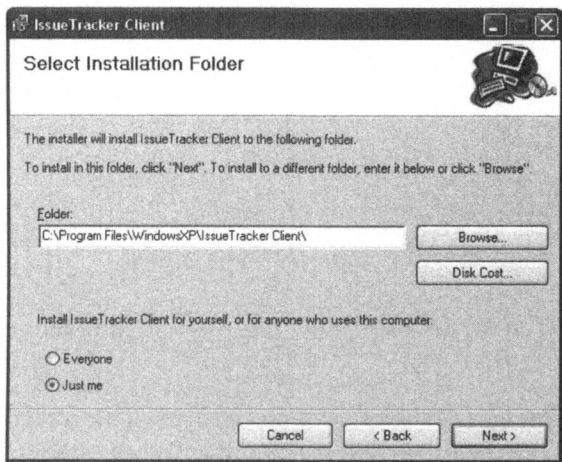

Figure 14-12. A runtime look at the desktop application setup program

When the installation completes, the application should exist in the specified directory. Always test the final installation application on a "clean" computer to ensure that all necessary files have been copied successfully. Also, check that the shortcuts have been created and that the necessary Registry values have been set.

Creating a Web Application Setup

The Web application deployment project is similar to the desktop application deployment project. The most significant difference is the support for deploying files into a virtual directory within the IIS server. The deployment project must specify the alias for the targeted virtual directory; the read, write, browse, and script execution permissions; and the default document to load. The remaining options for specifying Registry values, file associations, launch conditions, and custom actions still apply.

The first step to implementing the Web application deployment project is to add the distributable application files. After creating the setup project within the IssueTracker solution, open the deployment File Editor. Next, select the Web Application Folder entry and choose Add ➤ Project Output from its context menu. In the Add Project Output Group dialog box, select WebUI as the source project and choose Primary Output, Localized Resources, and Content Files for the distributable files.

Visual Studio checks the dependencies associated with the WebUI project and adds them to the Detected Dependencies list. It adds dependencies in the form of .dll files to the Web application's bin directory. Also, it adds the WebUI project's created .dll file to the Web application's bin directory.

Next, you need to add related Web application content to the distribution. From the deployment File Editor, select the Web Application Folder and choose Add ➤ Web Folder from its context menu. Rename the new Web folder to *images* or to another content directory. Next, select the newly created Web folder and choose Add ➤ File from its context menu. Browse to the source content directory and select the files to be included.

Most applications will need to write application properties, such as product version or database connection information, to the system Registry. To add create a new Registry key on the target computer, open the deployment Registry Editor. Expand the Registry hierarchy to HKEY_LOCAL_MACHINE\Software\ [Manufacturer]\[Program Name]. Choose New ➤ String Value from its context menu and edit the properties of the new Registry value. Set the Name property to Version and the Value property to 1.0.0. You can add any number of additional keys and values as needed.

After building the setup project, start the .msi file and step through the wizard, as shown in Figure 14-13. Determine if you should add or remove any of the Setup Wizard steps. Because IIS settings are being changed, the user installing the Web application must have administrative access to the computer.

When the installation completes, the Web application should exist in the specified virtual directory. Test the installation by opening a Web browser and pointing to the locally hosted Web application to ensure that all necessary files have been copied successfully.

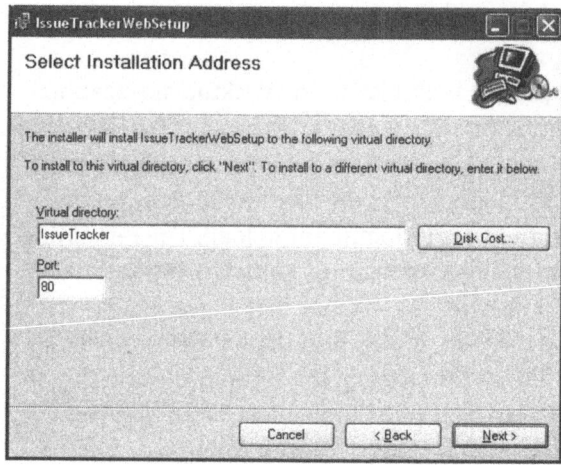

Figure 14-13.A runtime look at the Web application setup program

Reusing Deployment Packages with Merge Modules

The merge module deployment project is similar to the desktop and Web deployment projects. However, because it is intended to represent only a part of the installation process, the user interface and launch conditions are omitted. In the deployment File Editor, there are two destination folders: Common Files Folder and Module Retargetable Folder.

Files packaged into a merge module's Common Files Folder are deployed to a directory specified by the merge module itself. Conversely, files packaged into a merge module's Module Retargetable Folder can be deployed to any directory specified by the host setup program. You set the overridden deployment directory using the merge module's exposed Module Retargetable Folder property.

To include an existing merge module into a desktop or Web deployment project, add the merge module project to the solution. Then, open the application deployment project's deployment File Editor and choose Add ➤ Project Output from the context menu. In the Add Project Output Group dialog box, select the merge module.

Once you have completed and distributed a merge module, you should never modify it. There is no integrated version control, and it is easy for an .msm file to be mixed up, causing the applications that rely on them to fail. Instead, create a new merge module for each successive version of the deployed package and ideally embed a version label into the .msm filename itself.

Deploying Device Applications with Cabinet Files

The CAB deployment project is probably the most different from the other deployment projects. This is largely because there are no custom deployment editors, and it does not interact at all with the Windows Installer. It is simply a compressed package file that contains multiple application files, much like a .zip file. Although it is little more than a convenient method of packing directories full of files, its greatest benefit is in building device deployment projects.

Device applications are typically simple in their organization. You can build and package a device application into a single cabinet file containing all application files. Once the cabinet file is moved to the device through a desktop synchronization, the contents of the file can be self-extracted into the appropriate device directory structure. This is actually how the .NET Compact Framework is deployed to devices.

To add device application files to a cabinet file, select the PocketUI project within the Solution Explorer and choose Build Cab File from its context menu. Visual Studio creates a new cabinet file in the project's output directory, complete with all device application files, the Compact Framework, and SQL Server CE. It creates multiple versions of the device deployment file for different device processors. You use the PocketUI_PPC.ARM.CAB file for deployment to a Compaq IPAQ running the Pocket PC operating system.

After copying the cabinet device deployment file to the device, the user can click it to trigger an automatic installation. All application files reside beneath the Program Files directory in a directory with the same name as the device application project. The device application will also appear in the ActiveSync application manager, as shown in Figure 14-14.

Figure 14-14. The ActiveSync application manager

As mentioned in Chapter 11, "Deploying .NET Applications on Wireless Devices," a device application built using the .NET Compact Framework first needs to deploy the Compact Framework to the device. The Compact Framework is also packaged into a cabinet file located in \Program Files\Microsoft Visual Studio .NET 2003\CompactFrameworkSDK\v1.0.5000\Windows CE\wce300. Beneath this folder are multiple cabinet files targeting the different device platforms, organized by device processor.

To install the Compact Framework on Compaq IPAQ, copy the cabinet files located within the arm directory to the device and click the file to initiate the self-extract process. After you have configured the Compact Framework on the device, the device application can follow.

Addressing Common Deployment Issues

Deploying an enterprise application introduces a different set of issues from deploying typical desktop applications. Enterprise applications need to be more aware of their target environments. This typically translates into lots of launch conditions and careful attention to redistributing system files.

Deploying the .NET Framework

Every application built upon the .NET Framework will require it to be installed on the target computer. You can deploy the .NET Framework to the most recent versions of the Windows operating system, as outlined in Table 14-1.

Table 14-1. Operating Systems Supporting the .NET Framework

SUPPORTED PLATFORM	REQUIRED SERVICE PACK
Windows 98	
Windows Millennium Edition	
Windows NT 4.0	Service Pack 6
Windows 2000	Service Pack 2
Windows XP Home/Professional	

Although all deployment projects include a launch condition to check for the presence of the .NET Framework, they do not actually install it. To quietly install the .NET Framework onto a target computer, you must invoke a special Setup.exe bootstrap application. Install the compiled sample bootstrap locally

458

after downloading it from the Microsoft Developer Network (MSDN) at
http://msdn.microsoft.com/downloads/sample.asp?url=/msdn-files/027/001/
830/msdncompositedoc.xml.

Next, replace the Setup.exe bootstrap and Setup.ini file that Visual Studio
provides in the deployment project's output directory with the version downloaded from MSDN. Edit the replacing Setup.ini file and set the Msi property to
identify the installation package to invoke after installing the .NET Framework.
Also, set the FxInstallerPath property to point to the actual binary file containing
the redistributable .NET Framework:

```
[Bootstrap]
Msi=IssueTrackerSetup.msi
FxInstallerPath=redist/
```

For a basic English installation of any .NET application, an application's final
distribution CD image should contain the files outlined in Table 14-2.

Table 14-2. The Application Deployment CD Image Files

FILE	DESCRIPTION
Setup.exe	The downloaded bootstrap startup program that checks for the .NET Framework and installs if not present
Settings.ini	The initialization file indicating the application deployment package and .NET redistribution package
MyApplication.msi	The packaged application file created by the deployment project
redist\dotnetfx.exe	The .NET Framework redistributable files

Deploying the Data Access Components

Any application that implements the .NET Framework data services will also
require the Microsoft Data Access Components (MDAC) library version 2.6
installed on the target computer. Deployment projects containing a data-driven
application will need to create a launch condition that detects if MDAC is
installed.

In the deployment Launch Conditions Editor, select the Search Target
Machine node and choose Add Registry Search from its context menu. Edit
the Root property to point to vsdrrHKLM. Set the RegKey property to point to
Software\Microsoft\DataAccess. Set the Value property to FullInstallVer and the
Property property to MDAC_SEARCH. Next, select the Launch Conditions node

and choose Add Launch Condition from its context menu. Set the Condition property to MDAC_SEARCH >= "2.6". The version number is in quotation marks because the Registry key is typed as a string.

During installation, this launch condition will check the Registry path to determine if an MDAC library greater than version 2.6 is installed. If so, the installation completes normally; otherwise, the user is notified and instructed to download the package, and the entire installation rolls back to its original state.

Determining the Presence of IIS

Web applications have an additional dependency upon IIS being present. You can add a launch condition to check the Registry for the presence of IIS as well as its version.

In the deployment Launch Conditions Editor, select the Search Target Machine node and choose Add Registry Search from its context menu. Edit the Root property to point to vsdrrHKLM. Set the RegKey property to point to Software\Microsoft\InetStp. Set the Value property to MajorVersion and the Property property to IIS_SEARCH. Next, select the Launch Conditions node and choose Add Launch Condition from its context menu. Set the Condition property to IIS_SEARCH >= "5".

During installation, this launch condition will check the Registry path to determine if the IIS Web server version is greater than or equal to 5. If so, the installation completes normally; otherwise, the user is notified and instructed to install the later version, and the entire installation rolls back to its original state.

Localizing Application Deployment

You need to be aware of two aspects of localized deployment: the localized contents of the distribution and the localized version of the setup program. To create a localized version of the setup program, you need to create a new deployment project that targets the specific local. It is not possible for a single setup application to render itself differently for each local. To create a deployment project for Germany, open the deployment User Interface Editor and set the Localization property to German. Also, you will need to manually translate each custom message in every user interface dialog box into German. Although Visual Studio continues to represent the user interface in English, the resulting dialog boxes will appear in German, as shown in Figure 14-15.

Another aspect of localized deployment is the distribution contents. Ideally, core application files should be locale independent and can therefore be packaged into a single merge module. You can package the remaining application files that contain locale specific code or resources separately. Ideally, identify the locale within the merge module name, such as images_german.msm.

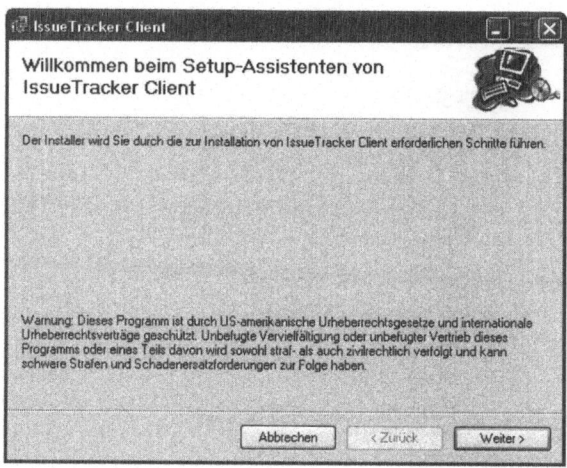

Figure 14-15. A German localized version of the setup program

For localized installers, you need to replace the default dotnetfxredist_x86.msm file with a .NET Framework merge module for the target locale, such as dotnetfxredist_x86_de.msm. You can obtain localized merge modules from Microsoft at `http://msdn.microsoft.com/downloads/default.asp?url=/downloads/` `sample.asp?url=/msdn-files/027/000/976/msdncompositedoc.xml`.

Configuring a SQL Server Database

One of the most important aspects of enterprise application deployment is the proper configuration of the application's database. Many enterprise applications treat this process as a secondary step after installation. Once completing an installation, a database administrator must create a database and execute a series of SQL statements that build the database schema.

The Windows Installer provides a better option through its extensibility features. In the IssueTracker application, you can create a custom user interface form, DatabaseSetupForm, in an extended class library package. You can code this form to read an .sql script file and create the entire database schema from a custom action defined within the deployment project.

Begin by adding a new Class Library project to the solution, named *DatabaseSetup*. Next, select the new project and choose Add ➤ Add New Item from its context menu. Select the Installer Class template and create an instance named *DatabaseSetup*, as shown in Figure 14-16.

The new DatabaseSetup class will serve as the entry point for the Windows Installer into the assembly. Listing 14-1 adds the necessary implementation to respond to the Windows Installer and activate a user entry form.

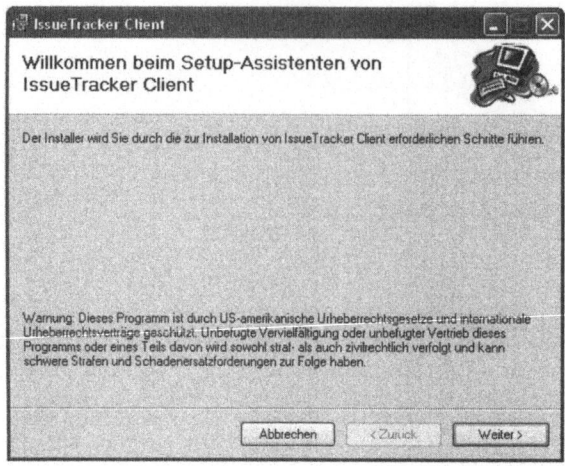

Figure 14-16. Adding a new installer class to the project

Listing 14-1. The DatabaseSetup Installer Class

```
[RunInstaller(true)]
public class DatabaseSetup : System.Configuration.Install.Installer
{
    DatabaseSetupForm formDatabase = new DatabaseSetupForm();
    private System.ComponentModel.Container components = null;

    public DatabaseSetup()
    {
        InitializeComponent();
    }

    private void InitializeComponent()
    {
        components = new System.ComponentModel.Container();
    }

    public override void Install(IDictionary savedState)
    {
        base.Install (savedState);
        formDatabase.ShowDialog();
    }

    public override void Commit(IDictionary savedState)
```

```
    {
        base.Commit (savedState);
        formDatabase.ShowDialog();
    }
}
```

The installer class derives from the System.Configuration.Install.Installer object, which manages the interaction with the Windows Installer. Two methods are overridden, Install and Commit. Both methods represent possibly entry points into the object, depending upon which custom action node activates the object. In either case, a new form, DatabaseSetupForm, displays.

Next, you need to create the new form to capture input from the user. Select the DatabaseSetup project and choose Add ➤ Add Windows Form from its context menu and set its name to DatabaseSetupForm.cs. This creates a blank Windows form, which in turn automatically creates references to the System.Forms and System.Drawing namespaces. Add form controls that capture the database server name, login name, and password, as shown in Figure 14-17.

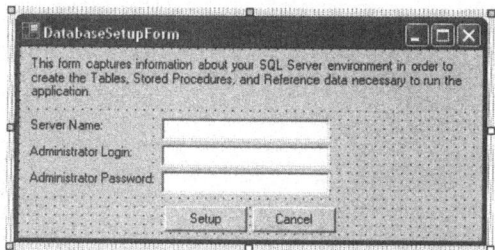

Figure 14-17. Creating a custom form to capture additional setup information

After creating the dialog form, you need to implement the Setup button handler to read an .sql script file and execute its table creation commands. Listing 14-2 implements the button handler that takes the server configuration settings, connects to the database, and creates the complete application schema.

Listing 14-2. Implementing the Create New Database Function

```
private void btnSetup_OnClick(object sender, System.EventArgs e)
{
    SqlConnection sqlConnection = new SqlConnection();

    try
    {
        //format the connection string
```

```
            string strConnString = "server=" + txtServer.Text + ";uid=" +
            txtLogin.Text + ";pwd=" + txtPassword.Text;

            //create the new database
            sqlConnection.ConnectionString = strConnString;
            sqlConnection.Open();
            sqlConnection.ChangeDatabase( "master" );
            SqlCommand sqlCommand = new SqlCommand( "CREATE DATABASE " +
                "IssueTracker", sqlConnection );
            sqlCommand.ExecuteNonQuery();


            //read the sql sourcefile
            Assembly assembly = Assembly.GetExecutingAssembly();
            string strAssemblyPath = assembly.GetName().Name + ".CreateDatabase.sql";
            Stream stream = assembly.GetManifestResourceStream( strAssemblyPath );
            StreamReader reader = new StreamReader( stream );

            //execute table create sql file
            sqlConnection.ChangeDatabase( "IssueTracker" );
            sqlCommand = new SqlCommand( reader.ReadToEnd(), sqlConnection );
            sqlCommand.ExecuteNonQuery();

            MessageBox.Show( "IssueTracker database setup complete.", "Succeess" );
        }
        catch( SqlException x )
        {
            MessageBox.Show( x.Message, "Database Setup Failed" );
        }
        finally
        {
            sqlConnection.Close();
        }
        return;
    }
```

This method begins by building a connection string from the user entry fields and opening a connection the database. Next, the connection points to the master table where the first SQL statement can create the IssueTracker database using the ExecuteNonQuery method. Next, the method obtains information about its assembly and retrieves the embedded .sql file for reading. Next, the connection points to the newly created database where the SQL statements within the embedded .sql file can be executed, again using the ExecuteNonQuery method.

The last step in the process is to create the SQL file. A new text file, CreateDatabase.sql, is created and added to the project with its Build Action property set to Embedded Resource. Appendix A, "Building the IssueTracker Database," outlines the SQL statements that create the application's data and validation tables.

Summary

Deployment is often the least considered element of an enterprise application. After spending months designing and developing the application, there is often little time remaining for putting together a well-planned setup application. From the user's perspective, smooth deployment is important. Just as books are judged by their cover, a good or bad setup program can set the tone for the rest of the user's experience.

Visual Studio provides tools for building smarter and easier-to-use setup programs, capable of detecting the environment they are targeting and selectively installing pieces of an application accordingly.

The following appendixes provide additional reference material for building the IssueTracker sample application as well as other .NET applications. Appendix A, "Building the IssueTracker Database," presents the SQL table create scripts necessary to build the IssueTracker sample database. Appendix B, "Understanding the IssueTracker Object Map," presents a diagram that outlines the business objects and collections referenced by the IssueTracker application. Appendix C, "Using String Format Specifiers," is a useful reference for formatting various data objects as strings. Appendix D, "Using XSLT Functions" is another useful reference that presents the most common XSLT instructions.

Building the IssueTracker Database

THIS APPENDIX SHOWS how to structure the create scripts for building the IssueTracker database, which is the sample application used throughout the book.

The Dat_Company table maintains a list of available reports to produce (see Listing A-1).

Listing A-1. Dat_Company

```
CREATE TABLE [dbo].[Dat_Company] (
    [CompanyID] [int] NOT NULL ,
    [UserID] [int] NULL ,
    [CompanyName] [char] (64) COLLATE SQL_Latin1_General_CP1_CI_AS NULL ,
    [Address1] [char] (128) COLLATE SQL_Latin1_General_CP1_CI_AS NULL ,
    [Address2] [char] (128) COLLATE SQL_Latin1_General_CP1_CI_AS NULL ,
    [City] [char] (64) COLLATE SQL_Latin1_General_CP1_CI_AS NULL ,
    [State] [char] (3) COLLATE SQL_Latin1_General_CP1_CI_AS NULL ,
    [Zipcode] [char] (10) COLLATE SQL_Latin1_General_CP1_CI_AS NULL ,
    [Country] [char] (32) COLLATE SQL_Latin1_General_CP1_CI_AS NULL ,
    [CreateDate] [datetime] NULL
) ON [PRIMARY]
GO
```

The Dat_Issue table contains data records related to individual issues logged in the database (see Listing A-2). Each issue will have a unique identifier, some attribute data, and references to look up values in other tables.

Listing A-2. Dat_Issue

```
CREATE TABLE [dbo].[Dat_Issue] (
    [IssueID] [int] NOT NULL ,
    [TypeID] [int] NULL ,
    [UserID] [int] NULL ,
```

```
        [EntryDate] [datetime] NULL ,
        [StatusID] [int] NULL ,
        [Summary] [char] (128) COLLATE SQL_Latin1_General_CP1_CI_AS NULL ,
        [Description] [text] COLLATE SQL_Latin1_General_CP1_CI_AS NULL ,
        [PriorityID] [int] NULL
) ON [PRIMARY] TEXTIMAGE_ON [PRIMARY]
GO
```

The Dat_User table contains data records related to the individual users who enter issues into the database (see Listing A-3).

Listing A-3. Dat_User

```
CREATE TABLE [dbo].[Dat_User] (
        [UserID] [int] NOT NULL ,
        [Password] [char] (16) COLLATE SQL_Latin1_General_CP1_CI_AS NULL ,
        [Firstname] [char] (32) COLLATE SQL_Latin1_General_CP1_CI_AS NULL ,
        [Lastname] [char] (64) COLLATE SQL_Latin1_General_CP1_CI_AS NULL ,
        [EmailAddress] [char] (256) COLLATE SQL_Latin1_General_CP1_CI_AS NULL ,
        [UserType] [int] NULL ,
        [CreateDate] [datetime] NULL
) ON [PRIMARY]
GO
```

The Val_IssueType table contains records that maintain a list of issue types (see Listing A-4). These types might include values such as Hardware, Software, or Networking. By storing lookup values within a database table rather than embedded within the application code, you can make product customizations for specific customers more quickly.

Listing A-4. Val_IssueType

```
CREATE TABLE [dbo].[Val_IssueType] (
        [TypeID]   uniqueidentifier ROWGUIDCOL  NOT NULL ,
        [TypeLabel] [char] (32) COLLATE SQL_Latin1_General_CP1_CI_AS NULL
) ON [PRIMARY]
GO
```

The Val_MailMessages table maintains a list of available reports to produce (see Listing A-5).

Listing A-5. Val_MailMessages

```
CREATE TABLE [dbo].[Val_MailMessage] (
    [MailMessageID] [int] NOT NULL ,
    [Format] [int] NULL ,
    [Priority] [int] NULL ,
    [Subject] [char] (128) COLLATE SQL_Latin1_General_CP1_CI_AS NULL ,
    [Body] [text] COLLATE SQL_Latin1_General_CP1_CI_AS NULL
) ON [PRIMARY] TEXTIMAGE_ON [PRIMARY]
GO
```

The Val_Priority table maintains a list of issue priorities (see Listing A-6). These priorities might include values such as High, Medium, or Low.

Listing A-6. Val_Priority

```
CREATE TABLE [dbo].[Val_Priority] (
    [PriorityID]  uniqueidentifier ROWGUIDCOL  NOT NULL ,
    [PriorityLabel] [char] (32) COLLATE SQL_Latin1_General_CP1_CI_AS NULL
) ON [PRIMARY]
GO
```

The Val_Reports table maintains a list of available reports to produce (see Listing A-7).

Listing A-7. Val_Reports

```
CREATE TABLE [dbo].[Val_Reports] (
    [ReportID] [uniqueidentifier] NOT NULL ,
    [ReportLabel] [char] (32) COLLATE SQL_Latin1_General_CP1_CI_AS NULL ,
    [ReportFilePath] [char] (256) COLLATE SQL_Latin1_General_CP1_CI_AS NULL
) ON [PRIMARY]
GO
```

The Val_Status table maintains a list of issue status conditions (see Listing A-8). These conditions might include values such as Open, Closed, or In Progress.

Listing A-8. Val_Status

```
CREATE TABLE [dbo].[Val_Status] (
    [StatusID]  uniqueidentifier ROWGUIDCOL  NOT NULL ,
    [StatusLabel] [char] (32) COLLATE SQL_Latin1_General_CP1_CI_AS NULL
) ON [PRIMARY]
GO
```

APPENDIX B

Understanding the IssueTracker Object Map

FIGURE B-1 SHOWS the object map for the example application, IssueTracker, that you'll be building throughout this book.

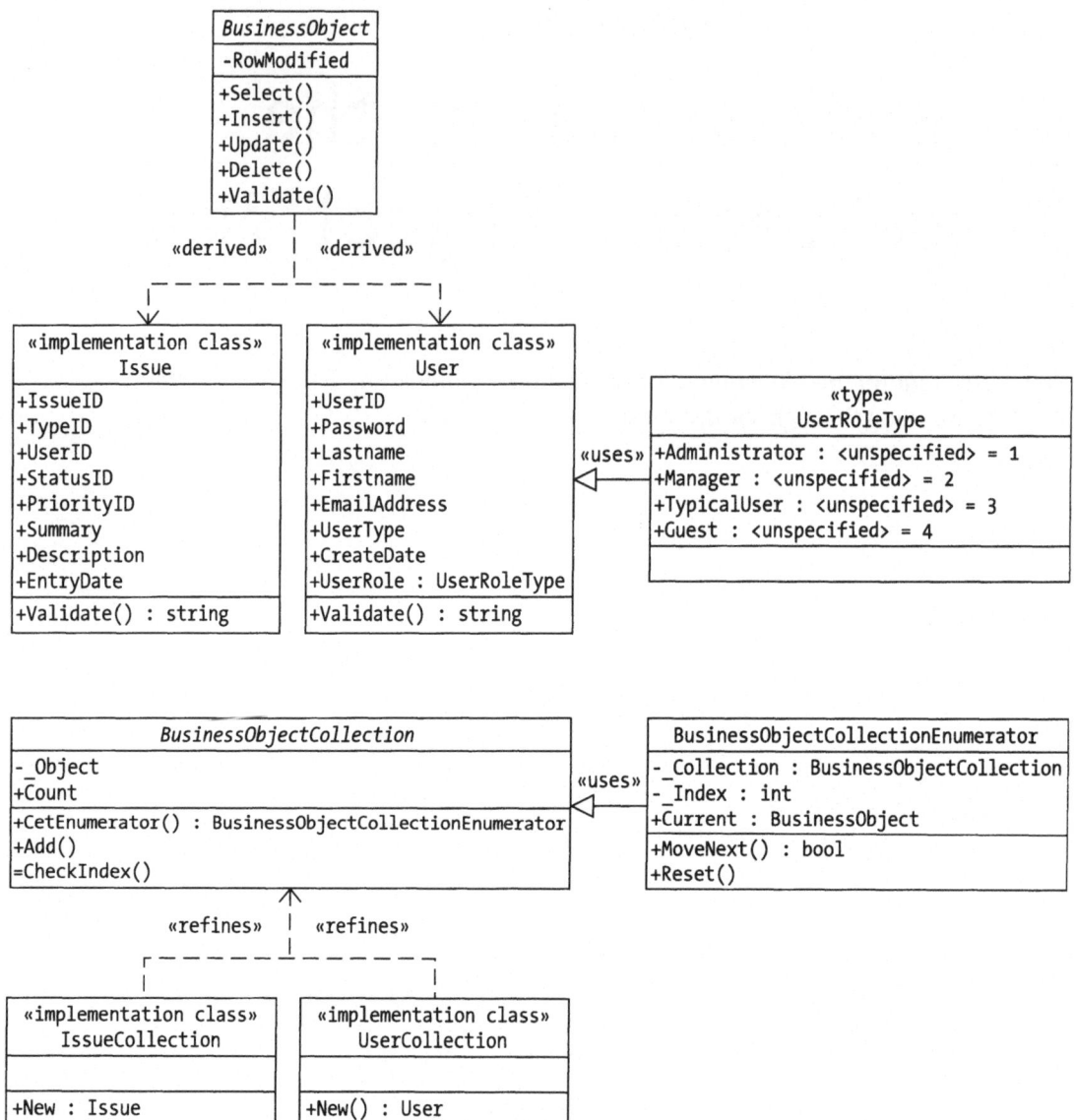

Figure B-1. The IssueTracker business object diagram

Using String Format Specifiers

THIS APPENDIX SHOWS YOU the string format specifiers you can use when developing enterprise applications using C#.

Formatting Numbers

A format specifier can quickly convert a numerical value into a properly formatted value string:

```
int i = 15;

Console.WriteLine( "{0:c} [" + string.Format( "{0:c}", i ) + "]" );
```

Table C-1 describes how to format numbers that take an integer value of 15.

Table C-1. Formatting Numbers Taking an Integer Value of 15

SPECIFIER	TYPE	FORMAT	OUTPUT
c	Currency	{0:c}	$15.00
d	Whole number	{0:d}	15
e	Scientific	{0:e}	1.500000e+001
e	Formatted scientific	{0:00e+0}	15e+0
f	Fixed point	{0:f}	15
g	General	{0:g}	15
n	Number with commas for thousands	{0:n}	15.00
x	Hexadecimal	{0:x4}	000f
#	Digit placeholder	{0:(#).##}	(15)

Table C-1. Formatting Numbers Taking an Integer Value of 15, continued

SPECIFIER	TYPE	FORMAT	OUTPUT
.	Decimal point	{0:0.0}	15.0
,	Thousand separator	{0:0,0}	15
,.	Number scaling	{0:0,.}	0
%	Percent	{0:0%}	1500%

Formatting Dates

A format specifier can quickly convert a DateTime object into a properly format-ted value string:

```
DateTime dateOutput = new DateTime( 2001, 1, 1 );

Console.WriteLine( "{0:d} [" + string.Format( "{0:d}", dateOutput ) + "]" );
```

Table C-2 describes how to format dates that take a DateTime object of January 1, 2001.

Table C-2. Formatting Dates Taking a DateTime Object Set to January 1, 2001

SPECIFIER	TYPE	FORMAT	OUTPUT
d	Short date	{0:d}	1/1/2001
dd	Day	{0:dd}	01
ddd	Day name	{0:ddd}	Mon
dddd	Full day name	{0:dddd}	Monday
D	Long date	{0:D}	Monday, January 01, 2001
t	Short time	{0:t}	12:00 AM
tt	A.M. or P.M.	{0:tt}	AM
T	Long time	{0:T}	12:00:00 AM
f	Full date and time	{0:f}	Monday, January 01, 2001 12:00 AM

Table C-2. Formatting Dates Taking a DateTime Object Set to January 1, 2001, continued

SPECIFIER	TYPE	FORMAT	OUTPUT
F	Full date and time (long)	{0:F}	Monday, January 01, 2001 12:00:00 AM
g	Default date and time	{0:g}	1/1/2001 12:00 AM
G	Default date and time (long)	{0:G}	1/1/2001 12:00:00 AM
mm	Minute 00–59	{0:mm}	00
M	Month/day pattern	{0:M}	January 01
MM	Month 01–12	{0:MM}	01
MMM	Month abbreviation	{0:MMM}	Jan
MMMM	Full month name	{0:MMMM}	January
r	RFC 1123 date string	{0:r}	Mon, 01 Jan 2001 00:00:00 GMT
s	Sortable date string	{0:s}	2001-01-01T00:00:00
ss	Seconds 00–59	{0:ss}	00
u	Universal sortable, local time	{0:u}	2001-01-01 00:00:00Z
U	Universal sortable, Greenwich Mean Time (GMT)	{0:U}	Monday, January 01, 2001 8:00:00 AM
Y	Year/month pattern	{0:Y}	January, 2001
f, ff, ...	Second fractions	{0:fff}	000
gg, ...	Era	{0:gg}	A.D.
fh	Two-digit hour	{0:hh}	12
HH	Two-digit hour, 24-hour format	{0:HH}	00
yy	Year, two digits	{0:yy}	01
yyyy	Year	{0:yyyy}	2001
:	Separator	{0:hh:mm:ss}	12:00:00
/	Separator	{0:dd/mm/yyyy}	01/00/2001

Formatting Enumerations

A format specifier can quickly convert an enumerated type into a properly formatted value string:

```
enum enumType
{
    TypeA = 1,
    TypeB = 2,
    TypeC = 3
}


enumType eVal = enumType.TypeB;

Console.WriteLine( "{0:g} [" + string.Format( "{0:g}", eVal ) + "]" );
```

Table C-3 shows how to format an enumeration that takes a value of enumType.TypeB.

Table C-3. Formatting an Enumeration Taking a Value of enumType.TypeB

SPECIFIER	TYPE	FORMAT	OUTPUT
G	Default (flag names if available, otherwise decimal)	{0:G}	TypeB
F	Flags always	{0:F}	TypeB
D	Integer always	{0:D}	2
X	Eight-digit hex	{0:X}	00000002

APPENDIX D

Using XSLT Functions

TABLE D-1 DESCRIBES the transformation methods used to complete an XSL Transformation (XSLT) document.

Table D-1. XSLT Functions

FUNCTION	DESCRIPTION
xsl:apply-imports	Raises the precedence of the current style sheet.
xsl:apply-templates	Invokes the best-match template rules against the node set returned by the select expression.
xsl:attribute	Returns an Extensible Markup Language (XML) attribute whose [local name] is name, whose [namespace URI] is namespace, and whose [children] are based on template.
xsl:call-template	Invokes the template rule named by name.
xsl:choose	Evaluates the template from the first xsl:when clause whose test expression evaluates to true. If none of the test expressions evaluate to true, then the template contained in the xsl:otherwise clause is evaluated.
xsl:comment	Returns an XML comment containing the template as its character data.
xsl:copy	Copies the current context node and associated namespace nodes to the result tree fragment.
xsl:copy-of	Returns the node set corresponding to the select expression.
xsl:element	Returns an XML element whose [local name] is name, whose [namespace URI] is namespace, and whose [children] are based on template.
xsl:fallback	Evaluates the template when the parent instruction/directive is not supported by the current processor.

Table D-1. XSLT Functions, continued

FUNCTION	DESCRIPTION
xsl:for-each	Evaluates the template against each node in node set returned by the select expression. The order of evaluation can be influenced using one or more xsl:sorts.
xsl:if	Evaluates the template if and only if the test expression evaluates to true.
xsl:message	Returns a message in a processor-dependent manner.
xsl:number	Returns a number based on the XPath number expression found in value.
xsl:processing-instruction	Returns an XML processing instruction whose [target] is name and whose [children] are based on template.
xsl:text	Returns the text found in #PCDATA. Escaping of the five built-in entities is controlled using disable-output-escaping.
xsl:value-of	Returns the string corresponding to the select expression.
xsl:variable	Declares a variable name and initializes it using the select expression or template.

Index